Imperial Inequalities

Manchester University Press

Postcolonial International Studies

Series Editors: Mustapha K. Pasha, Meera Sabaratnam and Robbie Shilliam

Postcolonial International Studies marks out a dedicated space for advanced critical inquiry into colonial questions across International Relations and beyond. The series embraces a multitude of methods and approaches, theoretical and empirical scholarship, as well as historical and contemporary concerns. It enquires into the shifting principles of colonial rule that inform global governance and investigates the contestation of these principles by diverse peoples across the globe. Critically re-interpreting popular concepts, narratives and approaches by reference to the 'colonial question', *Postcolonial International Studies* opens up new vistas from which to address the key political questions of our time.

Originally presented as *Kilombo*, this series retains the ethos reflected by the bricolage constituency of Kilombos – settlements of African slaves, rebels and indigenous peoples in South America who became self-determining political communities that retrieved and renovated the social practices of its diverse constituencies while being confronted by colonial forces.

Published by Manchester University Press

The rise of global Islamophobia in the War on Terror: Coloniality, race, and Islam

Edited by Naved Bakali and Farid Hafez

Previously published by Rowman & Littlefield:

Meanings of Bandung
Edited by Quỳnh N. Phạm and Robbie Shilliam

Politics of African Anticolonial Archive
Edited by Shiera S. el-Malik and Isaac A. Kamola

Asylum after Empire
Lucy Mayblin

Decolonising Intervention
Meera Sabaratnam

Global Development and Colonial Power
Daniel Bendix

The Postcolonial African State in Transition
Amy Niang

South Africa, Race and the Making of International Relations
Vineet Thakur and Peter Vale

Postcolonial Governmentalities
Edited by Terri-Anne Teo and Elisa Wynne-Hughes

Beyond the Master's Tools?
Edited by Daniel Bendix; Franziska Müller and Aram Ziai

Creative Presence
Emily Merson

Domination Through Law
Mohamed Sesay

Diplomatic Para-citations
Sam Okoth Opondo

Selective Responsibility in the United Nations
Katy Harsant

Imperial Inequalities

The politics of economic governance across European empires

Edited by

Gurminder K. Bhambra and Julia McClure

MANCHESTER UNIVERSITY PRESS

Copyright © Manchester University Press 2022

While copyright in the volume as a whole is vested in Manchester University Press, copyright in individual chapters belongs to their respective authors, and no chapter may be reproduced wholly or in part without the express permission in writing of both author and publisher.

Published by Manchester University Press
Oxford Road, Manchester M13 9PL

www.manchesteruniversitypress.co.uk

British Library Cataloguing-in-Publication Data
A catalogue record for this book is available from the British Library

ISBN 978 1 5261 6614 2 hardback
ISBN 978 1 5261 9126 7 paperback

First published 2022
Paperback published 2025

The publisher has no responsibility for the persistence or accuracy of URLs for any external or third-party internet websites referred to in this book, and does not guarantee that any content on such websites is, or will remain, accurate or appropriate.

EU authorised representative for GPSR:
Easy Access System Europe – Mustamäe tee 50,
10621 Tallinn, Estonia
gpsr.requests@easproject.com

Typeset
by Cheshire Typesetting Ltd, Cuddington, Cheshire

Contents

List of figures   *page* vii
List of tables   x
Notes on contributors   xi
Preface: Fiscal democracy and the legacy of empire – *Quinn
Slobodian*   xiv
Acknowledgements   xix

Introduction: Imperial Inequalities – *Gurminder K. Bhambra and
Julia McClure*   1

Part I: Institutional and fiscal issues

1   The great gage: Mortgaging Ireland to finance an empire –
    David Brown   19
2   The cost of thrift: The politics of 'financial autonomy' in the
    French colonial empire, 1900–14 – *Madeline Woker*   37
3   Madagascar and French imperial mercantilism: Foreign trade
    and domestic crises, 1895–1914 – *Samuel F. Sanchez*   57
4   The right to sovereign seizure? Taxation, valuation, and the
    Imperial British East Africa Company – *Emma Park*   79
5   Internal inequalities: Taxpayers, taxation, and expenditure in
    Sierra Leone, c. 1890s to 1937 – *Laura Channing*   98

Part II: Taxation and welfare

6   Taxation, welfare, and inequalities in the Spanish imperial
    state – *Julia McClure*   121
7   Political economies of welfare of the Spanish Empire: Tax
    and charity for the Hospital de los Naturales of Potosí –
    Camille Sallé   138

8   Poverty, health, and imperial wealth in early modern
    Scotland – *Andrew Mackillop*   157
9   Compromise and adaptation in colonial taxation: Political-
    economic governance and inequality in Indonesia – *Maarten
    Manse*   177
10 Imperial revenue and national welfare: The case of Britain –
    Gurminder K. Bhambra   198

Part III: Post-colonial legacies

11 Making investor states: Haitian foreign debt and neocolonial
    economic governance in nineteenth-century France – *Alexia
    Yates*   219
12 The lure of the welfare state following decolonisation in
    Kenya – *Lyla Latif*   240
13 From capitation taxes to tax havens: British fiscal policies in a
    colonial island world – *Gregory Rawlings*   259
14 Imperial extraction and 'tax havens' – *Alex Cobham*   280
15 The Crown Agents and the CDC Group: Imperial extraction
    and development's 'private sector turn' – *Paul Robert Gilbert*   299

Afterword: Imperialism and global inequalities – *Heloise Weber*   319

Index   329

Figures

2.1 Front page of *Le Grelot* ('The Bell'), 28 June 1896. Available at https://digi.ub.uni-heidelberg.de/diglit/grelot1896/0105   43

3.1 Madagascar imports and exports (1895–1911). Source: *Journal Officiel de Madagascar*, *Statistiques générales de Madagascar et dépendances*, 1905–11; author's compilation   59

3.2 Origin of imports in Madagascar (1883–1911). Source: *Journal Officiel de Madagascar*, *Statistiques générales de Madagascar et dépendances*, 1905–11; author's compilation   63

3.3 Destination of Madagascar's exports (1883–1911). Source: *Journal Officiel de Madagascar*, *Statistiques générales de Madagascar et dépendances*, 1905–11; author's compilation   64

3.4 Main export products of Madagascar (1896–1911). Source: *Journal Officiel de Madagascar*, *Statistiques générales de Madagascar et dépendances*, 1905–11; author's compilation   65

3.5 French imports from French colonies (1896–1911). Source: Jacques Marseille, *Empire colonial et capitalisme français: histoire d'un divorce* (Paris: Albin Michel, 2005); author's compilation   67

3.6 French exports to French Colonies (1896–1911). Source: Jacques Marseille, *Empire colonial et capitalisme français: histoire d'un divorce* (Paris: Albin Michel, 2005); author's compilation   68

3.7 Main budgetary resources in Madagascar (1897–1910). Source: *Journal Officiel de Madagascar*, *Statistiques générales de Madagascar*, 1905–10, Final Accounts of Income and Expenditure, 1901–10; author's compilation   71

3.8 Main budgetary expenditures in Madagascar (1899–1910). Source: *JOM*, *Statistiques générales de Madagascar*, 1905–10, Final Accounts of Income and Expenditure, 1901–10; author's compilation   72

List of figures

5.1 Comparative proportion of direct tax in total revenue in Freetown vs. the Protectorate, 1898–1940. Source: Municipality: British Foreign and Commonwealth Office [BFCO], Colony of Sierra Leone Financial Reports, 1922–31; BFCO, Colony of Sierra Leone Financial Reports, 1932–41; Sierra Leone National Archives [SLA], MP 3429/1900 Estimates of Revenue and Expenditure of the Municipality for 1900–01; SLA, MP 4768:1907 Estimates 1907–8 – Transmission of; The National Archives, UK [TNA], A 39/1910 Observations on the Accounts of the Municipality of Freetown for the Financial Year Ended 31.10.10; TNA CO 267/560/37126 Freetown Municipality 1912–13; CO 267/565–22805 Freetown Municipality Accounts 1913–14; CO 267/574/10615 Freetown Municipal Estimates 1916–17; CO 267/580/18882 Freetown Municipality Estimates 1918–19. Protectorate: TNA, CO 272/74–117 Sierra Leone Blue Books 1897–1940   106

5.2 Freetown City Council spending, various years 1898–1938. Source: BCFO, Colony of Sierra Leone Financial Reports, 1922–31; BCFO, Colony of Sierra Leone Financial Reports, 1932–41; SLA, MP 3429/1900 Estimates of Revenue and Expenditure of the Municipality for 1900–01; SLA, MP 4768:1907 Estimates 1907–8 – Transmission of; TNA, A 39/1910 Observations on the Accounts of the Municipality of Freetown for the Financial Year Ended 31.10.10; TNA CO 267/560/37126 Freetown Municipality 1912–13; CO 267/565–22805 Freetown Municipality Accounts 1913–14; CO 267/574/10615 Freetown Municipal Estimates 1916–17; CO 267/580/18882 Freetown Municipality Estimates 1918–19   108

5.3 Breakdown of general expenditure, 1898–1937. Source: TNA, CO 272/75–114 Sierra Leone Blue Books, 1898–1937   112

9.1 Value of exported goods from Java to the Netherlands compared to Dutch gross national income in fl. (guilders) 1,000, 1830–1910. Source: W. Korthals Altes, 'De betalingsbalans van Nederlandsch-Indië 1822–1939' (PhD thesis, Erasmus University Rotterdam, 1986); J. P. Smits, E. Horlings, and J. L. van Zanden, *Dutch GNP and its components, 1800–1913* (Groningen, 2000); author's compilation   180

9.2 Total colonial profits vs. Dutch gross national income (including colonial profits), 1856–65. Source: J. de Jong, *Van Batig Slot naar Ereschuld: De Discussie over de Financiële Verhouding tussen Nederland en Indië en de Hervorming van de Nederlandse Koloniale Politiek, 1860–1900* ('s-Gravenhage: SDU, 1989), p. 40; author's compilation ... 180

9.3 Government spending in the Dutch East Indies in fl. 1000, 1848–1938. Source: J. L. van Zanden, P. van der Eng, J. Th. Lindblad, D. Marks, and J. Mellegers, 'Government expenditure in the Netherlands East Indies 1848–1940' (Dataset; Amsterdam: IISH, 2003); author's compilation ... 183

11.1 Letter signed Veuve Lalleux, *c.* 27 June 1877. Source: FR-MAE Centre des archives diplomatiques de La Courneuve 752SUP 342 ... 227

11.2 Petition from bondholders Chappey, Caron, and Jances, September 1853. Source: FR-MAE Centre des archives diplomatiques de La Courneuve 752SUP 312 ... 232

13.1 The Western Pacific. Source: Map prepared by Les O' Neill, Archaeology and Social Anthropology Programmes, University of Otago, Dunedin, New Zealand ... 262

Tables

7.1 Estimation of the regional contribution to the medio peso (in pesos) from the mita contribution (1578–1610)   149

9.1 Head and land tax revenue levied on Java and the 'Outer Territories' in fl. (guilders), 1870–1920. Source: J. L. van Zanden, P. van der Eng, J. Th. Lindblad, D. Marks, and J. Mellegers, 'Government expenditure in the Netherlands East Indies 1848–1940' (Dataset; Amsterdam: IISH, 2003); author's compilation   182

9.2 Average direct tax assessments per capita in the 'Outer Territories', in fl. (guilders), around 1913. Source: J. Roest, 'Vergelijkend overzicht van de Buitenbezittingen van de inlandsche bevolking geheven directe belastingen over 1913', *Tijdschrift voor het Binnenlandsch Bestuur* 48 (1913), 518–29   185

14.1 The UK spider's web is the dominant 'tax haven' actor. Source: Tax Justice Network   291

Contributors

Gurminder K. Bhambra FBA is Professor of Postcolonial and Decolonial Studies at the University of Sussex. She is author of the award-winning *Rethinking Modernity: Postcolonialism and the Sociological Imagination* (Palgrave, 2007), *Connected Sociologies* (Bloomsbury, 2014), and, with John Holmwood, *Colonialism and Modern Social Theory* (Polity, 2021). She is also co-editor of *Decolonising the University* (Pluto Press, 2018).

David Brown is Archival Discovery Lead for Beyond 2022, Ireland's virtual record treasury. His monograph *Empire and Enterprise: Money, Power and the Adventurers for Irish Land during the British Civil Wars* was published by Manchester University Press in 2020. He is based at Trinity College Dublin.

Laura Channing is Assistant Professor of Economic History at Durham University. She completed her PhD at the University of Cambridge in 2021 and has held fellowships at the Institute of Historical Research, the London School of Economics, and Princeton University. Her research is on the history of taxation in West Africa and her work has been published in the *Journal of Imperial and Commonwealth History*.

Alex Cobham is chief executive of the Tax Justice Network, and a commissioner for the Scottish Government's Poverty and Inequality Commission. Recent publications include *The Uncounted* (Polity Press, 2019) and *Estimating Illicit Financial Flows* (Oxford University Press, 2020, with Petr Janský).

Paul Robert Gilbert is a Senior Lecturer in International Development at the University of Sussex. His current research focus is on for-profit contractors and consultants in 'Aidland'. Recent publications address speculative finance and racialised imaginaries in the extractive industries (*Economy & Society*, 2020), and the treatment of investor-state dispute settlement in post-colonial international law (*London Review of International Law*, 2019).

Lyla Latif is a finance, corporate, and human rights lawyer based in Kenya. She lectures at the University of Nairobi, School of Law and is currently working on her doctorate at Cardiff Law and Politics. Her research focuses on the interplay between law, finance, and development.

Andrew Mackillop researches the overlapping nature of British nation and empire building during 'the long eighteenth century', c. 1690–c. 1830. He explores Scottish involvement in empire, especially in the English East India Company, and comparisons with patterns of Irish and Welsh participation. His most recent monograph, *Human Capital and Empire: Scotland, Ireland, Wales and British Imperialism in Asia, c. 1690–c. 1820*, was published by Manchester University Press's Studies in Imperialism in 2021.

Maarten Manse currently lectures at Vrije Universiteit in Amsterdam and conducts postdoctoral research at Linnaeus University. His scholarly interests include the socio-economic, legal, political and diplomatic history of Southeast Asia and in particular the development of colonial mechanisms of governance. His PhD research focused on the development of modern taxation in the Dutch East Indies.

Julia McClure is Senior Lecturer in late medieval and early modern global history at the University of Glasgow. She is a specialist in the global histories of poverty, inequality, and charity with a particular focus on the Spanish Empire.

Emma Park is an Assistant Professor in the Department of History and co-director of the minor in Capitalism Studies at the New School for Social Research, New York. Her book project, titled *A Partible Sovereignty: Infrastructural Attachments, Austerity, and the Politics of Expertise in Kenya*, charts the dynamic interplay among infrastructural development, state building, capital accumulation, and the politics of expertise in Eastern Africa from the nineteenth century to the present.

Gregory Rawlings is Head of the Social Anthropology Programme in the School of Social Sciences at the University of Otago in New Zealand. His research on taxation has been published in *Law and Policy*, *Accounting Forum*, and *International Small Business Journal*, together with a number of book chapters in edited collections. His research increasingly seeks to identify the relationships between citizenship and taxation.

Camille Sallé is a PhD Candidate at the European University Institute of Florence (Italy). Her research project investigates the multifaceted provision of assistance to the sick and those unable to work in the colonial viceroyalty of Peru during the sixteenth and seventeenth centuries.

Samuel F. Sanchez is Maître de conférences in contemporary history (Université Paris 1 – Panthéon Sorbonne, Institut des Mondes Africains). His research focuses on the standard of living, construction of states, and trading networks in the western Indian Ocean, especially Madagascar, in a long-term perspective.

Quinn Slobodian is Marion Butler McLean Associate Professor of the History of Ideas at Wellesley College. His most recent book, *Globalists: The End of Empire and the Birth of Neoliberalism* (Harvard University Press, 2018), was awarded the George Louis Beer Prize by the American Historical Association.

Heloise Weber is Senior Lecturer in International Relations and Development, School of Political Science and International Studies, The University of Queensland. She is the co-author of the seventh edition of *Development and Social Change: A Global Perspective* (Sage, 2021), editor of *Politics of Development – A Survey* (Routledge, 2014), and co-author of *Rethinking the Third World: International Development and World Politics* (Palgrave Macmillan, 2014).

Madeline Woker is a Lecturer in the History of Modern France and the Francophone World at the University of Cambridge. She is also a research associate at the Centre for History and Economics and a fellow of Newnham College. She is currently working on a book about the politics of taxation in the French colonial empire between the 1850s and the 1950s and her academic work has appeared in the *Journal of Global History*. She has also written about the politics of international taxation for a wider audience, notably in *The Nation*.

Alexia Yates is Senior Lecturer in Modern History at the University of Manchester and has held fellowships at the Center for History and Economics, Harvard University, the Center for Global History at the Freie Universität, and the Centre for Research in Arts, Social Sciences, and Humanities at the University of Cambridge. She is the author of *Selling Paris: Property and Commercial Culture in the Fin-de-siècle Capital* (Harvard University Press, 2015).

Preface: Fiscal democracy and the legacy of empire

Quinn Slobodian

We should love taxes. They are the central institution of economic citizenship, our channel for giving to the state that which we and those needier than ourselves will receive back in a different form. And yet we don't. Who but the purest among us rejoices when they file their annual paperwork to find they owe more than expected? What is wrong with us? Are we hard-hearted materialists unable to match our pocketbook to our principles? Perhaps. But another possibility is that we have reason to distrust the system itself. Many of us feel the tax code is distorted, designed to deepen rather than lessen – let alone redress – economic inequality. And, if we live in the United States anyway, we are right. Emmanuel Saez and Gabriel Zucman show that the American tax code, once the most progressive in the world, is now effectively a giant flat tax, regressive at the top. Everybody pays between 25% and 30% of their income to taxes of various kinds – except the rich, who barely pay 20%.[1]

Tax injustice undercuts political legitimacy. Polls find well over half of Americans are bothered 'a lot' by their belief that neither corporations nor wealthy people pay their fair share of taxes.[2] What Saez and Zucman call 'fiscal democracy' and Alex Cobham calls, in this volume, 'tax citizenship', implies a sense of proportionality and accountability: a belief that fairness is wired into the economic machinery. Among the most important contemporary thinkers to draw attention to the problem of economic inequality and propose a solution is Saez and Zucman's collaborator, Thomas Piketty. He suggests what he calls 'participatory socialism'.[3] This is a kind of utopia of taxation. Inheritance, wealth, and carbon taxes dovetail with progressive income taxes to restore balance to the wild tilt of the economic scales. A premier example of socialism after its mellowing into social democracy, Piketty's blueprint dismisses predistribution in favour of redistribution. No longer must one seize the means of production. One must only seize the means of printing the tax code.

Taxes are politics. There is no question. But if so, why are they so hard to politicise? Why do they so easily take on the eye-glazing sheen of technocracy? The latest occasion to see this in action came in late 2021 when the International Consortium of Independent Journalists announced a dump of nearly twelve million records from fourteen different offshore tax services – a scalpel opening the guts of what Chuck Collins calls 'the wealth defence industry'.[4] The revelations of the so-called Pandora Papers were technically damning. Former prime minister Tony Blair, the supposedly anti-corruption crusaders of Slovakia and Kenya, Vladimir Putin, and many others, were all avoiding taxes through the use of offshore trusts and other 'vehicles', in the jargon. The news outlets with the scoop did everything they could to make the story land with a broad audience. They did not skimp on the interactive graphics that sought to explain once and for all how a 'trust' worked, how it had gone from a practice used by crusaders to protect their property in the case of their death while heading off to reclaim the Holy Land to a screen for every member of the 0.1% with wherewithal. They once again offered cartographies of small islands in the Caribbean and pointed out how South Dakota had recently surged into the ranks of tax havenry. They boggled minds once more with the idea that tens of thousands of businesses could be registered at a single 'brass-plate' location.

But, despite their mediagenic quality, the data dumps of Pandora, like their consonant siblings Paradise and Pegasus, seeded neither grassroots mobilisations nor social movements. After I gave a talk that touched on tax havens to University of Chicago law students in 2020, a student followed up to say they had been inspired and wanted to know which campus organisations were devoted to matters of tax justice. I was nonplussed. I could think of none. Asking around later, I found this was for a good reason: there were none to think of. It is a challenge that people either too young to have paid taxes themselves or little enough savvy to think about the regressive nature of taxation in places like the United States find it hard to connect to tax as an issue. Much easier is the inverse of debt, felt more viscerally, the seed of the Occupy movement which was, until the George Floyd protest wave of 2020, the most sizable mobilisation of the decade.

Curious about the limp public reaction to the chain of leaks, I put a poll on social media asking why the disclosures had had so little effect. Was it because of (1) information overload, (2) weaponised impunity, (3) institutional capture, or (4) political fatigue? When the results came in, they were: all four. A friend suggested that the tax haven leak had become a genre. It followed conventions. There were the usual characters showcased by the media—the former politicians, the Central Asian oligarchs, the sub-Saharan dictators. The genre plays a social role of cohesion but the details are ultimately interchangeable. Thus, like any other genre product, whether film or novel, we were distracted by it for a while before turning away.

Of course, to say taxes are difficult to politicise is only true from the left. For the right, the fight to reduce taxes of all kinds has been a forty-year victory march, beginning with the tax revolt of 1978 in California that culminated in the passage of Proposition 13, which locked in ultra-low property taxes and required supermajorities to adjust taxes to raise new revenues, capturing the state in permanent austerity. Opponents of taxation have lots of fodder. They can always gesture to a long history of uneven application and oppression through what Gurminder Bhambra, in this volume, cites Martin Daunton as calling the 'relations of extraction' without attendant 'relations of redistribution'. Tax has an ugly past.

The challenge of the volume that follows is to wind its way through these two political realities: to paint a merciless portrait of the colonial history of taxation without somehow rendering the project of taxation politically irredeemable. While the journalists of the data dumps rely on shock and anecdote, the scholars in this volume rely on explanation over time, pulling on the thread of path dependency as it winds over borders and oceans. Bhambra points out that scholars of redistributive justice assume the bounded space of the nation that contains the community of both donors and beneficiaries. The history of empire allows for no such conceits.

Were the imperial subjects and post-colonial citizens at the heart of this book to be asked about fiscal democracy, they might respond as Gandhi did about 'Western Civilisation': it would be a good idea. Fiscal democracy has many preconditions and we find out here why so few were on hand in post-colonial states. In sites and at moments around the world across the last five centuries, the authors show us systems of taxation used less as prelude to redistribution than as mechanisms to push people into relationships of monetised exchange. This is almost always a dynamic of duty without rights – 'Only taxation! No representation!' as Emma Park has it in her chapter on the British East Africa Company. What Madeline Woker calls the 'low-cost' French Empire of the late nineteenth century was funded by taxation in the colonies; conquered populations were compelled to pay the salaries of their own occupiers. If taxation is a social contract, it was signed here at the barrel of a gun. Refusal was not an option. Resistance to tax injustice was met with violent repression. Gregory Rawlings reports the murder of sixty indigenous Solomon Islanders by the British over a tax dispute. Laura Channing describes a Hut Tax War in Sierra Leone that stretched over six months. Woker cites tax revolts in Madagascar, Indochina, and the French Congo in a single decade. In his chapter on Madagascar, Samuel Sanchez reminds us that the poll tax was called the *capitation*, after the counting of heads. This should be the enumeration of the body politic. But recall the protests against Margaret Thatcher's poll tax in 1990 that brought hundreds of thousands of people into the streets and led to its withdrawal. To count each person equally is regressive in an unequal society. Paying the year's head tax took a Malagasy between one and four months of labour.

Sovereignty achieved after decolonisation was itself only partial. Beyond the absence of a tradition of accountability mediated through taxation upon which to build, new nations were incorporated into the world system on a model of what Adom Getachew calls 'unequal integration'.[5] Formally equal, new nations still operated through asymmetrical relationships encased in law. Lyla Latif explains in her chapter on Kenya how the post-colonial taxing state enjoyed no honeymoon period. It was seen as a 'new form of coercion-intensive Leviathan' which was also offering special treatment for corporations and foreign investors. Double tax treaties denied the post-colonial country fiscal jurisdiction. International investment law layered on guarantees for investors that assured them extraordinary privileges. Referring to the work of Friedrich Hayek, I have called these 'xenos rights', using the Greek word for the guest-friend or the stranger. In a system where the xenoi have more rights than the citizens, the ideal type of taxation as a social contract in a fiscal democracy has been inverted. What remains, as Latif writes, is 'a legacy of the old empire reconstituting its inequalities in the post-colonial era'.

To turn the tide of tax injustice towards a better future, we need more than another disclosure, more than another dozen terabytes of unsavory memos and emails, paper trails to another hidden mansion on the Riviera or a townhouse in Belgravia. What the authors in this volume provide is something more subtle than another sordid slice of plutocratic malfeasance or a world-systems tale of how the West underdeveloped the South. In their telling, taxation is a material matter, plunder by other means in many cases. But it is also an immaterial matter – the invisible tissue of legitimacy and the faith people have in their governments. As Cobham writes, government is not funded by taxation; it is an 'an *outcome* of taxation'. The state comes into being through fiscal mediation.

Post-colonial governments started with a double deficit: they were required to leave in place the asymmetrical forms of taxation instituted by colonisers in order to attract all-important foreign direct investment, and they were burdened by a toxic domestic legacy of distrust towards the tax-collecting state. Why should people trust the taxman to be the handmaiden of social justice when he had so long been the parasite if not the hangman? To make tax justice into effective politics, we need to see it in three dimensions as the authors do here, working from a highly uneven terrain where distrust of the state has deep and justified roots. Tax justice is not a a problem of information, accounting, or legal design. It is one part of the task of rebuilding democracy in a world where the language of sacrifice and 'giving back' has been travestied and abused by the petty tyrants of colony, post-colony, and workplace alike. Tax justice will not be achieved by deepening a sense of individual ownership, a bespoke clientelism for every citizen. It will be achieved by building a commons which, as the historical record shows, is as yet unbuilt.

Notes

1. Emmanuel Saez and Gabriel Zucman, *The Triumph of Injustice: How the Rich Dodge Taxes and How to Make Them Pay* (New York, NY: W. W. Norton, 2019).
2. Amina Dunn and Ted Van Green, 'Top tax frustrations for Americans: The feeling that some corporations, wealthy people don't pay fair share', *Pew Research Center* (30 April 2021), available at https://www.pewresearch.org/fact-tank/2021/04/30/top-tax-frustrations-for-americans-the-feeling-that-some-corporations-wealthy-people-dont-pay-fair-share/ (last accessed 15 March 2022).
3. Thomas Piketty, *Capital and Ideology* (Cambridge, MA: The Belknap Press of Harvard University Press, 2020), p. 966.
4. Chuck Collins, *The Wealth Hoarders: How Billionaires Pay Millions to Hide Trillions* (London: Polity, 2021).
5. Adom Getachew, *Worldmaking after Empire: The Rise and Fall of Self-Determination* (Princeton, NJ: Princeton University Press, 2019), p. 2.

Acknowledgements

The idea for this volume came about in the 'before-times' – before the coronavirus pandemic swept the globe. We had anticipated holding a workshop that would bring colleagues together to discuss ideas around colonialism, taxation, and welfare. This was curtailed as we went into a variety of lockdowns and international travel effectively ceased. As we discussed the best way to proceed, Alex Cobham, from the Tax Justice Network, suggested that we hold the workshop online and further suggested that we do a subsequent online public-facing event. We would like to thank Alex and colleagues at the Tax Justice Network for their considerable support in facilitating these meetings and ensuring that the project proceeded so effectively.

Both events – the workshop and the public-facing conference – were immensely valuable in allowing contributors to share their initial ideas and to begin to develop common themes across the chapters. We also learnt much from other contributors at the events who addressed the history of empires in creating contemporary inequalities and the pathways to global reparative justice today. In particular, we would like to thank the keynotes at the conference, Vanessa Ogle and Ndongo Samba Sylla. We would also like to thank other contributors to the conference whose insights were very valuable for the development of the themes within this volume. In particular, we thank Steven Dean, Clair Quentin, M. J. Rodríguez-Salgado, and Yvonne Tan. Special thanks also go to the Tax Justice Network members for their intellectual and organisational support: Helena Rose, Naomi Fowler, Liz Nelson, John Christensen, and Alex Cobham. Their insights were particularly useful for enabling us to connect the historical analysis of inequalities and empires with the ways in which taxation regimes continue to reproduce global inequalities today.

The editors would like to thank Tom Dark and the reviewers at Manchester University Press, whose comments helped in shaping the volume. We are also very grateful to Robbie Shilliam for his perceptive advice in developing and framing the volume and to Quinn Slobodian and Heloise Weber for contributing their reflections on the chapters and the broader themes.

Gurminder K Bhambra, University of Sussex
Julia McClure, University of Glasgow

Introduction: Imperial Inequalities

Gurminder K. Bhambra and Julia McClure

The coronavirus pandemic that started in 2020 has put global inequalities into sharp perspective. The issues are not only the severe disparities in access to vaccines and treatments, but also the disparities in the experience of environmental crises. Global patterns of land grabs and dispossession are widely seen as disrupting ecological balances in the relation of human and animal contact, thus facilitating transmission of disease. At the same time, there have been beneficiaries of the pandemic, primarily large corporations like Amazon and big pharmaceutical companies with shareholders in the West. These companies have generated large profits but have largely been exempt from taxation. Global populations in poor countries experience the 'external' costs of capitalist expansion at the same time as Western elites find profit in financialising those costs. Further, richer countries are able to mobilise their wealth to provide welfare for citizens, while poorer countries struggle to provide basic services.

In this volume we address the origins of various regimes of private property and taxation and redistribution. Importantly, the contributors treat taxation and welfare as integral to the configuration of structures of contemporary inequality. Whereas most approaches to political economy place private property and capital accumulation at the centre, the contributors here argue that accumulation and distribution through different modes of taxation have also played a fundamental part, thereby reinforcing the role of the political within political economy.

The elision of taxation in discussions of accumulation and distribution derives, in part, from a failure to understand the nature of the modern state not as a 'nation-state' (the typical focus of discussions of taxation), but as a colonial and imperial state. The contributors begin from the colonial histories that are typically absent in treatments of global inequality. Many scholars, for example, regard global inequality simply to be the sum of national inequalities understood in aggregate form.[1] Others suggest that what is needed is to construct a global comparative analysis based on data concerning inequality within nations.[2] Such approaches, with their focus on the nation, fail to recognise that global inequality has global, that is colonial, conditions for its emergence.[3]

Maintaining the nation as the dominant unit of analysis is inadequate given that the political entities under discussion were rarely nations over the *longue durée*, but empires. In the light of this, we argue that global inequalities need to be understood in the context of the colonial and imperial histories that have shaped them.[4] We use the term 'imperial inequalities' as we examine processes of fiscal governance that were not confined to either nations or colonies, but rather transcended the normative spatial and temporal boundaries of these units of analysis. As such, this volume utilises the idea of 'imperial inequalities' as a conceptual frame for thinking about the long-standing colonial histories that are responsible, in part at least, for the shape of present inequalities.

Over the two decades since the first global historical turn, we have become increasingly aware of the global dynamics of economic capital, but this has insufficiently transformed our understanding of the global dimensions of our political units of analysis. In short, states and empires have continued to be treated as separate rather than co-constitutive entities. One reason for this is that global historical analysis has often focused upon economic processes, rather than the political projects governing these processes. While previous scholarship has placed the development of the fiscal state in a more global historical context,[5] this volume focuses on the transregional imperial dynamics of the collection and redistribution of resources across political communities, questioning how the political boundaries of these political communities has been historicised. Further, by shifting the focus to the politics of economic governance, this volume challenges historical accounts which see global inequality as the natural outcome of economic processes and signposts possible future directions for post-colonial approaches to global history.

Imperial Inequalities takes Western European empires, and their legacies, as the explicit starting point for discussion. It addresses the institutional and fiscal processes involved in the modes of extraction and hierarchies of distribution across Europe's global empires. It looks at the ways in which particularities of economic governance across European empires have shaped forms of inequality in the present and their ongoing implications for contemporary political economy. Specifically, it examines the ways in which European empires mobilised forms of taxation across the territories they governed and addresses how this was understood, both in the metropole and the imperial hinterlands.

The volume further addresses the different forms of welfare provided within the imperial polity in terms of who contributed, who had access, and how this was differentiated across its broader reaches. The relationship between taxation and welfare can be regarded as central to the dynamics of modern nation-states, yet the role of imperialism has rarely been addressed. Nor has the relationship been discussed within the literature addressing issues of economic governance across imperial domains. The volume culminates by looking at the various taxation regimes in operation in different European empires and how their post-colonial legacies continue to shape our world. In sum, the volume provides historical insights into the shaping of structures of inequality through an examination of the complex interplay between forms of extraction and differential redistribution which continue to have repercussions in the present.

Rethinking our conceptual frameworks: From nation to empire

Nation-states and empires tend to be understood as the two dominant political forms configuring the modern world order.[6] They are also usually presented as distinct conceptual categories. While scholars often accept that a number of European states extended their powers beyond national boundaries through colonial and imperial activities – that is, by establishing empires – recognition of this co-extensive and overlapping activity rarely calls into question their categorisation as analytically distinct. In contrast, this volume looks beyond established historiographical approaches to regard nation-states and empires as co-constitutive political and economic endeavours. In particular, it identifies empires and not nations as the dominant modes of political organisation at the time that modern global inequalities were being established. This key insight provides a theoretical frame for the chapters in this volume which explore the complexities of entangled histories of empire and nation.

Many theorists of global inequality argue that such trends derive from historically unprecedented processes of economic growth that began, fitfully, in the sixteenth century and became sustained from the nineteenth. Initially, these trends were considered to be the result of developments endogenous to European societies, the so-called 'European miracle'. Classical, and later neoclassical, liberal economics held that a free market generated economic growth, while orthodox Marxist theory saw class relations and the value of labour as key. Different theories emerged to bridge the gaps between these positions. New Institutional Economists, for example, argue that European economic growth was made possible by strong institutions and constitutional arrangements that protected private property.[7] Others have looked beyond institutions, addressing the importance of innovation and invention, to argue for the importance of a 'culture of growth' that developed in Europe.[8] Across these various views, one factor remains constant:

that change and innovation occurred first in Europe and was primarily a consequence of developments internal to European societies and cultures that (in the resonant phrase of W. W Rostow[9]) experienced a 'take-off' that left others behind.

In contrast, we argue that the production and reproduction of global inequality trends was not primarily driven by factors internal to Europe, but by the global context of European colonialism and the modes of economic governance they established.[10] This position contributes to an established field of scholarship which has shown that attention to colonial histories reminds us, time and again, that the poverty of what comes to be understood as the Global South and the wealth of the Global North are intrinsically connected. That is, the very same historical processes that generated the wealth of European countries are ones that made other places poor.[11] From the early work of scholars such as Dadabhai Naoroji[12] and Lajpat Rai[13] in the context of India, and that of scholars such as C. L. R. James[14] and Eric Williams[15] in the context of the Caribbean, and those such as Walter Rodney[16] and Samir Amin[17] in the context of Africa, and then Eduardo Galeano[18] addressing South America, there is a long and substantial tradition of scholarship that points to the ways in which Europe became wealthy directly at the expense of the places it colonised.

Subsequent theoretical frameworks, such as dependency theory and world-systems analysis, set out the pathways by which the Global North became rich at the expense of the Global South, but these theories tended to prioritise the logic of capital over the logic of imperialism. The global historical turn that began with the publication of Pomeranz's *Great Divergence* demonstrated how European economic growth benefited from colonial subsidies, but the economic and the political have often been treated as separate spheres.[19] As such, we argue for the need for the politics of economic governance to be situated in terms of an understanding of colonial global economy.[20] In the following section, we draw out the significance of this by looking specifically at modes of taxation and welfare that were established across a variety of European empires.

Beyond these approaches – and related initiatives within the fields of dependency theory and underdevelopment theory – for much of the twentieth century, histories of nation states and empires continued to be treated as separate historical entities. Yet, from the emergence of the world's first global empires in the sixteenth century, projects of state and empire formation were intrinsically linked through economic flows of revenue and political discourses of the common good, justice, and welfare. When the economies of some European states began to experience sustained growth and diverged from the rest of the world in the nineteenth century, they were benefiting more from the colonial subsidies from their global empires than from endogenous sources.

In the twentieth century, in the post-war period, formal empires were dismantled around the world at the same time as modern welfare states came into existence in Europe, thereby reinforcing the idea that the two were separate. While they have often been treated as separate processes, this volume invites readers to follow the colonial and global historical turn and to look for the connections between such processes. In the post-colonial context of the twenty-first century, countries in the Global North often cite the need to protect national welfare from migration from the Global South (see Bhambra's chapter in this volume). Yet the wealth of the nation-states of the Global North and their capacity to provide welfare, together with the poverty of the nation-states of the Global South, are connected through the histories of colonialism.

Post-colonial nation-states, which emerge through struggles for self-determination and decolonisation, necessarily understood themselves in relation to their previous colonisers and their previous subjugated position within a larger imperial state. We suggest that the modern nation-states within Europe should be understood similarly as they too emerged as nation-states after the dismantling of empire.[21] Prior to that, we suggest, there may have been national(ist) projects, but these existed within imperial polities. An address of these complex and overlapping concerns is facilitated through a consideration of regimes of taxation and modes of extraction across imperial polities. Further, examining how these remain in place in post-colonial contexts after formal decolonisation is also illuminating in terms of understanding patterns of global inequality today, themes that are taken up in each of the parts of the volume and which are discussed in more detail below.

The politics of economic governance: Taxation and welfare

A focus on taxation – and the distributed returns to citizens of that taxation – clarifies the nature of economic governance by the state, its limits and its boundaries. While taxation was initially seen to be a significant factor in the state's ability to wage war, by the mid-twentieth century it became more extensively bound up with its execution of domestic issues of welfare. Although scholars of distributive justice frequently postulate the necessity of boundaries to the possibility of just distribution, what is rarely considered is where the resources that are to be redistributed come from. Further, and relatedly, there is little discussion of what the entitlements are of those broader constituencies who have contributed to the building up of those collective resources, but who are under the rule of the political community without being seen to be part of it. As such, one of the themes this volume examines is the link between colonial extraction on the one hand and state and public expenditure in the domestic national interest on the other. It also looks at how these processes were managed within the imperial polities that then went on to establish themselves as national states. This, in turn, provides us with a new way to conceptualise contemporary issues of global inequality that we suggest are consequent to the historical establishment of imperial inequalities.

Both states and empires accumulated revenue through taxation, simultaneously an economic and a political project. Brown's chapter in this volume demonstrates how, from the start of its colonial project, England leveraged both private finance as well as public taxation to finance colonialism in Ireland and generated profits to expand its colonial enterprise across the Atlantic. Taxation revenue could be in cash or kind (also known as tribute), and revenue extracted in this way was imagined as a public good. What differentiated taxation, at least hypothetically and often legally, from other forms of coerced extraction, was the notion that the taxpayer could expect some kind of return. There were expectations that economic revenues extracted through taxation would be put to the service of the political community, through the provision of protection, justice, or welfare. That this was not always the case is cogently demonstrated in the chapters by Sanchez (pointing to the ways in which metropole France established colonial markets exclusively for its own benefit) and Park (discussing the ways in which taxation could be seen as sovereign seizure).

Taxation was often an insurmountable economic burden for those at the margins of society, but taxpaying often also demarcated the boundaries of citizenship or other forms of belonging within a given political community and a stake, at least hypothetically, in the benefits of that political community. This theme is developed in the chapter by Woker, who shows how the need to maintain the consent of metropolitan French taxpayers limited the extent to which the French state could invest in its colonial enterprise. It is also picked up in Yates's chapter which examines continued extraction from post-colonial Haiti as central to debates around citizenship and entitlement in metropolitan France. Rawlings's chapter develops a related theme, concerning how colonial taxation helped construct racial inequalities of citizenship in the Pacific. From a different angle, Manse addresses the ways in which colonial resistance to taxation also shaped its particular configurations.

Different states and empires conceptualised the political membership and socio-economic rights of their subjects in different ways. In the Roman Empire of antiquity, for example, all citizens paid taxes and received identical tokens (tesserae) to receive the same amount of grain whether or not they were poor.[22] In the Spanish Empire in the early modern period, colonised indigenous Americans were classed as subjects of the Crown like other subjects in the Iberian Peninsula, but different groups were subject to different taxation and redistribution regimes (see the chapters by McClure and Sallé). In the French Empire, the ways people were categorised in empire changed during the nineteenth and twentieth centuries. In the 'old colonies' people were classed as citizens, but in the newer colonies (the so-called 'second' French Empire) people were classed as subjects, and across the French nation and empire people were taxed and governed differently (see Woker's chapter in this volume). In the British Empire, the way in which different people were taxed and governed was part of a conscious strategy to structure inequalities (see the chapters by Channing and Latif). Across national and imperial spaces, ruling powers needed to manage not only the extraction but also the distribution of resources and the different expectations of access to public goods in both colonies and metropoles. Mackillop's chapter demonstrates the ways in which imperial wealth flowed back to the metropole and was put in service, partly, to the maintenance of the health of citizens there.

The sinews of taxation and welfare that bound states and empires through the flow of economic and political resources were the same structures that helped create and maintain many of the inequalities that came to characterise the modern world. There is a growing body of literature on the ways in which political projects of taxation created inequalities historically. Guido Alfani and M. Di Tullio have shown that in pre-modern Europe taxation regimes had tended to increase inequality as the poor were taxed more than the rich.[23] The implication is that the rise of citizenship rights within states begins to produce a change in regimes of distribution, but it is an argument that is restricted to the nation and, therefore, misses how the 'pre-modern' regime identified by Alfani and Di Tullio is continued as an aspect of modern colonialism and imperialism. For example, historians such as Martin Daunton have conducted case studies on the ways in which taxation of colonial subjects helped increase economic inequalities between the metropole and its colonies.[24] Global histories by Fibiger Bang and C. A. Bayly have looked at the role played by taxation in holding large-scale empires together.[25] Economists such as Stanley L. Engerman and Kenneth L. Sokoloff have followed the methodologies of New Institutional Economics and asked what role colonial taxation regimes have played in the creation of post-colonial patterns of global inequality.[26] More recently, Vanessa Ogle has shown that the emergence of tax havens during the processes of decolonisation helped maintain many of the patterns of economic inequality that emerged under colonialism (see also the chapters by

Cobham, Gilbert, and Rawlings).[27] The chapters in this volume contribute to this literature and show that taxation regimes varied across national and imperial spaces and created inequalities in different ways. This volume makes a critical intervention in the global history of inequality by exploring how not only the economics of taxation but also how the broader political project of taxation and the concomitant enterprise of welfare shaped the socio-economic contours of inequality.

Earlier, Joseph Schumpeter set out a stadial theory of state formation which placed the development of certain tax regimes at the centre of genealogies of state formation, depicting states transitioning from domain states to tax states.[28] Taxation has been recognised as important to the emergence of states and is central to the birth of political economy that governed these states, but this history is seldom read in relation to its imperial and colonial contexts. Placing the history of state formation in a global context has helped challenge the Schumpeterian model, highlighting the complexities and diversities of fiscal state formation,[29] but such histories still tend to focus upon the importance of taxation, overlooking welfare and highlighting the importance of the nation-state rather than imperial spaces.

Histories of state formation have often focused upon the development of tax structures within national boundaries and the expenditure on warfare internationally. The sociologist Charles Tilly, for example, argued that state formation was driven by capital and coercion, that states developed the infrastructure for taxation in order to meet the costs of war.[30] Histories of state formation have tended to focus upon the collection of taxes nationally for the costs of war internationally. Yet not only warfare but also political projects of welfare were important to the development of states and empires. The economic historian Martin Daunton observed that the relationship between taxation and welfare provision shaped the way states developed in the modern period,[31] but such studies have been confined to nation-states in the modern period.[32] Indeed, the formative role of welfare in the ongoing political projects of empires has often been overlooked (see Sallé's chapter in this volume).[33] For example, as is set out in various chapters in this volume, political projects of welfare, broadly defined, have been important to the dynamics of state and empire formation for far longer.

The chapters in this volume help us to understand welfare more broadly as a political project, by reading it in relation to taxation and understanding its role in the politics of the economic governance across national and imperial spaces. As Bhambra and Holmwood have demonstrated, taxation of, and the extraction of resources from, colonial dependencies are part of the explanation for the growth of the resources available for the establishment of national welfare states.[34] However, there is little work that explicitly traces such connections. As Daunton himself notes, 'surprisingly little has been written about the taxation of the British empire from the point of view of the colonies, and the decisions about the mode of extraction of revenue'.[35] Further, the role of welfare in the history of the development of empires is also poorly understood,[36] although there is growing awareness of the roles played both politically and economically of charity and philanthropic institutions and practices in empires (see the chapter by Mackillop in this volume).[37]

Welfare, broadly defined as resources for the public good, has both political and economic functions in society. As Daunton has observed, the history of welfare is far from a simple story.[38] The history of welfare needs to be situated in its proper context as a tool of governance for both states and empires. In this volume, welfare is understood variously across the different chapters in terms of being a common good, of public expenditure on institutions such as hospitals and schools and public goods such as roads, and private expenditure on charity and philanthropic practices.

Structure of the volume

This volume is an interdisciplinary collaboration that prioritises historical and sociological approaches, although some chapters also take an economic history lens. The various contributions seek to reframe familiar subjects of colonial extraction and the national distribution of resources through an understanding of the connections that bound colonies to metropoles – that is, in the context of imperial polities. The focus of the volume is on the need to understand the politics of economic governance across national and imperial spaces, rather than providing cost–benefit analyses of colonialism.[39] The chapters, collectively, address the role of the politics of taxation and welfare in governing the movement of capital across states and empires. They further point to the significant implications of such endeavours for the establishment of pathways of global inequality. Further, examining the relationship between states and empires from the perspective of the political projects of taxation and welfare also demonstrates the permeability of the boundaries between public and private capital. This opens up new avenues of inquiry for mapping the different ways in which colonialism was responsible for the inequalities that configure our present.

The volume examines the institutional and fiscal issues at stake in the modes of extraction within Europe's global empires. It looks at the different forms of welfare provided within the imperial polity in terms of who contributed, who had access, and how this was differentiated. It also addresses the various taxation regimes in operation in different European empires and how these play out in post-colonial times. The volume, as a whole, explores the 'nationalisation' of imperial and colonial revenues, the formation of (and local resistance to) taxation regimes across empire, and the consequences for contemporary, that is, post-colonial social and political structures of welfare. Further, the volume questions the extent to which national public expenditure on welfare and private expenditure on philanthropy was possible due to imperial extraction, and what role public and philanthropic expenditure played in legitimating and normalising trends of global inequality more broadly. Today, all of the top ten – and eighteen of the top twenty – countries with the highest expenditure of gross domestic product (GDP) on welfare are European countries (Japan and New Zealand are also in the top twenty; the USA is twenty-first). To what extent has this European project of public expenditure on welfare been made possible by histories of colonial extraction?

The chapters establish a diachronic and transnational comparative framework for exploring these key questions, stretching from the early modern period to the present day, and encompassing the Spanish, French, Dutch, and British empires. This diverse selection of case studies and approaches do not aim to tell a single story about the role of taxation and welfare in connecting empires and nations, but rather help us to draw new insights into the collection and distribution of resources across national and imperial units and the patterns of inequality they create. The aim is not necessarily to draw new empirical conclusions but to probe the gaps in our understanding of the role of taxation and welfare in the relationship between states and empires and to participate in a conversation about the politics of economic governance across imperial spaces. As such, the chapters signpost the different ways of looking at the historic relationships between states and empires and the role played by the politics of economic governance in the creation and reproduction of global inequalities.

The volume is organised into three parts: 'Institutional and fiscal issues', 'Taxation and welfare', and 'Post-colonial legacies'. Part I offers chapters which examine the meaning of colonial 'financial autonomy' and the right of sovereign seizure, the ways in which taxation shaped imperial projects, and the development of fiscal capacity in the broader empires. Part II explores the ways in which beneficiaries of imperial extraction justified wealth inequalities using notions of the common good, spiritual economy of charity, philanthropy, or welfare provision. These notions were informed variously by humanistic ideas of ideal political community, religious ideas of obligation and return, and theories of morality or civilisation. The final part explores the legacies of imperial inequalities that were created through unequal colonial taxation regimes and the ways in which these shape contemporary economic policies through tax havens and the ongoing influence of former colonisers on the shapes of redistributive regimes in nominally post-colonial countries.

The Preface, by Quinn Slobodian, draws out the contemporary political implications of the scholarly research presented in the volume and highlights its relevance for thinking about such issues in the present. In particular, he highlights the ways in which tax injustice undercuts political legitimacy and calls for the remaking of democracy – the building of a new commons – that would rest on an accountability of past injustice in its contemporary mission of redress.

David Brown's chapter opens the first part which examines the fiscal innovations and strategies of governing groups to fund and maintain empires. In his chapter, Brown explains how England's imperial expansion into Ireland in the seventeenth century helped fund future imperial expansion and established a model of using public funds, raised through taxation, for the benefit of private interests. In particular, he sets out the ways in which Irish resources – comprising the population, produce, and land – were central to British imperial expansion and its involvement in the 'triangular trade'. This is followed by a chapter by Madeline Woker that charts how, from the start of the twentieth century, the French Empire devolved aspects of financial autonomy to its colonies so that the colonial subjects effectively paid for their own governance through direct taxation. This fiscal delinking both increased the extraction of tax from colonised populations and, at the same time, explicitly limited welfare, or 'national solidarity', to hexagonal France. Samuel F. Sanchez goes on to explain how the French Empire was able to profit from its invasion of Madagascar in the late nineteenth century by cannibalising the pre-colonial royal tax system and manipulating it to establish Madagascar as a key market for the French economy. These developments upset the economic and social relations within Madagascar with longer term consequences for the state after colonialism.

Emma Park examines the relationship between taxation and sovereignty by looking at how the Imperial British East Africa Company used the structures of taxation for imperial extraction in Eastern Africa. She sets out the complex relationship between the assertion of corporate sovereignty and the seizure of monies (tax) and the difficulties in reconciling these as corporate profits – difficulties that shape the way in which such issues continue to be debated in the present. In the final chapter of this part, Laura Channing demonstrates how the British imperial state established taxation regimes in Sierra Leone which were organised in terms of its different geographical units – protectorate, colony, and municipality. These differences exploited and reinforced local hierarchies, including in relation to how and where the taxes collected were spent, and created an enduring legacy of inequality.

The second part explores how taxation and welfare regimes spanned national and imperial spaces and played conjoined roles in the construction of states and empires. Julia McClure examines how taxation and welfare helped create the inequalities of the Spanish imperial state in the sixteenth century. She argues that the public–private pathway to imperial state formation gave sovereignty a more contractual nature, which heightened the need for taxation to be reciprocated with provisions of justice and welfare, but both taxation and welfare increased rather than decreased inequality. Camille Sallé then provides a focused example of the way the Spanish Crown taxed colonial subjects to fund their welfare provision in hospitals specifically for indigenous workers in the colonial mines of Potosí in the viceroyalty of Peru. The mines of Potosí have been recognised as important to the history of empires and global inequalities, as the site from which resources were extracted using various forms of Amerindian and African forced labour, but they have been underexplored as a site of political governance where inhabitants were subjected to regimes of taxation and welfare.

This is followed by a chapter by Andrew Mackillop which examines what the British Empire meant for Scottish nation building and how imperial wealth helped fund welfare provision in Scotland. Mackillop examines the connections between notions of health and wealth across national and imperial spaces, how empire was perceived to fit with national discourses of 'improvement', and how imperial revenues were used to mitigate some of the destabilising effects of imperial migration. Maarten Manse focuses upon the Dutch colonial tax system between the end of the nineteenth and beginning of the twentieth century. He complicates our understanding of the role of taxation simply as an extractive tool of empire, demonstrating how colonial subjects reshaped, reinterpreted, and resisted certain taxation policies in ways which had a lasting legacy on local politics and social organisation in the East Indies. Manse explains how taxation was used as a political tool to govern colonial society in Dutch Indonesia, which was made more effective by use of the pre-colonial indigenous tax systems. In the final chapter of this part, Gurminder K. Bhambra examines the relationship between taxation and welfare in the British state. In particular, she argues that the imperial boundaries of Britain were constructed through relations of extraction (that included the payment of income tax by colonial subjects in India), while the national project came into being through relations of redistribution, or welfare, that were primarily limited to the island.

The final part explores the legacies of the relationships between colonial taxation regimes, national welfare states, and global inequalities through the periods of decolonisation to the present day. Alexia Yates explains how

France continued to benefit economically from its former colony Haiti, even after its independence, through the way it structured its debt obligations. She further sets out the ways in which involvement in international debt established modes of political engagement within France and demonstrated the character of its ongoing imperial relations. In the following chapter, Lyla Latif demonstrates that, much as in Channing's example of Sierra Leone, the bureaucratic structures of the British Empire in Kenya, including its taxation regimes, created the enduring inequalities of the independent state of Kenya. Latif argues that the British Empire left Kenya structured towards the extraction of its resources (first through colonial taxation and later through neoliberal economics) which left it unable to finance its own development of a welfare state.

As many scholars have argued, decolonisation did not mean the end of empire but the evolution of new forms of imperial formation. In his chapter, Gregory Rawlings demonstrates how, between the nineteenth and twentieth centuries, Pacific islands transitioned from being sources of revenue through colonial taxation by European powers to sources of revenue for global elites through the creation of tax havens. As both forms of empire and capital mutate, the colonial 'periphery' still facilitates capital accumulation for global elites via the manipulation of local taxation regimes. This is followed by Alex Cobham's chapter in which he argues that taxation regimes are as important to maintaining global inequalities in today's globalised financial system as they were during the age of formal empires. In particular, he examines how the trend of the private accumulation of wealth in tax havens developed through imperial processes. Paul Gilbert, in the final chapter, looks at the role of Crown Agents and the CDC Group (formerly the Commonwealth Development Corporation, and prior to that the Colonial Development Corporation) since the decline of Britain's formal empire. He highlights how these institutions effectively continue aspects of imperial taxation and colonial administration into the present day.

The Afterword, by Heloise Weber, offers a perceptive reflection on the chapters and discusses the broad themes of the volume as read through a lens of international development. It addresses the significance of the histories set out in the volume to contemporary configurations of inequality and the possibilities of their redress.

As a whole, the volume provides a distinctive examination of various contours of global inequality through an explicit address of the historical legacies of colonialism. It mobilises historical research to transform the parameters of how we think about issues of political economy and, specifically, the politics of economic governance across European empires and their post-colonial legacies.

Notes

1 Branko Milanovic, *Global Inequality: A New Approach for the Age of Globalization* (London: Harvard University Press, 2016).
2 Thomas Piketty, *Capital and Ideology*, trans. Arthur Goldhammer (Cambridge, MA: Harvard University Press, 2020).
3 For further discussion, see Gurminder K. Bhambra, 'Narrating inequality, eliding empire', *British Journal of Sociology* 72.1 (2021), 69–78.
4 Heloise Weber, *The Politics of Development: A Survey* (London: Routledge, 2014).
5 Bartolomé Yun-Casalilla, Patrick K. O'Brien, and Francisco Comín Comín, *The Rise of Fiscal States: A Global History, 1500–1914* (Cambridge: Cambridge University Press, 2012).
6 Elisabeth S. Clemens, *What is Political Sociology?* (Cambridge: Polity, 2016).
7 Douglass C. North and Barry R. Weingast, 'Constitutions and commitment: The evolution of institutions governing public choice in seventeenth-century England', *Journal of Economic History* 49.4 (1989), 803–32.
8 Joel Mokyr, *A Culture of Growth: The Origins of the Modern Economy* (Princeton, NJ: Princeton University Press, 2016); S. R. Epstein, *Freedom and Growth: The Rise of States and Markets in Europe, 1300–1750* (London: Routledge, 2000).
9 W. W. Rostow, *The Stages of Economic Growth: A Non-Communist Manifesto* (Cambridge: Cambridge University Press, 1960).
10 See, for example, Quinn Slobodian, *Globalists: The End of Empire and the Birth of Neoliberalism* (Cambridge, MA: Harvard University Press, 2018).
11 For example, Kenneth Pomeranz, *The Great Divergence: China, Europe, and the Making of the Modern World Economy* (Princeton, NJ: Princeton University Press, 2000); Prasannan Parthasarathi, *Why Europe Grew Rich and Asia Did Not: Global Economic Divergence, 1600–1850* (Cambridge: Cambridge University Press, 2011).
12 Dadabhai Naoroji, *Poverty and UnBritish Rule in India* (London: Swan Sonnenschein & Co., Ltd, 1901).
13 Lajpat Rai, *England's Debt to India* (1917).
14 C. L. R. James, *The Black Jacobins: Toussaint L'Ouverture and the San Domingo Revolution*, 2nd edn (New York: Vintage, 1989 [1963, 1938]).
15 Eric Williams, *Capitalism and Slavery* (Chapel Hill: University of North Carolina Press, 1944).
16 Walter Rodney, *How Europe Underdeveloped Africa* (London: Bogle-L'Ouverture Publication and Dar-es-Salaam: Tanzania Publishing House, 1972).
17 Samir Amin, *Unequal Development: An Essay on the Social Formations of Peripheral Capitalism*, trans. Brian Pierce (New York: Monthly Review Press, 1976).
18 Eduardo Galeano, *Open Veins of Latin America: Five Centuries of the Pillage of a Continent*, trans. Cedric Belfrage (New York: Monthly Review Press, 1971).

19 Pomeranz, *The Great Divergence*. Pomeranz overturned the ideas of the 'European miracle' established by Eric Jones. Eric Jones, *The European Miracle* (Cambridge: Cambridge University Press, 1981).
20 Gurminder K. Bhambra, 'Colonial global economy: Towards a theoretical reorientation of political economy', *Review of International Political Economy* 28.2 (2021), 307–22.
21 Gurminder K. Bhambra, 'The postcolonial state', in Robbie Shilliam and Olivia Rutazibwa (eds), *Routledge Handbook of Postcolonial Politics* (London: Routledge, 2018), pp. 200–9.
22 Peter Brown, *Poverty and Leadership in the Later Roman Empire* (Hanover; and London: Brandeis Press), p. 5.
23 Guido Alfani and M. Di Tullio, *The Lion's Share: Inequality and the Rise of the Fiscal State in Preindustrial Europe* (Cambridge: Cambridge University Press, 2019).
24 Martin Daunton, 'Tax transfers: Britain and its empire, 1848–1914', in Holger Nehring and Florian Schui (eds), *Global Debates on Taxation* (Basingstoke: Palgrave, 2007), pp. 137–57.
25 Peter Fibiger Bang and C. A. Bayly, *Tributary Empires in Global History* (Basingstoke: Palgrave Macmillan, 2011).
26 Stanley L. Engerman and Kenneth L. Sokoloff, 'Colonialism, inequality, and long-run paths of development', *NBER Working Paper* 11057 (2005).
27 Vanessa Ogle, '"Funk money": The end of empires, the expansion of tax havens and decolonization as an economic and financial event', *Past & Present* 249.1 (2021), 213–49.
28 Joseph Schumpeter, 'The crisis of the tax state'. Enlarged version of a lecture Schumpeter gave before the Wiener Soziologische Gesellschaft. Published in 1918 under the title 'Die Krise der Steuerstaates' as issue number 4 of *Zeiqragen azu dem Gebiet der Soziologie*. An English translation, by Wolfgang F. Stolper and Richard A. Musgrave, appeared (1954) in *International Economic Papers* 4. For a broader discussion on the role of taxation in the rise of states, see Richard Bonney (ed.), *The Rise of the Fiscal State in Europe c.1200–1815* (Oxford: Oxford University Press, 1999).
29 Yun-Casalilla, O'Brien, and Comín, *The Rise of Fiscal States*.
30 Charles Tilly, *Coercion, Capital, and European States, AD 990–1992* (Oxford: Blackwell, 1990).
31 M. J. Daunton, 'Payment and participation: Welfare and state-formation in Britain 1900–1951', *Past & Present* 150 (1996), 169–216.
32 Joseph Schumpeter saw the provision of common welfare as something enabled by the transition to the modern fiscal state; Schumpeter, 'The crisis of the tax state'. T. H. Marshall explained the importance of the development of the modern welfare state in relation to the evolution of citizenship; T. H. Marshall, 'Citizenship and social class', in D. Held, J. Anderson, B. Gieben *et al.*, *States and Societies* (Oxford, 1983, first printed in 1948). On the formation of the liberal welfare state, see Pat Thane, *Foundations of the Welfare State*, 2nd edn (London: Longman, 1996).

33 See Julia McClure, 'Poverty and empire', in David Hitchcock and Julia McClure (eds), *The Routledge Handbook of the History of Poverty in Early Modern Europe* (Abingdon: Routledge, 2020), pp. 39–59.
34 Gurminder K. Bhambra and John Holmwood, 'Colonialism, postcolonialism and the liberal welfare state', *New Political Economy* 23.5 (2018), 574–87; see also Robbie Shilliam, *Race and the Undeserving Poor: From Abolition to Brexit* (London: Agenda Publishing, 2018).
35 Daunton, 'Tax transfers', p. 137.
36 James Midgley and David Piachaud called for more research into the way European imperialism shaped the development of the world's social welfare institutions; James Midgley and David Piachaud, *Colonialism and Welfare, Social Policy and the British Imperial Legacy* (Cheltenham: Edward Elgar, 2012).
37 See Julia McClure, 'Introduction', 'Empires of Charity Special Edition', *New Global Studies* 12.2 (2018), 123–30, and the articles in this special edition.
38 Daunton, 'Payment and participation', p. 212, cites Maier, 'Introduction', in Charles S. Maier (ed.), *Changing Boundaries of the Political: Essays on the Evolving Balance between State and Society, Public and Private in Europe* (Cambridge: Cambridge University Press, 1987), p. 2.
39 This has been debated by global economic historians; for example, see Patrick K. O'Brien, 'The costs and benefits of British imperialism 1846–1914', *Past & Present* 120 (1988), 163–200.

Part I

Institutional and fiscal issues

1

The great gage: Mortgaging Ireland to finance an empire

David Brown

Despite two decades of civil wars, England achieved a great imperial expansion in the mid-seventeenth century. The Wars of the Three Kingdoms, 1638–60, had left Ireland economically flattened and Scotland in not much better shape, while England slowly nursed the social and political changes brought about by its revolution. This revolutionary period at home was book-ended by two disastrous naval wars with Spain that left England's merchants, and their rulers, in no doubt as to which European state was the pre-eminent colonial power in the Atlantic. In 1651, English merchants were forced out of their sole trading post on the Gambia River and England's parliament had to send its own navy to reassert control over British colonies in Virginia and the Caribbean. Between 1663 and 1669, however, despite plague and the Great Fire of London, £2 million in manufactured goods were exported through the port of London.[1] This transformation of England's trade was an astonishing turnaround that gathered pace throughout the reign of Charles II, from his restoration in 1660 until his death in 1685, when the three kingdoms once again fell into a period of conflict. By then, however, English merchants had established a major trading post at Mumbai, factories to trade in gold and enslaved people at several points along the coast of West Africa, while Barbados had become entrenched as the most profitable component of Britain's empire through the exploitation of the labour of more than 40,000 enslaved Africans.[2]

It had taken 500 years for sputtering British colonial ambitions to advance to this stage of development. Britain's first colony was in Ireland, invaded from Wales in the late twelfth century and controlled in parts from a Pale of Settlement centred on Dublin.[3] Colonisation expanded greatly during the early years of the seventeenth century, when the development of English and Scottish plantations in Ireland was at its peak. This activity coincided with the early development of English colonies in the wider Atlantic. The promoters and investors in these colonial activities were often active in multiple geographical regions.[4] Britain's colony in Ireland was almost lost with the Irish rebellion of October 1641 and the establishment of the Irish Confederacy at Kilkenny in its aftermath.[5] To crush the Irish rebellion, an almost equally rebellious English parliament colluded with Charles I in April 1642 to launch the Adventure for Irish Land. The aim of this Adventure was to collect £1 million from private investors to send an army to Ireland and crush the rebellion. The investors were to be repaid with the landed estates of defeated rebels, a collective punishment that encompassed all Catholic Irish landowners.

England's reconquest of Ireland became, therefore, a private enterprise in line with the financing models of all of England's other colonial undertakings up to this point. Britain's Atlantic expansion in the early decades of the seventeenth century had been achieved by an eccentric mosaic of private trading companies and individual plantation enterprises. These ranged from well-organised joint stock companies – the Virginia Companies and Massachusetts Bay Company being prominent examples – to Robert Rich, the 2nd earl of Warwick's Bermuda Company that was essentially a playground for rich young noblemen.[6] A second approach was to award huge tracts of unknown lands to favoured courtiers, irrespective of whether the British Crown had any claim to these territories. Examples of these undertakings were grants of the Caribbean to Sir James Hay, 1st earl of Carlisle, and of Nova Scotia to William Alexander, both Scottish nobleman who were to encroach on the Spanish and French empires respectively.[7] Most of these endeavours ended in repeated failures. The Virginia Company became bankrupt three times before its trade in tobacco was taken over by a competent and well-financed group of London merchants in the 1630s. The other Atlantic colonies followed a similar path, so by the time the Irish revolt came about in 1641, solving colonial difficulties using private enterprise had become the norm, rather than an outlier.[8] Having endured widespread opposition to his ship money tax in the 1630s, the king had become more receptive to deploying resources other than taxation to resolve his increasing burden of difficulties.

It was not without precedent, therefore, that the state turned to private finance as an alternative to taxation to prosecute the early phases of the Wars of the Three Kingdoms. In 1642, London's colonial merchants, sensing an opportunity to acquire the landed estates of the rebellious Irish for a fraction of their value, aggressively promoted the forfeiture and redistribution of the estates of Catholic Ireland as the solution to the king's problems. This land, high-quality productive agricultural land that had been carefully husbanded over many centuries, was priced between one and a half and six pence per acre, a similar value to the nominal cost of undeveloped land in England's North American colonies. The eventual scheme, the Adventure for Irish land, was enabled by an act of the Westminster parliament and was published with the assent of Charles I on 19 March 1642.[9] Significantly, the Irish parliament was not consulted and from this point had only a small role to play in major policy decisions concerning Ireland. Politically, Ireland became England's colony. Practically, one quarter of Ireland was mortgaged to merchants as a desperate gamble to preserve British colonial ambitions. Buried in the Adventurer's Act, intended as a bribe to encourage Charles's assent to what was a parliamentary undertaking at the outbreak of the First English Civil War, was a transformative annual tax on land, the Quit Rent, to be calculated at an average rate of three pence on each acre of land. The yield to the Crown would be roughly £10,000 per year, enabling much of the royal household's day-to-day expenses to be met by taxing Ireland, rather than the king's subjects in England. In the event, the money, and the army that had been raised, were both used by Parliament against Charles I. Despite this diversion, the Adventure had become law and its contributors devoted considerable energy over the ensuing years to collect their winnings.

Ireland remained in rebellion until 1648, when a peace treaty with Charles I brought all of Ireland not under the control of English parliamentary forces into the royalist camp. Virginia and Barbados, the most economically important of England's Atlantic colonies, had also sided with the royalist cause. The senior colonial merchants, however, those who were profiting the most from colonial trade, were on the side of the parliamentarians. Unwilling to shoulder the financial burden of bringing the colonies to heel themselves, these colonial merchants orchestrated a series of political, and then military initiatives to ensure that the cost of securing their commercial empires came from the pockets of taxpayers, rather than their own. The most significant new arm of the state was the Council of Trade, formed in 1650 to formulate a new external trade policy for the Commonwealth and staffed almost entirely by merchants.[10] The Council of Trade's Navigation Act in 1651, the centrepiece of which was a ban on all non-English shipping from interacting with the colonies, was a statement of the monopolistic aspirations of the Council's members.[11] In October 1651, however, the Navigation Act was merely aspirational; it would have to be imposed on the colonies. For the first time, the re-conquest of the colonies was entrusted to Parliament's navy and its Navy Commissioners.[12] Until 1651, the colonial planters, merchants, chartered trading companies, and shippers had been expected to manage their own affairs and to send out their own vessels to protect these investments. The state would sometimes issue official letters of *marque* to effect reprisals against foreign vessels, but in most cases acts of encroachment or piracy were left to the merchants to sort out. The English naval expeditions of 1651, intended to secure the private business interests of merchants in the Atlantic colonies, were financed with public funds, in this case the proceeds from sequestered estates. With this change, the state was no longer the passive beneficiary of taxes on colonial produce. The state was now subsidising colonial production. For the first time, the Atlantic colonies had become a primary responsibility of the state, in which treasure must be invested rather than merely extracted, and the colonies had reached such a level of economic and strategic importance that they could no longer be left to private interests. The colonies had, in fact, become like Ireland – with the significant difference that Ireland had its own supply of labour. The English slave trade also emerged permanently from the shadows in 1651, as an integral part of the colonial strategy of the Council of Trade.

In 1649, Oliver Cromwell was selected by Parliament to lead the expeditionary force to Ireland, with £535,000 committed to the campaign.[13] The entire apparatus of state finance was placed at Cromwell's disposal. A £20,000 per month subsidy for Ireland was implemented, a general tax on the population based on either income or wealth.[14] By the standards of Civil War England, this tax was collected with brutal efficiency, and a respectable £108,500 was raised from a target of £120,000, with £87,000 of that paid directly to Cromwell's campaign and the remainder to suppliers.[15] Two treasurers were appointed to manage the collection and disbursement of the tax: Thomas Andrews and Maurice Thomson. Andrews was an old hand at state finance and was treasurer of the Adventure for Irish Land of 1642. The investors in the Adventure would reap the rewards of Cromwell's Irish campaign. Maurice Thomson had been the treasurer for a smaller speculation in the conquest of Ireland in 1642, the additional sea adventure.[16] Thomson was also the senior figure on the Board of Trade and personified the links between the conquest of Ireland and England's broader colonial ambitions. The invasion fleet was commanded by George Ayscue, who would next be sent to Barbados, in 1651, to execute a similar mission. Large amounts of cash were delivered directly to Ireland, by, for example, the arrival of the *Guinea Frigate* at Cork in January 1650 with thirty barrels of freshly minted Commonwealth coin.[17]

Oliver Cromwell's brutal Irish campaign, 1649–50, paid for by English taxpayers for the benefit of private investors, laid a foundation for England's early modern empire. By the 1650s, the war in Ireland had dragged on for so long that the adventures, the vouchers to claim lands, were changing hands for a fraction of their original value in 1642.[18] Although Cromwell himself left Ireland in May 1650, never to return, the war between royalists and parliamentarians dragged on until 1653 and was even then only replaced with guerrilla fighting.[19] In the late 1640s, a total of £2 million was collected from English taxpayers to finance the conquest of Ireland, but even this enormous sum was not enough.[20] When in direct command, Cromwell scrupulously ensured that his soldiers were well and regularly paid. After Cromwell left Ireland, however, arrears of pay spiralled rapidly out of control. Cromwell was occupied in Scotland and there was nothing left in Ireland to tax. To add to the misery of the Adventurers for Irish Land who stood to gain the most from Cromwell's taxpayer-funded conquest of Ireland, in 1652 Cromwell stated that all arrears of pay for the huge army still serving in Ireland would also be redeemed in seized land. This promise was enshrined in what became the legislative foundation for the Irish land settlement, 'An Act for the Setling of Ireland', in August 1652.[21]

England's first great imperial project of the early modern period, the conquest of Ireland, was a vast transfer of wealth from two major groups of the population to a small number of well-connected investors and speculators. The first cohort of contributors were the ordinary taxpayers of England, as the military conquest was paid for in the first instance with a tax on income and assets, and later with a portion of the English excise.[22] The second cohort was Irish landowners, irrespective of whether they had participated in the rebellion of 1641. The landed estates of Catholic Ireland that were the security for the Adventure were awarded in full to the original investors or their descendants, by the Acts of Settlement and Explanation of 1662–66. In the general changing of the guard that followed the fall of the Cromwellians, the value of debentures for Irish land continued to fall, enabling speculators and courtiers to snap up some 640,000 acres in Ireland at rock-bottom prices. It was the largest transfer of land in Western Europe during the early modern period. For the beneficiaries of the Restoration land acts, this sequestered land had cost almost nothing but represented an unexploited store of value on a scale that London's financial markets had not experienced before.[23]

While this great expanse of Irish land was being acquired, a great advance in banking practice had taken place in London during the 1650s. The scrivener's bank of Clayton and Morris had perfected the long-term mortgage, meaning that once Irish land had been acquired for a low value, it could be mortgaged at its real, higher value, freeing up large amounts of capital for the new landowner.[24] Their methodological advance took the form of the estate particular, a detailed set of documents that set out the exact measurements of the land, any debts or other encumbrances that may have been registered against it, the annual rental income that could be expected from the estate, and, ideally, a list of tenants.[25] This new form of mortgage had advantages for both borrower and lender. For the borrower, the repayment term of perhaps ten years was far longer than the six months to one year traditionally available from merchant lending. For the lender, land was excellent security that could not be spirited away in the middle of the night, and the estate particular represented irrefutable proof of the value and provenance of the asset. The difficulty for the banker was that estate particulars were very expensive documents to produce.

Fortunately, however, the forfeited Irish estates were already supplied with estate particulars of the desired quality. These had been prepared in the 1650s at public expense and are known as the Civil and Down surveys.[26] The Civil Survey, 1654–56, was an inquisition made by local commissioners at dozens of locations across Ireland under the direction of Benjamin Worsley, formerly secretary to the Board of Trade and promoted to the position of Surveyor General of Ireland. The Civil Survey determined the rightful owner of the land in 1641, recovered a typical rent roll from before the conflicts and an inventory of the normally small number of buildings left standing after years of war. The Down Survey, 1655–59, was a mapped survey prepared under the direction Sir William Petty, who was also chairman of a committee for assigning land to army officers to settle their claims for arrears of pay.[27] Taken together, these two surveys could not have been better designed for servicing the burgeoning mortgage market pioneered by Clayton and Morris. Petty travelled frequently between Dublin and London to ensure that his work was up to the standards required by investors while London's financial community gathered for the feast.

Throughout the 1650s, the upper echelons of the Protectorate government in London and their vassals in Dublin had clung to a fantasy that included the colonisation of Ireland with English soldiers stranded after the wars, and large-scale investment in stock raising and commodities for export. These delusions were promoted through the publication of works such as Gerard Boate's *Ireland's Naturall History* in 1652, an exposition on the profits to be made from colonising Ireland and published by no less a figure than Samuel Hartlib. Boate had travelled to Ireland with Cromwell and died there while Benjamin Worsley and William Petty were amongst Hartlib's camp followers. Petty brought Hartlib's ideas to the newly formed Royal Society, when it was founded with a grant of Irish land in 1660.[28] The fallacy of a colonial Ireland that imprinted itself on the minds of intellectual London was almost entirely at odds with the intentions of the primary recipients of most of the land. Many of the soldiers simply wanted to go home and sold their entitlements to their officers or through brokers as soon as possible. The Adventurers, having patiently marshalled Charles II back to his throne, patiently brokered a series of changes to the law that would allow them to maximise their profits when they placed their own lands on the market.[29]

Like the intellectual circles that flattered Protestant landowners in Ireland into purchasing forfeited land at a healthy mark-up, London's merchant community had their own plans for Ireland, within their emerging vision of an imperial trading network. Ireland had many advantages in terms of a temperate climate, a large skilled population, and land which the Adventurers intended to acquire for a mere one tenth of the cost of land in England. The

Adventurers and Restoration-era merchants who piled into the land market wanted to convert Ireland into a great centre for raw materials, to supply cheap wool and flax into England, where artisans would convert it into the cloth that was the foundation of early modern England's international trade.[30] Cheap Irish wool would give England a huge competitive advantage in the international market, especially when it came to competing with the Dutch West India Company for access to markets for enslaved people in West Africa. English merchants were blocked from most Irish ports during the civil wars of the 1640s, so Irish goods, especially cloth, was instead brought to Africa by Dutch merchants.[31] The Irish Confederates were desperate for Dutch supplies, especially gunpowder, which kept prices low. By 1649, Irish commodities became so important within the Dutch Atlantic trading system that one of Charles I's last acts before his execution was an attempt to broker a trading alliance between the Irish Confederates and the Dutch Republic.[32] When war broke out between England and Spain in the late 1650s, large numbers of English tradesmen, desperate for work, moved to Holland to circumvent the Spanish ban on English finished cloth. English merchants could see the negative effects of mass skilled emigration from home and their petition demanded the recall of the tradesmen. Skilled manufacturing would stay in England while Ireland would produce the raw commodities, the classic imperial economic structure. Recalling how their last period of extended prosperity coincided with peace between England and Spain in the early seventeenth century, these merchants with an interest in Ireland needed an end the Anglo-Spanish war.[33] In 1660, therefore, they patiently marshalled Charles II back to his throne and brokered a series of changes to the law that would allow them to maximise their profits when they placed their own lands on the market.[34]

The first step in this legal process was to abolish the ancient rights associated with Irish land. These rights included feudal tenures, obligations to provide military support, and specific reliefs for inheritances, wardships, and marriages. These rights, built up by aristocratic families in Ireland over centuries, were integral to balancing the rights of private ownership against the power of the state to create arbitrary taxes, but were simply swept away by Westminster. The ancient rights had the potential to undermine the simple freeholds that England's authorities in Ireland were intent on issuing for the forfeited Catholic land. Once the sequestered estates were stripped of any customary advantages, the land could be valued in purely monetary terms.[35] Other holdovers from the Cromwellian era that reduced the value of the land were also quietly dropped. Provisions from the 'Act for Setling Ireland' of 1652, that leases to tenants could only be granted for a maximum period of seven years and land could only be purchased by English Protestants, were abolished.[36] Most significantly, the Cromwellian requirement that Irish Catholics must transplant to Connaught in the west of Ireland to make way for English settlers was quietly dropped.[37] Keeping former Irish landowners as tenants on their former estates guaranteed the rent roll and allowed the land to be mortgaged at the highest possible value.

Irish resources, its people, produce, and finally land, were an essential component of the earliest British imperial experiments in the wider Atlantic world. Lacking supplies in England, in the 1630s Sir Nicholas Crisp and his partners in the original Guinea Company turned to Richard Boyle, 1st earl of Cork, for supplies of bar iron to trade in Senegambia for gold and the enslaved.[38] The Guinea Company established a brisk trade in iron for gold, bartering iron sourced from Bandon, County Cork. Bar iron became a widely accepted currency in Senegambia during the early decades of the seventeenth century, and these cheap imports, together with other European manufactured goods, transformed the fortunes of local rulers within easy reach of the Europeans.[39] For Crisp, the alchemy of converting Irish iron into African gold landed him a lucrative share in the farm of the English customs in 1640.[40] Crisp could bring his gold to the Mint, where it was converted into the coin of the realm and loaned, at interest, to the state. For thirty years, 1630–60, England's Africa trade was developed by private merchants who clustered around Sir Nicholas Crisp and Maurice Thomson and kept the state at arm's length from their business. These merchants, however, were also deeply entangled in English tax farms and a licence for a monopolistic hold on the Africa trade was at once a reward to the merchants for supporting the state, and the financial means that enabled them to do so.

The interests of English investors in sequestered Irish land and in the burgeoning English trade in enslaved Africans converged in 1660. The detailed particulars of lands in Ireland, derived from the Cromwellian surveys, enabled land to be converted into cash on London's money markets. These estates, with their simplified titles, were worth a multiple of their annual rent but the land was often acquired for less than the rent for one year. Prominent among these investors was the scrivener banking firm of Sir Robert Clayton and William Morris, who aimed at first to emulate the iron-for-gold business, established in the 1630s by the earl of Cork and Sir Nicholas Crispe.[41] Clayton and Morris put detailed plans in place to finance the construction of an iron mine and foundry in Enniscorthy, County Wexford.[42] The land was acquired from Colonel Robert Phayre, a Protestant soldier from Ireland who, in 1649, held Charles I prisoner while the order for Charles's execution was being drawn up. Phayre was arrested in 1660 and taken to the Tower of London. He was released in July 1661, with £2,000 proceeds from Irish land allocated to him by the Cromwellian regime for his pay arrears. Robert Clayton and John Morris financed this land purchase, and subsequently mortgaged the land for £30,000 to finance the construction of their ironworks.

Profits on this scale attracted many of the leading figures from London's financial circles. Sir Martin Noel, for example, an on-and-off partner of Thomson who had speculated heavily on land in Barbados in the 1640s, was granted 200 houses in the port town of Wexford, the hub of the Irish herring industry.[43] Clayton and Morris's ironworks at Enniscorthy was only a few miles away. In 1658, Noel went into partnership with another London merchant/financier, Alexander Bence. Bence had made a fortune financing Parliament's navy under Cromwell. Bence's son, also called Alexander, was sent to Dublin to coordinate trade with a kinsman who maintained a trading office in Seville to purchase wine. Bence and Noel made natural business partners as the exchange of fish for wine was the foundation of Britain's trade with Spain. Their partnership was so profitable that Bence and Noel agreed to farm the entire Irish customs and excise later in 1658, as the duties on these key commodities would become, in effect, payable to them. These farms were continued over the objections of the Irish Convention parliament in June 1660.[44] With these profits and their Spanish connections, Bence and Noel, with their immediate siblings based in London and Seville, became central to Charles II's plans to develop England's trade in enslaved Africans.

The Stuarts, in the person of Prince Rupert, realised the importance of the slave trade to England's colonial ambitions at a relatively early stage. It was Rupert, when in command of the English royalist fleet, who had forced Maurice Thomson's Guinea Company merchants from their foothold in the Gambia in 1651. On 18 December 1660, Charles granted the Africa trade to Rupert, James Duke of York, several other family members, leading nobles, and forty-six named merchants, including Bence and Noel.[45] This association was known as the Company of Royal Adventurers trading into Africa. Of these merchants, fully twenty-one were engaged in acquiring cheap land in Ireland, mainly from the representatives of army officers who were desperate to sell their entitlements for any price they could get and return home.[46] A similar grant was issued to the Duke of York and a smaller group of merchants on 11 September 1661 to establish the 'Morocco Company'.[47] The Morocco Company was intended to commercially exploit England's seizing of Tangier and, once again, the company was dominated by men who had recently received vast tracts of Irish land that could be exploited. Sir John Cutler, one of the Royal Adventurers trading into Africa, used his contacts in Bristol to source the skilled men and specialist equipment that would make Clayton and Morris's ironworks a reality. In 1661, Bence and Noel assigned the farm of the excise for the barony of Scarwalsh, in which the ironworks was situated, to Clayton and Morris's partnership. These partners could then exempt their mine from the excise, eliminating both these costs and the need to make returns at the port of Wexford. Cutler travelled to Ireland to oversee the completion of the building work and by 1662 the ironworks was in full production.[48] Twenty-four tons of irons were shipped through Kinsale to Virginia in this first year.[49] The largest customers, however, were in Bristol and Bridgewater, in the Bristol Channel. The client in Bridgewater was Benjamin Blake, a shipping contractor for the Company of Royal Adventurers.

While this work was underway, Charles's personal income from Ireland, in the form of the Quit Rent, failed to materialise. Earmarked by the Irish parliament to meet the costs of the military establishment until patents for land had been passed, soldiers were told to go to the sequestered estates and collect the rents themselves. One group of soldiers squatted near Clayton and Morris's iron mine until they were offered work cutting down trees as an alternative.[50] In 1662, Charles traded some of his sequestered land for the right to a permanent custom and excise, which was promptly farmed to Noel.[51] A hearth tax (a form of poll tax levied on every hearth in the country) and an ale tax were also imposed in 1662. In 1663, an alnage duty, a tax on cloth for export, was introduced that protected both English cloth exports to Africa and the iron mine. These taxes, taken together with the Quit Rent, increased the king's notional hereditary revenue from £35,000 per year before the Restoration to an expected £250,000 once the new taxes began to be collected. Charles expected a surplus for his own enjoyment of at least £100,000.[52] Although almost none of this money ever made it past the hands of the farmers to the Royal Household, Charles II seemed content to reward his new partners in the Company of Royal Adventurers with more concessions. This policy caused trouble in Ireland. In June 1666, for example, the garrison of troops stationed at Carrickfergus, in the north of Ireland, rebelled when they heard that taxes that had been collected for their pay had been spirited away to Dublin and into the hands of the farmers.[53]

None of this deterred the Stuarts. After a sputtering start, the Company of Royal Adventurers trading into Africa received a renewed charter on 20 January 1663. The officers of the company commenced regular meetings, once or twice a week, on 11 March 1664, and made the Duke of York its governor.[54] The company envisaged two arenas of commercial activity. Their first goal was to use the new base at Tangier to service Spain's demands for enslaved people through this outpost in North Africa.[55] Their second goal was to reoccupy and rebuild the abandoned outpost on the River Gambia. The Company of Royal Adventurers was run by a court of assistants that included the cohort of Irish land grantees. The most striking feature of the rolls of attendance for the company's meetings, however, is the presence at almost all of them of both royal princes, the Duke of York and Prince Rupert. Their attendance underlines the royal family's careful stewarding of England's slave trade during these early years, and their hopeful expectation of the financial bonanza that might accrue from their shareholding. James initially purchased £2,000 worth of shares and the next most important investors were Noel and Bence with investments of £1,000 and £900 respectively.[56] While the Irish land settlement completed its tortuous process through a Court of Claims in Dublin, and innumerable other legal challenges, the merchants at the court of the Company of Royal Adventurers indulged the three Stuarts – Charles II, James Duke of York, and their cousin Prince Rupert – in their dream of an empire in Africa. The Africa Company provided a novel opportunity for ordinary merchants to have regular audiences with the royal family. Unsurprisingly, these meetings came to the attention of more senior figures in London's financial circles, and in May 1664 the shareholders' ranks were swelled by the leading goldsmith bankers Sir Andrew Riccard and Sir Thomas Viner, who could provide the company with all the capital it needed.

Cheap manufactured goods to trade on the African coasts were central to the plans of the founders of the Company of Royal Adventurers to maximise their profits. When new patentees were appointed to the Company of Royal Adventurers in 1672, the company was expected to deliver enslaved Africans to the English Caribbean for approximately £17–£19 per person.[57] At the company's factory at Offra, an enslaved person was stated as costing 12 bars of iron.[58] There were normally around 72 bars of iron to a ton, meaning a merchant could obtain six people for one ton of iron.[59] The difficulty for the English slave traders was that England was not self-sufficient in iron in the mid-seventeenth century – almost half of the iron used in English manufacturing had to be imported.[60] England could only produce around 14,000 tons of iron per year, with limited land and diminishing forests from which to obtain timber for charcoal. Irish iron, produced for £12 per ton and sold in England for £16 with no excise, offered the Company of Royal Adventurers' shareholders a highly profitable opportunity.[61] Excluding freight costs, which were considerable, £12 worth of Irish iron could return £72 with the sale of an enslaved person at Bridgetown, Barbados. By 1663, when this supply chain was in place, Bence, Noel, the cream of London's early banking community, and the royal family made preparations to re-establish English trade in the Gambia and elsewhere.

On 11 May 1664, Charles confirmed a grant to Roger earl of Orrery and John Lord Kingston of the farm for licensing alcoholic drinks in Ireland and the excise due on them.[62] This farm was immediately sold on to Alexander Bence and his associates. Simultaneously, George Villiers, 2nd Duke of Buckingham and the largest aggregator of sequestered Irish land after the Duke of York, began his regular attendance at the meetings of the Company of Royal Adventurers.[63] The three key foundational pillars of the company were in place: cheap Irish land that could be mortgaged to provide capital, cheap Irish produce that could be exported to the company free of taxes, and the profits from the Irish tax farms that were available for the key promoters of the company to exploit. The capacity for Irish produce to service export markets is hinted at by the creation in Dublin of the short-lived Canary Company to corner the barter market for Canary Islands wine.[64] English merchants were fearful that the tax farmers, led by Alexander Bence, would corner the entire wine market worth £30,000 per year and break into the lucrative market supplying the enslaved to the Spanish Empire through intermediaries in the Canary Islands. The Canary Company was snuffed out while two agents of the Company of Royal Adventurers, Sir James Modyford and Sir John Colleton, signed a firm contract with the holders of the monopoly for the supply of enslaved people to Spanish America, Domingo Grillo and Ambrogio Lomellini.[65] This business was to be managed through the Bence family's agency in Seville.[66] The strategic goal of the Company of Royal Adventurers was to transform Barbados and Jamaica from sleepy producers of sugar into the principal slave markets in the Caribbean. With this lofty ambition, the Company of Royal Adventurers knew from the outset that it would require naval support to encroach on its principal competitor in Africa, the Dutch West India Company. Prince Rupert announced at the meeting of the court of assistants on 15 August that Charles II would provide the support of the navy to unseat the Dutch West India Company from some of its strongholds in West Africa.[67] In another disaster that resulted from English mercantile aggression, the Second Anglo-Dutch War of 1665–7, the Company of Royal Adventurers lost its entire stock and capital of £175,000.[68] Many of the investors in the Company of Royal Adventurers were wiped out financially, but all did not suffer equally. The two shareholders who were also farmers of the Irish customs, John Bence and Joseph Deane, were authorised by the king to keep £27,500 of Irish tax revenue as compensation for their losses.[69]

Following this disaster, more capital and fresh merchants were needed to keep Charles's imperial dream alive. In 1666 an Act of Explanation for the Irish land settlement was finally passed at Westminster, greatly improving the permanence of the land settlement and opening it up to further exploitation through the mortgage markets. John and Alexander Bence were appointed collectors for any revenue due from the land acts in 1667.[70] On 12 July 1669, Charles granted the farm of his entire suite of new taxes in Ireland to a consortium of merchants headed by John Forth, an alderman and sheriff of London.[71] William and John Dashwood, both of London, were recruited with five others to raise finance in London to loan against these future taxes, and two further men were recruited in Dublin to organise the collections. Forth and the Dashwoods were prominent among the first investors into a new Royal Africa Company stock that opened in November 1671.[72] Ford arranged a bridging loan for the Irish exchequer to tide it over until the farmers' team in Dublin had collected the taxes, but no further money was remitted.[73] The result was a stop of the Irish exchequer on 10 June 1671, a harbinger of England's stop the following year.[74] It would be easy to ascribe this sequence of events to the incompetence or larceny of the farmers, but there is evidence of collusion and intense familiarity at the highest level of England's administration in Ireland. Arthur Capel, 1st earl of Essex, was appointed Lord Lieutenant of Ireland in 1672. Upon his arrival in Dublin on 5 August, his first call was to the house of Sir Alexander Bence where the new appointee was royally feasted.[75] In this comfortable environment, the most urgent business of state could be agreeably transacted. John Bence and George Dashwood were asked to cover the army's pay in Ireland and a further consortium of farmers was cobbled together who were placed in complete control of the Irish exchequer. This consortium was empowered to collect taxes and to make payments on behalf of the state, while money was to be loaned to the state at interest until the taxes were collected. The Stuarts had fallen into the trap of repeatedly attempting to do the same thing and expecting a different result. Within four years, over £100,000 had gone missing.[76]

This was the great gage, the mortgaging of Irish land and Irish taxes to finance the formation of the Royal Africa Company in 1671. In the month that the newly re-formed company was open for subscriptions, ending on 10 December 1671, £111,600 was committed to the Stewart monarchy's largest trading venture. These investors belonged to a specific cohort of investors in Irish land and Irish state finance. Out of an initial 198 named subscribers for shares in the new company, 68 individuals, or their immediate relatives, had received Irish land under the Act of Settlement or were involved in Irish tax farming.[77] Furthermore, these individuals had received more than half of the sequestered land. By comparison, of the major creditors of the English exchequer at the stop of 1672, only seven were invested in the Royal Africa Company by 1674, none had been involved in farming Irish tax revenue, and only Robert Backwell had a significant financial stake in Ireland.[78]

Britain's imperial expansion during the reign of Charles II did not happen entirely by accident. Neither can the transformation of England's small colonies be attributed solely to a peculiar gift for commercial opportunity or a sudden surge in maritime or fiscal innovation. A select group of financial speculators, who were closely supervised and supported by the royal family, followed a clear and sustained strategy of exploiting tax farming and cheap

Irish produce to finance the emerging trade in enslaved Africans. The first colony became the fuel for its successors.

Notes

1. Ralph Davis, 'English foreign trade, 1660–1700', *The Economic History Review*, Second Series, 7.2 (1954), 154–60.
2. Russell R. Menard, *Sweet Negotiations: Sugar, Slavery and Plantation Agriculture in Early Barbados* (Charlottesville: University of Virginia Press, 2006), 47.
3. For an introduction to the colonial administration of Ireland, see Peter Crooks, 'The structure of politics in theory and practice, 1210–1541', in Brendan Smyth (ed.), *The Cambridge History of Ireland*, vol. 1: *600–1550* (Cambridge: Cambridge University Press, 2018), 441–68.
4. David Brown, *Empire and Enterprise: Money, Power and the Adventurers for Irish land during the British Civil Wars 1640–1660* (Manchester: Manchester University Press, 2020), 22–43.
5. For an overview, see Micheál Ó Siochrú, *Confederate Ireland, 1642–1649: A Constitutional and Political Analysis* (Dublin: Four Courts Press, 2008).
6. There is a wealth of literature on the development of the early British Atlantic corporate world, but for some introductory perspectives see David Armitage and Michael Braddick (eds), *The British Atlantic World, 1500–1800* (Basingstoke: Palgrave Macmillan, 2002); Alison Games, 'The English Atlantic world: A view from London', *Pennsylvania History: A Journal of Mid-Atlantic Studies* 64 (1997), 46–72; W. Frank Craven, 'The Earl of Warwick, a speculator in piracy', *Hispanic American Historical Review* 10.4 (1930), 457–79; Karen Ordahl Kupperman, *Providence Island, 1630–1641: The Other Puritan Colony* (Cambridge: Cambridge University Press, 1993); Robin Law, 'The first Scottish Guinea Company', *The Scottish Historical Review* 76.202, Part 2 (1997), 185–202; Frances Rose-Troup, *The Massachusetts Bay Company and Its Predecessors* (New York: Grafton Press, 1930).
7. Alexander Fraser, *Nova Scotia, The Royal Charter of 1621 to William Alexander* (Toronto: University of Toronto Press, 1922); Roy Schrieber, 'The first Carlisle, Sir James Hay, first earl of Carlisle as courtier, diplomat and entrepreneur, 1580–1636', *Transactions of the American Philosophical Society* 74, Part 7 (1984), 1–202.
8. The deployment of private capital to the strategic needs of the state was an important and steeply developing trend. See David Parrott, *The Business of War: Military Enterprise and Military Revolution in Early Modern Europe* (Cambridge: Cambridge University Press, 2012).
9. *Statutes of the Realm*, vol. 5: *1628–8* (London: HMC, 1819), pp. 168–172.
10. James E. Farnell, 'The Navigation Act of 1651, the First Dutch War, and the London merchant community', *The Economic History Review*, New Series, 16.3 (1964), 439–54.

11 C. H. Firth and R. S. Rait, *Acts and Ordinances of the Interregnum*, vol. II (London: HMSO, 1911), 559–62, 'October 1651: An Act for increase of Shipping, and Encouragement of the Navigation of this Nation'.
12 Samuel Rawson Gardiner (ed.), *Letters and Papers Relating to the First Dutch War 1652–54*, vol. I (London: Navy Records Society, 1899), p. 54.
13 *Journal of the House of Lords: Volume 6, 1643* (London: His Majesty's Stationery Office, 1767–1830), p. 15. To place this figure in context, Parliament's entire naval expenditure from January 1643 to May 1645 was £641,000, and £450,000 of this money came from customs. The Irish campaign was a huge financial undertaking compressed into a relatively short time.
14 The National Archives [hereafter TNA], SP 28/ 350/7, f. 1.
15 TNA SP 28/350/7, f. 30.
16 David Brown, 'The sea adventure to Munster and Connacht, July and August 1642', in Patrick Little (ed.), *Ireland in crisis: War, Politics and Religion, 1641–50* (Manchester: Manchester University Press, 2020).
17 Gregory Moule, *The Irish Mercury* (London, February 1649), p. 2.
18 William Petty reported that, in 1653, debentures for land were being sold for five shillings in the pound and the value fell still further as the decade ground on. See Sir William Petty, *The Economic Writings of Sir William Petty, together with The Observations upon Bills of Mortality, more probably by Captain John Graunt*, 2 vols, ed. Charles Henry Hull (Cambridge: Cambridge University Press, 1899), vol. 1, p. 150.
19 Micheál O'Siochrú, *God's Executioner: Oliver Cromwell and the Conquest of Ireland* (London: Faber & Faber, 2008), pp. 200–7.
20 Hugh Hazlett, 'The financing of the British armies in Ireland 1641–9', *Irish Historical Studies* 1 (1938), 37.
21 Firth and Rait, *Acts and Ordinances of the Interregnum 1642–60*, vol. II, pp. 598–603, 'August 1652: An Act for the Setling of Ireland'.
22 D'Maris Coffman, 'Towards a New Jerusalem: The Committee for Regulating the Excise, 1649–1653', *The English Historical Review* 128.535 (2013), 1418–50, p. 1435.
23 See John Habakkuk, 'Presidential Address: The land settlement and the Restoration of Charles II', *Transactions of the Royal Historical Society* 28 (1978), 201–22.
24 Frank T. Melton, *Sir Robert Clayton and the Origins of English Deposit Banking 1658–1685* (Cambridge: Cambridge University Press, 2002), pp. 55–60.
25 Melton, *Sir Robert Clayton and the Origins of English Deposit Banking*, pp. 156–62.
26 R. C. Simington, *Books of Survey and Distribution: being abstracts of various surveys and instruments of title, 1636–1703*, vols 1–4 (Dublin: Irish Manuscripts Commission, 1949–67); *The Civil Survey*, vols 1–10 (Dublin: Irish Manuscripts Commission, 1931–61); *The Transplantation to Connacht 1654–8* (Shannon: Irish University Press, 1970).
27 Library of the Joint Houses of the Oireachtas, Ms DCA 071, *Minute Book of Sir William Petty*.

28 For much more on Hartlib, see The Hartlib Papers, an online edition of 25,000 pages of his letters and papers edited by the University of Sheffield: http://dhi.ac.uk/hartlib/. For the impact of Hartlib's intellectual circle, see Toby Barnard, *Improving Ireland? Projectors, Prophets and Profiteers 1641–1786* (Dublin: Four Courts Press, 2008), pp. 14–40.

29 Brown, *Empire and Enterprise*, pp. 201–28.

30 See Thomas Leng, *Fellowship and Freedom: The Merchant Adventurers & the Restructuring of English Commerce 1582–1700* (Oxford: Oxford University Press, 2020). This work is a long overdue examination of the Fellowship of Merchant Adventurers and also serves as a survey of England's cloth trade during the period under discussion.

31 K. Ratelband, *Vijf Dagregisters van het kasteel Sao Jorge Da Mina aan de Goudkust, 1645–47* (The Hague: Martinus Nijhoff, 1953), pp. 293–5.

32 Brown, *Empire and Enterprise*, pp. 157–9.

33 Richard Baker, *The marchants humble petition and remonstrance to his late Highnesse, with an accompt of the losses of their shipping, and estates, since the war with Spain ...* (London, 1659).

34 Brown, *Empire and Enterprise*, pp. 201–28.

35 William Francis Finlason, *The History of Law of Tenures of Land in England and Ireland* (London: Stevens & Haynes, 1870), pp. 50–62.

36 Bodliean Lbrary, Ms Rawlinson A 14, f. 168 *Proposals Concerning Ireland*.

37 For the sustained presence of Irish landowners on their own estates, see Séamas Pender (ed.), *A Census of Ireland circa 1659* (Dublin: Irish Manuscripts Commission, 1959).

38 J. M. Gray, *A History of the Gambia* (Cambridge: Cambridge University Press, 1966), p. 23.

39 Toby Green, *A Fistful of Shells: West Africa from the Rise of the Slave Trade to the Age of Revolution* (London: University of Chicago Press, 2019), pp. 89–91.

40 R. Porter, 'The Crispe family and the African trade in the seventeenth century', *Journal of African History* 9.1 (1968), 57–77, p. 66.

41 Alexander Balloch Grosart, *The Lismore Papers of Richard Boyle, First and 'Great' Earl of Cork* (London, private printing, 1886), p. 318.

42 National Library of Ireland (NLI), Ms 30: Clayton/Greenwell correspondence, ff. 2–3v.

43 Toby Barnard, *Cromwellian Ireland: English Government and Reform in Ireland 1649–1660* (Oxford, Oxford University Press, 2000), p. 59.

44 Neil Johnson, 'State formation in seventeenth-century Ireland: The Restoration financial settlement, 1660–1662', *Parliaments, Estates and Representation* 36.2 (2016), 115–36, p. 122.

45 George F. Zook, *The Company of Royal Adventurers Trading into Africa* (Lancaster, PA: New Era Publishing Company, 1919), p. 8.

46 These transactions are tabulated in the Books of Survey and Distribution that were compiled using the Cromwellian surveys and Restoration land grants and provide a means to compare soldiers' and Adventurer's allocations against the

eventual purchasers. A complete set of the Books of Survey and Distribution is preserved at the National Archives of Ireland, QRO/1/1/3/1–20.
47 W. Noel Sainsbury, *Calendar of State Papers Colonial, America and West Indies*, vol. 5: 1661–1668 (London: HMC, 1880), p. 55.
48 John Rylands Library, Rylands Charter 3643: Clayton Papers, 11 July 1662.
49 NLI Ms 30, f. 22v.
50 NLI Ms 30, f. 4r.
51 Thomas J. Kiernan, *History of the Financial Administration of Ireland to 1817* (London: P. S. King & Son, 1930), p. 82.
52 Kiernan, *History*, p. 89.
53 *The London Gazette*, 1–11 June 1666, p. 2.
54 TNA T70/75, f. 7r. I am very grateful for the generosity of Paul Dryburgh of the National Archives, a colleague on the Beyond 2022 project, who photographed several volumes of Royal Africa Company records during the 2020 lockdown to enable the research for this chapter to be completed.
55 Sainsbury, *Calendar of State Papers*, p. 179.
56 TNA T70/75, f. 12v.
57 Sainsbury, *Calendar of State Papers*, p. 119.
58 Robin Law (ed.), *The English in West Africa 1681–1683: The Local Correspondence of the Royal Africa Company of England, 1681–1699 Part 1* (Oxford: Oxford University Press, 1997), p. 222. Letter from John Thorne, Offra in Arda, 19 August 1681.
59 Goran Ryden and Chris Evans, *Baltic Iron in the Atlantic World in the eighteenth Century* (Boston, MA: Brill, 2007), pp. 163–72.
60 Peter King, 'The production and consumption of bar iron in early modern England and Wales', *The Economic History Review*, 58.1 (2005), 1–33.
61 NLI Ms 30, f. 9v.
62 TNA SP 63/316, f.190 The King to the Lord Lieutenant for Peter Harvey and Others.
63 TNA T70/75, f. 11.
64 TNA SP 63/346, f. 223. Memorandum by the Farmers of the Irish Customs on the Canary Company's patent.
65 TNA T70/75, f. 16. Minutes, 20 June 1664.
66 TNA SP29/200, f. 100.
67 TNA T70/75, ff. 18r–22r.
68 TNA SP 29/144, ff. 18r–18v. 2 January 1666.
69 TNA SP 63/318, f. 93. Entry of the king to Joseph Deane and John Bence.
70 TNA SP 63/330/3, f. 72.
71 TNA SP 63/325, f. 141.
72 Ralph Davis, *The Rise of the English Shipping Industry in the Seventeenth and Eighteenth Centuries* (London: Macmillan, 1962), p. 60.
73 TNA SP 63/325, No. 36, Observations by Mr. Muschamp, one of the Commissioners or Farmers of the Irish revenue, concerning the same at the time Lord Ranelagh and his partners contracted with the King.
74 TNA SP 63/333, f. 53.

75 *The London Gazette*, 12–15 August 1672.
76 TNA SP 44/55, f. 262.
77 National Archives of Ireland, QRO/1/1/3/1–20. Books of Survey and Distribution, *passim*. In addition to place and personal names, this invaluable source also lists the acreages granted to new patentees under the various acts of forfeiture.
78 Li Ling-Fan, 'The stop of the exchequer and the secondary market for English sovereign debt, 1677–1705', *Journal of Economic History* 79.1 (March 2019), 176–200.

2

The cost of thrift: The politics of 'financial autonomy' in the French colonial empire, 1900–14

Madeline Woker

This chapter examines how the early twentieth-century French imperial state financed itself, why French colonies were eventually asked to draw on their own fiscal resources, and what consequences this carried for colonised populations. Very much like other European empires examined in this volume, the French Empire was largely funded by the wealth it was able to extract in the colonies. This principle was in fact legally enshrined in 1900 when colonial financial self-sufficiency or 'autonomy' became the organising rule of French imperial financial relations. Indeed, the consolidation of democratic republicanism and the timid emergence of state-run welfare programmes in late nineteenth-century France created new exigencies of accountability and care towards French citizens in hexagonal France, prompting republican political elites to curtail the fiscal costs of empire. This doctrine remained largely uncontested until the First World War when new debates about the financing of colonial development began to challenge this logic.

This fiscal delinking owed much to the specific circumstances of late nineteenth-century French imperialism and the evolution of French colonial doctrine from 'assimilation' to 'association', which meant that colonies were no longer expected to become replicas of the metropole but rather self-sustaining polities at the service of French investors and manufacturers.[1] While the debate initially centred around the 'old colonies' of the French Caribbean and Indian Ocean whose local assemblies were routinely accused of mishandling French metropolitan monies, and Algeria, then largely viewed as a costly 'economic failure', this thorough reform of the French colonial financial regime owed much to the resumption of formal imperialism and the set-up of civil administration in recently occupied territories in Africa and Southeast Asia.[2]

In this chapter I argue that metropolitan debates about the cost of imperialism at the turn of the twentieth century and the necessity to preserve a fragile fiscal bargain at home caused a subsequent turn to a 'low-cost empire' in 1900. Practically, this meant that the metropole strongly curtailed financial transfers to the colonies by declaring them financially 'autonomous'. This transformed the French Empire into a flurry of smaller colonial fiscal states able to borrow on metropolitan markets and responsible for raising their own fiscal resources. This increased the tax burden of colonised populations and also limited the bounds of national solidarity to European France.[3] This fiscal separation between the metropole and the colonies had deep consequences on the structuring of imperial inequalities: while it helped mitigate the effects of extreme economic inequality in the metropole by shielding average French taxpayers from a significant portion of the cost of empire, it also entrenched a racialised imperial fiscal hierarchy where the interests and livelihoods of metropolitan white citizen-taxpayers stood firmly above those of colonial subject taxpayers.

In 1900, deputies at the French Assembly capped years of heated debates about financial relations between the metropole and its colonial realm by voting a series of laws granting 'financial autonomy', first to the French territories which then fell under the purview of the Ministry of Colonies, and then to Algeria, whose northern part was administratively integrated to metropolitan France.[4] Although these 1900 laws are only mentioned in passing in studies of colonial taxation, they enacted a much stricter budgetary partition which effectively shifted the tax burden of empire onto colonial taxpayers while offering little in the way of representation.[5] In the minds of French imperialists, colonial 'autonomy' did not equate any form of financial self-determination for the millions of French colonial subjects living in Africa and Asia. Instead, they envisaged it as a disciplining device which would give the metropole greater control over imperial expenditures and ultimately make colonies more productive for the metropole and less costly for its taxpayers, in line with the protectionist spirit of the time.[6]

Article 33 of the 13 April 1900 budget law thus made local colonial budgets responsible for all 'civilian' and 'police' expenditures and introduced a provision stating that colonies could in the future be requested to reimburse military expenditures incurred on their soil. This last provision was left deliberately vague as it remained unclear whether colonies should legitimately be asked to bear the burden of 'sovereignty expenditures', commonly understood as expenditure items primarily destined to maintain national standing and prestige.[7] A very similar wording was used in the 19 December 1900 law granting financial autonomy and a special budget to Algeria. Its expenditures had hitherto been covered by different sections of the metropolitan budget and local colonial authorities and settlers, not to mention colonised populations, did not enjoy much leeway in determining how to cover them.[8]

This chapter is divided into three sections. The first section explains why the French metropolitan state became increasingly unwilling to bear the cost of empire. France's concomitant entry into the age of mass democracy and expansive formal empire forced metropolitan authorities to cheapen their imperial endeavours, reneging on past assimilationist policies and colonial bailouts. The second section explores how various political groups and public figures mobilised the political category of the 'metropolitan taxpayer' in order to advocate a 'low-cost' empire in the 1890s, an era when growing welfare obligations and discussions about tax justice forced politicians to pay much greater heed to the consent of citizen-taxpayers. Finally, the third section explores the aftermath of the 1900 laws and their lasting effects on colonial taxpayers, especially non-citizens.

A more 'rational' imperialism

The 1880s saw France's entry into the geopolitical game of high imperialism. By the early 1900s, France had won decisive victories in its wars against local rulers in North Africa, Western and Central Africa as well as Southeast Asia, effectively extending its territorial grip to nearly 13 million square kilometres.[9] As the era of military occupation seemed to be drawing to a close, a growing number of French imperialists hailed the dawn of a new period of more rationally conducted 'economic conquest'.[10] Concretely, this meant that political elites were now ready to pave the way for private investment in infrastructure and public works with the ultimate aim of boosting trade and economic activity within France's expanding colonial empire. But in the early twentieth century, a large part of France's external capital exports still went to Europe and Latin America and observers routinely deplored the fact that even though colonial expenditures had amounted to roughly 1.4 billion francs between 1885 and 1899, representing 2.69% of total metropolitan expenditures during this period, the overall colonial trade volume and reverse flows to the metropole remained disappointingly low.[11]

We now know that military and civilian expenditure in the empire never made up more than 0.8% and 0.14% respectively of the metropole's GDP between 1833 and 1962 and that colonial ventures probably generated sizable private profits.[12] Yet authorities at the time were obsessed with the supposedly high costs of empire. In the mid-1880s, republican France still counted staunchly anti-colonial voices, and arguments against further expansion often included concerns about costs and the spilling of the 'gold and blood' of France in faraway lands.[13] By the early 1890s, however, most republicans had come to accept the 'necessity' of imperial expansion.[14] Members of the French Assembly even began to organise in small but powerful groups tasked with colonial propaganda, leading to the creation in November 1890 of the Committee of French Africa and of the informal 'Colonial Party' in 1892.[15] The latter was mostly made up of progressive and moderate republicans and deputies from the colonies but many still disagreed about the most effective way to rule over and pay for empire.[16] While some supported policies of national prestige, others were primarily concerned with making colonies safe for French capital exports and did not necessarily favour annexation.[17] A crucial question, however, was how to reconcile territorial control with as little public money transfers as possible.

This became especially urgent as large new territories were now being added to the empire, making the assimilationist policies of the past increasingly less attractive.[18] Praising the British example, French imperialists came to favour a much stricter separation between the metropolitan budget and local budgets.[19] At the French parliament, deputies rallied behind the opinion that the cost of empire should be borne by the colonies themselves. In 1886, the conservative deputy and rapporteur of the 1887 state budget, Edmond Turquet, exclaimed in the Chamber that 'colonies have to be able to sustain themselves and the metropole should only take on sovereignty expenditures reduced to the strict minimum', and seven years later, the republican Adolphe Chautemps, budget rapporteur for 1893 and 1894, went further and explained to other deputies that 'colonies, as well as departments, have to pay for their own military expenses, just like their civilian expenses, unless they lack resources; they have to contribute, in proportion to their ability to pay, to the general expenses of the state'.[20]

Besides the supposed colonial drain on the metropolitan budget, another point of contention concerned the haphazard nature of the French colonial project – and more precisely, the lack of budgetary legibility.[21] As politicians debated colonial spending in the Chamber, in the Senate and in the press, some questions were constantly brought up: what exactly constituted 'colonial expenditure', which ministry was responsible for it, who ought to pay for it, and, most importantly, could one exert effective control over it? The denomination 'colonial budget' was indeed rather murky. Did it refer to the 'budget established by the colonies'? Or the budget allocated to colonial troops? Or was it the budget of the Ministry of Colonies? In fact, the 'colonial budget' only referred to the portion of the metropolitan state budget allocated to the Ministry of Colonies and encompassed all the expenditures that the metropole spent on the colonies as well as the compensatory receipts that it received to offset a portion of these expenditures, notably the maintenance of colonial troops outside of metropolitan France. Next to the colonial budget sat the 'colonial troops' budget', which fell under the purview of the War Ministry and paid for troop maintenance on metropolitan soil. 'Local colonial budgets', in turn, referred to the budgets of individual colonies.[22] Yet this confusing set-up only nourished widespread suspicions of colonial budgetary mismanagement.

These ongoing controversies prompted the Minister of Colonies to nominate a special commission on local budgets in January 1899. Headed by the colonial governor and inspector Albert Picquié, the commission reiterated many of the conclusions made in past colonial budget reports and noted that no other European imperial power was spending as much on colonial matters, calling for an end to 'unproductive' expenditures in the colonies.[23] A close reading of the parliamentary debate which took place on 8 December 1899 shows that a few of the most evocative figures presented in the Picquié report had made their way into the minds of deputies: for instance, the alleged fact that 'metropolitan taxpayers' were forced to cover 44% of the expenditures generated by the colonies whereas colonial taxpayers were only shouldering 56% of their 'own expenditures'.[24] It is also during this debate that the French liberal diplomat and pacifist Paul D'Estournelles de Constant took to the pulpit to make a forceful speech against the direction taken by the Third Republic's colonial policy. One sentence resonated particularly as he exclaimed ironically that 'there are two things in our colonial policy: first, the joy of conquest and then the bill to pay'.[25] This widespread preoccupation with the 'bill to pay' is indeed what drove the Minister of Colonies Albert Decrais to make a long speech a few days later where he announced that colonies would soon be required by law to cover all their civilian and public order expenditures.[26]

Shielding the metropolitan taxpayer

The necessity to make empire pay for itself was also deeply linked to France's domestic context and new understandings of the principles underlying taxation, redistribution, and welfare. Consent to taxation in late nineteenth-century Third Republic France was still fragile and had only been obtained through the granting of exemptions and the slow routinisation of collection methods.[27] Furthermore, intellectual debates about tax justice remained quite vivid given the highly regressive nature of the French fiscal state at the time.[28] Members of the Republican majority even began to voice the idea of a progressive income tax, which was already in place in a number of European countries but faced strong liberal opposition. In this context, no politician or government wanted to be found guilty of breaking this feeble balance, and the respective burdens weighing on metropolitan and colonial taxpayers thus soon became a focal point. Invoking a principle inherited from the French Revolution, the deputy Camille Chautemps reminded his parliamentary audience in 1893 that 'all Frenchmen, whether they live in the colonies or in the metropole, are equal before taxation'.[29] Similarly, the well-known colonial theorist Arthur Girault opined that there could not be 'two categories of Frenchmen: the ones maintained at the expense of the others'.[30] Although not all French commentators agreed on exactly how much tax should be borne by non-European and European taxpayers in the colonies, the necessity to shield the metropolitan taxpayer had nevertheless become a pressing political imperative.[31]

The idea that French metropolitan taxpayers were being unfairly asked to pay for France's 'civilising mission' was quite common and sometimes made it to the front pages of widely read satirical newspapers. In 1896, a late June issue of Le Grelot ('The Bell') featured an evocative and starkly racialised political caricature which showed a proud Marianne, the national personification of the French Republic, standing at the helm of a long line of recently emancipated colonial subjects while, immediately beneath them, crawling French metropolitan taxpayers were painstakingly pulling a heavy cart loaded with sacks of various sizes (see Figure 2.1).[32] Upon closer scrutiny, readers would have quickly noticed that the sacks were tagged with distinct tax names: labour taxes, customs taxes, direct and indirect taxes, and so on. At the bottom of the image, the legend read: 'The Chamber of Deputies just abolished slavery in Madagascar. To the great joy of the French worker!' Six days earlier, the Chamber had indeed unilaterally voted the abolition of native slavery in Madagascar to justify conquest in a context of growing public discontent about the fiscal and human cost of the second Franco-Hova war.[33]

The journalists were clearly invested in conveying the idea that French metropolitan taxpayers were now being transformed into slaves themselves and forced to pay the costs of France's imperial ventures and the emancipation of French colonial subjects. Political caricatures portraying oppressed taxpayers were a relatively common feature of the *fin de siècle* (1870–1914) satirical press, given ongoing debates about the legitimacy and justice of taxation. However, this image stands out for its stark illustration of the intersection between domestic distributional conflicts and colonial expansion.[34]

This kind of critique also came from the far ends of the French political spectrum which had been crucially recast by a series of political convulsions, notably the Boulanger crisis of 1889, the Panama scandal of 1892, and the Dreyfus affair. On the right, a racist and exclusivist nationalist commentariat appropriated the question of empire's costs to lash out at the financial corruption of republican elites.[35] In 1894, the journalist Adrien Henri Canu famously published a pamphlet titled *La Pétaudière Coloniale* ('Colonial Mess'), which presented the reader with a litany of colonial

'Financial autonomy' in the French colonial empire

Figure 2.1 Front page of *Le Grelot* ('The Bell'), 28 June 1896.

financial scandals. Canu had served in Indochina in the 1880s and thus felt particularly entitled to comment on the unsavory underpinnings of colonial railway concessions, notably in sub-Saharan Africa. Canu accused various colonial businessmen of squandering taxpayers' money in shady schemes and snarled at the growing colonial budget, the creation of the Ministry of Colonies in 1894 and the fact that it constituted yet another 'call on the purse of taxpayers'.[36] Front-page articles in Cassagnac's far-right paper *L'Autorité* similarly pointed to the 'millions' spent on colonial ventures.[37]

The left also challenged republican colonial policy but did so in the name of antimilitarism and to expose the Third Republic's regressive tax system, thus articulating an original critique of the distributive effects of imperialism. In 1895, the French Workers' Party Congress adopted the motto 'not a penny, not a man' for colonial conquest and two years later, a major mouthpiece called the *Revue Socialiste* published a series of articles by a young thinker named Paul Louis whose essay 'Colonisation and the French parliamentary system' leveled an all-out attack on the 'few thousand individuals, relatives of ministers … already gorged with gold' for whom 'French citizens ha[d] been sent to die under burning climates', forcing the 'public treasury' to discharge 'its fecund wealth on the desert sand'.[38] A few months earlier, the same Louis had defended the joint introduction of a progressive tax on income and capital and a state monopoly on alcohol in order to uplift the French working class and enlist rural masses, the same social groups that the protectionists were then trying to 'buy' with the promise of a partial land tax exemption.[39] According to this critique, metropolitan protectionism and the creation of captive foreign markets through informal and formal rule were easily explained by the unwillingness of powerful sectional interests to redistribute income and wealth in the domestic realm.

Faced with these internal constraints and international competition, ministers and deputies sought to reform the functioning of French imperial finance in ways that would assuage, or at least not interfere with, contentious domestic fiscal politics.[40] On 13 April 1900, deputies voted to approve the 1900 budget law which contained article 33 that extensively modified French colonies' financial regime. As of 1 January 1901, all civilian and police (*gendarmerie*) expenditures were to be carried by the colonies' local budgets. The law also stated that military expenditures would *eventually* have to be transferred to the colonies and that the colonies' contributions to military expenses would see a steady increase. Furthermore, local budget expenditures in colonies endowed with general councils (this concerned mostly the 'old colonies') were to be divided into 'non-compulsory' and 'compulsory' expenditures, with the latter including debt servicing, civil servants' salaries, police and justice salaries as well as the hospitality expenses of the governor general's office. In these colonies, council members retained some deliberative powers over the tax base, tax rates and collection rules, but these powers did not extend to the tariff regime which largely remained the prerogative of the metropole in accordance with the protectionist law of 11 January 1892. Yet in a clear break with past practices, these deliberations had now become conditional upon approval by the Council of State in Paris. The law said very little about recent colonies organised in government generals (notably Indochina and West Africa) and this silence effectively gave greater powers to governors general whose financial powers would only be fully codified twelve years later.

As for Algeria, similar debates occurred in the Chamber of Deputies throughout 1900 amidst growing controversy over widespread financial corruption and budgetary confusion.[41] Algeria had experienced a major political crisis in the late nineteenth century, prompting the most autonomist settlers to ask for full or 'integral' budgetary autonomy, but officials in the metropole did not trust them to responsibly manage a fully independent Algerian budget. Given previous experience with 'old colonies' and their chronic deficits, Paris wanted to be able to keep the last word on expenditures and contain potential future bailouts. During a debate in the Chamber in March 1900, the Oran deputy and mastermind of France's colonial strategy Eugène Etienne cited article 33 of the 13 April 1900 law and expressly asked that its dispositions be transposed to Algeria. After all, he argued, Algeria also deserved to be granted its own budget. Waldeck-Rousseau, then Minister of Interior, remarked that it was indeed necessary for Algeria to vote its own taxes but also to 'learn how to earmark' them.[42]

In June 1900, the parliament sent an inquiry commission to Algiers to determine the most suitable budgetary organisation, and this was followed by further discussion in the parliament until mid-November when the new law was read aloud and voted on unanimously by the deputies.[43] Its first article granted Algeria its own 'civil personality' while article 3 stated that 'Algeria's budget ceases to be encompassed in the state budget'. Not unlike what the April 1900 law had done for other colonies, Algeria had now become responsible for its own civilian and police expenditures. The law also organised expenditures into 'compulsory' and 'non-compulsory' ones, thus effectively constraining the margin of manoeuvre of the newly created Financial Delegations.[44] Finally, articles 6 and 7 stated that the budget would be established by the governor general and then debated and voted by the Financial Delegations following the guidelines issued by the Delegations' finance commission, itself composed of four settlers, four non-settlers, and three Algerian 'native' delegates.[45]

The consequences of financial 'autonomy'

Ten years after the passing of the laws, Adolphe Messimy, a military officer, member of the National Assembly and later briefly Minister of Colonies, published a lengthy overview of France's colonial empire where he examined the functioning of France's imperial finances and described the financial and political configurations of Indochina, Madagascar, West Africa, Equatorial Africa, and other smaller colonies.[46] *Notre œuvre coloniale* drew from Messimy's parliamentary reports on the colonial budget and the first section exposed the 'budgetary and financial development' of French colonies since 1895. With the help of elaborate graphs and figures, Messimy showed that the 1900 laws had drastically increased local budgets and somehow curbed the expansion of the metropolitan colonial budget which now mostly funded military expenditures.[47] Meanwhile, colonial contributions paid to the metropolitan state had expanded while metropolitan subventions to the colonies had decreased considerably 'under article 33 of the 13 April 1900 budget law'.[48] Finally, the amounts of the loans contracted by French colonies had gone up by nearly 240% between 1900 and 1905, allowing Messimy to claim that the 1900 law had 'bore fruit'.[49]

But the 1900 law was not always received favourably by colonial deputies and would again become an object of intense political debate after the First World War. Left-wing deputies and those representing the 'old colonies' of the Caribbean and Indian Ocean voiced the strongest disagreements because the law deprived local assemblies of most of their powers. At a parliamentary session in November 1900, the deputy from French Guiana, Henri Ursleur, deplored the fact that the law had put these territories in an impossible situation because their lack of fiscal leeway did not allow them to 'to save the money they were being asked to save'.[50] In October 1902, the centre-left deputy from the Ardennes, Lucien Hubert, issued a resolution proposal meant to modify the law in order to move from mere 'budgetary autonomy' to real 'financial freedom'.[51] In some colonies, local assemblies even refused to apply the law – Tahiti, for instance, where the colonial council voted against the introduction of land taxes and taxes on commodities which, it argued, would fall disproportionally on local taxpayers.[52]

In other parts of the empire, financial autonomy led to the creation of local federal budgetary structures, notably in Indochina and West Africa and Equatorial Africa. This increased the overall tax burden and spurred the systematisation of personal taxes, leading to violent tax revolts and contentious tax politics. The first decade of the twentieth century was indeed shaken by highly publicised tax revolts in Madagascar, Indochina, and the French Congo, prompting French imperialists to ponder over the distinctive 'issue' of colonial taxation.[53] While tax debates in hexagonal France were now increasingly concerned with justice and progressivity, colonial taxation was essentially viewed as a 'moralising' and 'civilising' tool meant to project French sovereignty and force colonial subjects into wage labour.[54] Expenditures were also largely biased in favour of the small number of French settlers and civil servants and served to build infrastructure meant to sustain an export-led economy at the service of the metropole.[55]

In Algeria, financial decentralisation resulted in the creation of twelve new taxes and other tax hikes. In 1907, for instance, colonial authorities severely increased the consumption tax on tobacco, which fell heavily on the local non-European population.[56] In Indochina, the creation of the three infamous monopolies on opium, alcohol, and salt were directly related to the turn to 'autonomy' and served to ensure the colony's credit on financial markets.[57] The ensuing consolidation of the Indochinese fiscal state translated into a slew of tax revolts, most notably in 1908. These violent episodes in turn triggered extensive debates about the disastrous effects of fiscal monopolies across metropole and colony.[58] In West Africa, capitation taxes were introduced shortly before or after 1900 and increased after the creation of a federal budgetary structure in 1904.[59] As Emma Park notes elsewhere in this volume, these were hardly viewed as taxes but rather as 'sovereign seizures' or tributes collected under duress.

These colonial seizures nevertheless normalised over time and a 1912 decree on the financial regime of French colonies even codified their functioning. The 1900 laws had provided little guidance on the everyday workings of 'financial autonomy' but the 1912 decree unified earlier texts and gave the empire a common document which today is still considered the 'financial constitution of overseas France'.[60] Indeed, by that time it had become essential to create 'a unified accounting system' for the colonies now that the government generals of West Africa and Equatorial Africa as well Indochina were fully formed. The 1912 decree overhauled the 1862 and 1882 decrees on colonial public accounting, and streamlined rules pertaining to budget making, tax collection, and organised metropolitan oversight.[61] It also delineated the oversight powers of the Audit Court (*Cour des Comptes*), an administrative court responsible for the financial audit of the French state, and of the Council of State (*Conseil d'Etat*), the highest French body for administrative litigation.[62] Tax-related cases often landed on its desks and in fact administrative cases stemming from the colonies most often concerned tax disputes.[63] The same kind of metropolitan oversight applied to protectorates and even territories officially placed under international governance.[64] Furthermore, all fiscal instruments instituted in the colonies (including Algeria) had to be initially approved by the metropole.

The 1912 decree also contained articles regulating the issuance of colonial loans. Article 87, for instance, stated which authority was entitled to contract debt: in colonies organised as government generals like Indochina or West Africa, only central governments, usually through the authority of the governor general himself, could decide to issue them. Articles 159 to 201 provided rules on tax assessment and collection and on the legality of colonial taxes and required that taxes be levied based on nominal rolls rather than numerical rolls whenever possible in order to get at a more 'individualised' assessment of the capacity to pay. Article 176 stipulated that taxes could only be levied by a competent authority sanctioned by the French colonial state; this was to avoid unlawful tax collection by tax farmers and various forms of corruption considered endemic in the colonies.[65] Finally, the 1912 decree also served as a yardstick and handbook for colonial inspectors sent to audit colonial tax systems and who often referred to the decree to determine the legality of certain taxes or comment on assessment or collection methods.[66]

Increased codification did not modify the basic rule, which remained that colonies should not be a burden on the metropole. Yet as the author of an oft-cited history of French colonial finance would put in 1938, the 'dream' of a costless colonial empire was also a 'dangerous' one as it had encouraged the metropole to 'hog too many things'.[67] Indeed, this situation of endemic imperial austerity generated renewed debates in the aftermath of the First World War, inaugurating a new era of contentious politics and imperial crisis.[68] While reformist and anti-colonial movements began to voice and fight for their own vision of tax justice, imperial authorities sought to rejuvenate a battered France through empire; however, colonial endeavours and public investment remained constrained by the untenable 1900 bargain. The 'father' of French inter-war colonial development policy, the Minister of Colonies Albert Sarraut, argued early on that 'the regime of the 1900 law ... had led to deplorable results' by generating 'a twenty-year delay in the development of our colonies', leading to 'botched public works, insufficient or done too slowly, not to mention the tax surcharge on natives'.[69] It thus became urgent to find a way to overturn article 33 of the 13 April 1900 law which, after all, was a 'mere law' and not a 'charter' of any sort.[70]

But Sarraut faced strong resistance in the Chamber in 1920 and 1921 as deputies discussed his ambitious colonial development plans. Opposition to greater colonial expenditure was still vivid and, more generally, France's post-war economic policy was then one of 'decontrol and retrenchment, not management and modernisation'.[71] The 1900 laws and the 1912 decree thus remained in place, effectively making the empire more reliant on private investment despite a few metropolitan loans granted in the 1930s.[72] The colonial financial autonomy policy continued to generate heated controversy during the inter-war period, both in the metropole and in the colonies. In Algeria, for instance, reformist nationalists strongly opposed the financial autonomy principle which, they argued, had ended up serving as a shield for European settler fiscal privilege and which reinforced the powers of the Delegations.[73]

The decision to run empire on the cheap and to strictly limit metropolitan transfers were both the result of the specific circumstances of late nineteenth-century imperialism and the product of contentious metropolitan politics. It allowed for the creation of smaller colonial fiscal states whose existence entrenched imperial inequalities because revenue now had to be raised locally. This effectively shifted the burden of empire from metropolitan taxpayers onto colonial taxpayers. Yet the colonial tax base was disproportionately composed of disenfranchised colonial subjects enjoying almost no democratic representation. The political fallout of colonial 'financial autonomy' was thus quite immediate and generated a flurry of tax revolts. This prompted several reformist colonial officials to rethink colonial financial relations in the aftermath of the First World War, yet the self-sufficiency doctrine would only come to an end in 1946 with the full emergence of 'developmentalist' colonialism.

Notes

1 On the transition from 'assimilation' to 'association', see Raymond Betts, *Assimilation and Association in French Colonial Theory, 1890–1914* (New York: Columbia University Press, 1961).
2 On nineteenth-century colonial Algeria as an economic failure, see David Todd, *A Velvet Empire* (Princeton, NJ: Princeton University Press, 2020), pp. 104–10.
3 On the rise of solidarity and 'solidarism' as the official doctrine of the Third Republic, see Serge Audier, *La pensée solidariste: aux sources du modèle social républicain* (Paris: Presses Universitaires de France, 2010).
4 I use 'colonies' as a shorthand here to refer to all the territories of the French colonial empire which fell under the purview of the Ministry of Colonies. These include the protectorates and colony which made up French Indochina, the colonies of French West Africa and Equatorial Africa, Madagascar as well as the 'old colonies' of the Caribbean and Indian Ocean. Northern Algeria was composed of three departments.
5 Historians of colonial taxation have clearly recognised the necessity that metropolitan governments felt to 'shield metropolitan taxpayers against [the] real burden of empire' and often integrate the 'revenue imperative' in their analysis, but they usually have paid less attention to what this imperial fiscal hierarchy entailed. See for instance Marlous Van Waijenburg, 'Financing the African colonial state: The revenue imperative and forced labor', *The Journal of Economic History* 78.1 (2018), 40–80; Ewout Frankema and Marlous Van

Waijenburg, 'From coast to hinterland: Fiscal capacity building in British and French West Africa, c. 1880–1960', in Anne Booth and Ewout Frankema (eds), *Fiscal Capacity and the Colonial State in Asia and Africa, c. 1850–1960* (New York: Cambridge University Press, 2020), p. 169.

6 By the early 1890s, France had made a sharp protectionist turn despite the temptation of liberal empire which lasted until the early 1880s. Given the smaller size of France's empire and limited industrial capacities, it could simply not afford British-style free trade imperialism. For a contemporary analysis comparing imperial protectionism to a sort of neo-mercantilism, see Etienne Grosclaude, 'Le Nouveau Pacte Colonial', *La Revue des Deux Mondes* 8.1 (1902), 49–85. Not all territories in the French empire fell under the metropolitan protectionist regime. Morocco, West African colonies, and the colonies situated in the 'conventional basin' of the Congo were subject to international trade treaties and subject to an 'open door' policy. Such policies still constrained their revenue structures. For a recent analysis of the historical consequences of trade liberalisation on revenue structures, see Julia Cagé and Lucie Gadenne, 'Tax revenues and the fiscal cost of trade liberalisation, 1792–2006', *Explorations in Economic History* 70 (2018), 1–24.

7 Economists writing on French colonial public finance typically treat military expenditure separately. See for instance Denis Cogneau, Yannick Dupraz, and Sandrine Mesplé-Somps et al., 'Fiscal capacity and dualism in colonial states: French Empire, 1830–1962', *Journal of Economic History* 81.2 (2021), 448 and 462. Experts at the time also considered that military expenditures were not specifically 'colonial' and would have remained the same even if France had not engaged in formal colonisation. See for instance L. Faulong, *Les rapports financiers de la métropole et de l'Afrique occidentale française depuis 1825 jusqu'à nos jours* (Paris: Giard & E. Brière, 1910), p. 143. It must also be noted here that the French sought (and managed) to actively 'indigenise' their colonial troops during conquest in order precisely to cut 'costs'. For estimates, see Bouda Etemad, *Possessing the World: Taking the Measurements of Colonisation from the Eighteenth Century to the Twentieth Century* (New York: Berghahn Books, 2007), pp. 42–6.

8 Auguste Chamborédon, 'La décentralisation financière en Algérie' (PhD dissertation, University of Lyon, 1907).

9 Auguste Terrier and Charles Mourey, *L'expansion française et la formation territoriale* (Paris: Emile Larose, 1910), p. vi.

10 Auguste Dardenne, *Les emprunts publics et le régime de décentralisation financière dans les colonies françaises et de protectorat* (Paris: Arthur Rousseau, 1908), p. 2.

11 For capital export figures, see Rui Pedro Esteves, 'The belle epoque of international finance: French capital exports, 1880–1914', *SSN Working paper* (2011). See also H. Van Kol, 'L'Algérie et la politique coloniale', *Le Mouvement Socialiste* (May 1903), 104–7, for an estimation of total colonial expenditures between 1885 and 1899. For total expenditure numbers, I relied on *Annuaire statistique de la France, 1885* (Paris: Imprimerie Nationale, 1885), *Annuaire*

statistique de la France, 1899 and the *Bulletin de Statistique et de législation comparée* (Paris: Imprimerie Nationale) for 1898 and 1899. This figure of 2.69% does not include Algerian expenditures, which are included in overall metropolitan expenditures (in 1898, Algerian expenditures represented 2.19% of metropolitan expenditures.) French imperialists often deplored the lack of economic interest in empire at the turn of the century; see for instance Louis Vignon, 'De la mise en valeur de notre domaine colonial', *La revue scientifique* 25 (16 December 1899), 769–84. Jacques Marseille showed that this changed shortly after 1900 ; see Jacques Marseille, *Empire colonial et capitalisme français: histoire d'un divorce* (Paris: Albin Michel, 2005), p. 143.

12 See Cogneau *et al.*, 'Fiscal capacity and dualism in colonial states', p. 24; 0.14% represents far less than the minimum aid ratio, which is set at 0.7% of GDP. We still know very little about private profits in the French empire. For a recent survey of the literature, see chapter 4 in Klas Rönnbäck and Oskar Broberg, *Capital and Colonialism: The Return on British Investments in Africa 1869–1969* (London: Palgrave Macmillan, 2019).

13 Raoul Girardet, *L'idée coloniale en France, 1871–1962* (Paris: La Table Ronde, 1972), p. 109. See also Georges Clemenceau's famous response to Jules Ferry's civilisational pretensions; Gilles Manceron, *1885: Le tournant colonial de la république* (Paris: La Découverte, 2007), p. 104.

14 By 'anti-colonialists' I refer to politicians who pronounced themselves in favour of the outright 'evacuation' of colonies. Candidates to the legislature made use of colonial themes in their platforms: in 1885, more than 100 candidates ran on anti-colonial platforms, but this number went down to 84 in 1889 and 28 in 1893. For these numbers, I rely on Boris Lesueur's preface to Adrien-Henri Canu, *La pétaudiere coloniale* (Paris: L'Harmattan, 2013), p. xi. For an analysis of radical republicans' progressive adherence to imperialism, see Gilles Candar, 'La gauche coloniale en France: socialistes et radicaux (1885–1905)', *Mil neuf cent. Revue d'histoire intellectuelle* 1.27 (2009), 37–56.

15 Julie d'Andurain, 'Réseaux politiques et milieux d'affaires: le cas d'Eugène Etienne et d'Auguste d'Arenberg', in Hubert Bonin, Catherine Hodeir, and Jean-François Klein (eds), *L'esprit économique impérial (1830–1970)* (Paris: Publications de la SFHOM, 2008), p. 98.

16 Inhabitants of the 'old colonies' of the Antilles and the Indian Ocean had been granted formal citizenship in 1848 and could send deputies to the French parliament. Some later additions to the empire, notably Algeria and Cochinchina, also sent (white) deputies to Paris. Although hardly representative, these colonial deputies would come to play a non-negligible role in parliamentary debates on French imperial finance at the turn of the century and were often members of influential pro-colonial lobby groups. Colonial 'representation' in the metropole has received little attention. For some additional information, see Jacques Binoche, *La France d'outre-mer et sa représentation parlementaire de 1789 à nos jours* (Paris: L'Harmattan, 2019). Sometimes, these deputies also sat on local colonial councils, notably in Martinique, Guadeloupe, Réunion, Guiana, Senegal, Tahiti, and later Cochinchina.

17 While many republicans still favoured flexible and indirect forms of colonial rule such as protectorates, for instance in Tunisia, others warned that indirect domination would grant too much political space to rival European powers and favoured colonial annexation. See for instance André Lebon, 'La pacification de Madagascar 1896–1898: du protectorat à l'annexion', *La Revue des Deux Mondes* 2 (15 May 1900), 331.

18 For a discussion of this 1900 turn to autonomy, see Raymond Betts, *Assimilation and Association in French Colonial Theory, 1890–1914* (Lincoln: University of Nebraska Press, 1961), pp. 106–54.

19 See for instance Joseph Caillaux, 'Les budgets, les finances des colonies en France et en Angleterre', *Questions diplomatiques et coloniales* (March 1899 and April 1899).

20 *Ibid.*, p. 80; Octave Thomas, *Nos colonies et le budget métropolitain* (Paris: Giard & Brière, 1906), p. 78.

21 On the lack of an 'overall plan' (*plan d'ensemble*), see Eugène Bonhoure, 'Les expédients et le remède', in *La Politique Coloniale* (24 January 1899). The law of 7 July 1900 forced the Ministry of Colonies to take on a greater number of military expenditures.

22 Pierre Paul Martin, *Le budget colonial* (Bordeaux: Y Cadoret, 1906), pp. 1–2.

23 On 30 January 1899, the French government placed Albert Picquié, an experienced colonial inspector who had served as governor general of New Caledonia between 1892 and 1894, at the head of the reform commission tasked with preparing the 1900 law. See Albert Picquié, 'Les budgets locaux des colonies', in Charles Mourey and Louis Brunel, *L'année coloniale* (Paris: Tallandier, 1899) pp. 27–8. On the Doumergue report, see Amaury Lorin, *Paul Doumer, gouverneur général de l'Indochine* (Paris: L'Harmattan, 2004), p. 157.

24 Journal Officiel de la République Française [hereafter JORF], Chamber of Deputies (8 December 1899), p. 2112.

25 JORF, Chamber of Deputies (8 December 1899), p. 2115.

26 JORF, Chamber of Deputies (11 December 1899), p. 2131.

27 On this process, see Nicolas Delalande, *Les batailles de l'impôt: consentement et résistances de 1789 à nos jours* (Paris: Seuil, 2011), p. 128.

28 On the implementation of a regressive fiscal state at the beginning of the Third Republic, see Stephen Sawyer, 'A fiscal revolution: Statecraft in France's early Third Republic', *American Historical Review* 121.4 (2016), 1141–66.

29 Thomas, *Nos colonies et le budget métropolitain*, p. 80.

30 Arthur Girault, *Principes de colonisation et de législation coloniale* (Paris: Sirey, 1927), pp. 664–5.

31 See for instance M. J. Charles-Roux, *Comment rendre nos colonies prospères: conférence faite sous le patronage de l'Union Coloniale Française* (Paris: Chailley, 1896), p. 22, who approvingly argues that the French emigrate to the colonies to 'avoid the excessive taxation which devours the main bulk of their labour in the metropole'.

32 *Le Grelot* (28 June 1896), available at https://digi.ub.uni-heidelberg.de/diglit/grelot1896/0105 (last accessed 17 March 2022).

33 On the circumstances of this vote, see Edouard C. André, *De l'esclavage à Madagascar* (Paris: Arthur Rousseau, 1899), pp. 165–73. On the expedition, see Jean Lémure, *Madagascar: L'expédition au point de vue médical et hygiénique. L'acclimatement et la colonisation* (Paris: Librairie J.-B. Baillère, 1896), p. 22, cited in Samuel Sanchez, 'De l'Etat royal à l'Etat colonial à Madagascar: ruptures et continuités des politiques économiques (fin XIXe–début XXe siècle)', in Mireille Razafindrakoto, François Roubaud, and Jean-Michel Wachsberger (eds), *Madagascar: d'une crise l'autre: ruptures et continuités* (Paris: Karthala, 2018), p. 88. In early 1897, French colonial authorities also dismantled the Merina kingdom and sent Queen Ranavalona III into exile.

34 For other examples of caricatures on taxation in the French satirical press between 1870 and 1914, see Nicolas Delalande, 'Consentement et résistances à l'impôt: l'Etat, les citoyens et le problème de la confiance sous la IIIe République' (PhD dissertation, Paris I Sorbonne, 2009), p. 652.

35 There was in fact a specifically right-wing form of French imperialism, but it defined itself in opposition to republican imperialism and in public discourse anti-republicanism often trumped pro-colonial sentiment. On imperialism and the French far right, see Aviel Roshwald, 'Colonial dreams of the French right wing, 1881–1914', *The Historian* 57.1 (1994), 59–74.

36 Adrien Henri Canu, *La pétaudière coloniale* (Paris: L'Harmattan, 2006), p. 168.

37 *L'Autorité*, 9 March 1899; 13 May 1899.

38 Paul Louis, 'La colonisation sous la troisième république', *La Revue Socialiste*, (April 1897) (Paris: Librairie de la Revue Socialiste), p. 170. In his 1897 essay he also excoriated the crass racism of settlers, especially in Algeria. 'The Arab pays,' he wrote, 'but he is unable to make his voice heard. We must be careful: we administer Algeria like the England administered India. Awakenings can be dangerous.' *Ibid.*, p. 168.

39 Nicolas Delalande writes that Paul Louis was dismissive of republican income tax projects but his opinion on direct taxation as a tool of redistribution was in fact much more complex. See Paul Louis, 'Le Monopole et l'impôt progressif', *La Revue Socialiste* 24 (July–December 1896) (Paris: Librairie de la Revue Socialiste), p. 406. On protectionism, agrarianism, and the politics of land tax exemption in the 1890s, see Delalande, 'Consentement et résistances à l'impôt', pp. 83–8.

40 See for instance the conversation on imperial financial relations at the International Colonial Institute: Maurice Chotard, 'Des rapports financiers entre la métropole et les colonies', *Compte-rendu de la séance tenue à la Haye* (May 1901), Institut Colonial International, p. 274.

41 On the politics of 'scandals' and corruption in late nineteenth-century Algeria (and metropolitan opinions on these), see Didier Guignard, *L'abus de pouvoir dans l'Algérie coloniale. Visibilité et singularité* (Nanterre: Presses Universitaires de Paris Ouest, 2010). On the process which led to the financial autonomy in colonial Algeria, see Jacques Bouveresse, *Un Parlement colonial? Les délégations financières algériennes, 1898–1945: l'institution et les hommes: Tome I* (Rennes: Presses Universitaires de Rennes, 2008):, pp. 49–76.

42 JORF, Chamber of Deputies (19 March 1900), p. 920.
43 Leon Rouye, *Le budget algérien, la colonisation. Contribution à l'enquête parlementaire (Juin 1900)* (Constantine: Adolphe Braham, 1900).
44 The 'Financial Delegations' were established in 1898 by the governor general Laferrière. Its proponents saw it as a form of 'business assembly' which would successfully depoliticise the rowdy Algerian settlers and 'protect' native Algerians against European electoral clientelism. It was modelled after the Consultative Conference in neighbouring Tunisia. See Henri Lorin, 'Dix ans d'autonomie financière: l'Algérie depuis 1901', *Revue des Deux Mondes* (1910), 426. For a recent overview, see Jacques Bouveresse, *Un Parlement colonial? Les délégations financières algériennes, 1898–1945: l'institution et les hommes: Tome I* (Rennes: Presses Universitaires de Rennes, 2008) and Jacques Bouveresse, *Un Parlement colonial? Les délégations financières algériennes, 1898–1945: le déséquilibre des réalisations Tome II* (Rennes: Presses Universitaires de Rennes, 2010).
45 JORF, Chamber of Deputies (13 November 1900), pp. 2031–2.
46 Adolphe Messimy, *Notre œuvre coloniale* (Paris: Emile Larose, 1910).
47 François Bobrie, 'Finances publiques et conquête coloniale: le coût budgétaire de l'expansion française entre 1850 et 1913', *Annales. Histoire, Sciences Sociales* 31.6 (1976), 1233.
48 *Ibid.*, p. 61.
49 *Ibid.*, p. 62.
50 JORF, Chamber of Deputies (26 November 1900), p. 2281. Ursleur had been president of Guiana's General Council between 1892 and 1898.
51 JORF, Chamber of Deputies, resolution project presented by Lucien Hubert (28 October 1902), p. 183.
52 See Etablissements français de l'Océanie, *Procès-Verbaux des séances du Conseil Général, Session extraordinaire et ordinaire 1902. Session extraordinaire de 1903* (Papeete: Imprimerie du Gouvernement, 1904), pp. 253–6. On Tahiti as an exception, see Isabelle Merle and Adrian Muckle, *L'indigénat: genèses dans l'empire français. Pratiques en Nouvelle-Calédonie* (Paris: CNRS, 2019), pp. 110–20. Paris reacted promptly to this refusal and ordered the council's dissolution in 1903, replacing it with a much more docile colonial council composed exclusively of nominated members. See Merle and Muckle, *L'indigénat*, p. 118.
53 See for instance Marcel Saint Germain, 'Théorie sur la fiscalité coloniale', *La dépêche coloniale*, 11 July 1905.
54 On taxation as a 'civilising' tool, see Guy Jacob, 'Gallieni et "l'impôt moralisateur" à Madagascar. Théorie, pratiques et conséquences (1901–1905)', *Revue française d'histoire d'outre-mer* 74.277 (1987), 431–73.
55 For a recent quantitative study of French colonial fiscal capacity building, see Cogneau *et al.*, 'Fiscal capacity and dualism in colonial states'.
56 Archives Nationales [hereafter AN]/Pierrefitte /602AP/2/Archives Joseph Desmars/Bilan de l'autonomie financière, 1912.
57 Gerard Sasges, *Imperial Intoxication: Alcohol and the Making of Colonial Indochina* (Honolulu: University of Hawai'i Press, 2017), p. 51.

58 For a more thorough analysis of these debates, see Madeline Woker, 'Empire of inequality: The politics of taxation in the French colonial empire, 1900–1950s' (PhD dissertation, Columbia University, 2020), especially chapter 3.
59 See for instance René-Pierre Anouma, 'L'impôt de capitation en Côte d'Ivoire de 1901 à 1908: modalités et implications d'un instrument de politique et d'économie coloniales', *Africa Zamani* 8–9 (1978), 153; Kimba Idrissa, 'L'impôt de capitation: les abus du régime de sur taxation et la résistance des populations', *African Economic History* 21 (1993), 105.
60 Jean-François Boudet, 'Les codes fiscaux d'outremer', *Comparative Law Journal of the Pacific*, Special issue on taxation in the South Pacific (2015), 56.
61 Centre des Archives Economiques et Financières [hereafter CAEF], B-0019192/1 'Réglementation sur le régime financier des colonies: interpretation du décret du 30 décembre 1912, correspondance, notes, 1906–1928'.
62 C.-M. Merly and Bernard Sol, *Le régime financier des colonies (annoté et mis à jour au 1er janvier 1931)* (Paris: Emile Larose, 1932). Archives Nationales de l'Outre-Mer [hereafter ANOM]/INDO/NF/3253/Intervention of the Cour des Comptes sur l'impôt personnel. See also ANOM/ALG/81F/1303/Décisions Conseil d'Etat sur la fiscalité and Jean Massot (ed.), *Le Conseil d'Etat et l'évolution de l'outre-mer français du XVIIe siècle à 1962* (Paris: Dalloz, 2007).
63 See Bernard Pacteau, 'Colonisation et justice administrative', in Massot, *Le Conseil d'Etat*, p. 60.
64 Georges Guénée, *Les finances tunisiennes* (Tunis: Louis Namura, 1932), pp. 78–9; André-Jean Godin, *Cours de législation budgétaire marocaine* (Paris: Quillet, 1929); Jacques Milleron and Louis Poveda, *Précis de législation budgétaire et de comptabilité administrative chérifiennes* (Rabat: L. Poveda, 1938).
65 ANOM/AP/2APOM/2/Devouton.
66 On the colonial inspection service, see R. Garner, 'Watchdogs of empire: The French colonial inspection service in action: 1815–1913' (PhD thesis, University of Rochester, 1970). These 'rules' were often violated on the ground, and it is quite unclear whether colonial administrators were always aware of their existence.
67 Albert Duchêne, *Histoire des finances coloniales de la France* (Paris: Payot, 1938), p. 168.
68 For an overview of political and economic crises in the French empire during the inter-war period, see Martin Thomas, *The French Empire between the Wars: Imperialism, Politics, and Society* (Manchester: Manchester University Press, 2005).
69 Albert Sarraut, *La mise en valeur des colonies françaises* (Paris: Payot, 1923); Archives départementales de l'Aude [hereafter ADA] Fonds Sarraut/12J184/ Budget des colonies: notes, presse, 1920.
70 ADA/Fonds Sarraut/12J184/Question de droit ou de forme: l'article 33, loi 1900.
71 Richard F. Kuisel, *Capitalism and the State in Modern France: Renovation and Economic Management in the Twentieth Century* (Cambridge: Cambridge University Press, 1981), p. 62.

72 On the reliance on private investment during the inter-war period, see Jacques Marseille, 'L'investissement français dans l'empire colonial: l'enquête du gouvernement de Vichy (1943)', *Revue historique* 252.2 (1974), 409–32.
73 See for instance "La Voix Indigène' and 'La Défense' se rencontrent pour manifester leur opposition à l'autonomie financière de l'Algérie', in ANOM/ALG/GGA/40G/28/ Revue de la presse indigène, 1936–38/February 1936.

3

Madagascar and French imperial mercantilism: Foreign trade and domestic crises, 1895–1914

Samuel F. Sanchez

In 1895, Madagascar's invasion by France appeared to be a decisive break, which led to a profound political, economic, and social crisis of unprecedented magnitude. With the development of an aggressive mercantilism induced by metropolitan France, only domestic production and trade remained as resources for the colonial state, which was obliged to extend the pre-colonial royal tax system. The French administration perpetuated and optimised the predatory system developed at the time of the Merina Kingdom[1] with regard to the domestic economy and especially to the peasantry. One must steer clear of the dichotomous periodisation which separates the pre-colonial period from the colonial period. The tax system of the royal state in the nineteenth century was characterised by a hybrid system that combined a non-market tributary system and a monetarised tax system of Euro-American inspiration.[2]

The purpose of this chapter is to study the evolution of Madagascar political economy through the economic resources used by the colonial administration to rule the island. It is therefore a question of understanding how the French administration was able to take over a large part of the pre-existing monarchical fiscal structures. However, imperial France profoundly modified the mechanisms, particularly customs, which provided the monarchical government with a large part of its resources. The shift from these two different governments gave rise to a crisis that upset the economic and social relations within the country. This chapter will largely deal with the type of resources used by the colonial administration. To what extent did French mercantilism, which colonial propaganda called the 'colonial pact', disrupt the fiscal and economic structures of Madagascar? And what kind of reciprocity could the population receive from the French rule? The chapter examines the ruptures and continuities in the relationship between Madagascar's political structures and the economy. The recent historiography of British and Portuguese colonisation in Africa shows a certain interest in taxation, in a comparative perspective.[3] For the French colonies, much remains to be done, even though economists are now working on a better understanding of budgetary organisation in a long-term perspective.[4] Although the continuities of fiscal issues after independance have been studied, very little has been written about the beginning of colonial administration and the legacy of pre-colonial practices in colonialism. The statistical data available for the colony of Madagascar make it possible for one to consider the effects of imperial customs policies on the local government's budgetary arrangements.[5]

The French administration collected its resources from domestic production and loans, leaving the export economy free. The analysis of the pre-colonial/colonial transition shows us that the autonomy of the royal Merina state was largely based on its capacity to control foreign trade. The imperial dogma of budgetary autonomy, intended to spare metropolitan taxpayers, deprived the local administration of resources and burdened its meagre attempts to develop public services (schools, hospitals, and so on). To compensate for the loss of customs revenue, the administration could only rely on direct taxes and taxes that weighed mainly on rural people. The French government took over a good part of the devices already put in place by the Merina monarchy. But it failed to develop an ethic of reciprocity that might have made the monarchical power bearable. The redistributive and tributary rites of the Merina monarchy had founded a kind of monarchical social pact – at least for free subjects, mainly in Imerina – while a penniless and materialistic administration had few services to offer in return for the labour of the population.

The socio-economic 'big bang' of the conquest

The defeat of the Merina Kingdom during the second Franco-Malagasy war (1895) – in which there was very little fighting – can largely be explained, alongside ideological reasons related to the desacralisation of royalty, by the structural weakening of the Malagasy state during the second half of the nineteenth century.[6] After the French conquest of 1895, economic structures evolved rapidly, under the impact of the socio-economic 'big bang' constituted by the almost simultaneous abolition of slavery (27 September 1896) and the aristocratic political and economic system (17 April 1897). These events shook the economic edifice of the country and disrupted the socio-political structures that had been so gradually and slowly erected throughout the nineteenth century,[7] to such an extent that a number of colonial civil servants seriously criticised the validity of these reforms. Two years after the social revolution caused by the conquest, some French administrators deplored the resulting social catastrophe: 'The multiplicity of regulatory prescriptions ... which, in two years, have done the work of a century in France, completely troubled people's minds. We are currently reigning over a crumbling society and a distraught population'.[8] The Menalamba revolt and its harsh repression during the 'pacification' also ruined a large part of the country, interrupting the smooth running of the cultivation calendar and causing subsistence crises, the human toll of which has not yet been clearly established.

Despite this unprecedented social crisis, if we examine the customs records of the French Ministry of Foreign Affairs and the Gouvernement Général de Madagascar, we notice that the value of Madagascar's foreign trade increased almost exponentially after 1895 (see Figure 3.1). The reasons for this increase are to be found in the tax exemption granted to imports from metropolitan France and in the relatively large investments made by the French government, which led to a sharp rise in consumption. While the trend expressed by these figures is significant, its magnitude should be put into perspective. The customs system more regularly recorded and better controlled by the state allows us to have access to more precise data than during the royal period. The figures in our possession are only a

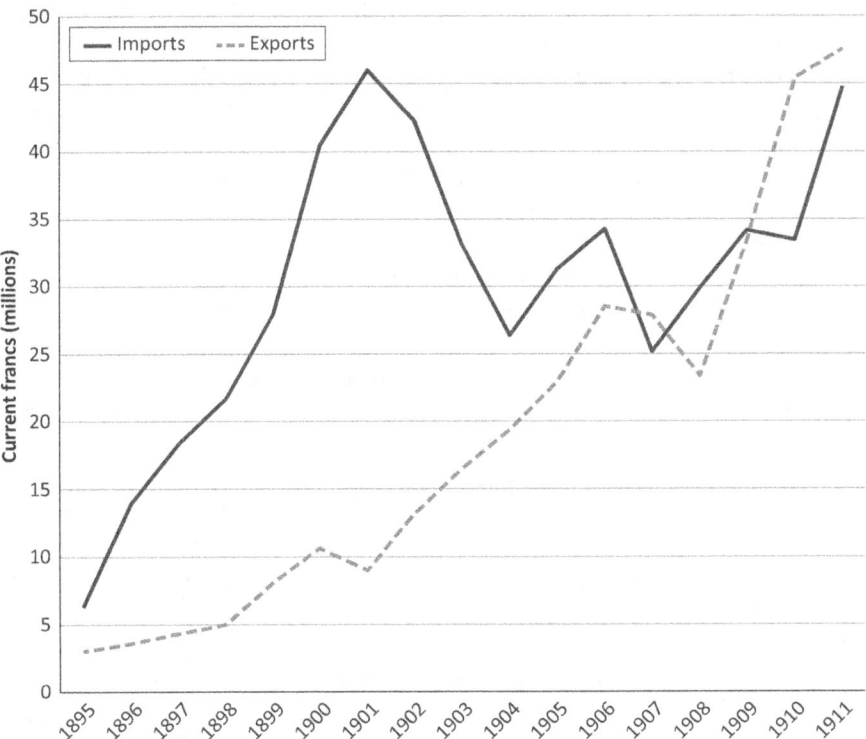

Figure 3.1 Madagascar imports and exports (1895–1911).

reflection of what the Gouvernement Général controlled, and we have relatively little data on Malagasy foreign trade before 1885.[9] Colonial statistics must also be taken cautiously, because a tradition of manipulating figures could have led civil servants to increase or decrease certain data for political or career reasons.

The colonial stakes of 'customs assimilation'

During the short period of the protectorate of Hippolyte Laroche (Dec. 1895–Sep. 1896) the former customs regulations of the Kingdom of Madagascar (10% on entry and exit) were initially maintained. The Comptoir National d'Escompte de Paris (CNEP, French bank) which controlled the Malagasy customs as part of the repayment of the loan of 15 million francs made in 1885 by the Malagasy government, retained control over several ports as part of the repayment of the Malagasy debt.[10]

With the annexation decree of 6 August 1896, a major reform was passed: customs came under the direct control of the Gouvernement Général, and trade with France and its colonies was freed from all taxes. The colony continued, however – for the sake of state continuity – to reimburse the Comptoir National d'Escompte de Paris. Ironically, the indigenous-status Malagasy taxpayers continued, after the French conquest and until the 1900s, to reimburse the French metropolitan banks for the compensations that France had extorted from the kingdom in 1885![11] The 10% *ad valorem* charge that was applied to all imports was now only applied to products coming from non-metropolitan areas. In 1897, following the advance of French troops during the pacification, twenty-six ports were equipped with customs posts and opened to international trade.[12]

However, the number of ports with a customs collector was soon limited to ten: Diego-Suarez, Vohémar, Sainte-Marie, Tamatave, Vatomandry, Mananjary, Fort-Dauphin, Nosy-Ve, Majunga and Nosy Be.[13] The commercial geography of the island was affected, as certain older posts disappeared completely, and the hierarchy between cities was disrupted, especially because of the extraordinary rise of Tamatave, the main gateway to the island.[14] It is only from 1897 that the Gouvernement Général was able to effectively control the major part of the Malagasy maritime boundaries, even if the immense coastline, especially in the west, left many gaps for dhows and schooners which practised all types of trade in these peripheral regions. As late as 1907, when confronted with a smuggling problem, the central authority was still obliged to issue circulars prohibiting maritime trade outside ports with customs.[15]

The French conquest was not inevitably synonymous with economic protectionism. In several colonies of the French Empire, particularly West Africa, France and Great Britain were bound by free trade agreements, and commercial freedom prevailed.[16] In the case of Madagascar, the French government initially favoured a protectorate. But the scandal caused by the disastrous Madagascar expedition – fuelled by Réunionese[17] deputies and industrial lobbies – was such that French metropolitan opinion demanded compensation for the loss of the 6,000 members of the contingent and reservists out of the 15,000 that had been sent to Madagascar.[18] The option of annexation was thus finally chosen. The question of Madagascar's customs regime was one of the central issues discussed at the National Assembly in 1896. Some deputies, such as Gaston Doumergue, did not fail to raise serious objections to the choice of annexation. Its economic consequence was feared, because making Madagascar an economically assimilated colony was bound to be costly, since the island was not very productive and essentially destined to absorb French industrial productions.[19] The Méline government (1896–98) finally passed the law of 16 April 1897 in the National Assembly, establishing Madagascar's new customs rules. It is not surprising that these protectionist laws were supported by a president of the Council who was an ardent defender of metropolitan agriculture, but also a deputy from the Vosges, a region renowned for its active textile industry[20], eager for colonial outlets, which then produced nearly half of French textile exports.[21] The Méline government thus successfully managed to make Madagascar a protected market, providing significant advantages to exports from French metropolitan industries, predominantly textiles.[22] As feared by the French liberals, the government's choice favoured the export of goods to the colony while maintaining a high taxation on Malagasy items exported to mainland France – thereby following the protectionist policy prevailing there. Indeed, some products, such as sugar or products derived from cattle production, could compete with metropolitan production or that of other colonies. The new colony, represented only as an outlet for metropolitan France, quickly aroused bitterness among the new colonial oligarchy of the island, composed essentially of concession holders who wished to export tropical products to metropolitan France. The products of these investors, who had campaigned for the annexation of the Big Island, were subject to heavy taxation when entering mainland France. Metropolitan importers of colonial products – particularly those from Marseilles – were also opposed to these regulations, which were unfavourable to their colonial investments and to the low-cost importation of the tropical products they needed.[23] In colonial Madagascar, the application of the 1892 metropolitan customs regime was considered unfair. It was pejoratively denounced in the newspapers as a 'semi-colonial pact' that in no way benefited domestic production. Indeed, the taxes on the products of the French colonies were only granted a 50% abatement compared to the tropical foodstuffs of the foreign colonies, which was insufficient to make the Malagasy exports competitive. According to planters' lobbies, metropolitan France only considered Madagascar 'an outlet to be monopolised'.[24] As colonial inspector Xavier Loisy said,[25] it was indeed a question of 'exceptional tariffs in favor of Metropolitan France, and no longer in favor of the colony'. The consequence of this choice weighed on the budget of the colonial state, which could no longer count on the contribution of taxes on foreign trade, to be consolidated.

Madagascar, French market with forced march

From 1897 onwards, trade was thus largely dominated by the importation of mainly manufactured goods (textiles) and alcohols from France (see Figures 3.2, 3.3, and 3.4). The situation was not only favoured by legislation, but also by the investments inherent to the conquest and colonial development of the territory, both of which were undertaken by the Gouvernement Général de Madagascar. The construction of the Tananarive–Tamatave railroad, the development of ports, the construction of roads,[26] the mechanisation of certain concessions, and the introduction of high value-added goods supplying the growing European community caused an explosion in demand and a consequent increase in the rate of French imports. In 1897–98, exports were slowed down by the troubled political situation caused by the Menalamba revolt in Imerina – the demographic and economic heart of Madagascar – and that of the Sambirano in the north.[27] Moreover, the abolition of slavery and aristocratic rights, which was decided in a relatively unprepared manner, affected productive and socio-economic structures, particularly in Imerina. The prohibition of cut silver coins that were used before the conquest made this situation worse.[28] It was not until the end of the 1900s that Madagascar's trade balance regained a certain equilibrium (see Figure 3.1).

In the meantime, French imports had imposed themselves on the island. In this area, France had levelled off at around 31% before annexation (see Figure 3.2). The United Kingdom, the United States, and Germany shared two thirds of the market. From 1896 to 1898, France seized Malagasy trade by skillfully overtaxing German-, American-, and British-made products. It managed to limit Gujarati and Chinese commercial penetration by introducing residence permits and specific patents at prohibitively high prices.[29] Their avowed aim was to stimulate French merchants to the detriment of those of foreign origin.[30] The tax exemption for French goods and residence

Madagascar and French imperial mercantilism 63

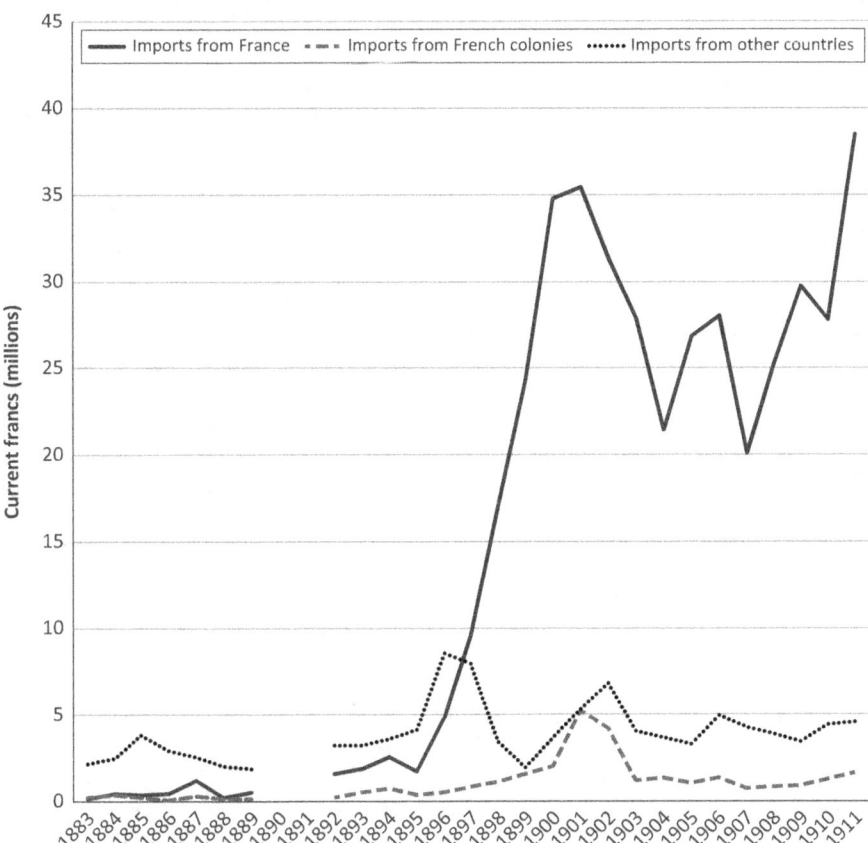

Figure 3.2 Origin of imports in Madagascar (1883–1911). Note: Missing data for 1890 and 1891; data from 1883 to 1895 come from the French Protectorate administration and must therefore be considered with caution (figures for the only ports with French residents).

permits explain the collapse of foreign imports over the period 1896–1902, during which 75% of goods arrived from France – and, marginally, from the French colonies (7%). The monopoly situation increased during the period 1903–11. Henceforth, only 12% of imports came from the other industrial powers. French industry flooded the Malagasy market with fabrics and manufactured articles that were free of all taxes (see Figures 3.2 and 3.3).

The customs system, amended with exceptions by the decrees of 28 July 1897, affected many articles, but was aimed primarily at fabric, the most important imported product (in terms of value). A battery of taxes specifically targeted the most popular cotton fabrics at Malagasy fairs. Fine

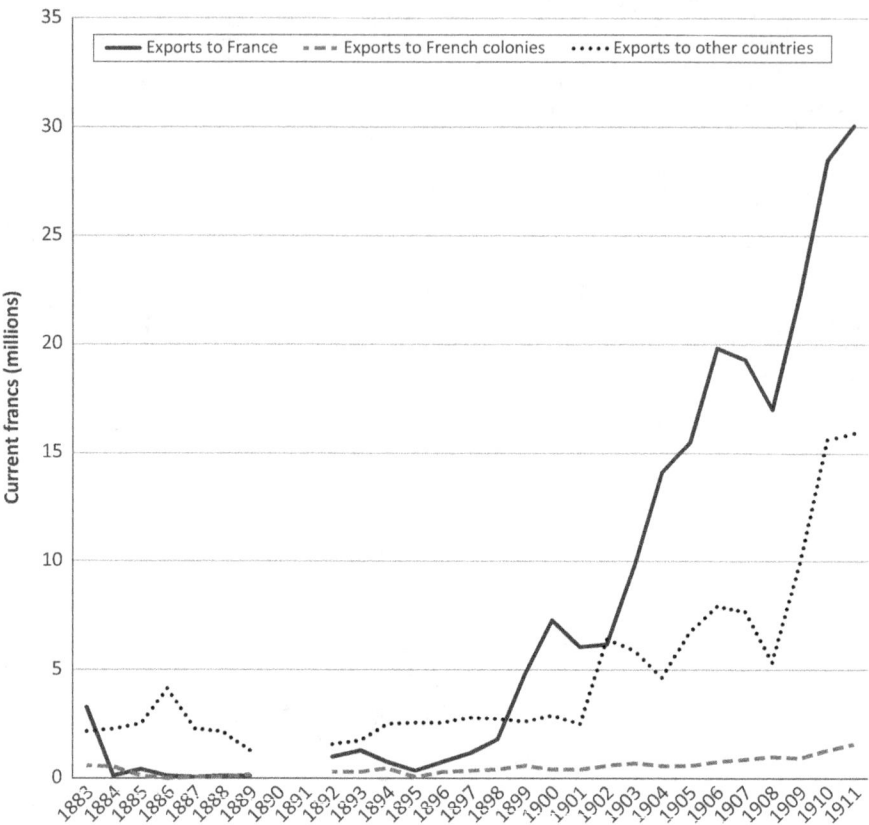

Figure 3.3 Destination of Madagascar's exports (1883–1911). Note: Missing data for 1890 and 1891; data from 1883 to 1895 come from the French Protectorate administration and must therefore be considered with caution (figures for the only ports with French residents).

top-of-the-range foreign textiles – an area in which the French industry excelled and had no need to fear competition – were practically tax free. On the other hand, the entry-level *merikani*-type cotton fabrics,[31] so popular in the southwestern Indian Ocean, were overtaxed.[32] The decree of 31 May 1898 further strengthened the monopoly of French manufacturers on the Malagasy market by raising the tax on entry-level foreign textiles to an exorbitant rate of 77 francs per 100 kg.[33] It took all the effort of the administration to oust American textiles from a market that valued them enormously. Foreign textiles could no longer compete with French fabrics. Taxes on these textiles were higher than in metropolitan France itself, which resulted in higher textile prices on the markets as French production was

Figure 3.4 Main export products of Madagascar (1896–1911).

unable to meet demand. Nevertheless, French and German traders skilfully circumvented the situation by importing American or English fabrics at low cost into metropolitan France, clearing them through customs and then introducing them duty free into Madagascar. This operation remained profitable because transport costs were largely amortised by the tax exemption. The publicity of this process led to an awareness of the shortcomings of the mercantile system that had been put in place, which ultimately benefited neither French industry nor the colony's budget.[34] Cotton fabrics were the main items of cash expenditure of Malagasy consumers and one can easily imagine the effect that these price increases due to customs manipulations had on the cost of living, in a context of cash shortages and fiscal pressure.

The situation was not the same regarding exports. While France's share was significant – 29% in the 1880s – the monopoly position was less clear-cut than that of imports during the years 1896–1902. France was certainly the first destination for Malagasy products, but 42% of these products were still being exported to Great Britain and Germany, which still had large trading houses in the country. Over the period 1903–11, France's share increased and reached its peak – which resulted both from the strength of German consumption and restrictive customs laws in metropolitan France. Nevertheless, the proportion of Malagasy foodstuffs destined for non-metropolitan markets remained at around 30% (see Figure 3.3).

In the field of exports, Germany gained considerable importance thanks to the networks of the companies O'Swald and DOAG (Deutsch-Ostafrikanische Gesellschaft). German industry was growing and consumed huge quantities of colonial products, including tannic plants, oil seeds, latex, gums, and skins. In Madagascar, as elsewhere in sub-Saharan Africa, German companies were very active, not only in their colonies, but also in the territories of other powers. In some of them, as in the French colony of Dahomey (present-day Benin), the export trade in 1910 was still more than 70% foreign oriented – and primarily to Germany. In the British colony of the Gold Coast around the same time, more than 50% of all the exports went to Germany. In Madagascar, despite the installation of colonial protectionist measures and borders, export trade continued to function more or less as before, relying on the same trade networks.[35] The companies continued their operations by diversifying their activities and buying French products, in order to maintain their business operations in French colonies. O'Swald and DOAG pursued their usual trading activity, balancing their purchases with French rather than German products as much as possible: cotton from Rouen, Vosges, northern France, and Lyons. German spirits were replaced by French wines.

The expansion of German companies suffered little from the protectionist laws imposed by the French, since they imported mainly non-German products, or types of products that were not (or rarely) produced in France – machines, for instance. Metropolitan France made sure that Madagascar consumed only French products; however, national tradesmen lost their hold on their distribution. With the law of 5 August 1913, colonial pressure groups managed to revise the trade relations between France and Madagascar. Malagasy products benefited from a tax reduction upon their arrival in France, which favoured exports and thus Malagasy production.

In the first decade of the twentieth century, foreign trade increased threefold. In 1910, Madagascar accounted for about 10% of France's colonial imports (third place behind Indochina and Afrique Occidentale Française [AOF]). The population was then estimated at 2.7 million inhabitants, making Madagascar a colony with a very high rate of trade openness compared to AOF, which, with a population four times larger, accounted for only 22% of metropolitan imports. At that time, Madagascar was a high-yield colony, as evidenced by a large influx of settlers: around 15,000 Europeans were settled in the island in 1910 (0.5% of the population),

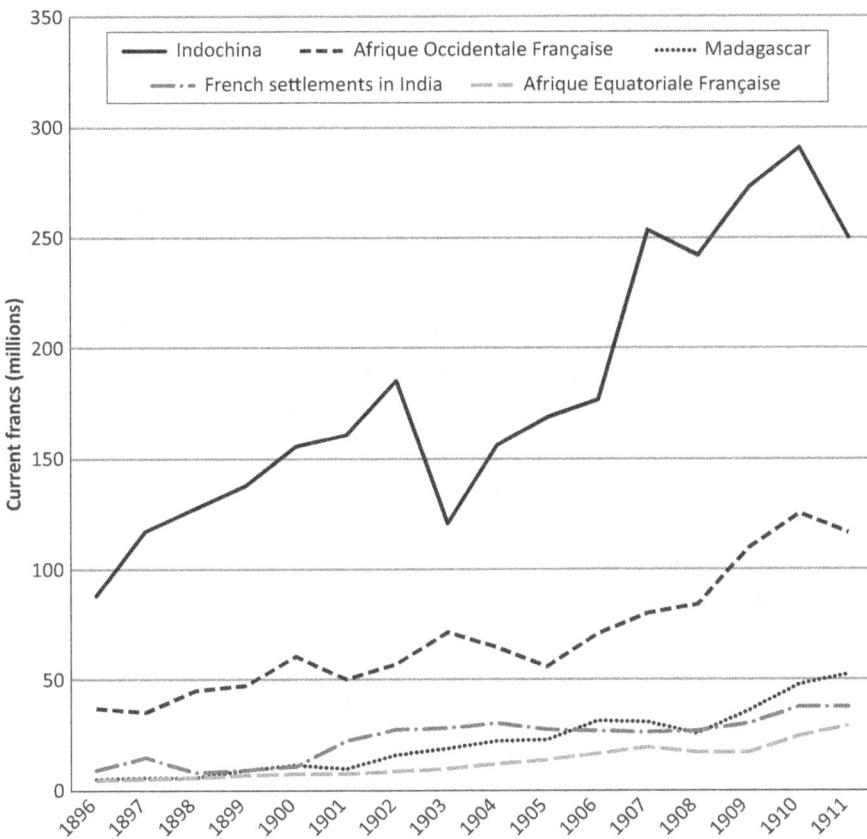

Figure 3.5 French imports from French colonies (1896–1911).

compared with only 7,800 for all the AOF (0.07% of the population). Even the colony of Senegal, which constituted the majority of Europeans in AOF, accounted for only 3,300 Europeans (only 0.25% of its 1.3 million people with indigenous status) (see Figures 3.5 and 3.6).

Crisis fiscality and domestic solutions

From its commencement, and following the protectionist principles that had prevailed from the beginning of the Great Depression (1873–96), the mechanism which had regulated the development of the colony of Madagascar was that of a budgetary autonomy – a guarantee for metropolitan France that the colony would not become a financial burden. The

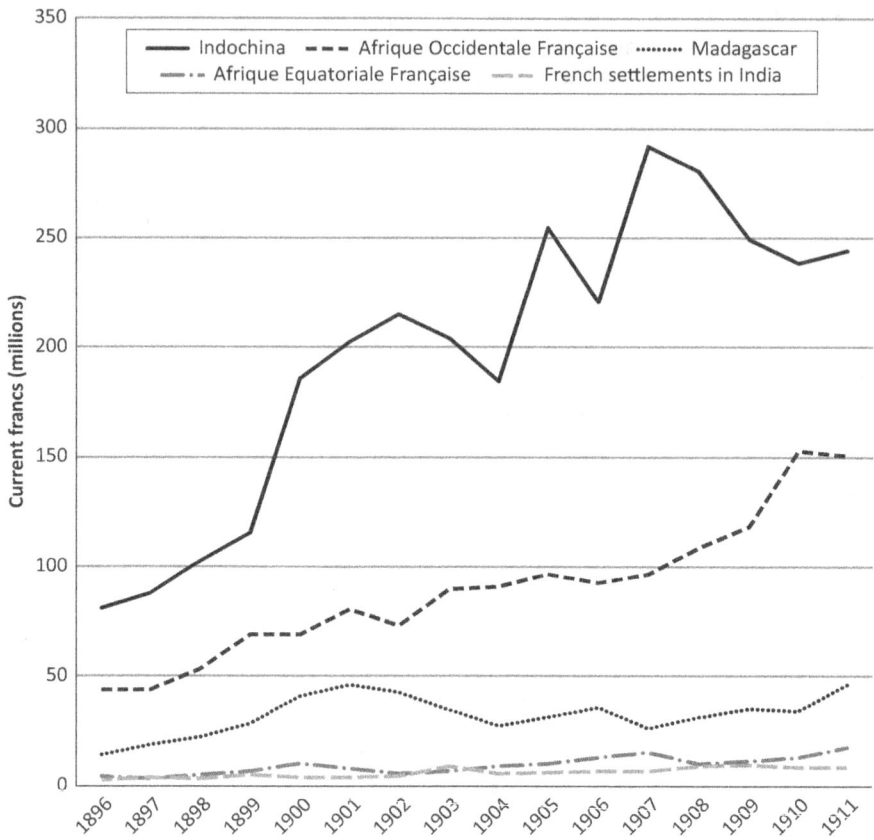

Figure 3.6 French exports to French colonies (1896–1911).

colony had to be self-financing. However, the exemption on the importation of French products caused a real loss for the budget of the Gouvernement Général de Madagascar, which had to ensure sufficient tax revenues to pay staff, assume the expenses of the various budgets, and ensure the reimbursement of the loans contracted through metropolitan organisations. Between 1896 and 1900, because of the island's low level of monetarisation, taxation on exports could have ensured a significant income, as most ports were controlled (see Figure 3.2). Madagascar's main exports at that time were raw products, with no added value. The total value of certain exports – such as gold, rubber, hides, and raffia – handled by concessionary companies exceeded one million francs (see Figure 3.4). Gold exports in particular reached 10 million francs in 1909, though the state gained no benefits from this extraction, which was extremely remunerative for the concessionary companies.[36] The absence of taxation on these exports caused a real loss of income for the colony, which in such conditions had no choice but to fall back on other resources to replenish its reserves.

In the aftermath of the conquest, and faced with the impossibility of taxing the population and trade throughout the island, the French authorities decided to develop the *prestations de travail* (sum of work due annually by individuals) system by instituting a legal duration of mandatory work and associating it with minimal financial compensation.[37] This system merely perpetuated, under a new French name, the principles of *fanompoana*: the former 'royal service' or 'corvée' (tribute labour) that free individuals owed to their sovereign in pre-colonial Madagascar. From this point of view, colonial taxation was largely inherited from the royal state.[38] The system of labour *prestations* thus enabled the government to mobilise taxpayers who could no longer raise the cash needed to pay their taxes. Construction of the necessary infrastructures and porterage between 1896 and 1901 were thus largely paid for by the inhabitants themselves. As Gallieni put it: 'We owe the rapid recovery of this country to [the *prestations*]'.[39] From 1901 onwards, following the doctrine of the *impôt moralisateur* ('moralising tax'), *prestations* were abolished and the per capita tax was reinforced to remedy their disappearance.[40]

The development of the *capitation* (per capita tax) and the repression against vagrancy were supposed to promote wage earning in the cities and colonial concessions, and to promote the monetarisation of the economy. This organisation aimed, through administrative coercion, to push workers, especially rural workers, into wage employment. The personal tax rate varied from region to region, depending on their economic development. It amounted to 30 francs in Antananarivo and 10 francs in the Menabe and southeast. The state extended and unified the cash tax to the entire island only in the mid-1900s.

But the colonial objective of founding a fully monetarised tax model was quickly abandoned. In the provinces, taxes were not easily collected, not only because population censuses were not accurate enough, but also because taxes were often too high in relation to the financial capacity of taxpayers – a fact that had been pointed out by many administration agents, such as General Pennequin. Between 1900 and 1903, it took about one month of labour for Antananarivo employees to pay the *capitation*; in the poorest provinces, three to four months were needed to collect the currency required by the administration. In rural areas, the requirement to raise currency boosted the collection of raw products intended for export, which in turn enriched colonial export companies. This generated a phenomenon of tax avoidance that caused significant regional migration.[41] Even in the prosperous regions of Imerina, peasants had difficulty in collecting the sums demanded by the administration's tax collectors. The government decided to act pragmatically and return to an intermediary solution, using new work *prestations* that were supposed to benefit the community of the *fokonolona* institution.[42] From 1902 onwards, the inhabitants of Imerina had to carry out collective work in this context. The principle was then gradually extended to all regions of the island. In some provinces, the peasantry is squeezed by crushing taxes and the diversion of benefits for private purposes, leading to peasant revolts, as in the Farafangana region (southeast) in 1904. In 1905, following some misappropriation that benefited certain settlers, the *fokonolona* corvées were more closely supervised. All Malagasy of indigenous status subject to the personal tax had to accomplish the 'corvées de fokonolona'. The duration of these *prestations* varied from year to year. It was determined by the Gouvernement Général after consultation with the heads of provinces. In practice, the *prestations* were not to exceed eight working days per year, for periods that did not exceed four consecutive days.[43] Urban dwellers and wealthy groups were rapidly able to buy back their *prestations* in cash. This was in line with the government's policy of monetarisation and extension of the salaried workforce in Malagasy society.

The question that remains is that of the redistributive nature of the tax system. All in all, can it be said that taxation at the beginning of the colonial period contributed to the public good? An examination of the colony's budgets between 1897 and 1910 (see Figures 3.7 and 3.8) shows that, from a structural point of view, revenues exceeded expenditures. The surpluses collected by the colonial administration were in fact due to the contribution of loans contracted by the colony for the construction of infrastructures dedicated to the opening up of the region (railways and roads).

In the structure of state revenue, the share of taxes on foreign trade remained minimal in this distribution, due to the *Pacte colonial* organisation. On the other hand, the share of taxes weighing directly on Malagasy people with indigenous status was increased. From 1901 onwards, the personal tax became the main budgetary source, accounting for almost 50% of state revenue (excluding loans). Other taxes such as the tax on rice fields, houses, and animals also increased the tax burden on rural dwellers.

The two main items of government expenditure were infrastructure development (railways, roads, telegraphs, etc.) and, as in the majority of French colonies, the remuneration of civil servants.[44] Railways and roads were largely financed through loans, and were therefore ultimately borne by the Malagasy taxpayers.

In these early years of colonisation, school and hospital expenses were low and the welfare system weak. The Malagasy taxpayers did not have much to expect from public services organised by the colonial

Madagascar and French imperial mercantilism 71

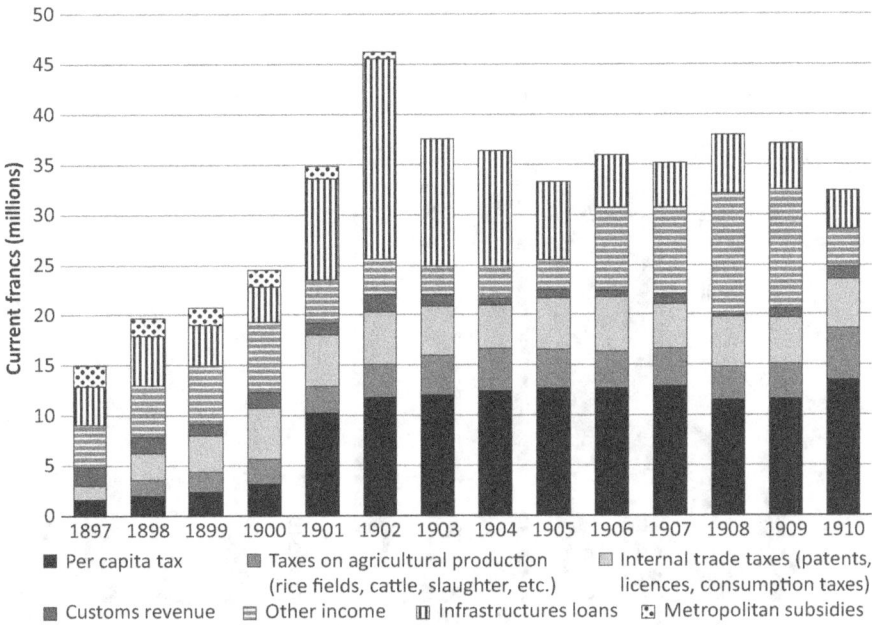

Figure 3.7 Main budgetary resources in Madagascar (1897–1910).

administration. In 1905, public education in the colony comprised 363 indigenous schools, in which 561 teachers (of which only 50 were French civil servants) taught 28,380 pupils. At the same time, eight public schools 'attended by European or assimilated children' with 13 teachers and 246 pupils were dedicated to the children of citizens. Until 1905, education was largely undertaken by Christian schools which, with their 3,134 schools, educated 159,215 pupils with 4,139 teachers. The Catholic missions alone had 45,693 pupils, while the largest Protestant mission (Norwegian Missionary Society) had 41,326 children.[45] Most of the education was financed directly by families or through the help of the congregations. Even after the application of the 1905 law, which acted on the separation of church and state (also in the colonial territories), and boosted the construction of schools in all districts to compensate the demise of several Christian schools, the private sector remained predominant in the country's school system.[46]

As for medical infrastructure, in 1904 Madagascar officially had 38 hospitals, 42 maternity wards, 28 dispensaries, and 11 leprosaria. Most of the facilities were concentrated in Imerina. Central Imerina had 7 hospitals, 9 maternity wards, and 9 dispensaries. The disparity in hospital coverage was very high. Unsurprisingly, medical coverage was relatively good in

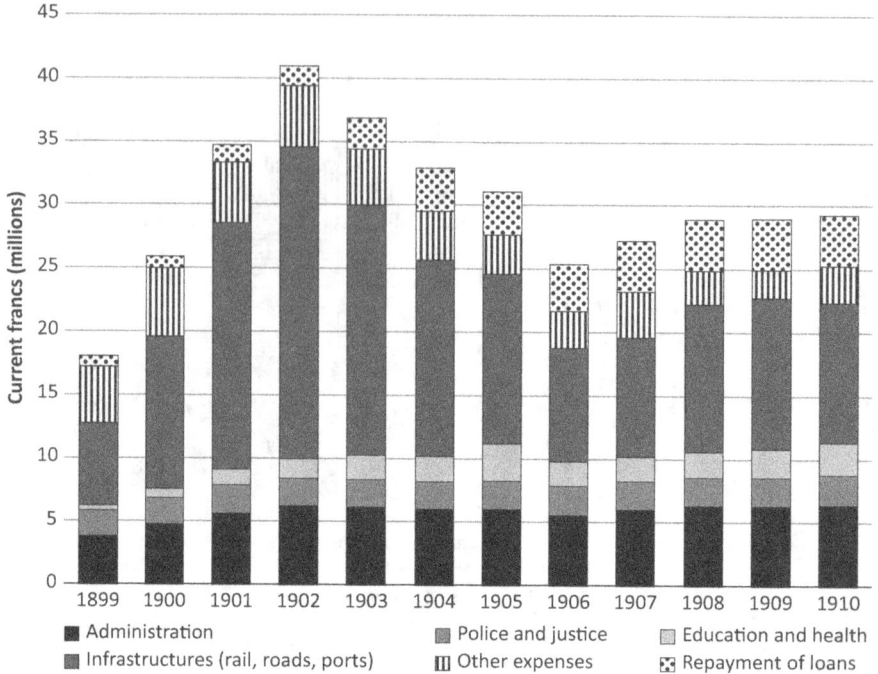

Figure 3.8 Main budgetary expenditures in Madagascar (1899–1910).

Tananarive-Ville where the inhabitants could count on important public services and a lot of Malagasy general practicians. The consultation rate there was 0.3 per inhabitant per year. At the other end of the spectrum, more remote and rural regions such as Fort-Dauphin (southeast) had only 0.01 consultations per inhabitant per year.[47]

While the repayment of the various loans taken out at the time of pacification for the construction of the Tananarive–Tamatave railway put a strain on the expenditure budget, social spending increased, especially after the First World War, as the rate of trade openness in the colonies increased.[48]

The tax burden on taxpayers (personal tax, tax on rice fields, tax on cattle and consumption) was therefore very high. But was it higher than before the conquest? It seems that the answer varies from one region to the next. Some provinces, such as Betsileo, experienced a 30-fold increase in capitation between 1896 and 1905.[49] In others, the pressure seems to have decreased relatively. Add to this the persistence of the *fanompoana*, which demanded several days of work from the peasants – a sacrifice that could prove dramatic during the harvest period.[50] It would be interesting to determine the evolution of working time per individual devolved to the state between the royal and colonial periods. The monetarisation of the economy makes this comparison difficult, but it would allow us to understand how the evolution was experienced in Malagasy households. As a general rule, the structure of revenues and expenditures shows us how the development of Madagascar's infrastructure and the upkeep of the administration were carried out solely with the resources, whether in currency or manpower, of the – essentially rural – Malagasy subjects, without any resort to levies on foreign trade.

Conclusion

In the early twentieth century, the Malagasy economy seemed in full transformation and singularly divided. It operated its transition between a non-market, tributary and symbolic model and a value system based on monetary and market exchange. The extroversion of the economy was excessively favoured by the French conquest in an anti-liberal perspective, and we witness an unprecedented expansion of foreign trade (multiplied by three, in terms of value, between 1898 and 1911). But this economic integration into an imperial economic system essentially benefited the French metropolitan industrial sector and the extractive sector, monopolised by French entrepreneurs (gold, rubber, etc.). The bulk of production, however, remained oriented towards rural self-consumption. France's quasi-monopoly, accompanied by an almost total exemption from taxes on foreign trade, created an unprecedented situation: the budget of the colonial state had to function in quasi-autarky, in a society with little monetarisation. Faced with the impossibility of taxing foreign trade, the French administration increased taxation on production and domestic trade. The recourse of the colonial state to the *prestation* regime, although theoretically opposed to the ideology of development advocated by Joseph Gallieni, was a pragmatic response to the prohibition by metropolitan France on taxing foreign trade.

Early colonial Madagascar was paradoxical in that it retained the structures of the former pre-colonial agrarian state, while emptying them of their sacred and tributary symbolism, and aggressively opening the economy to French interests.

This situation produced certain perverse effects reminiscent of other periods in Madagascar's history. It is tempting to relate the economic policy of the early years of colonisation – struck by the diktat of budgetary autonomy and stuck in the stranglehold of the relations between the colony and mainland France – to the situation of autarky that prevailed during the recurrent periods of isolation in the nineteenth century. During these periods – which generally originated from conflicts with Europeans (reign of Ranavalona I; Franco-Malagasy conflicts in the 1880s) – similar dynamics were at play: state retreat to its agrarian base, extensive and massive use of *fanompoana*, enrichment of predatory oligarchies, and so on. The state's inability to derive income from foreign trade led it to drain domestic production and trade, causing a drop in the standard of living of local communities.

In closing this chapter, it is also tempting to hypothesise that the fiscal domination of the contemporary Malagasy state, due in large part to the very low taxation of corporations and extractive industries,[51] has its roots in the ancient practices of entrepreneurial and political oligarchies, particularly during the colonial period and even before.

Notes

1 The Merina Kingdom or 'Kingdom of Madagascar' was a state developed in the highlands of Madagascar, in the region of Imerina. In 1817, the Merina Kingdom was recognised by Great Britain as sovereign of the whole island of Madagascar, whereas it was only one kingdom among many others. From then on, the official term to refer to this state became 'Kingdom of Madagascar', although this state never controlled the entire Great Island. See Pier Larson, *History and Memory in the Age of Enslavement: Becoming Merina in Highland Madagascar, 1770–1822* (Portsmouth, NH: Heinemann, 2000); Françoise Raison-Jourde, *Bible et pouvoir à Madagascar au XIXe siècle* (Paris: Karthala, 1991).
2 Samuel F. Sanchez, 'The value of the 'Royal Bath' (Fandroana): Tributary exchanges and sovereignty in the Kingdom of Madagascar in the 19th century', *Revue d'histoire du XIXe siècle* 59.2 (2019), 71–94.
3 Ewout Frankema, 'Colonial taxation and government spending 1880–1940: Maximizing revenue or minimizing effort?', *Explorations in Economic History* 48.1 (2011), 136–49; Philip J. Havik, Alexander Keese, and Maciel Santos (eds), *Administration and Taxation in Former Portuguese Africa, 1900–1945* (Newcastle upon Tyne: Cambridge Scholars, 2015); Leigh Gardner, *Taxing Colonial Africa: The Political Economy of British Imperialism* (Oxford: Oxford University Press, 2012).
4 Denis Cogneau, Yannick Dupraz, and Sandrine Mesplé-Somps, 'African states and development in historical perspective: Colonial public finances in British and French West' (2018), available at https://halshs.archives-ouvertes.fr/halshs-01820209 (last accessed 20 March 2022); Denis Cogneau, Yannick Dupraz, and Sandrine Mesplé-Somps, 'Fiscal capacity and dualism in colonial states: The French Empire 1830–1962' (2020), available at https://hal.archives-ouvertes.fr/halshs-01818700v4 (last accessed 20 March 2022).
5 Data compiled by the author mainly from *Statistiques générales de Madagascar et dépendances*, 1905–11.

6 Stephen Ellis, *L'insurrection des Menalamba: Une Révolte à Madagascar, 1895–1899* (Paris and Antananarivo: Karthala-Ambozontany, 1998); Guy Jacob, 'Influences occidentales en imerina et déséquilibres socio-économiques avant la conquête française', *Omaly sy Anio* 5–6 (1977), 223–31.
7 Gabriel Rantoandro, 'Après l'abolition de l'esclavage à Madagascar, le devenir immédiat des esclaves émancipés', in Ignace Rakoto, *L'esclavage à Madagascar. Aspects Historiques et Résurgences Contemporaines* (Antananarivo: Institut de Civilisation-Musée d'art et d'archéologie, 1997), pp. 273–90.
8 Archives Nationales de l'Outre-Mer [hereafter ANOM] Madagascar 2D39: Notebook: Report on penetration of 4th military territory, dossier C, pp. 45–6, chap. pol. situation 1898–99.
9 Attempts in historiography to establish a comprehensive picture of the Big Island's foreign trade are currently at the draft stage: Gwyn Campbell, *An Economic History of Imperial Madagascar, 1750–1895: The Rise and Fall of an Island Empire*, African Studies Series 106 (New York: Cambridge University Press, 2005).
10 This debt stems from trade treaties between King Radama II (1861–63) and several French investors. Following a palace revolution, the new Rasoherina (1863–68) government, led by Prime Minister Rainilaiarivony, unilaterally denounced these treaties, which was considered by the French government as a reason for breaking up. This situation was one of the causes of the Franco-Merina war in 1883–85. The treaty of 1885 ratified the principle of an indemnity due to the heirs of the aggrieved merchants. To pay this compensation, the Merina government had to take out loans from Parisian banks.
11 For debt history in colonial Africa, see Leigh Gardner, 'Trading sovereignty for capital? Public debt in West Africa, 1871–1914', in Nicolas Barreyre and Nicolas Delalande (eds), *Global Politics of Public Debts from the Late 18th Century* (Basingstoke: Palgrave Macmillan, 2020), pp. 175–200.
12 They were Diego-Suarez, Loky, Vohémar, Maroantsetra, Fénérive, Sainte-Marie, Tamatave, Andevoranto, Vatomandry, Mahanoro, Mananjary, Vangaindrano, Farafangana, and Fort-Dauphin, on the east coast; Hell-Ville and Ambanoro in Nosy Be, Ampasimena (Ampasindava Bay), Andranosamonta, Nosy Lava, Maevarano, Ambenja (Mahajamba), Majunga, Marovoay, Soalala, Manombo, and Nosy-Ve on the west coast. See *Journal Officiel de Madagascar*, 22 June 1897, p. 603.
13 *Journal Officiel de Madagascar* [hereafter *JOM*], decree of 22 August 1897.
14 Samuel F. Sanchez, 'L'État et les matières premières à Madagascar. Éléments historiques sur le contrôle du commerce extérieur par l'État (XIXe–XXe s.)', *Afrique contemporaine* 251.3 (2014), 157–66.
15 Madagascar National Archives, Série Navigation Maritime, dossier 11, circ. 23 March 1907.
16 Hubert Bonin, 'Des négociants français à l'assaut des places fortes commerciales Britanniques: CFAO et SCOA en Afrique occidentale anglaise puis anglophone', in Hubert Bonin and Michel Cahen (eds), *Négoce Blanc En Afrique Noire* (SFHOM-Alterna, 2001).

17 La Réunion island was a French colony with a special status. Since the abolition of slavery in 1848, all male inhabitants were citizens. They elected deputies who sat in the National Assembly in Paris. The colony considered itself as a 'colonising colony' and played a key role in French imperialism in the Indian Ocean.
18 Eric T. Jennings, *Perspectives on French Colonial Madagascar* (New York: Palgrave Macmillan, 2018).
19 See 'Approbation de la loi déclarant Madagascar et les îles qui en dépendent colonie française', in *JORF, Débats parlementaires*, Thursday 18 and Saturday 20 June 1896.
20 H. Mager, *Rapport Adressé Aux Chambres de Commerce de Rouen et Des Vosges*, 2 vols (Rouen: Lapierre, 1897).
21 Jacques Marseille, *Empire Colonial et Capitalisme Français Histoire d'un Divorce* (Paris: Seuil, 1989).
22 The 'Méline' protectionist law of 11 January 1892 was applied in the colony in 1897. *JOM*, 22 June 1897, p. 605.
23 Francis Koerner, *Madagascar: Colonisation Française et Nationalisme Malgache, XXe Siècle* (Paris: L'Harmattan, 1994); Olivier Lambert, *Marseille et Madagascar, Histoire d'une Aventure Outre-Mer Entrepreneurs et Activités Portuaires, Stratégies Économiques et Mentalités Coloniales (1840–1976)*, Histoire Du Commerce et de l'industrie de Marseille, XIXe–XXe Siècle 14 (Marseilles: Chambre de commerce et d'industrie Marseille-Provence, 2000).
24 *Le Progrès de Madagascar*, 5 June 1909.
25 Xavier Loisy, *Madagascar. Etude Économique* (Paris: A. Challamel, 1914).
26 Jean Fremigacci, *État, économie et société coloniale à Madagascar de la fin du XIXe siècle aux années 1940*, Hommes et sociétés (Paris: Karthala, 2014).
27 Ellis, *L'insurrection des menalamba*.
28 Albert Ralaikoa, *Pression Fiscale et Appauvrissement Chronique Sur Les Hautes Terres Centrales Malgaches, 1896–1945*, Lille-Thèses (Lille 3: ANRT, 1987); C. André (ed.), *De la condition de l'esclave dans la société Malgache avant l'occupation Française et de l'abolition de l'esclavage* (Paris: A. Rousseau, 1899); Guy Jacob, 'La France et Madagascar de 1880 à 1894. Aux origines d'une conquête coloniale' (thesis, Paris IV, 1996).
29 *JOM*, Decree of 3 November 1896 on residence permits; Decree of 26 July 1897 on patents.
30 Joseph-Simon Gallieni, *Rapport d'ensemble Sur La Pacification, l'organisation et La Colonisation de Madagascar (Octobre 1896 à Mars 1899)* (Paris: Henri-Charles Lavauzelle, 1899).
31 *Merikani* were bleached cotton sheets manufactured in Massachusetts factories that were very popular in the Indian ocean in the second half of the nineteenth century. See Pedro Machado, Sarah Fee, and Gwyn Campbell (eds), *Textile Trades, Consumer Cultures, and the Material Worlds of the Indian Ocean* (Basingstoke: Palgrave Macmillan, 2018).
32 'Décret portant fixation des exceptions au tarif général des douanes', *JOM* 131 (14 August).

33 *JOM* 257 (4 June 1897), p. 1942.
34 Loisy, *Madagascar*.
35 Leonhard Harding, '"À la pêche dans l'eau des autres": Les sociétés de Négoce allemandes en Afrique noire au tournant du xxe siècle', in Hubert Bonin (ed.), *Négoce Blanc en Afrique Noire* (Paris: SFHOM-Alterna, 2001).
36 Gwyn Campbell, 'Gold mining and the French takeover of Madagascar, 1883–1914', *African Economic History* 17 (1988), 99–126.
37 At the very beginning of French colonisation, the legal duration of the *prestations* could, depending on the needs, be up to fifty days per year, with a maximum of nine hours per day. Only men were concerned. An allowance of 0.2 francs per day was granted. *JOM*, 'Arrêté au sujet des prestations des indigènes', 6 November 1896.
38 Guy Jacob, 'Gallieni et "l'impôt moralisateur" à Madagascar: théorie, pratiques et conséquences (1901–1905)', *Revue française d'histoire d'Outre-Mer* 74.277 (1987), 431–73.
39 *JOM*, supp. Com., 'Instructions relatives à la suppression de la prestation indigène', 17 January 1901.
40 *JOM*, 'Arrêté du 31 décembre 1900, supprimant le régime des prestations et portant augmentation de la taxe personnelle'.
41 Jacob, 'Gallieni et 'l'impôt moralisateur' à Madagascar'.
42 The *fokonolona* originally referred to a lineage identity, but became synonymous with a village community in a *fokontany* territory with the colonial decree of 9 March 1902. See Georges Condominas, *Fokon'olona et collectivités rurales en Imerina* (Paris: Orstom, 1961).
43 *JOM*, 'Arrêté du 6 mars 1907'.
44 Cogneau *et al.*, 'Fiscal capacity and dualism in colonial states'.
45 *Statistiques générales. Situation de la colonie au 1er janv. 1905* (Melun: Imp. Administrative, 1906), p. 73.
46 Simon Duteil, 'Laïcisation dans les colonies françaises. Le cas de Madagascar (1904–1913)', in Patrick Weil (ed.), *Politiques de la laïcité au XXe siècle* (Paris: Presses Universitaires de France, 2007), pp. 265–84; Faranirina V. Esoavelomandroso, 'Langue, culture et colonisation à Madagascar: malgache et français dans l'enseignement officiel (1916–1940)', *Omaly sy Anio* 3–4 (1976), 105–65, and 'Politique des races et enseignement colonial à Madagascar (jusqu'en 1940)', *Omaly sy Anio* 5–6 (1977), 245–56.
47 *Statistiques générales. Situation de la colonie au 1er janv. 1905* (Melun: Imp. Administrative, 1906), pp. 83–4.
48 Denis Cogneau, Yannick Dupraz, and Sandrine Mesplé-Somps, 'African states and development in historical perspective: Colonial public finances in British and French West', available at https://halshs.archives-ouvertes.fr/halshs-01820209 (last accessed 21 March 2022).
49 Jacob, 'Gallieni et 'l'impôt moralisateur' à Madagascar'.
50 Faranirina V. Rajaonah and Samuel F. Sanchez, 'De l'engagisme au salariat dans le sud-ouest de l'océan Indien. La colonie de plantation de Nosy Be, Madagascar (1840–1960)', in Eric Guerassimoff and Issiaka Mandé (eds), *Le*

Travail Colonial. Engagés et Autres Travailleurs Migrants dans les Empires 1850–1950 (Paris: Riveneuve, 2016), pp. 245–82.
51 Jean-David Naudet and Linda Rua, 'Madagascar: La spirale de l'échec public', in Mireille Razafindrakoto, François Roubaud, and Jean-Michel Wachsberger (eds), *Madagascar, d'une Crise l'autre: Ruptures et Continuité* (Paris: Karthala, 2017).

4

The right to sovereign seizure? Taxation, valuation, and the Imperial British East Africa Company

Emma Park

In 1892, Ernest Berkeley, an official working in Eastern Africa, wrote back to his superiors regarding what he understood to be a matter of some sensitivity. 'I am not prepared at present', he wrote,

> to actually lay down a positive opinion regarding the levying of taxes on shambas [Swahili for farms] situated along the road ... The Natives already inhabiting the track through which the road is intended to run would probably in their present undeveloped state, fail to recognize in it such advantages as would warrant in their eyes the levying of a tax from them.[1]

The link between market economies and civilisational uplift is a common refrain in the colonial archive. However, this official did not work for the state, but was an employee of the Imperial British East Africa Company (IBEA). For this employee of the corporation, then, at issue was not simply uncertainty regarding people's willingness to pay the 'tax', but the more vexing question regarding how to stabilise the relationship between the assertion of corporate sovereignty and seizure, or what this administrator perhaps self-consciously referred to as 'a tax'.

That this administrator could weigh in on the legitimacy of the corporate state's nascent taxation regime was the outgrowth of earlier, never fully stabilised distributions of sovereign authority. While the IBEA's parent company had worked in the region since the 1870s, it was not until 1888 that the IBEA received a Royal Charter which authorised the firm's operations in the region on behalf of the Crown. This sanctioned the IBEA's place in the region, the Company having secured a Concession from the territorial sovereign along the Coast, the Sultan of Zanzibar, the year before. These legal arrangements were pursued on the dual promise that the corporation would 'open up this unknown region' in the interests of 'Commerce and Civilisation'.[2]

The capaciousness of its mandate notwithstanding, all parties to these negotiations – the Crown, the Sultan, the IBEA – seemed to agree that at the centre of claims to sovereignty was the right to engage in what I refer to as *sovereign seizure*, the Company being sanctioned to raise taxes and impose and collect customs dues, as well as administer justice and sign treaties. Taken together, these prerogatives sanctioned the IBEA to assume 'the powers of government within a specified area'.[3] Profits, not least in the form of novel regimes of sovereign seizure, would be the outgrowth investors were promised. Though short-lived, this delegation of political and fiscal authority rendered the IBEA the de jure sovereign power in the region until the Company's collapse in 1893.

While today it is widely accepted that some right to sovereign seizure is a common feature of all existing polities, this framework is premised on the normative relationship between sovereign power and taxation. As the introduction to this volume notes, what has historically been assumed, 'at least hypothetically and often legally, [to differentiate taxation] from other forms of coerced extraction, was the notion that the taxpayer could expect some kind of return'. What, then, are we to make of a tax regime haphazardly developed and administered by a corporation and designed not simply to bind the ruler to the ruled but to enrich corporate shareholders? Beginning in the 1880s, I thus chart the emergence of what to contemporary readers might appear to be an 'institutional innovation': the corporate state. However, the IBEA shared much with the joint-stock companies that launched many imperial powers to the height of their dominance. From the British East India Company to the Dutch East India Company, various strategies of company rule were long the normative modality through which empires enacted their authority. Taxation, as this suggests, must be considered beyond the narrow field of the 'political' and attention must be directed to the ways that political aspirations were shunted to the sphere of the 'economic' as fiscal and administrative sovereignty was delegated to firms such as the IBEA, a corporation that was also the bearer of sovereign authority.[4] Following this, I examine the fiscal and political strategies of the IBEA, focusing on the mechanisms (namely the expropriation of land and efforts to consolidate a labour regime) and conceptual frameworks the IBEA deployed as it worked to translate its de jure right to administration through taxation into de facto acceptance of its status as regional sovereign. When and where it succeeded, the monies seized would be transformed as they moved, a portion of the taxes collected being used to offset the costs of 'administration' and 'development' – namely the construction of road networks – and a portion becoming corporate profits and shareholder dividends. However, and as I show, administrators faced severe limitations in securing a monopoly over valuation as they confronted competing visions of the relationship between seizure and political authority. Taken together, and when told from the vantage of the corporate state, taxation appears not as a stable category binding the ruler to the ruled, then, but as a flexible though ideologically dense claim on the public hoard, one which calls into question the very epistemological status of taxation in its connection to sovereignty.

A divisible sovereignty

The distribution of administrative and fiscal authority the Sultan and the Crown delegated to the IBEA was not unusual in the nineteenth century. As Henry Sumner Maine candidly wrote in 1892:

> [s]overeignty is a term which, in international law, indicates a well-ascertained assemblage of separate powers or privileges ... there is not, nor has there ever been, anything in international law to prevent some of those rights being lodged with one possessor and some with another. Sovereignty has always been regarded as divisible.[5]

Sovereignty, then, was not a unitary formation, but was conceived of both in practice and in law as a partible entity whose constituent elements could be strategically unbundled and distributed in varying configurations across a variety of bodies.[6] This shape shifting has led political theorist David Ciepley to argue that historically corporations were neither wholly private nor wholly public but were 'amphibian' legal forms that straddled the waters of the public and the shores of the private.[7]

According to its supporters, the wisdom of mobilising the IBEA as a means of enacting imperialism 'on a shoestring' was well established by 'the principles of Political Economy', which made it 'manifest' that only such a firm had access to the capital required to move the 'lever of the powerful engine necessary for so tremendous an enterprise'.[8] Unwilling to use its own revenues, the state thus appealed to the 'large and influential company, [finding it] competent to give the necessary guarantees, [and able to raise] the gigantic capital required for such an undertaking'.[9] As Frederick Lugard, one-time Company employee wrote, 'merchant adventurers', such as the men of the IBEA, could mobilise finance capital, which they would put to the task of 'development', accepting 'the responsibility which the government shunned'. These legal arrangements 'would not only afford a revenue for administration and defence, but also a prospect of profit'.[10] Many accepted that corporate profits were the appropriate reward for a company willing to take on the work of empire which the Crown 'shunned'. Nor did they question that these profits would largely come in the form of monies seized through exacting sovereign seizure, namely in the form of taxation and customs dues.[11] The IBEA itself was confident in the soundness of these arrangements, arguing that it could be 'safely be asserted ... that the capital so employed will ... yield, as an investment, a dividend not only good and reasonable but also perfectly safe'.[12]

While the Charter operated simply as 'a letter of no objection' sanctioning the IBEA's work, the Crown's political support was central to the firm's prospective profitability.[13] As the Company acknowledged, the Crown's Charter reassured prospective shareholders of the security of their investments, its political backing enabling the Company to raise subscriptions valued at £240,000.[14] Carving out spaces for the speculative investment of British capital was, then, a 'spatial fix' that was as much political as it was economic in character.[15] Mobilising the IBEA also allowed the Crown to engage in the project of imperial expansion without burdening either the treasury or British taxpayers whose 'purses' would be protected from 'rash encroachment in the name of Empire'.[16] Put simply, the British public's private hoards would be put to the task of imperial expansion not in their capacity as taxpayers, but in their capacity as private investors and profit-seekers.[17]

Despite the IBEA's confidence in the soundness of these arrangements, many were less certain. For Tories, the 'failures' of the East India Company (EIC) during the Indian Uprising of 1857 had demonstrated the problem of mobilising commercial enterprises as the agents of empire.[18] Others were concerned about the Company's limited knowledge of the extant grammars of sovereignty and seizure operative on the coast and in the interior. While it seemed apparent that the Sultan had 'all manner of nominal rights ... no one ... [could] exactly ascertain [their limits] ... which', this author dismissively wrote, the Sultan 'hardly ... [understands] himself'.[19] At the centre of these thorny issues was the relationship between territorial control and the Company's right to engage in sovereign seizure, which to be exacted would require a 'clear understanding' as to the Sultan's authority over both 'territory and taxation'.[20] These issues concerned the Company as well, as its appropriation and extension of the Sultan's revenue regime was to form the basis of returns for investors.

The men of the IBEA, not deaf to their critics, argued that the Company was not seeking 'a monopoly for any single company, [but was intent on opening up the territory] ... for the [benefit of the] large commercial enterprise of the country at large'. Profits, they assured critics, were 'merely prospective'. Its operations were not simply those of a private capital firm, however. It had been deputised by the Crown to pursue 'aims and ends' which were 'Imperial and immediate'.[21] Political and commercial dominance were viewed as being two sides of the same coin, and this dual mandate sat at the centre of the IBEA's aspirations. Indeed, the terms of the Berlin Conference – which mandated that European powers must ensure 'effective occupation' – notwithstanding, the IBEA was the governing authority in the region until the Foreign Office took over in 1894. In other words, in Eastern Africa, the Crown and the Sultan did not simply sanction the corporation's operations, but granted the IBEA the right to act like a state.

This state-like power was one the corporation symbolically performed with aplomb, enacting its amphibious character through a repertoire which

> radiated an aura of late Victorian respectability. With a Court rather than a Board, a President rather than a Chairman, its own specifically-commissioned flag [which read 'Light and Liberty', and its own currency] ... it created for itself an image as an organisation that was closer to government than to ... ordinary business.[22]

But the semiotics of sovereignty were never to be sufficient, and the Company struggled to translate its de jure authority into de facto acceptance of its sovereign status on the ground.

Enacting corporate sovereignty and the politics of space

Enacting corporate sovereignty was an incremental and protracted process that emerged piecemeal over the course of a decade out of an entangled series of overlapping contracts which the Company wielded to reconfigure the 'layered sovereignties' that characterised the region's spatial order.[23] After lengthy negotiations, by 1877 the Sultan had 'shown himself disposed, to enter into negotiations with the company ... [it having] capital sufficient to take upon themselves, for a certain agreed term, the "General Administration and Government" of his whole domain'.[24] At the centre of the proposed Concession was the sovereign prerogative to engage in forms of seizure, the Concession granting the IBEA the right to monies made through the customs house as well as the 'right' to collect 'all duties or taxes either direct or indirect which may be existing *or may be established by the company*'.[25] In exchange for this acquisition of administrative and fiscal authority, the Company agreed to pay the Sultan an annual 'rent' raised through the collection of customs dues.

In the first year of the Company's operations, customs amounted to US$56,000, or 119,000 rupees,[26] but it was confident that should its labours of marketisation prove successful these revenues were 'capable of considerable increase'.[27] Any 'surplus' over and above the requisite rent would be put to the task of 'development', the remainder being relocated to the pockets of shareholders in the form of dividends.[28] This 'surplus' amounted to £2,595 in 1890, £4,618 in 1891, and an estimated £8,000 in 1892.[29] The Sultan stood to gain personally from this arrangement, having been granted 'Original Founders' Share No. 1' as a term of the Concession.[30]

With these arrangements in place, the Company worked to expand its revenue regime into the interior. This proved to be no easy task. As they moved through the countryside, the men of the IBEA struggled to convince local leaders that they were bearers of a novel yet legitimate sovereign order backed by the Sultan. It quickly became clear to these men that the region boasted a lively and changing social topography, one over which the Sultan had little control. And people brought their own ideas regarding the relationship between political authority and seizure to bear as they interpreted the IBEA's presence. These competing visions of sovereign authority critically shaped dynamics at the colonial 'interface'.[31]

To get at these other grammars of sovereignty we must follow Company men as they tried to assert their authority in the region, a protracted process daily revealed as they moved across the territory. Space, for these men, was a problem to be managed through its transcendence, a prospect that would be enabled by laying out a road network, which, they believed, would territorially instantiate the centralisation of political and fiscal control in Company hands. It is perhaps no surprise, then, that contests over valuation often played out on the IBEA's roads, an imagined infrastructural web that was at the centre of the IBEA's plans to open up the region to 'commerce and civilisation'.

By contrast to IBEA officials, for the fissiparous communities living in Eastern Africa not all spaces were equally open to human intervention.[32] As John Ainsworth noted of the ubiquity of unoccupied corridors: '[t]hese areas were in no way looked upon as lands belonging to any of the tribes concerned'.[33] These zones fell outside of proprietary claims, but this was not tantamount to their existing exterior to human social relations. Indeed, as Ainsworth noted, these zones were routinely crisscrossed materially and ideationally by shifting trade networks and durable practices of kinshipping. 'It should be borne in mind', he advised, 'that native law and custom usually provides for natives of any other tribe being received into and adopted by another tribe on the stranger complying with certain formalities and paying his footing.'[34] A one-time tribute in goods and conformity with extant practices of sociality eased the flow of people across spatial and cultural lines, securing new relations of kinship in the process. These zones, in other words, were deliberate but permeable socio-spatial gaps.

Paying one's 'footing' was but one of a whole host of charges that communities levied on one another in the nineteenth century. Over the course of its tenure, Company administrators had to conform to these shifting boundaries of social life and sovereign authority. As one report noted, 'You should carefully ascertain and advise me of the basis on which hongo [or tribute] is charged at each point by the various tribes and the amount and description of each article levied, sending samples of some.'[35] Company officials were acutely aware that different regimes of valuation extended throughout the territory. And their movements were circumscribed by the patchwork ideas of sovereignty and space, debt and deference, that governed the interior.

While Company officials' movements were contingent on the writ of the Sultan, his authority was often insufficient for local officials. Company administrators routinely lamented their inability to convince local leaders that the Sultan had, indeed, vested them with his authority; this the first step in the bid to consolidate the sovereign rights of the corporate-state. Absent the Sultan's letter, local authorities routinely demanded 'a lot of money' in exchange for allowing the IBEA to cut roads through their territories, chastising administrators for the 'strange' hubris of coming to their lands with 'no letter' in hand.[36] Others criticised company men for arriving with 'no representative of the Sultan'.[37] Others examined the letter and 'ignored it altogether'.[38] The Sultan's authority was simply not considered legitimate by many in the interior, it being largely circumscribed to the '10 mile zone' along the shore and extending 'only a comparatively short distance inland'.[39] The Sultan's authorisation, while a crucial first step in 'materially ... dealing with these chiefs', was evidently not sufficient, forcing Company administrators to concede to the demands of local sovereigns.[40]

The interior was, indeed, a busy and competitive world of valuation. Paying attention to these shifting repertoires was of the utmost importance for Company men who struggled to comprehend the different metrics of value that extended throughout the territory. In some periods in the interior gold watches, guns, money, and silver were in high demand.[41] In other instances, beads of specified size and colour, and cotton cloth were at a premium.[42] And so, aspirations notwithstanding, IBEA officials were routinely forced to pay tribute to pass through the lands of local authorities. Tribute was often augmented by the mixture of bodily fluids, blood brotherhood between Company officials and local 'chiefs' accepted as rites critical to securing relations of trust and mobility.[43] Boundaries, bodies, and ideas of sovereignty were porous in this period. Distributed sovereignty, itself the logic underwriting the IBEA's Charter and Concession, was taken as standard.

The problem of seizure and the politics of valuation

These negotiated exchanges were struggles over valuation, as the IBEA worked to establish a monopoly over the meaning of the material transfers requisite for the operations of the corporate state. These dynamics were a source of profound anxiety for Company officials, who tried to impress on local 'sultans' that these 'gifts' did mark the inauguration of a dynamic of routine payment. They were not paying *hongo*, they insisted, but a one-time *Ada* or 'customary gift' for which leaders should express gratitude, for the IBEA's real gift came in the form of the capital the Company had invested for the 'good of the country'.[44] Put simply, Company officials worked to convince leaders that these exchanges were not evidence of their fealty to local sovereigns; that Company officials were patrons rather than clients.

The claim that these gifts were temporally circumscribed transactions was a ruse, however, Company officials viewing the distribution of gifts as inaugurating a dynamic of debt that attached leaders to the IBEA. In exchange for *Ada*, these local interlocutors were to begin repayment in the form of raising labour required for 'clearing the jungle' in preparation for road building. This was the most important return leaders could make 'for the monied payments we may have ... [made] to secure their friendship'. The return of labour was critical if the Company was to avoid 'such payments being viewed as [local leaders] levying ... "black mail" on the Company'.[45] Incrementally, Company officials hoped, their sovereign authority would extend spatially, moving out from the infrastructural networks they tried to conscript local leaders into constructing.

The exchange of currency and gifts was accompanied by the signing of treaties which in Company hands operated as commercial instruments signalling the marketisation of sovereignty. These dynamics were geared towards commodification of a different kind, however.[46] Gifts of *Ada* were exchanged for land, or so officials claimed, thereby undermining the layered sovereignties that had governed the region's spatial order. As one official argued, 'the sum [spent on gifts]' was 'not extravagant when one thinks of the enormous tracts of land which it practically gives the Company the freehold rights over'. The coercive nature of these processes notwithstanding, this official wrote that there was no 'doubt of the beneficial influence [this process of expropriation] ... exercised over the entire native mind'.[47]

Newly cut roads would not only facilitate the creation of a land market, theoretically increasing customs duties seized at the coast, but their construction would justify the expansion of the IBEA's nascent taxation regime, with communities living along the new roads being 'subject to the payment of a suitable tax for the facilities of transport accorded'.[48] Whether in the form of custom dues or taxation, the expansion of the IBEA's regime of sovereign seizure would comprise prospective returns to corporate investors in the form of dividends, enriching (mainly) British shareholders located an ocean away. While this exchange of tax for access to these networks of mobility was taken to be common sense, in practice administrators acknowledged that 'the market' was not a self-evident good but was a cultural construct that would require work to enact.[49]

People would thus need to be eased into this new arrangement which inaugurated both novel notions of sovereignty and reconfigured dynamics of seizure, and that would see claims to *hongo* move from the hands of local leaders to those of the company state which, in an ideologically dense act of discursive gymnastics, variously rebranded its forms of sovereign seizure as a 'tax', a 'toll', a 'duty'.[50] This discursive reframing was intimately connected to the ideological claims grounding the legitimacy of the IBEA as a bearer of 'civilisation'. In the hands of the Company, *hongo*, or 'tribute', was rebranded a 'barbaric' form of 'blackmail',[51] to be contrasted against the 'civilised' forms of value capture inaugurated by the corporate state. The Company sought to replace these 'uncivilised' modes of value capture with their quintessentially 'modern' variant, a tax. This was not merely discursive quibbling. The claim that the Company's form of sovereign seizure was distinct from existing regimes was part of the ideological armature embedded in the dual mandate of 'commerce and civilisation' that justified the presence of the firm in the region. As one observer noted, it was only 'under a European flag [that it would be] … possible to prevent divided and often hostile chiefs from levying the inland transit duties, which, better than any other barbarian contrivance, throttle trade'.[52] In European hands, arbitrary forms of seizure would be routinised, rationalised, and centralised; rather than acting as an obstacle to trade, they would facilitate its expansion. Stabilising the relationship between new modes of seizure and novel distributions of sovereign authority would require work and time, however – of this, administrators were well aware.

Coining conquest and transforming work into labour[53]

These vernacular forms of valuation placed limits on IBEA impositions, particularly as it pertained to the labour regime they tried to conjure into being. In the early days, people exchanged their work for currency as well as non-currency media of value and exchange: brass wire, beads, muskets, and *merikani* cloth, all of which were in high demand by the 1840s.[54] Company administrators were well aware of the need to be alive to the changing tastes of the communities living in the region as they solicited them for favours, requesting permission to cut new roads, and asking local leaders to call people up for work.[55] 'Runners' were routinely sent back to camp with information 'detailing the beads, cloth &c. that are necessary'.[56] Generalities were not sufficient, instead these men were to report on the 'article most in favour with the natives for barter'.[57]

Administrators came to realise that getting people to accede to new rhythms that, they hoped, would transform work into labour would be difficult. People routinely abandoned work if they found the terms undesirable, relocating to other locales where the terms of payment and the media of the same were more suited to their repertoires of valuation. Others left mid-'contract' when the rhythms of the nascent labour regime contravened the seasonal rhythms of the harvest.[58] Part of the problem, from the perspective of the IBEA, was the proliferation of value forms and their lack of subsumption – either formal or real – into a hierarchy of worth. What was needed was a medium over which the IBEA held a monopoly; one which could act as a fiscal attachment, tying people to new regimes that could transform work into labour. Administrators saw in currency one such attachment. 'Money as a medium of exchange was unknown among the natives of the interior [in the early days]', Ainsworth noted, 'the buying of food, any payment for services etc. was done by way of barter.'[59] Just as the spatial order was crisscrossed with competing visions of sovereignty and cultured space, so too was this a busy and competitive realm when it came to units of account, stores of value, and media of exchange.

Indeed, by the time the IBEA received its charter, the use of the Indian rupee was common throughout the region, the coins operating as a means through which regional economies interfaced with global circuits of capital.[60] This presented a problem for the sovereign aspirations of the company-state, and administrators fixated on gaining control over a single, and centralised, legitimate medium of value. As one report noted: 'I think it is desirable that we should at once issue our own coin.'[61] And so, in the 1880s, the Company introduced IBEA-minted rupees as a mechanism to assert a monopoly over valuation.[62]

IBEA rupees were not simply symbolic of an aspirational dominance. Administrators hoped that the Company currency could displace the Indian rupee as well as non-currency units of value, such as livestock, cloth, and beads.[63] To achieve this, the Company shifted its focus from ascertaining people's preferences in non-currency units of exchange to working to understand what coins people willingly integrated into their repertoires of value. As one report noted, 'By separate parcel I send you specimens of the ... coin most in circulation, which we will largely require for payment of labour.'[64] The goal was to produce Company coins as near facsimile copies of circulating tokens, Company administrators engaging in overt mimicry. It would be wise, a report noted, 'to keep to the style of the latest coin minted by the Sultan'.[65] The circulation of IBEA coins was, then, a struggle over valuation. In both symbolic and material terms, the IBEA viewed gaining a monopoly over valuation as being essential to its assertion of corporate sovereignty, but a form of sovereignty that was premised on its divisibility, distributed as it was across the Sultan, the IBEA, and the Crown.[66] As for the people they hoped to coerce into labouring on Company infrastructures, the structures of sovereign authority at play were significantly more numerous, flexible, complex, and layered.

Some people came to accept Company coins as legitimate stores of value. There was a networked spatiality to this shift in units of account, which radiated out from the nascent infrastructural networks and the emergent disciplinary regimes and new economies of desire with which they were associated. And Company administrators were anxious to ensure that their coins were operating as messengers of a new sovereign order, the IBEA sending representatives into the countryside who reported back on the ubiquity of their circulation.[67] But gaining a monopoly over units of account was geared to enact more thoroughgoing transformations. Paying wages in a standardised unit of value was designed to reconfigure diverse lifeways and forms of work, by rendering both time and labour equivalent to a single unit of account. But at this stage, there was no monopoly over the measures of value with multiple currencies and stores of value jostling for authority.[68]

'Taxing' infrastructures and the 'failure' of the IBEA

Currencies, IBEA-issued or otherwise, were not robust infrastructural attachments. They could not, on their own, tie people to the road and the revenue regime with which it was associated. Rather, what was needed was a fiscal technology capable of binding people to new regimes of labour and the infrastructures and profit margins of which they were to be generative. In taxation Company administrators saw one such possibility, hoping that new regimes of sovereign seizure could act as infrastructural attachments, forcing people into the wage-labour economy. But we would miss much if we saw in taxation a simple instrumentalism. For administrators, these new regimes of seizure were ideologically dense; they were core components of the civilisational value of labour itself.[69]

But what were people being taxed for? In theory, people were taxed for their proximity to a work of 'public utility' – an infrastructure – which would in turn enable their entry into new markets.[70] However, people had their own ideas regarding the appropriate relationship between infrastructures and work which they brought to bear as they considered this nascent regime of sovereign seizure. As one report noted: 'I ought ... to mention that the natives ... feel themselves ... aggrieved by this tax ... since the Canal is solely the labour of their own hands.'[71] For many, the idea that people should be taxed for the use of infrastructures they had constructed rang hollow. As Lugard wrote, reflecting on the early days of British occupation, 'the imposition of ... taxation' had generated an 'amount of friction quite disproportionate to the advantage gained'.[72]

Drawing connections among infrastructures, sovereignty, and legitimate forms of seizure was, evidently, difficult for the corporate-state, helping us understand the words of the IBEA official with whom we began who advised caution on laying 'down a positive opinion regarding the levying of taxes on shambas situated along the road'. The reason for this was explicated in civilisational terms: 'The Natives ... in their present undeveloped state, [would] fail to recognise in it such advantages as would warrant in their eyes the levying of a tax from them.'[73] There was nothing natural about the benefits of the 'market' on this framing, which had to be enacted and cultivated before it could be naturalised. And for this to succeed, incommensurate systems of valuation would need to be brought into alignment.

But these regimes of sovereign authority and seizure were wildly out of synch. For African communities, if anyone ought to have been the beneficiaries of these emergent proximities, it was the communities living in the areas through which IBEA infrastructures ran. It should have been the corporation that paid its 'footing' as an acknowledgement of the privilege of this proximity; this in line with long-standing spatial practices mediating the patchwork of forms of sovereignty that governed the region. Administrators tacitly conceded the point. People would need to be eased into this new system of valuation. 'In regard to the toll to be charged over the road', the report concluded, 'this should not be imposed until the road is somewhat actively used by the natives, who having once appreciated its utility, would be more likely to pay the toll cordially.'[74]

Conclusion

By 1892, the IBEA was functionally bankrupt, and the Foreign Office took over the administration of the region, along with a range of corporate debts, in 1894. The IBEA had evidently failed in its efforts to enact its twin goals of 'commerce and civilisation' through exacting what administrators variously referred to as a 'toll', a 'tax', and a 'due', which it contrasted against the 'barbaric' systems of seizure well established in the region. It failed, in other words, to gain a monopoly over valuation, a project geared towards establishing social, cultural, and economic hegemony critical to asserting corporate sovereignty.

However, it was not simply that the IBEA had failed to gain a monopoly over valuation, which would have required the de facto acceptance of the firm as *the* sovereign in the region. Indeed, central to its collapse was its inability to establish a regime of taxation that could be translated into corporate profits. Shareholders expected dividends on their investment, monies that the Company hoped to accrue through rolling out novel repertoires of sovereign seizure. Put simply, while the right to 'tax' was an ideologically dense claim proffered by the company-state, the epistemological status of such forms of seizure was much less straightforward as monies so seized moved. The emphasis here was on the ways in which the status of monies could be discursively reframed as the monies themselves were translated from taxes paid in rupees (and ideally IBEA currency) to profits that would, ultimately, be denominated in British pounds. One man's tax, another man's return on investment. Commerce and civilisation were, indeed, two sides of the same coin, a coin that East Africans had little interest in having, much less the regimes of sovereign seizure and labour which they portended.

One might imagine this to have been the end of the story, but that would be to accept the ideological claims of the nascent colonial state which took the place of the amphibious corporate-state following the demise of the IBEA. British administrators, too, claimed that taxation was necessary to bring development to the region. They, too, argued that taxes were a form of debt owed by colonial subjects to the state. However, they operationalised their regime of sovereign seizure in novel ways, namely through enforcing a regime of direct taxation.[75] Theoretically extracted from all able-bodied men, direct taxation operated as a robust infrastructural attachment, which administrators hoped would force people into the wage-labour economy. This difference notwithstanding, as in the case of the IBEA, taxes so collected were rarely reinvested in 'native' areas, but were instead used to shore up the infrastructures required for the commercial farms established by white settlers.[76] Put simply, while the institutional arrangement that gave rise to the IBEA unravelled, the fiscal strategies developed by the corporation not only persisted but became more pronounced.

These continuities raise questions about the epistemological status of a 'tax' in its relation to sovereignty, and directs attention to the complex interplay of monetary policy, race, and empire. The battle cry of the white settlers during the American revolutionary war was 'no taxation without representation', a demand that elided the racialised forms of extraction and exploitation upon which (white) American wealth rested. In the racialised geographies of the rest of the British Empire, however, the role of race in shaping colonial monetary policy was explicit, colonial officials enacting policies premised on a different logic, 'Only taxation! No representation!' as they worked to enrich white investors by seizing the surpluses of racialised colonial subjects to both fund the administration of the colonial state and line the pockets of the white, settler minority.

Notes

1. Ernest J. L. Berkeley to Sec. London, 28 January 1892, Box 72, File 49, Mackinnon Papers, School of Oriental and African Studies [hereafter SOAS].
2. Roland Oliver, 'Some factors in the British occupation of East Africa, 1884–1894', *Uganda Journal* 15.1 (1951), 56.
3. P. L. McDermott, *British East Africa or IBEA: A History of the Formation and Work of the Imperial British East Africa Company* (Ulan Press, 2012), p. 392.
4. Nancy Fraser, 'Behind Marx's hidden abode: For an expanded conception of capitalism', *New Left Review* 86 (2014), 55–72.
5. Henry Sumner Maine, *Sir Henry Maine: A Brief Memoir of His Life* (New York: Henry Holt & Co., 1892), p. 322. See also Philip J. Stern, *The Company-State: Corporate Sovereignty and the Early Modern Foundations of the British Empire in India* (Oxford: Oxford University Press, 2012), p. 9.
6. Lauren Benton, *A Search for Sovereignty: Law and Geography in European Empires, 1400–1900* (Cambridge: Cambridge University Press, 2009), p. 5.
7. David Ciepley, 'Beyond public and private: Toward a political theory of the corporation', *American Political Science Review* 107.1 (2013), 156.
8. 'Draft of the Contract to be entered into between Sultan of Zanzibar and Company to be formed for the Administration of his Domain', NA. File 8, Box 65, PP MS 1 IBEA/Mackinnon Papers, SOAS. Sara Berry, 'Hegemony on a shoestring: Indirect rule and access to agricultural land', *Africa* 62.3 (1992), 327–55.
9. 'Draft of the Contract to be entered into between Sultan of Zanzibar and Company to be formed for the Administration of his Domain', NA. File 8, Box 65, PP MS 1 IBEA/Mackinnon Papers, SOAS. As Marie J. De Kiewiet writes, 'No matter what Salisbury's own views might be, in 1888 neither Parliament nor public was yet ready to pay the cost of outright annexation. In these circumstances the East African chartered company was a most useful instrument of imperial policy'. See Marie J. De Kiewiet, 'History of the Imperial British East Africa Company 1876–1895' (PhD dissertation, King's College London, 1955), p. 98.
10. Frederick Lugard, *The Dual Mandate in British Tropical Africa* (London: Forgotten Books, 2012 [1922]), p. 14.
11. Lugard, *The Dual Mandate*, p. 14.
12. 'Draft of the Contract to be entered into between Sultan of Zanzibar and Company to be formed for the Administration of his Domain', NA. File 8, Box 65, PP MS 1 IBEA/Mackinnon Papers, SOAS.
13. De Kiewiet, 'History of the Imperial British East Africa Company', p. 36.
14. Raj Kumar Tivedi, 'The role of Imperial British East Africa Company in the acquisition of East African colony in the second half of the nineteenth century', *Proceedings of the Indian History Congress* 33 (1971), 619. The Company was oversubscribed within two months of the first issue. See John S. Galbraith, *Mackinnon and East Africa, 1878–1895* (Cambridge: Cambridge University Press, 1972), p. 138.

15 David Harvey, 'Globalization and the 'spatial fix'', *Geographische Revue* 2 (2001), 24.
16 [No author], 'The East African Chartered Company', *The Economist*, 3 October 1891.
17 Though the first subscription was not open to the public at large. As De Kiewiet writes, 'An agreement of April 18, 1888 set forth the terms by which the IBEA Company was financed and directed. The nominal capital was set at one million pounds. The first issue was limited to 250 000 bounds in 100 pound shares. The subscribers to this issue, which was not open to the public, received special voting privileges.' See De Kiewiet, 'History of the Imperial British East Africa Company', p. 99.
18 For his part, Adam Smith wrote that 'the government of an exclusive company of merchants ... [was] perhaps the worst of all forms of government'. Adam Smith, *An Inquiry into the Nature and Causes of the Wealth of Nations* (New York: The Modern Library, 1994), p. 302.
19 [No author], 'The Danger of Trouble in East Africa', *The Economist*, 19 April 1890.
20 *Ibid.*
21 George S. Mackenzie, 'Evacuation of Uganda, opinion of the Company', 28 September 1892, Newspaper cutting, newspaper not indicated. File 46, Box 71, PP MS 1 IBEA/Mackinnon Papers, SOAS.
22 Forbes J. Munro, *Maritime Enterprise and Empire: Sir. William Mackinnon and His Business Network, 1823–1893* (Woodbridge: Boydell & Brewer, 2003), p. 422. The Company's motto of 'Light and Liberty' was reported in 'Imperial British East Africa Company', *Anti-Slavery Reporter*, May and June 1889.
23 Frederick Cooper, 'Alternatives to empire: France and Africa after World War II', in Douglas Howland and Luise White (eds), *The State of Sovereignty: Territories, Laws, Populations* (Bloomington: Indiana University Press, 2008), p. 106.
24 P. L. McDermott, *British East Africa or IBEA: A History of the Formation and Work of the Imperial British East Africa Company* (London: Chapman & Hall, 1895), p. 3; 'Draft of the Contract to be entered into between Sultan of Zanzibar and Company to be formed for the Administration of his Domain', NA. File 8, Box 65, PP MS 1 IBEA/Mackinnon Papers, SOAS.
25 'Draft of the Contract to be entered into between Sultan of Zanzibar and Company to be formed for the Administration of his Domain', NA. File 8, Box 65, PP MS 1 IBEA/Mackinnon Papers, SOAS (emphasis added). Some of the provisions of this document contravened the rights of other powers, notably the maintenance of a fixed import duty to citizens of France, Britain, Germany, and the United States. Galbraith, *Mackinnon and East Africa, 1878–1895*, p. 57. There were other stipulations. The IBEA could levy tolls on quays and jetties, but it could not prevent competitors from landing goods on the beach. Similarly, while the IBEA could levy tolls on roads, it could not stop people from using the existing routes that crisscrossed the territory. Galbraith, *Mackinnon and East Africa, 1878–1895*, p. 59.

26 McDermott, *British East Africa or IBEA*, p. 232.
27 NA to the Secretary of the Imperial British East Africa Coy. 14 November 1888, File 1A, Box 63, 'Mombasa Letters, Sept 1888–Jan 1889', PP MS 1 IBEA/Mackinnon Papers, SOAS.
28 'Appendices to 1893 Shareholders Agreement', File 50, Box 72, PP MS 1 IBEA/Mackinnon Papers, SOAS. [No author], 'Case to Advise on Behalf of the Imperial British East Africa Company', N.D. File 49, Box 72, PP MS 1 IBEA/Mackinnon Papers, SOAS. Imperial British East Africa Company, The Scotsman, 25 July 1894, p. 5.
29 'Appendices to 1893 Shareholders Agreement', File 50, Box 72, PP MS 1 IBEA/Mackinnon Papers, SOAS; [No author], 'Case to Advise on Behalf of the Imperial British East Africa Company', N.D. File 49, Box 72, PP MS 1 IBEA/Mackinnon Papers, SOAS. In file 50, box 72 this amounts to Rs. 38,929 in 1890, Rs. 70,192 in 1891, and Rs. 67, 257 in 1892.
30 [No author], 'Deed of Settlement of the Imperial British East Africa Company, 1889', 1889, File 51, Box, 72, PP MS 1 IBEA/Mackinnon Papers, SOAS.
31 Jane Guyer, *Marginal Gains: Monetary Transactions in Atlantic Africa* (Chicago, IL: University of Chicago Press, 2004), pp. 5–9.
32 See Fernando Coronil, *The Magical State: Nature, Money, and Modernity in Venezuela* (Chicago, IL: University of Chicago Press, 1997), especially chapter 1.
33 John Ainsworth to Chairman, 'Kenya Land Enquiry Commission', Nairobi. September 1931. MSS. Afr. S. 381 (2), Bodleian Library, University of Oxford.
34 *Ibid.*
35 MacKenzie to Lt. Swayne RE. 11 October 1888, 'Mombasa Letters, Sept 1888–Jan 1889', PP MS 1 IBEA/Mackinnon Papers, SOAS.
36 [No author], 13 July 1877, File 3, Box 64, PP MS 1 IBEA/Mackinnon Papers, SOAS.
37 [No author], 'Extract of Letter Dated', Zanzibar, 24 August 1877, File 3, Box 64, PP MS 1 IBEA/Mackinnon Papers, SOAS.
38 [No author], 'Extract of Letter Dated', Zanzibar, 24 August 1877, PP MS 1 IBEA/Mackinnon Papers, SOAS.
39 Illeg. To Kirk, 9 January 1877, File 1c, Box 64, PP MS 1 IBEA/Mackinnon Papers, SOAS. Jonathan Glassman, *Feasts and Riot: Revelry, Rebellion, & Popular Consciousness on the Swahili Coast, 1856–1888* (Portsmouth, NH: Heinemann, 1995), p. 182.
40 Illeg. To Kirk, 9 January 1877, File 1c, Box 64, PP MS 1 IBEA/Mackinnon Papers, SOAS.
41 Mackenzie to Sec of IBEAC, 4 January 1889, 'Mombasa Letters, Sept 1888–Jan 1889', PP MS 1 IBEA/Mackinnon Papers, SOAS.; F. Moir to W. Mackinnon, 3 December 1877, File 9, Box 65, PP MS 1 IBEA/Mackinnon Papers, SOAS.
42 H. Leakey, 'Kenya Land Commission', *Evidence*, 1865 as cited in Charles H. Ambler, *Kenyan Communities in the Age of Imperialism: The Central Region in the Late Nineteenth Century* (New Haven, CT: Yale University

Press, 1988), p. 126. On beads as stores of value, see Jeremy Prestholdt, *Domesticating the World: African Consumerism and the Genealogies of Globalization* (Berkeley: University of California Press, 2008), p. 74; G. S. Mackenzie wrote to the Secretary of the IBEA reporting on the delivery of the gift of Maxim guns to the Sultan; G. S. Mackenzie to Hon. Secretary IBEA Co., 3 December 1888, Box 63, PP MS 1 IBEA/Mackinnon Papers, SOAS; Frederick Lugard, *The Rise of our East African Empire; Early Efforts in Nyasaland and Uganda*, vol. 1 (Emeryville, CA: Franklin Classics, [1893] N.D.), p. 274.

43 J. Sangard [maybe] to Sir William Mackinnon, 20 October 1890, Dagoretti. For an analysis of the role of blood brotherhood, see Luise White, 'Blood brotherhood revisited: Kinship, relationship, and the body in East and Central Africa', *Africa* 64.3 (1994), 359–72.

44 F. Moir to W. Mackinnon, 3 December 1877, File 9, Box 65, PP MS 1 IBEA/ Mackinnon Papers, SOAS.

45 George Mackenzie to the Hon Sec of IBEAC, 25 September 1888, File 1A, Box 63, 'Mombasa Letters, Sept 1888–Jan 1889', PP MS 1 IBEA/Mackinnon Papers, SOAS.

46 Steven Press, *Rogue Empires: Contracts and Conmen in Europe's Scramble for Africa* (Cambridge, MA: Harvard University Press, 2017), p. 10.

47 George S. Mackenzie to The Secretary, Imperial British East Africa Coy., 15 January 1889, File 1A, Box 63, 'Mombasa Letters, Sept 1888–Jan 1889', PP MS 1 IBEA/Mackinnon Papers, SOAS.

48 Ernest Bentley, Acting Sec to The Administrator, Mombasa, 10 November 1891, File 49, Box 72, PP MS 1 IBEA/Mackinnon Papers, SOAS.

49 Ernest J. L. Berkeley to Sec. London, 28 January 1892, File 49, Box 72, PP MS 1 IBEA/Mackinnon Papers, SOAS.

50 *Ibid*; 'Draft of the Contract to be entered into between Sultan of Zanzibar and Company to be formed for the Administration of his Domain', NA. File 8, Box 65, PP MS 1 IBEA/Mackinnon Papers, SOAS; John Kirk to Gerald Waller, May 12 1878, File 60, Box 77, PP MS 1 IBEA/Mackinnon Papers, SOAS.

51 For a discussion of the emergence of 'local sultans' in seams of Barghash bin Said's authority, see Chayya Goswami, *The Call of the Sea: Kachchhi Traders in Muscat and Zanzibar, c. 1800–1880* (Hyderabad: Orient Blackswan, 2011), 168; Lugard, *The Rise of Our East African Empire; Early Efforts in Nyasaland and Uganda*, vol. 1, p. 325.

52 [No author], 'The policy of creating reigning companies', *The Economist*, 15 September 1888.

53 The title of this section is deeply indebted to Wambui Mwangi's brilliant article, 'Of coins and conquest: The East African Currency Board, the rupee crisis, and the problem of colonialism in the East African Protectorate', *Comparative Study of Society and History* (2001), 763–87.

54 H. Leakey, 'Kenya Land Commission', *Evidence,* 1865 as cited in Ambler, *Kenyan Communities in the Age of Imperialism*, p. 126. G. S. Mackenzie wrote to the Secretary of the IBEA reporting on the delivery of the gift of Maxim guns

to the Sultan; G. S. Mackenzie to Hon. Secretary IBEA Co., 3 December 1888, Box 63, Mackinnon Papers, SOAS.
55 G. S. Mackenzie, Zanzibar to Lt. Swanye, October 1888, Box 63, Mackinnon Papers, SOAS. For a wonderful discussion of the importance of consumer 'taste' in Eastern Africa and how it shaped global markets in commodities for consumption, see Prestholdt, *Domesticating the World*.
56 Mackenzie to FJ Jackson Esq. 10 November 1888, File 1A, Box 63, 'Mombasa Letters, Sept 1888–Jan 1889', PP MS 1 IBEA/Mackinnon Papers, SOAS.
57 Mackenzie to Lt. Swayne RE. 11 October 1888, File 1A, Box 63, 'Mombasa Letters, Sept 1888–Jan 1889', PP MS 1 IBEA/Mackinnon Papers, SOAS.
58 Beardall to Waller 11 December 1879, Box 77, File 61, PP MS 1 IBEA/Mackinnon Papers, SOAS.
59 John Ainsworth, 'East Africa "Kenya" Reminiscences', MSS. Afr. s. 380, Bodleian Library, University of Oxford.
60 Mwangi, 'Of coins and conquest', p. 770. As Mwangi suggests, to look to these histories of currencies offers a different narrative trajectory for the history of empire, one which moves not from metropole to colony, but one that traversed colonial spaces, connecting India to Eastern Africa.
61 George S. Mackenzie to Sec IBEAC, 23 October 1888, 'Mombasa Letters, Sept 1888–Jan 1889', File 61, Box 77, PP MS 1 IBEA/Mackinnon Papers, SOAS.
62 John Ainsworth, 'East Africa "Kenya" Reminiscences', MSS. Afr. s. 380, Bodleian Library, University of Oxford.
63 Mwangi, 'Of coins and conquest', p. 778.
64 Mr Dick to Sir W. Mackinnon, 2 December 1890, File 24, Box 68, PP MS 1 IBEA/Mackinnon Papers, SOAS.
65 George S. Mackenzie to Sec IBEAC, 23 October 1888, 'Mombasa Letters, Sept1888–Jan 1889', File 61, Box 77, PP MS 1 IBEA/Mackinnon Papers, SOAS.
66 Mwangi, 'Of coins and conquest', p. 771.
67 Mackenzie to [not indicated], 13 May 1889, File 16, Box 67, PP MS 1 IBEA/Mackinnon Papers, SOAS.
68 Mwangi, 'Of coins and conquest', p. 771.
69 'Fort Hall District, Handing Over Report, 1926', Kenya National Archives [hereafter KNA] DC/FH/12/1a.
70 'Draft of Proposed Concessions to be Obtained from His Highness the Sultan of Zanzibar', File 2, Box 64, PP MS 1 IBEA/Mackinnon Papers, SOAS.
71 Mackenzie to Col. CB Euan Smith, 27 December 1888, 'Mombasa Letters, Sept 1888–Jan 1889', File 1a, Box 63, PP MS 1 IBEA/Mackinnon Papers, SOAS.
72 Lugard, *The Rise of Our East African Empire*, p. 645.
73 Ernest J. L. Berkeley to Sec. London, 28 January 1892, Box 72, File 49, Mackinnon Papers, SOAS.
74 Ernest L. Bentley, Acting Secretary to Admin Mombasa, 22 April, 1892, Box 72, File 49, BIEA Co., SOAS.

75 Mathew Forstater, 'Taxation and primitive accumulation: The case of colonial Africa', in Paul Zarembka (ed.), *Research in Political Economy* (Greenwich, CT: JAI Press, 2005), pp. 51–64; Janet Roitman, *Fiscal Disobedience: An Anthropology of Economic Regulation in Central Africa* (Princeton, NJ and Oxford: Princeton University Press, 2005).
76 Bruce Berman, *Control & Crisis in Colonial Kenya: The Dialectic of Domination* (London: James Currey, 1996).

5

Internal inequalities: Taxpayers, taxation, and expenditure in Sierra Leone, c. 1890s to 1937

Laura Channing

All empires governed different people differently. Through the process of incorporating new territories and peoples into the overarching structure of empire, European powers deliberately maintained and exacerbated diversity and inequalities.[1] Fiscal history is a revealing lens through which to examine this phenomenon. In a frequently quoted phrase, the fiscal sociologist Rudolf Goldscheid described fiscal history as revealing the 'skeleton of the state'.[2] Who were the colonial taxpayers? How was each group taxed? And how did their categorisation into such groups, and the built-in inequalities of empire, structure the tax system and patterns of expenditure? In most colonies, there was no single tax for which all subjects were liable. While European countries, and others including the United States of America, were moving towards income taxes, by the early twentieth century, that assigned the same fiscal weight to each individual subject, colonial systems were instead dividing up their taxpaying populations.[3] Historians have noticed these broad trends, and Martin Daunton argues that in the colonies, 'unlike in Britain, the administrators showed little concern for balance and equity in the tax system: it was biased between groups, as a deliberate act of policy'.[4]

Scholarship on colonial taxation has taken off in the last two decades with a focus on colonial and imperial fiscal policy, balancing budgets, and the source composition of revenue. It is now well established that the most important factor shaping fiscal systems was the pressure for colonies to achieve financial self-sufficiency amid serious resource constraints. The balance of different sources in a particular budget was overwhelmingly a product of local resources and conditions rather than any metropole-determined framework, and empires often minimised effort rather than maximising revenue.[5]

While much of the initial work on colonial taxation has prioritised the differences between colonies, scholars have also begun to turn their attention more explicitly towards the differences *within* them.[6] Many of these efforts have concerned the differences between white settlers and Black African taxpayers in colonies such as Kenya and South Africa.[7]

This chapter will focus on a single colonial fiscal system, that of Sierra Leone, and is concerned with the interaction between the tax system and inequality: how existing inequalities informed the design of the tax system, and, in turn, how the spending of tax revenue could exacerbate or ameliorate inequalities.[8] These channels of inequality intersected with the 'revenue imperative' and the tendency for empires to govern different people differently, and it is argued here that this led to a patchwork of colonial tax categories that both reflected and further entrenched existing inequalities. The approach taken is that of a within-colony comparison of taxpayer categories designed to capture the internal heterogeneity of colonial tax systems. The focus is on direct taxation, as this was both administratively more challenging for the state to assess and collect, revealing differences in the forms of wealth, geographical and legal status of taxpayers, and available information across Sierra Leone, and was also more 'visible' from the point of view of taxpayers than indirect taxes on trade. Once collected, the allocation of tax revenue and the potential for redistribution was an important feature in maintaining inequalities between groups of taxpayers, meaning that it is essential also to consider expenditure. While most studies of colonial taxation examine tax revenue at the whole-colony level, looking at the sub-colony level, and including the expenditure side, can reveal a more complex situation where expenditure was potentially redistributive at a regional level but not in the aggregate.

Sierra Leone is a particularly good case with which to examine this. While the reputation of the 'Scramble for Africa' in the late nineteenth century gives the impression that colonial boundaries were created and hardened overnight, in Sierra Leone in particular, their development had been underway for a century, creating what Catherine Boone has described as an 'uneven institutional topography'.[9] As Britain's oldest West African colony, Sierra Leone was originally founded in the late eighteenth century as a settlement of freed slaves. Black settlers from London, Nova Scotia, and Jamaica, followed by Liberated Africans from slave ships intercepted by the British Navy, arrived during the late eighteenth and early nineteenth century, populating Freetown and the Western Peninsula. Initially run by the Sierra Leone Company, the British government took over in 1808 and Sierra Leone became a Crown Colony. After only a few decades, the population was already a diverse, multilingual mixture that also included indigenous Africans from the surrounding areas. Padraic Scanlan has pointed to important distinctions between the settlers in Freetown and the Liberated Africans in the villages, describing, by 1822, the existence of 'two Sierra Leones': the urban area of the European merchants and Maroon and Nova Scotian settlers, and the hinterland villages of the Liberated Africans.[10] Ruled as a stand-alone Crown Colony for much of the nineteenth century, in 1893 a Municipal Council with a Black settler majority was created in Freetown and in 1896 neighbouring territory was annexed as the Protectorate. By 1896, then, 'two Sierra Leones' were now three: Municipality, Crown Colony, and Protectorate.

Drawing on primary sources, particularly regional, provincial, district, and municipal level tax records pertaining to each category of taxpayer, alongside reports, minute papers, budgets, and ordinances, this chapter argues that the establishment and development of taxpayer categories in a single colony reflected and further entrenched internal inequalities. The next section examines the legal differences between inhabitants of the three main geographical regions of Sierra Leone and their respective forms of colonial governance. The second section turns to the functioning of the tax system, examining the taxing institution in each area and how different methods of assessment and collection were employed, before briefly considering the relative economic importance of direct taxes to demonstrate the insights that a within-colony comparison can provide to debates on the source composition of revenue. A third section considers, finally, patterns of expenditure and the scope for redistribution.

Administrative structure

Rather than integrating the Protectorate with the Crown Colony in a single administrative structure, it was incorporated in 1896 as a separate entity based on different legal principles.[11] Annual Colonial Reports set out this distinction in clear terms. They describe the Colony as 'founded on English law, with such modifications as are required by local circumstances', while the Protectorate was governed by the 'laws of the native chiefs modified by the Protectorate Ordinances' in order to 'abolish slave dealing and to eradicate such native customs as are repugnant to civilisation'. While the constitutional system in the Colony could be compared to those of the 'old-established Crown Colonies', with a governor aided by executive and legislative councils, that of the Protectorate was more similar to the 'East African Protectorates', where administrative principles recognised the use of 'native' customary law between African peoples, attempted to preserve and strengthen the authority of the local rulers, and granted to all 'non-natives' (which included the inhabitants of the Colony and Municipality as well as European officials) in the Protectorate 'the protection of the English law to which they had formerly been accustomed'.[12] This arrangement led to what Joseph Alie has called a 'dual nature of citizenship'.[13] The Colony was considered a 'British possession', or, in the words of Sierra Leonean lawyer Samuel Lewis, 'a settlement of British subjects', with inhabitants officially recognised as such since an act of parliament in 1853.[14] In contrast, the Protectorate remained a 'foreign territory', over which the British Empire exercised a more limited kind of sovereignty.[15] Its inhabitants were 'protected peoples', prevented from acquiring the same subjecthood as their neighbours in the Colony.[16]

In the Protectorate, from its creation in 1896, 'administration on the cheap' was upheld by a 'thin white line' of European officials.[17] This was grafted onto a reconstituted framework of 'native' power associated with British indirect rule and resembling the 'peasant-export' type of colonial economy based on African control of production. Initially, the official presence was skeletal, with one District Commissioner allocated to each of the five districts, supported by a small handful of other officials.[18] While this essential framework remained the same before 1937, districts were reshaped and resized both to reflect and encourage changes in economic geography and the distribution of local political power, especially during the construction of the railway.[19] The main administrative unit was the chiefdom, and rather than imposing an elaborate and expensive imperial structure, the colonial government either co-opted existing chiefs into the administrative framework, or simply created new chiefs to suit their needs.

In contrast, the deep-rooted precedent of settler self-government led to a much tighter administrative framework in Freetown. Municipal government had been established in 1893 and was representative, comprising a mayor and fifteen councillors, three appointed by the government and the remaining twelve elected by the residents of Freetown, meaning the Council operated with an African majority. Despite this representative basis, the franchise was extremely narrow, and was 'not a formula for the politicisation of the masses': only male British subjects who owned or occupied buildings of an assessed value of £6 could vote, despite a third of urban properties being owned by women.[20] The main duties of the Council were the assessment and collection of rates, the fixing of licence fees, and the provision of water services and other social goods like cemeteries, markets, and a fire service.

The final region, the Crown Colony, was based less recognisably on representative principles than the Municipality but retained some of the closeness of administration, attempting to balance elements of both Colony and Protectorate administration in a compromise described as 'both intricate and clumsy'.[21] Every district, each a collection of villages, was served by an unelected Local Advisory Board whose members were local religious leaders and teachers appointed by the Governor.[22] Whilst not technically representative, the existence of these boards and their inclusion of local residents was designed to ensure that taxes would be spent on works benefiting these specific groups of taxpayers.

Three taxation regimes

The type of taxation levied in each region was closely tied to these administrative structures and the precise form of colonial governance in each place. Until 1898, none of the three regions was taxed directly by the colonial government and the largest contributor to revenue was customs taxation levied on imports, with the rest made up by fees, licences, and grants.[23] From the 1890s, the incorporation and maintenance of new territory in the form of the Protectorate, with only limited transport and communication facilities and sparse knowledge about the population, was too significant to be absorbed by existing sources of revenue, already under pressure from international trading competition. The legislation establishing British annexation of the Protectorate contained provisions for a direct 'native' tax to cover the costs of administration.[24] Beginning in 1898, this was levied on each house, or hut, at a dual rate: 5s. for houses with three or fewer rooms and 10s. for those with four or more. Assessment and collection were undertaken by the chiefs and payment was initially accepted in either cash or goods.

Famously, the imposition of this tax preceded an anti-colonial rebellion, the Hut Tax War, which lasted for around 6 months and involved separate rebellions in the northern and southern parts of the new Protectorate. Despite this period of intense violence which became a warning for other colonial governments considering direct taxation, and the recommendation by Special Commissioner Sir David Chalmers that the tax be abandoned, the levy remained in place and revenue collection increased incrementally.[25] The dual rate, clearly beyond the administrative capacity of the government, was swiftly abandoned and the tax was imposed as a regressive flat rate of 5s. per hut. Alongside this tax, the colonial government also required a certain number of unpaid labour days on public works projects, mostly road building and maintenance close to railway lines.[26] This was explicitly classified as a tax in an attempt to avoid increasing international pressure against slavery and forced labour applied by the International Labour Organization and the League of Nations.[27]

Both of these taxes relied on local chiefs for administration, who were responsible for counting the number of huts in their villages, collecting and handing over tax revenue, and responding to requests for labourers from the Public Works Department. The light official presence in the Protectorate and consequent reliance on indirect rule was driven by, and in turn drove, discrepancies in the quantity and quality of information available to colonial policymakers. A lack of the basic demographic and economic information needed to design tax policies led to simple byt regressive flat rates to reduce the prohibitively high transactions costs of obtaining the relevant information for a more nuanced tax based on income or wealth.[28] Instead, the colonial state collected information about the chiefs – their reliability, character, and relationship with the colonial government – which was both easier to obtain and more useful in facilitating this kind of village- and chiefdom-based communal taxation.[29]

As well as administering these central taxes, chiefs themselves taxed their populations at the chiefdom level. These were paid mainly in labour days or as a percentage of produce from farms, although there were efforts to commute these payments to a cash sum.[30] This meant the Protectorate population was paying taxes at the central or colonial level and at the communal level, in cash, goods, and labour days. These taxes were geographically specific to the Protectorate, but also legally specific to the 'native' Protectorate population. Traders from the Crown Colony and Freetown travelling or resident in the Protectorate were instead subject to an annual 'non-native' tax. This was regulated and institutionalised as a poll tax of £2 from the 1930s to clear up confusion about the obligations of other categories of taxpayer when crossing geographical subdivisions but had been in place more informally before this as an annual sum paid to the chief of the area in which they were resident. The discovery of minerals in the late 1920s and setting up of mines in the early 1930s triggered another shift in fiscal structure with a tax of up to 27.5% on the profits of mining companies, particularly the Sierra Leone Selection Trust.[31]

Direct taxes had a chequered history in Freetown. Attempts throughout the nineteenth century to introduce taxes on roads, horses, carriages, and other items proved short-lived and rarely made significant contributions to revenue.[32] Eventually, the colonial government gave up trying to impose taxes itself and set up the Municipal Council so that the residents of Freetown could 'tax themselves'.[33] The City Rate was introduced in 1899 and was proportional on the assessed value of land and buildings, initially at the rate of 5%.[34] Transparency and accountability were key: rates were published in the local newspapers, alongside other practical information about assessment and collection.[35] A new tax in the form of a Water Rate was introduced in 1906, assessed in the same manner as the City Rate, beginning at 2.33%, and specifically channelled towards water provision.[36] By 1925, the combined rates had reached 13% of the assessed value of property. Alongside direct taxes, other sources of municipal income included licences, fees, fines, market dues, and an annual grant from the colonial government. The liability for the tax was officially on the owner of the property, not on the occupier. This distinction could, however, become complicated, with the burden shifted to the tenant by the owner compounding the rate into the rental value.[37] Taxes were levied on the property of individuals and companies alike whilst all colonial and imperial property, either owned or rented, was exempted, which dealt a considerable blow to the Municipal Council's income while also causing tension with the colonial government.[38]

The Crown Colony was the final area to receive a direct tax. A degree of economic necessity lay behind this decision, as competitive trading and the threat of smuggling meant indirect tax revenue couldn't be increased through higher import duties.[39] The organisation of much of the Colony as a system of villages, described as 'incipient municipalities', led to suggestions of adopting the same arrangement as Freetown.[40] On paper, the tax rate calculations resemble a mix between the graduated system of Freetown and the regressive flat tax in the Protectorate.[41] Like Freetown, tax was levied on property, which included 'dwelling houses' and any stores, warehouses, shops, tenements, or buildings 'used or occupied as a place of abode or business'.[42] Properties were classified into two groups: those with an annual value that exceeded £5 were taxed at a proportional rate of 1s. in the pound on the annual rent or value, whilst houses with an annual value below £5 paid a regressive flat rate of 5s. per house, much like the hut tax in the Protectorate. The Colony district funds comprised the fewest number of revenue sources, with tax revenue providing almost the entire annual revenue. Unlike Freetown, the burden of the tax was officially on the occupier, but if there was 'no such occupier' or if he was absent and could not be found, the owner would be liable.[43]

The relative contribution of these population groups was controversial. This issue has been discussed with reference to other colonies, particularly those with white European settlers where relative contributions were divided on racial lines.[44] However, these tensions were present even in colonies like Sierra Leone that lacked a substantial European settler population. Discussion of the imposition of direct taxation on settlers and their descendants in the Colony and Freetown intensified during the Hut Tax War. The fact that direct tax had initially been imposed exclusively in the Protectorate was cited as a cause of jealousy and a contributing factor in the insurrection. Confusion and resentment stemmed from the perception in the Protectorate that 'every other law has come through them to us' while 'this law has jumped over them and come to us'.[45] The Colonial Secretary regretted imposing the tax in the Protectorate first, arguing that the Colony should be on an 'equal footing'.[46] Freetown lawyer Samuel Lewis agreed that direct tax should be imposed across the regions of Sierra Leone and that 'the same principle should be made to apply to [the Colony] as to Freetown', with other places paying a 'rate of a like nature', although in an effort to make it 'acceptable to the people', the funds raised would be applied specifically for local improvements.[47]

The relative economic importance of direct taxation

The efforts of the colonial tax literature to disaggregate budgets by source has focused much attention on the balance of indirect and direct taxation. Some broad patterns have been established: in general, colonial governments in all empires relied as much as possible on indirect taxes levied on trade, only then imposing direct taxes. East African colonies, which received a far smaller proportion of overall revenue from trade taxes, were forced to rely more heavily on administratively challenging direct taxes, while West African colonies seemed in a fortunate position with the option mostly to cover their expenses from indirect sources.[48] While East African colonies routinely relied on direct levies for at least 50% of their overall budget, in Sierra Leone the figure was never much more than 15%.[49] However, even this was not an inconsiderable contribution, and in some difficult years could mean the difference between a balanced budget and deficit.

Focusing instead on the internal heterogeneity of direct taxes, a different picture emerges. As discussed above, municipal direct taxes fed into the budget of the Freetown City Council, not the overall colonial government revenue, and local tax records show that at this level, direct taxation was the largest single contributor to municipal finances, providing between 40% and 60% of the annual budget. While full budget figures do not exist for the Crown Colony house tax funds, it can be assumed, given the lack of alternative means of funding, that direct taxes were also important here. Figure 5.1 compares the proportion of direct taxes in the overall colonial revenue with those at a municipal level and shows that the City Rate was providing around half of municipal revenue in most years, while the figure for the Protectorate, recorded in statistical overviews like the Blue Books, is much lower. Also missing from these sources are the gains made from labour taxes used on road construction and maintenance. Instead of appearing as part of the budget, a short note in the reports of the Public Works Department indicated the scale of savings made through this tax. In 1924, labour taxes were worth an estimated £24,000, and although this was less than half the revenue collected that year in respect of the hut tax (just over £60,000), it still represents an important contribution to government revenue.[50] While historians and economists debate the motivations behind the introduction of direct taxes in colonies, whether purely for extraction, for developmental purposes, to force Africans into the labour

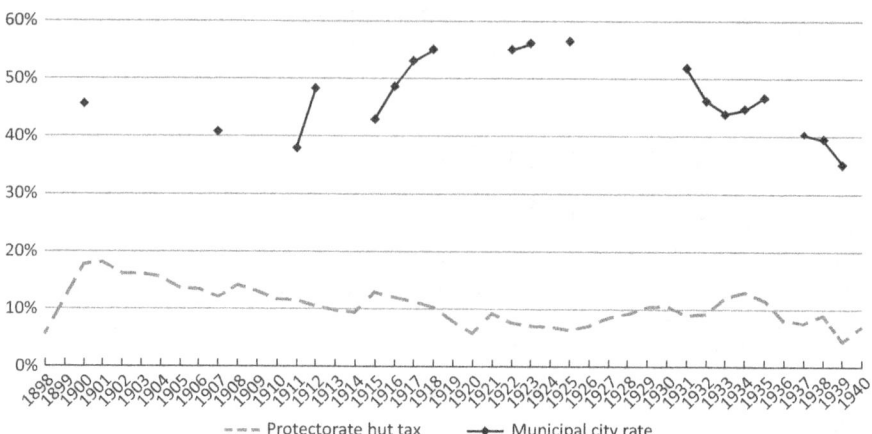

Figure 5.1 Comparative proportion of direct tax in total revenue in Freetown vs. the Protectorate, 1898–1940. N.B. This graph shows only the City Rate and City Fund figures. It must be kept in mind that from 1906 the Water Rate was also levied and funnelled into a separate account used specifically for water provision, a social service.

market, or increase the circulation of cash, from this disaggregated perspective, the fiscal importance of direct taxes is clear.

Expenditure: Restricted redistribution

A comprehensive picture of colonial fiscal structure and taxpayers requires taking into consideration expenditure as well as taxation policy. While tax rates and revenue in a given society are important in their own right, the ability of governments and interest groups to exert power over the spending of this revenue makes it necessary to examine taxes and spending in tandem. While tax structures might look progressive in isolation, this could always be compromised by regressive patterns of expenditure. Thandika Mkandawire has called the relationship between taxes and spending 'profound', extending far beyond a simple budgetary calculation and instead signalling the 'fundamental values' and the 'balance of social forces' in a society.[51] So far, work on expenditure has been more thorough for settler colonies: historians, economists, and political scientists have called attention to the impact of racial distinctions resulting from the presence of white settlers and their restrictive land, labour, and tax policies.[52] Taxes in settler areas were acceptable because redistributive expenditure was restricted to within the settler population, and, through the segregation of local authorities, settlers could guarantee that no taxes gathered there could leak into other sections of the population.[53] The 'dual' nature of these settler states 'attenuated' the progressive tendency of direct taxes.[54] While there was no white settler population in Sierra Leone, we can learn from how the settler literature treats segregated local authorities and institutions. Sharp divisions existed everywhere, and by including the expenditure side and approaching the topic at the sub-colony level for Sierra Leone it will be shown here how different taxation systems underpinned different patterns of expenditure that had important implications for redistribution.

Targeted spending in Freetown and the Crown Colony

In both Freetown and the Crown Colony, tax revenue was retained and spent in the areas from which it was collected. The African-majority Municipal Council took care of most spending in the city, although the maintenance and repair of streets remained in the hands of the colonial government, and they later also took over sanitation, to the frustration of the Municipal Council.[55] Revenue from the two direct taxes was channelled into respective funds: the City Fund, for general expenditure, and the Waterworks Fund, for water services. Unlike the Crown Colony and the Protectorate, revenue was collected and spent by an African-controlled local institution specific to the urban area. The proportional rate and spending on collectively beneficial items like streetlights, cemeteries, and markets meant the tax had redistributive potential locally but not at the whole-colony level.

As early as 1900, over half of annual municipal expenditure was devoted to public services and works, including infrastructure projects, sanitary improvements, streetlights, and a fire brigade (see Figure 5.2).[56] Municipal reports disaggregate spending to a minute level and provide an insight into the kind of city that settler self-government was creating. Spending on street lighting was vast, growing from £366 in 1900–01 to £1,323 in 1915 to £1,483 by 1918. Of this, in 1915, £400 was spent on wages for thirty-three lamplighters and three head lamplighters, employed 365 days of the year. Oil for these lamps was £600 in 1915 and 1916, rising to £800 by 1917 and 1918. The Council also took its responsibility for maintaining the markets and public areas of the city seriously. It spent £1,000 on a new slaughterhouse on Bombay Street in the east of the city in 1915. Between £300 and £500 was spent on the general upkeep of markets each year, including the salaries of market keepers. A similar portion of revenue was spent on cemeteries, including repairing drains and walls, building chapels, and digging graves. Gravediggers were employed 365 days of the year. The

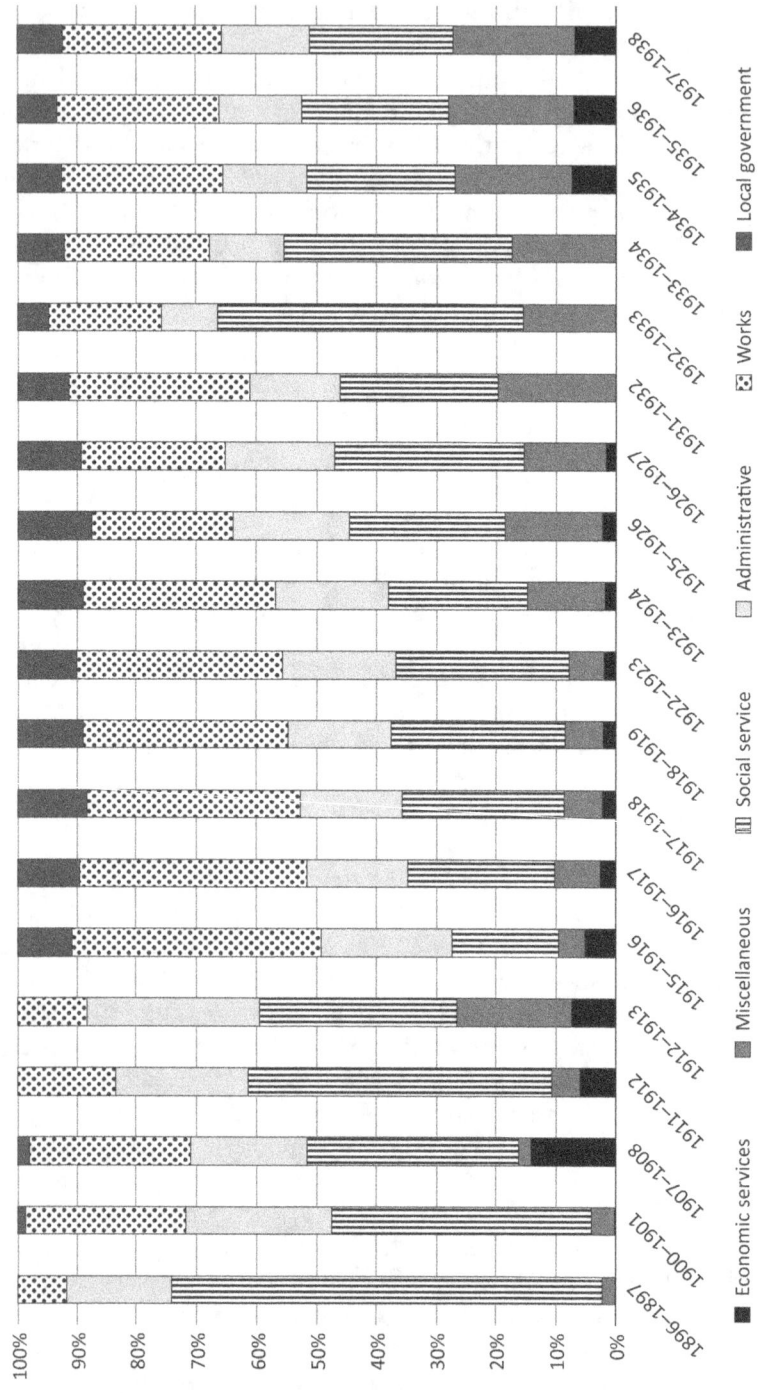

Figure 5.2 Freetown City Council spending, various years 1898–1938.

Water Rate was spent on the labour, materials, and expertise required to maintain the existing waterworks in operation and construct extensions and improvements.[57]

The Municipal Council also devoted funds to self-preservation, protecting this African-controlled level of urban government for the urban area from encroachments from the colonial government. The Council paid for the rental, insurance, and upkeep of the local government premises in the centre of the city, funded a City Bailiff's department, rented and staffed polling stations, constructed valuation lists, tax books, and paid the salaries of tax assessors, all of which ensured the continued functioning of the Council itself, the reproduction of a narrowly defined electorate, and a loose but mostly functional enforcement mechanism for urban taxation.

The Municipal budgets do not show significant spending on health care or poor relief. Charitable giving, however, was an important feature of public and religious life and reports in the local press indicate that Freetown residents were giving to local causes fairly regularly.[58] But this goodwill was not unlimited. When the colonial government indicated its intention to transfer the financial burden of poor relief to the Municipality through a new tax, there was outrage among the professional classes of the city who worried it would encourage migration from the Protectorate and lead to increased crime and unemployment, and the proposal was dropped.[59]

In much the same way as Freetown, revenue collected in the Crown Colony was retained in the area in which it was collected and 'expended on works of improvement in such district' on the advice of Local Advisory Boards.[60] As these were not representative institutions, they could only recommend to the Governor any works which were considered to be priorities to be undertaken in their districts. Each district was comprised of a network of villages, and tax revenue could be redistributed among these to reflect the spending priorities of the district as a whole, but no revenue was transferred for spending outside this unit.

Spending in the Colony covered a mixture of social and public works items. Evidence for these is scattered and was not compiled in an itemised budget like in Freetown. Instead, annual expenditure across all the Colony districts was compiled into a long list including location, item, amount spent, and the district fund from which the money came. A majority of revenue, over half of total spending in six out of nine districts in 1912, was spent on items falling into the category of 'public works'.[61] Unlike in the Protectorate, this category of spending did not aim above all else to increase the export productive capacity of the region, but served multiple ends including sanitation, safety, social services, and economic development. Water supply, including the building of latrines and wells, and the building of local roads and bridges, were frequently listed, and streetlights were constantly discussed and lobbied for, serving as both a sign of development, an enhancement of safety, and a measure to reduce crime. In 1913, the expenditure list includes examples of social services spending and funds designated for the repair and maintenance of local services, as well as larger amounts for the construction of new infrastructure, including a new 1,000 gallon water tank in Bonthe to increase water supply and £50 towards building a new latrine. In Kent, £25 went towards improvements on a public well, £240 in Hastings provided for a supply of lamps and standpipes, and £25 in Madonkia went towards repairing a bridge at Waterloo.[62]

Street lamps were a common item of expenditure in the Colony districts. A great deal has been written about the developmental aspect of street lighting, not only in an African context, but associated with progress and Enlightenment in all areas of the world.[63] An application for street lamps in Kissy and Wilberforce districts was submitted in 1912 and gives an insight into the practicalities of spending.[64] Only two out of thirteen villages across the two districts had any form of public lighting, but initial proposals were ridiculed as 'absolutely ludicrous' and far too expensive to be covered by each tax district fund. For example, Kissy town had asked for twenty-four lamps, which would cost £168 plus an additional £84 in upkeep annually. Their total tax collection annually amounted to around £140, 'from which has to be deducted ¼ as the headman's share for local purposes, leading £105 to be carried to the House Tax general fund, ¾ of which it is proposed to spend on lighting the village'. Eventually a smaller number was agreed, meaning a more realistic financial commitment from local tax revenue. The committee of Aberdeen stated that they 'preferred to do without the lamps in view of the more pressing needs of an improved water supply'.[65]

The Protectorate and the general revenue

Unlike Freetown and the rest of the Colony, in the Protectorate spending was directed centrally and there was no meaningful role for local-level institutions in spending decisions until after the creation of Native Treasuries in 1937.[66] Instead, tax revenue was collected by chiefs and handed over to District Commissioners in each part of the Protectorate before being subsumed into the general revenue.[67] District and Provincial administrations did have some spending powers but this was mostly over the salaries and allowances of the officials stationed there, the construction of buildings in the district headquarters and the encouragement of export production. During the early years of colonial rule, spending was designed to serve the priorities of the central colonial government, not the rural taxpayers themselves, and tended to concentrate in the areas of the Protectorate that showed the most potential for export production. Spending in the Protectorate initially was designated to security and to smoothing the relationship between colonial officials and 'native' chiefs through stipends and annual presents and the provision of salaries and transport for the 'thin white line' of European officials stationed there.[68]

Public works and infrastructure were allocated large sums and, within a decade of the annexation of the Protectorate, had become the largest categories of expenditure (see Figure 5.3). In contrast to the Municipality and Colony, this spending wasn't directed specifically to the areas from which taxes had been collected, and there was no correlation between higher tax capacity and more developmental spending and little obvious recompense for the payment of taxes. Funds were channelled into areas that could increase export production, most noticeably the railway line and feeder roads constructed linking the port in Freetown with the areas in the south that produced the highest volumes of palm products. The salaries and pensions of colonial officials were paid from this fund, as were all administrative expenses of government departments and the repayment of loans. While there was no direct transfer of tax revenue through state institutions to Britain, the volume and proportion of revenue devoted to salaries of European officials, who were not taxpayers in Sierra Leone, represented an indirect transfer of wealth.

Spending on 'social services' includes the Medical Department, the Sanitary Department, and Education, and increased throughout the period. Social services were 7% of total spending in 1900, rising to 10% in 1920 and eventually 13% by 1937.[69] Also included in this infrastructural spending was a substantial amount of spending on works in Freetown. In 1921, of a total of £112,012 spent on Public Works, an examination of the individual items of spending reveals that £48,660, or 43.5% of this, was spent in Freetown and the Colony, particularly on sanitation items and road repairs (visible in Figure 5.3).[70]

The discrepancies between spending in different areas of Sierra Leone was the cause of disagreements and complaints both within regions and between them. In 1909, deliberating where to invest the general revenue, Governor Probyn felt under pressure to devote funds to public works and improvements in Freetown, which would mean little funding available for the 'development of the wealth and well-being' of the Protectorate for several years, which he judged as a 'disastrous' outcome. The 'native interest' in the Protectorate was vocal in its desire for a share of the expenditure

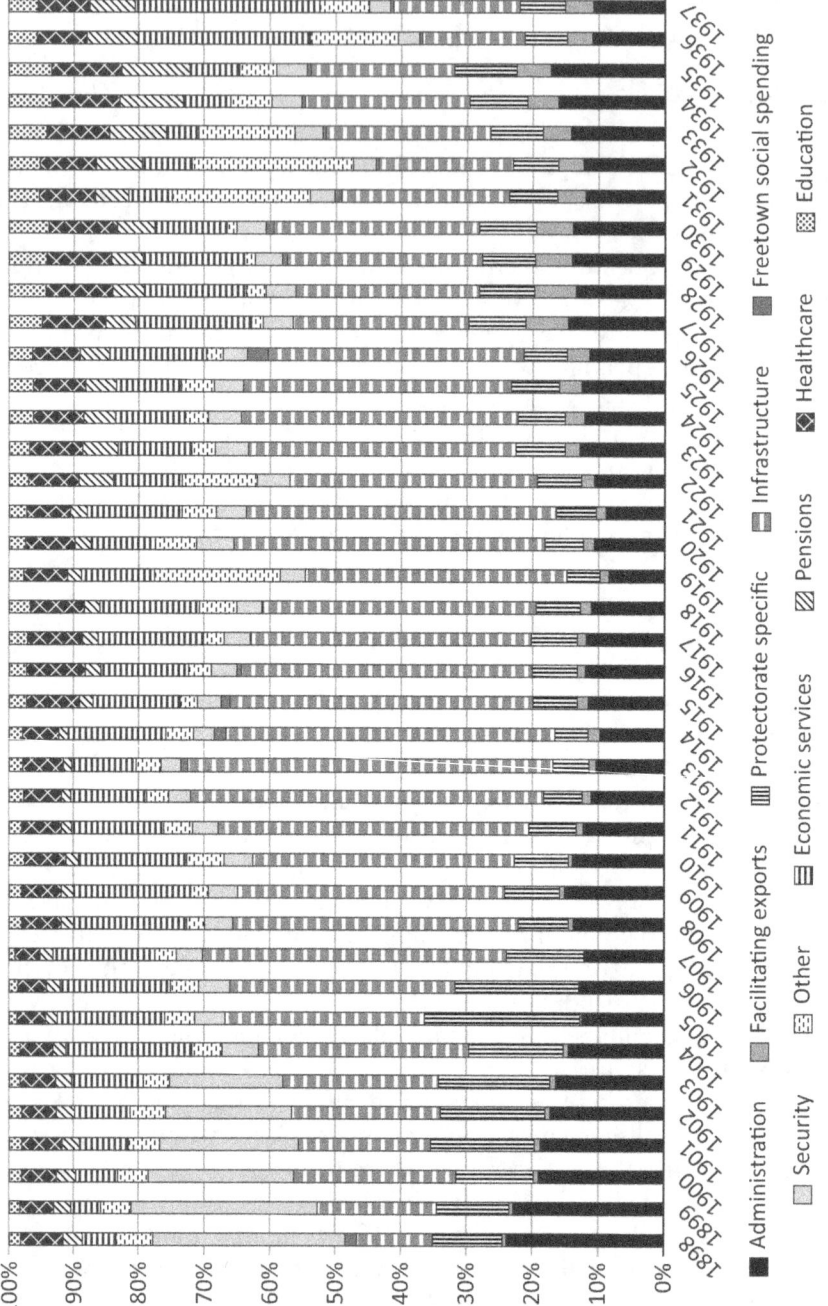

Figure 5.3 Breakdown of general expenditure, 1898–1937.

and was unable to understand or accept why taxes in the Colony and Freetown were spent on works benefiting taxpayers there while the whole Protectorate house tax was subsumed into the general revenue.[71] Pa Saba, a chief in the Karene District in the north of the Protectorate, lobbied the Governor on behalf of fifteen chiefs that the district should receive 'direct benefit' from the payment of the house tax. While there was no indication that chiefs might refuse to pay taxes, there was a 'growing feeling that other districts and the Colony were being preferred to Karene'. Probyn admitted that while Karene paid around £10,000 a year in tax, it was yet to receive 'any direct benefit from public expenditure of the kind which has so greatly advanced the material welfare of the Mendi and Yonni people' in the palm-producing districts of the south. While Probyn suggested ensuring by law that Protectorate tax revenue should be spent in the region, the proposal was dismissed in favour of a balance between 'non-productive' works in Freetown and 'productive' works consisting of railways roads and bridges in the relevant areas of the Protectorate.[72]

Conclusion

Cross-colony approaches, largely favoured by economists in efforts to facilitate vast geographical and chronological coverage, have extended our understanding of types of colonial states and tax system variation between colonies. However, the internal differences within these colonial states were just as important for the experience of taxpayers as variations between them. Inequalities in the ways different regions and groups were incorporated into the colonial state were reflected in the design of tax systems, which in turn served to embed these distinctions more deeply. The 'revenue imperative' constrained the options of colonial governments, and as such, the type of information available to taxing institutions varied widely across the colony, from annual assessments of individual properties in Freetown to a lump sum based loosely on the number of huts in each chiefdom. These tax categories were defined by both geographical units, the Protectorate, Colony, and Municipality, and partly by legal statuses, including 'native' and 'non-native'.

Removing taxation from its exclusive association with an overarching colonial state reveals an additional layer of complexity in the relationship of taxpayers to taxing institutions in a colonial context. These differences are particularly clear when expenditure is taken into account. The provision in the tax legislation for the revenue to be spent in the areas where it was collected meant that urban-settler tax revenue was explicitly retained for these areas while Protectorate taxes disappeared into the overall budget. While regional redistribution could occur, at the whole-colony level the segregation of local authorities meant that tax revenue was restricted to certain areas, with spending skewed by devolved institutions and by the perceived export potential of certain areas.

Notes

1 J. Burbank and F. Cooper, *Empires in World History: Power and the Politics of Difference* (Princeton, NJ: Princeton University Press, 2010), pp. 8, 2.
2 J. A. Schumpeter, 'The crisis of the tax state', in Richard Swedberg (ed.), *Joseph A. Schumpeter: The Economics and Sociology of capitalism* (Princeton, NJ: Princeton University Press, 1991), p. 108. Originally published in 1918 under the title 'Die Krise der Steuerstaates' as issue no. 4 of *Zeitfrangen aus dem Geibet der Sociologie*. This has been the foundation of a move towards an interdisciplinary 'New Fiscal Sociology'; see I. W. Martin, A. K. Mehrotra, and M. Prasad (eds), *The New Fiscal Sociology: Taxation in Comparative and Historical Perspective* (Cambridge: Cambridge University Press, 2009).
3 See A. K. Mehrotra, *Making the Modern American Fiscal State: Law, Politics, and the Rise of Progressive Taxation, 1877–1929* (Cambridge: Cambridge University Press, 2013); M. Daunton, *Just Taxes: The Politics of Taxation in Britain, 1914–1979* (Cambridge: Cambridge University press, 2002); M. Daunton, *Trusting Leviathan: The Politics of Taxation in Britain, 1799–1914* (Cambridge: Cambridge University Press, 2001).
4 M. Daunton, 'Tax transfers: Britain and its empire, 1848–1914', in M. Daunton, *State and Market in Victorian Britain: War, Welfare and Capitalism* (Woodbridge: Boydell Press, 2008), p. 145.
5 L. A. Gardner, *Taxing Colonial Africa* (Oxford: Oxford University Press, 2012); L. A. Gardner, 'Decentralization and corruption in historical perspective: evidence from tax collection in British colonial Africa', *Economic History of Developing Regions* 25.2 (2010), 213–36; E. Frankema, 'Raising revenue in the British empire, 1870–1940: How "extractive" were colonial taxes?' *Journal of Global History* 5.3 (2010), 447–77; E. Frankema, 'Colonial taxation and government spending in British Africa, 1880–1940: Maximizing revenue or minimizing effort?', *Explorations in Economic History* 48.1 (2011), 136–49, p. 147; E. Frankema and M. van Waijenburg, 'Metropolitan blueprints of colonial taxation? Lessons from fiscal capacity building in British and French Africa, c. 1880–1940', *Journal of African History* 55.3 (2014), 371–400; B. De Roo, 'Taxation in the Congo Free State, an exceptional case? (1885–1908)', *Economic History of Developing Regions* 32.2 (2017), 97–126.
6 K. Alexopoulou and D. Juif, 'Colonial state formation without integration: Tax capacity and labour regimes in Portuguese Mozambique (1890s-1970s)', *International Review of Social History* 62.2 (2017), 215–52; T. Mkandawire, 'On tax efforts and colonial heritage in Africa', *Journal of Development*

Studies 46.10 (2010), 1647–69; T. Feger and J. Asafu-Adjaye, 'Tax effort performance in Sub-Saharan Africa and the role of colonialism', *Economic Modelling* 38 (2014), 163–74. A recent edited collection explicitly looks at social taxonomy in empires through taxation; see S. Albiez-Wieck, (ed.), *Taxing Difference: Empires as Spaces of Ordered Inequality* (Röhrig Universitätsverlag, 2020).

7 E. Lieberman, *Race and Regionalism in the Politics of Taxation in Brazil and South Africa*, Studies in Comparative Politics (Cambridge: Cambridge University Press, 2003); L. Gardner, 'New colonies, old tools: Building fiscal systems in East and Central Africa', in E. Frankema and A. Booth (eds), *Fiscal Capacity and the Colonial State in Asia and Africa, c. 1850–1960* (Cambridge: Cambridge University Press, 2019), pp. 193–229.

8 This is a point well made in K. L. Sokoloff and E. M. Zolt, 'Inequality and evolution of institutions of taxation: Evidence from the economic history of the Americas', in S. Edwards, G. Esquivel, and G. Márquez (eds), *The Decline of Latin American Economies: Growth, Institutions and Crises* (Chicago, IL: University of Chicago Press, 2004), pp. 83–136.

9 C. Boone, *Political Topographies of the African State: Territorial Authority and Institutional Choice*, Cambridge Studies in Comparative Politics (Cambridge: Cambridge University Press, 2003), especially chapters 1 and 2.

10 P. X. Scanlan, 'MacCarthy's skull: The abolition of the slave trade in Sierra Leone, 1792–1823' (PhD dissertation, Princeton University, 2013), pp. 1–407, p. 301.

11 A. Renner-Thomas, *Land Tenure in Sierra Leone: The Law, Dualism and the Making of a Land Policy* (Milton Keynes: AuthorHouse, 2010), pp. 26, 29.

12 Parliamentary Papers [hereafter PP], Sierra Leone, Annual Colonial Reports, No. 460 (1904), p. 4; No. 648 (1909), p. 5; No. 694 (1910), p. 5.

13 J. Alie, *A New History of Sierra Leone* (Freetown: Sulaiman International, 2016), chapter 11, 'Local government and decentralization'.

14 PP, D. Chalmers, *Report on the Subject of the Insurrection in the Sierra Leone Protectorate, 1898*, 2 vols (London, 1899) (henceforth C. R. I–II), Vol. II, Sir Samuel Lewis, 19 August 1898, p. 136; Renner-Thomas, *Land Tenure*, pp. 16–17; PP, C. R., Vol. II, Sir Samuel Lewis, 19 August 1898, pp. 136, 152; B. E. Everill, *Abolition and Empire in Sierra Leone and Liberia*, Cambridge Imperial and Post-Colonial Studies Series (Basingstoke: Palgrave Macmillan, 2013), p. 164; A. Wyse, *The Krio of Sierra Leone: An Interpretive History* (London: Hurst, 1989), p. 6.

15 Renner-Thomas, *Land Tenure*, pp. 16–17.

16 PP, C. R. II, Sir Samuel Lewis, 19 August 1898, p. 152; M. Mamdani, *Citizen and Subject: Contemporary Africa and the Legacy of Late Colonialism* (Princeton, NJ: Princeton University Press, 1996), p. 18.

17 A. H. M. Kirk-Greene, 'The thin white line: The size of the British colonial service in Africa', *African Affairs* 79.314 (1980), 25–44; J. Herbst, *States and Power in Africa* (Princeton, NJ: Princeton University Press, 2000), pp. 72–4.

18 The National Archives, UK [hereafter TNA], CO 272/73–77, Sierra Leone Blue Books, 1896–1900.

19 Alie, *A New History*, p. 154.
20 TNA, CO 272/70–117 Sierra Leone Blue Books 1893–1940; Sierra Leone National Archives [hereafter SLA], Valuation for Central Ward, Freetown, 1925–26 shows the proportion of female property owners in the Central Ward was substantial, around 33%; A. J. G. Wyse, 'The dissolution of Freetown City Council in 1926: A negative example of political apprenticeship in colonial Sierra Leone', in M. Last and P. Richards (eds.), *Sierra Leone 1787–1987: Two Centuries of Intellectual Life* (Manchester: Manchester University Press, International African Institute, 1987), pp. 422–38, pp. 423–4; T. N. Goddard, *The Handbook of Sierra Leone* (London: Grant Richards, 1925), p. 124.
21 Goddard, *Handbook*, p. 101.
22 SLA, Local Minute Papers 444/1912 Application for Street Lamps.
23 Select exports were taxed until 1887, when these levies were abandoned in favour of slightly higher import duties, and weren't reintroduced until 1918. See PP, C.R. Vol. II, Memo of W. J. P. Elliott, Collector of Customs, 26 August 1898, p. 671.
24 D. F. Wilbraham and E. T. Packard, *A revised edition of the ordinances of the colony of Sierra Leone*, Vol. IV 1904–09, London: Waterlow & Sons, 1909, pp. 1475–6.
25 N. A. Cox-George, *Finance and Development in West Africa: The Sierra Leone Experience* (London: Dennis Dobson, 1963), pp. 70–1.
26 TNA, CO 267/ 578/2558 Labour for Road Construction, 15 January, 1919; for road building in other colonies, see K. O. Akurang-Parry, 'Colonial forced labor policies for road-building in Southern Ghana and international anti-forced labor pressures, 1900–1940', *African Economic History* 28 (2000), 1–25; C. Ash, 'Forced labor in colonial West Africa', *History Compass* 4.3 (2006), 402–6.
27 Marlous van Waijenburg's study is by far the most thorough in viewing forced labour through a fiscal lens: M. van Waijenburg, 'Financing the African colonial state: The revenue imperative and forced labour', *Journal of Economic History* 78.1 (2018), 40–80.
28 M. Levi, *Of Rule and Revenue* (Berkeley and Los Angeles: University of California Press, 1989), p. 23.
29 SLA, Information Regarding Protectorate Chiefs, 1912.
30 TNA, CO 267/502/11256 Labour Commutation System; TNA, CO 267/510/36837 Commuted Payments to Chiefs.
31 British Foreign and Commonwealth Office [hereafter BFCO], Financial Report for Sierra Leone, 1935.
32 Cox-George, *Finance and Development*, pp. 57–67.
33 PP, C. R., II, Sir Frederic Cardew Governor of Sierra Leone, 16 November 1898, p. 547.
34 TNA, CO 272/75–117 Sierra Leone Blue Books, 1898–1940; Wilbraham and Packard, *Ordinances*, Vol. III, 1905–1908, Freetown Municipality No. 28 of 1908 An Ordinance to consolidate and amend the Law relating to the Municipality of Freetown, p. 1301.

35 PP, Sierra Leone, Annual Colonial Report, No. 299 (1899).
36 TNA, CO 272/82–91 Sierra Leone Blue Books, 1905–14.
37 Wilbraham and Packard, *Ordinances*, Vol. III, Freetown Municipality No. 28 of 1908 An Ordinance to consolidate and amend the Law relating to the Municipality of Freetown, p. 1304.
38 *Ibid.*
39 PP, C. R., II, Mr Buckley, 24 September 1898.
40 *Ibid.*
41 The exception to these arrangements was Bonthe, administered by a Local Advisory Board until 1905, when it became a municipality and was renamed the Port of Sherbro District. The municipal board never managed consistently to balance the budget and was abolished in 1912; PP, Sierra Leone, Annual Colonial Reports, No. 759 (1912); No. 808 (1913); No. 851 (1914).
42 Wilbraham and Packard, *Ordinances*, Vol. II, 1900–1904, House Tax, No. 11 of 1900, p. 359.
43 *Ibid.*
44 For example, Gardner's work on Kenya and Northern Rhodesia; see Gardner, *Taxing Colonial Africa*, especially chapter 5.
45 PP, C. R., II, Mr Macaulay, J.P., 14 August 1898, p. 168.
46 PP, C. R., II, Lieutenant-Colonel Gore, Colonial Secretary, 17 November 1898, p. 537.
47 PP, C. R., II, Sir Samuel Lewis, 19 August 1898, p. 161.
48 Gardner, *Taxing Colonial Africa*; Frankema, 'Colonial taxation'; Frankema, 'Raising revenue'.
49 See Gardner, *Taxing Colonial Africa*, figure 1.3, p. 7.
50 BFCO, Sierra Leone Public Works Department Report, 1924, pp. 3–4.
51 Despite this, Mkandawire does not consider the expenditure side of fiscal policy and instead prioritises identifying the balance of sources of revenue over asking questions about how this revenue was distributed. Mkandawire, 'On tax efforts', p. 1664.
52 Gardner, *Taxing Colonial Africa*, especially chapter 5; Lieberman, *Race and Regionalism*, especially chapter 2.
53 Mkandawire, 'On tax efforts', pp. 1654–5; S. Bowden, B. Chiripanhura, and P. Mosley, 'Measuring and explaining poverty in six African countries: A long-period approach', *Journal of International Development* 20.8, Special Issue: Historical Roots of Poverty (2008), 1049–79.
54 L. Gardner, 'New colonies, old tools: Building fiscal systems in East and Central Africa', in E. Frankema and A. Booth (eds), *Fiscal Capacity and the Colonial State in Asia and Africa, c. 1850–1960* (Cambridge: Cambridge University Press, 2019), p. 210.
55 The government had planned to hand over the responsibility once the street and drainage scheme in progress had been completed. See PP, Sierra Leone Annual Colonial Report, No. 460, 1904.
56 SLA, MP No. 3429/1900 Estimates of revenue and expenditure of the Municipality for 1900–01.

57 Wilbraham, *Ordinances*, No. 35 of 1901, Freetown Waterworks, pp. 517–18.
58 For example, donations were made after a fire in the West Ward in 1914; see *Sierra Leone Weekly News*, 11 April 1914, Fire Relief Fund Subscriptions, pp. 504–5.
59 *Sierra Leone Weekly News*, 2 April, 1921, p. 511; 9 April, 1921, p. 531; 16 April, 1921, p. 543.
60 PP, Sierra Leone, Annual Colonial Report, No. 289/1902.
61 SLA, House Tax (Colony) Fund: Abstract of Revenue & Expenditure for the year 1912.
62 SLA, Minutes of the Executive Council of the Colony of Sierra Leone for the half year ended 30th June 1913.
63 R. Porter, *The Enlightenment: Britain and the Creation of the Modern World* (London: Allen Lane, 2000), p. 44.
64 SLA LM 444/1912 Application for Street Lamps, p. 11.
65 *Ibid*.
66 Native Administrative was established in Sierra Leone in 1937, comparatively late compared to other British West African colonies, and involved the establishment of Native Treasuries to which a portion of tax revenue was given; see L. Gardner and J. Bolt, 'How Africans shaped British colonial institutions: Evidence from local taxation', *Journal of Economic History* 80.4 (2020), 1–35.
67 Initially this was enumerated under its own heading, but eventually found its way into fees, charges, and fines.
68 TNA, CO 272/73–76 Sierra Leone Blue Books, 1896–99.
69 TNA, CO 272/77, 97, 114 Sierra Leone Blue Books, 1900, 1920, 1937.
70 TNA, CO 272/98 Sierra Leone Blue Books, 1921.
71 TNA CO 267/574/17212 Protectorate Mal-Administration.
72 *Ibid*.

Part II

Taxation and welfare

6

Taxation, welfare, and inequalities in the Spanish imperial state

Julia McClure

Introduction

Like other European polities, Spain developed in the early modern period as a state at the same time that it was developing as an empire. States and empires are often treated as different political units with distinct historiographies; however, the development of states and empires have been intrinsically connected. Burbank and Cooper set out criteria for distinguishing between states and empires, arguing that 'the concept of empire presumes that different peoples within the polity will be governed differently'.[1] However, this distinction between states and empires collapses in the case of many polities. Burbank and Cooper discuss 'empire as a type of state',[2] but we can also think of the state as a type of empire. The idea that different people were ruled differently was already at work in the composite monarchies that developed in medieval and early modern Europe.[3] Different status groups had different privileges and tax exemptions. The Spanish imperial state was already accustomed to ruling and taxing different people differently in ways that reinforced inequalities before its expansion across the Atlantic in the sixteenth century, but its transition to a global imperial state created new layers of inequalities which became increasingly racialised across the early modern period.

Taxation and inequality: Medieval foundations in the Iberian Peninsula

Taxation did increase inequality, but the Crown also had obligations to its subjects in return for this taxation. In the Iberian Peninsula this was a legacy of the way in which the expansion of the Spanish imperial state had been financed. To finance expansion the Spanish Crown leveraged some of its sovereign powers of taxation. The Crown granted *mercedes* (rewards) such as tax exemptions to those leading military conquest and it granted towns the privilege of raising their own taxation. In order to finance expansion, the Crown had effectively pawned sovereign powers, including privileges of taxation, in ways that had long-lasting implications for the landscape of inequality.

The expansion of the Spanish imperial state across the Muslim territories of the Iberian Peninsula during the Middle Ages was financed by a variety of public–private partnerships, whereby the Crown leveraged sovereign powers, such as the notionally public economic revenue stream of tax collection, in order to reward those who supported military conquest and resettled former Muslim territories (known as *Repoblación*). This meant that the Iberian imperial state was a patchwork of privilege, and this was reflected in its tax codes. The Crown granted tax exemption as rewards for subjects and so the taxation system both reflected and reinforced the status inequalities of the Spanish imperial state. Those with noble status (*hidalguía*) were often exempt from taxation. Hidalgos were not a homogeneous group. Ortiz identified five different sub-categories, ranging from the very rich to those living by their own labour.[4] This pattern of tax exemptions meant that the poorest were often left to shoulder the burden of taxes. These lower-class taxpayers (*pecheros*) paid the royal head tax (*pechero*), which made up the tax receipt paid by the towns to the Crown (known as the *servicio*). This tax burden increased in the second half of the sixteenth century;[5] according to one calculation, 'by 1590 one-third of the average peasant's income in a good year was consumed in tax'.[6] This meant that the Spanish imperial state never became a rentier state: as Vassberg summarises, 'gold and silver from Mexico and Peru were a windfall for the royal treasury, but the sums derived by the Spanish crown from the Americas comprised a small proportion of its total revenue, rising from about 11% in 1554 to some 20% in 1598' and 'most of the rest was paid, directly or indirectly, by the Castilian peasant'.[7] The taxation regime reflected the hierarchy of status that constituted the Iberian world and helped structure its inequalities.

The Crown issued *fueros* (law codes) and *cartas pueblos* (municipal charters) to the towns of newly conquered territories and placed the surrounding countryside in the jurisdiction of the towns. These fueros and cartas pueblos conceded a range of privileges (*privilegios*), exemptions (exenciónes or *franquezas*), and freedoms (*libertades*).[8] The fueros were upheld by the *Cortes* (parliaments) and represented a constitutional arrangement. This meant that the Iberian Peninsula could be described as a commonwealth of city-states.[9] The fueros granted the cities a degree of autonomy. This autonomy included the freedom of self-taxation. The cities and surrounding countryside were obligated to pay a direct tax (*servicio*) to the crown, but the towns, represented by the *procuradores* of the Cortes, were able to negotiate the terms of this taxation. As many individuals, and sometimes whole towns, had been granted tax exemption, the tax burden often fell to those in the countryside who could least afford it.[10] In order to finance expansion, the Crown effectively pawned part of its sovereignty by granting to the towns the power to negotiate the terms of taxation, and this reinforced existing inequalities.

The transactions of grants of sovereign privileges in exchange for political and economic support continued long after the conquest of Muslim territories. During this period, the Crown consolidated its power by pawning its sovereignty. The Trastamara dynastic control of Castile began with the reign of Enrique II (1369–79) who issued grants of royal towns, including royal jurisdiction and powers of taxation (except royal taxation), to supporters. These *mercedes Enriqueñas* were permanent, and as Helen Nader summarises, 'transferred sovereignty in perpetuity as a hereditary, private possession to the lords'.[11] Dispute over these privileges led to civil war. The first claims of absolutism came in to justify these grants.[12] Isabel inherited the Crown of Castile during the civil war caused by the disputes over privileges, but this didn't deter her from continuing this strategy of selling sovereign privilege. In 1495 Isabel began selling the cities the privilege of collecting their own taxes, *encabezamiento*. In royal and seignorial towns, the royal treasury sold tax farming (*arrendamiento*) contracts to the highest bidder, which resulted in higher taxation.[13] *Encabezamiento* enabled towns to collect tax themselves or sell tax collecting contracts.

The sale of tax exemption and tax collection was important to the fiscal strategy of the Spanish imperial state. This strategy created short-term fiscal liquidity but long-term political compromises for the Crown. At the end of the Middle Ages the Spanish imperial state was a patchwork of privilege. The differentiations of status were reflected in the tax codes, and to raise new revenues the Crown had to negotiate with the Cortes. The Cortes would grant new taxes, but they expected returns for this taxation and respect for due procedure. When the young Charles of Habsburg (1500–58), Duke of Burgundy, Lord of the Netherlands, and heir to the Holy Roman Empire, inherited the Spanish imperial state in 1516, he would learn the hard way that the sovereign power of taxation was bound in a contractual system of reciprocal obligations. Taxes could be collected – but in return for upholding the justice which respected the variated landscape of status.

Sixteenth-century transformations: The *comunero* tax revolt, causes and consequences

In 1517 Charles V landed in Spain for the first time and in 1518 he asked the *procuradores* of the Cortes for money.[14] But Charles V was entering a difficult world. He had inherited the Spanish Crown in 1516 even though he had never been to Spain and his mother, Joanna of Castile, known as Juana la Loca (Joanna the Mad), was still alive. When the Cortes first met in 1518 in Valladolid they initially did not recognise him as king. Despite inheritance disputes, the Cortes recognised Charles V as King of Castile and Leon as he promised to defend Spain,[15] while the Cortes of Aragon recognised Charles as joint ruler with his mother. The Cortes granted funds but made it clear that the Crown had obligations in exchange for taxation. Charles V swore an oath to uphold law,[16] and his spokesperson, Pedro Ruiz de la Mota, presented Charles as committed to protecting the liberties of the cities.[17] The *procuradores* were clear in their petitions that they would grant taxation but the king had to uphold justice.[18]

Following the model of sovereignty that had developed in the Iberian Peninsula in the Middle Ages, the king had to provide justice in return for taxation. The *procuradores* asked the Crown for reforms, especially in the process and distribution of justice. Among other things, the representatives of the Cortes wanted the Crown to help with assistance to the poor and give tax exemption for those struck by epidemics and famines.[19] The towns expected justice and welfare for their taxation. The chronicler Sandoval reported that the rebels asked that the king look out for the common good of all (*bien comun de todos*).[20]

The Crown did not take action to implement the reforms requested by the Cortes in exchange for taxation in 1518, and when Charles tried to raise more revenue in 1520 he met with resistance. People in Spain did not want to fund foreign wars, or what they saw as Charles's private costs for the elections for Holy Roman Emperor, as they wanted to see returns for their taxation. In 1520 Charles had created enemies amongst people from across different statuses by trying to change the tax code to end *encabezamiento* (the towns' privileges of self-taxation) and to the tax exemptions of the hidalgos. When, in 1520, Charles's chancellor, Mercurino Gattinara, summoned the Castilian Cortes to give more taxes, the uprising known as the *comunero* revolt, or war of the communities, began. Charles resorted to bribery to pass demands for taxation in the Cortes of Santiago de Compostela. As the Cortes wanted their issues discussed, he temporarily suspended them. He reconvened them to pass a new tax in the Cortes of Corunna. The revolt broke out in Toledo, where some on the city council tried to pass the approval for new Crown taxation by sending away opponents. Instead a crowd assembled and drove out those prepared to pass the new taxation. The revolt was not a class war but included rich and poor. The revolt was led by, amongst others, Juan de Padilla, who was an urban elite opposed to the threat to his tax-exempt status. The conflict escalated to military confrontation in Segovia, and unrest spread to other cities.

The rebels established their own Cortes, the *Santa Junta de las Comunidades* (Holy Assembly of the Communities), later renamed as the *Cortes y Junta General del Reino* (General Assembly of the Kingdom) as an alternative government to represent the autonomy of the cities.

In 1520 the Junta issued a manifesto and a petition articulating the grievances of the comuneros, indicating that sovereignty comes from upholding the public good. The 1520 demands of the comuneros indicated the importance of justice: they stated that the king should not decide the *corregidores* (district magistrates) but rather that these should be elected from each city and town, that both nobles and commoners should be elected, and that certain office holders should have a minimum age.[21] The demands of the comuneros also indicated concern for the public good and welfare of the people, stating that the Crown could not export the key foodstuffs of bread and meat without the permission of the Cortes.[22] The demands of the comuneros made clear that the Crown had to uphold justice. The Crown had also tried to increase the taxation of the Church, and consequently many religious personnel supported the rebels. One letter reminded the king that 'he was chosen to rule and govern in peace and justice'.[23]

The comuneros were ultimately defeated in the battle that took place near Villalar in 1521, but this was not simply a victory of the Crown or an indicator of the absolute power of the Spanish imperial state. Charles had learned valuable lessons about the moral economy of his Iberian inheritance, and that the expectations of the Crown to uphold distributive justice and welfare in return for sovereign rights to taxation were more than rhetoric. Following the resolution of the comunero revolt, Charles needed to innovate to standardise revenues for imperial state projects.

Charles set about a programme of institutional reform and fiscal innovation, led by Juan Tavera (1472–1545), who was president of the council of Castile from 1524 to 1539. In 1536 Charles began his own sale to the towns of the authority to collect their own taxation (*encabezamiento*). Despite the difficulties in levying new taxes, according to Mauricio Drelichman, 'by the end of the sixteenth century, Castile has managed to increase its tax revenues and fiscal pressure to levels far above those of competing powers'. Tavera's reforms regularised Charles's taxation revenues, but Tavera also warned Charles about the dangers of overtaxing, especially the poorest in society, and especially during periods of famine and epidemic, such as during the bad harvest of 1530/1.[24]

The Crown could raise taxation but had to demonstrate accountability and the provision of distributive justice. One result of the comunero revolt was that Crown needed to demonstrate its obligations to the people, and especially its obligation to uphold law and justice in exchange for taxation. In 1522, in order to restore order in the wake of the comunero revolt, the

Crown confirmed municipal autonomy, especially their power to tax themselves. The people expected law and justice to be upheld for the price of their taxation. This justice included socio-economic justice and the maintenance of their welfare. In 1523 the Crown granted a significant *merced* for the Cortes: the right to address petitions and grievances before discussing subsidy amounts. This concession was a reminder that the Crown's sovereignty was contractual and dependent upon upholding the moral economy. Espinosa reports that 'from 1523 to 1533, the *procuradores* calculated the amount of subsidies on the basis of Charles's implementation of their petitions',[25] and that 'most of the demands that followed pertained to the economic welfare of the nation and the royal patrimony.'[26]

Charles V recognised that providing justice and welfare was important to the legitimacy of his sovereignty, and the comunero revolt had taught Charles that this was more than rhetorical. Charles engaged in his own programme of welfare reform. He took interest in the debates on new systems of poor relief and the programme implemented in Ypres in 1525. In 1526, one year after the trial of the Ypres scheme, the Valencian humanist Juan Luis Vives wrote *De Subventione Pauperum* whilst living in Bruges (published in 1530), which extended the case for the increased regulation of the lives of the poor and systems of charity. Charles requested a copy of Vives's *De Subventione Pauperum* and used this as a basis for his poverty legislation. In 1531 Charles sanctioned charitable reform in the Netherlands, including the ban on begging and the attempt to create a Common Fund for poor relief. Back in Spain, Charles listened and responded to the petitions of the *procuradores* of the Cortes about the problem of poverty and the number of poor in the cities. For example, in 1534 they asked that a new office be established to license the begging of the poor. Charles issued a new poor law which gave the *corregidores*, *justicias*, and *alcaldes* of the *Cortes* the power to prosecute the wandering poor, so that the poor of one place, who were not able to wander, were provided for,[27] and stipulated that in addition to the *alcaldes de corte*, the mayors of the court, and the *justicias*, two good people should be deputies to take care of the administration of the poor in accordance with the new poor laws.[28] Charles issued a further substantial piece of poverty legislation in 1540, creating the position of 'Fathers of the Poor' (*padres de pobres*) in every town and proposing that beggars be provided for in institutions. The 1540 poor law also instructed cities and towns to ensure that the so-called shame-faced poor (*envergonzantes*), those for whom poverty was against their socio-economic status, were provided for.

Charles's welfare reforms responded to the *procuradores*' petitions and the fears they expressed over migration, the rise of urban poverty, and increased pressure from 'outsiders' on existing welfare provision. Charles's response, influenced by the work of Vives, was to find ways of limiting welfare to people who could prove their '*naturaleza*', or citizenship status.[29] For example, Book VII, Chapter XXXIX, Law I of the *Novísima recopilación* ruled that the poor should not wander about but only solicit alms in their own '*naturaleza*'.[30] As Tamar Herzog has shown, this emphasis on linking people to categories of *naturaleza* and also *vecinidad* were important to the project of constructing a community of natives in the kingdoms of Spain, which was part of Spain's project of nation building.[31] Citizenship came to matter for welfare provision, and it was driven by the complaints of the *procuradores* of the Cortes who were the ones who negotiated taxes with the Crown.

Taxation and inequality: Sixteenth-century foundations of colonial Latin America

As in the Iberian Peninsula, the Spanish imperial state expanded in the New World via contracts (*asientos*, or *capitulaciones*) and licences (*licencias*). These contracts set out a mixed financial model of public–private partnerships. Many conquistadors funded expenses privately in return for a share of the future public revenue from conquered lands. For example, in 1529 Charles V issued an *asiento* to Hernán Cortés for the 'discovery and conquest of the islands and mainlands of the ocean sea'. The Crown granted privileges to Cortés to compensate the costs he had incurred in making conquests in the name of the Crown, but also reserved supreme jurisdiction.[32] The Crown underlined its political authority as the font of justice, but conceded potential economic revenue to finance the expansion.

The Crown claimed a significant share, known as the '*quinto real*' (royal fifth) of the spoils of war and any high-value goods such as gold, silver, and pearls. Conquistadors invoked the sovereign's obligation to uphold justice and the common good in order to negotiate privileges, including political authority. In 1519, during his power struggle with rival conquistador Diego Valazquez, Hernán Cortés wrote to Charles V:

> having thus completed our business and being all together in our council, we decided to write to Your Majesties and send You all the gold, silver and jewels which we have obtained in the land, over and above the fifth which belongs to Your Royal revenues by law, for we decided that by sending You all the first spoils from these land, and in keeping nothing for ourselves, we should serve Your Royal Highness and demonstrate the very great satisfaction we have in Your service, as we have shown before by venturing our persons and possessions ... And in the name of this town and council beg Your Royal Highnesses to favour us with certain things necessary for the service of God and Your Majesties and from the common and public good of this town.[33]

Cortés offered the king more than the obligatory royal fifth, but he expected in return more political power and more resources to uphold the public good on the Crown's behalf.

The colonisation of the Americas was organised via contracts between the Crown and private individuals, the *caudillos*, or leading conquistadors. This public–private partnership pathway to imperial state formation was similar to the mechanism of expansion into Muslim territories in the Iberian Peninsula in the Middle Ages. Private conquistadors were rewarded for their role in conquering the Americas on behalf of the Crown with leases of the right to extract goods and labour from indigenous people. The first of these systems was the *encomienda*, from *encomendar*, meaning to entrust. *Encomienda* contracts leased Amerindian labour to *encomenderos* as a kind of tribute. *Encomenderos* did not own the land and they could not be bought, sold, or inherited. There were laws against enslaving the Amerindians, but the conditions of the *encomiendas* were often little different from slavery. The Crown had not made encomienda grants permanent as it wanted to avoid the construction of feudal fiefdoms and the kind of entrenched privilege that would undermine its authority. The Crown used concern for the welfare of the Amerindians, based on denunciations made by Bartolomé de Las Casas and others, to limit the legislatation against encomiendas and restrict the power of the encomenderos.

In 1542 the Crown passed the New Laws of the Indies which aimed to end the abuse of the Amerindians and to bring about the end of the *encomienda* system. Article 10 declared: 'the Indians are free persons and vassals of the Crown, and it has always been the royal purpose to have them treated as such. The Council of the Indies is therefore commanded to see to the execution of the laws for their benefit and protection.'[34] The Crown asserted itself as the ultimate distributor of justice to the Amerindians, ruling that lawsuits involving Indians no longer be tried in the Indies, or by the Council of the Indies, but must be pleaded before the King himself.[35] Claiming authority as the protector of the Amerindians, the Crown limited the scale and scope of encomiendas, preventing the power of *encomenderos* from becoming entrenched. The New Laws ruled: 'All Indians held in *encomienda* by the viceroys, by their lieutenants, royal officers, prelates, monasteries, hospitals, religious houses, mints, the treasury, etc., are to be transferred forthwith to the Crown', and 'those *encomenderos* who have mistreated their Indians are to lose their *encomiendas*, which will be placed in the Crown'.[36] In the New Laws of 1542 the Crown used the sovereign principles of justice and welfare to expand its own authority and limit that of the encomenderos. The New Laws were not intended as an end to Amerindian tributes. Article 42 ruled: 'the tributes of newly discovered Indians are to be fairly assessed and delivered to the royal treasurer'.[37] The discourse of fairness was important to constructing the legitimacy of the continuation of the tribute system. The New Laws also tried to show fairness to the conquistadors, and ruled that those without *encomienda* should be provided for by the other tributes that Amerindians outside *encomiendas* provided.[38]

The New Laws established another form of appropriation of Amerindian labour, that of *repartimiento*, a term derived from *repartir*, 'to allot or distribute'. In theory, *repartimiento* labour was supposed to be used for public works projects, or forms of production essential to public welfare.[39] In reality, of course, it was used to build the imperial infrastructure; the system was open to abuse and *repartimiento* labour could be leased to various private projects. Technically, private labour drafts were classed as *servicio personal*, but in reality *repartimiento* contracts were abused. Labour framed as for the public good was often in private interest. The oppressive labour tributes of *encomienda* and *repartimiento* indicated that the Amerindians were treated differently from Spanish settlers, creating a new form of proto-racial inequality, but despite this difference Amerindians were also recognised as Crown subjects.[40]

The Spanish Crown officially recognised the indigenous property and patterns of land tenure. Even during attempts to resettle indigenous communities into civic and religious *congregaciónes*, Amerindians still technically retained their landholdings and reverted to them when *congregaciónes* broke down.[41] Recognising Amerindian landholdings and allowing continued agricultural and artisanal production was of benefit to the Crown in the establishment of the imperial state as it could tax this production and help feed the expanding population of Spanish settlers. Many Iberians saw their movement across the Atlantic as a way to change their status, and although many had been farmers in Spain, few wanted to return to the manual labour of the fields. This helped construct the newly emerging proto-racial inequality between Amerindians and Spanish settlers. It also placed pressure on food systems, especially as Amerindian populations were declining as a result of diseases brought by the Spanish and the excessive demands of the *encomienda* and *repartimiento* systems.

Recognising Amerindian property gave the Crown the advantage of being able to tax it. In New Spain as in Spain, head towns (*cabaceras*) collected the head tax from heads of households in subject towns (*sujetos*). In some areas Amerindians were allowed to pay their tributes in maize, to ensure the continuation of local food production, but in other areas they were asked to pay it in wheat. In this case Amerindians could shift production, or buy it from elsewhere to meet the payments as many did not want to turn their agricultural land to wheat production.[42] Whereas in the Iberian Peninsula Castilian peasants met the Crown's tax bill, in the Americas the declining Amerindian population could not keep pace with the growing food demands of the Spanish. Population data for the tax bill was often overestimated, often intentionally, resulting in increasing tax demands falling on fewer and increasingly poorer subjects,[43] and this resulted in petitions from *sujetos* for autonomy.

The Amerindian tribute system reinforced and deepened patterns of inequality in the New World, just as the tax system had in the Old. Pre-conquest Amerindian communities were stratified and socio-economic hierarchies tended to survive conquest, even as indigenous communities overall became poorer. Wealthier Amerindians (the *caciques*, or lords) might be able to buy their way out of labour extraction while poorer groups (*macehuales*, or commoners) that could not make any payments in kind might have to work more, leading to the neglect of their own lands and deepening their poverty.[44] As in the Iberian Peninsula, different people were taxed differently. Amerindians with lord status or certain office holders could be exempt from direct taxation (tribute). As Adrian Masters summarises, 'through grace (*gracia*) petitions which established an array of special privileges for crown loyalists and virtuous vassals, some ethnicities and political confederations also managed to carve out a status somehow different from their neighbors, distinguishing Indians from other Indians'.[45] The continuation of pre-conquest status inequalities varied by region. *Cacicazgos* (estates of indigenous lords) persisted into the colonial era, but perhaps most strongly in the region of Oaxaca.[46] In the seventeenth century the Crown confirmed in law that these indigenous lordships should be hereditary and not appointed.[47]

Welfare and inequalities across the Spanish imperial state

Taxation was not a one-way street and monarchs needed to be seen to be offering returns in the form of protection but also justice and welfare. From the twelfth century, the translation and reception of classical texts impacted on the history of political thought in Europe. Important amongst these was Aristotle, who had written that good government should promote justice and well-being.[48] Aristotle defined a king as someone who cares for his subjects 'with a view to their well-being, as a shepherd does his sheep'.[49] This pastoral metaphor was also important in Christianity: the Gospel of John described all the people of the world as one flock in need of one shepherd to care for them, '*unum ovile et unus pastor*' (John 10:16). Scholastic thinkers such as Thomas of Aquinas established the place for Aristotelian thought within Christian moral philosophy in the thirteenth century, and these ideas influenced the neo-Scholastic and neo-Thomist trends in political thought that were important in the Iberian world in the sixteenth century.

While commutative justice was important to criminal law (as all should be punished equally for mortal sins such as homicide), distributive justice was important to welfare (as different people needed maintaining in different conditions in society according to their status).

The provision of welfare was important to sovereignty and the stability of the political community before the development of the welfare state (and the comunero revolt had taught Charles V that this was more than rhetorical). The Crown provided welfare in a variety of ways. One of these we have met before, the *merced*. The merced was the reward that could be given for military service, but was also given to lawyers and clergy and was one of the ways the Crown bought loyalty. These rewards, which were issued according to the recipient's status in society, were seen as a matter of justice. As Espinosa summarised, 'medieval Spanish kings believed that, by granting *mercedes*, they fulfilled their obligations as the fount of justice'.[50] As the Crown was seen as the ultimate protector and provider of justice, subjects were able to write petitions on a range of issues. In response to *gracia* petitions the Crown issued privileges, which, as Adrian Masters summarises, 'included grants of Indian tribute, pensions, preeminences, pardons, crown offices, and other royal prerogatives'.[51] In these petitions people could claim poverty according to their relative status and could be granted resources. The Crown also managed the payment of alms (*limosnas*) on an ad hoc basis, often in response to petitions. In addition to payments to individuals, the Crown funded welfare institutions, namely royal hospitals, but there were numerous attempts to make these institutions self-funding rather than a drain on the public purse. In the remainder of this chapter, I will indicate ways in which the Crown used imperial revenue to fund this welfare and how the welfare regime of the Spanish imperial state tended to reinforce inequalities of status.

The Crown used some of its imperial revenues to fund its welfare obligations. It funded pensions for men who had given military service to the Spanish Empire, their widows, and other Crown dependents. Murdo J. Macleod reports that by the end of the sixteenth century much of the tributary revenue from the Americas went to fund 'a pension system with many of the awards going to the widows and other dependants of poverty-stricken *benemeritos*, or to court retainers in Madrid who seldom if ever saw the Indies, far less the Indians "entrusted" to them'.[52]

Pensions are a common form of welfare payment. Throughout the pre-modern period the Crown issued pensions on an ad hoc basis, to military officers and other types of elites. Widows or heirs could benefit from these pensions, which were important to upholding relative status in society. The mariner Juan Sebastián Elcano, who had led the circumnavigation of the world after the death of Fernand Magellan, was granted a pension by the Crown of 500 gold ducats a year, and his heirs launched a court case after his death for access to this pension.[53] The relatives of Amerindian elites could also write to the Crown regarding pensions according to their status. For example, in 1569 Don Pedro de Moctezuma, the son of the former Aztec emperor, wrote to the Crown regarding an annual pension of 3,000 pesos.[54] Imperial funds could be used to make pension-style payments to elites and those with particular status, such as prominent members of religious orders, on both sides of the Atlantic. Not all the costs of those in need of pensions were met directly by the Crown; instead, imperial institutions, such as the Council of the Indies, could order private individuals to make pensions to orphans and widows to whom they were related. For example, in 1531 the Council of the Indies mandated that Francisco de Arteaga, a merchant, provide for the daughter of Juan de Ribera from the funds he received from a bond left by her deceased father.[55] Pensions did not begin to become a formal state system open to a cross-section of the population until the eighteenth century. In 1761 the Bourbon monarch Charles III created the *Monte Pío Militar*, a pension system for the families of military offices according to their rank and status.[56]

The Crown used imperial revenues to make ad hoc charitable payments (*limosnas*). For example, in 1531 the Crown issued a royal decree to the officers of the House of Trade and other justices of the kingdoms to pay Fray Francisco de Arévalo (Order of the Holy Trinity) an annual payment of 25,000 *maravedis* to cover his debts and support his mother.[57] Again the Crown did not always simply grant alms directly, but approved licences for people to go to the Americas and beg there for funds for their religious and charitable institutions.[58] The Crown did not only grant alms payments of cash to individuals and charitable institutions but certain other goods of empire. For example, it issued Royal Decrees to the House of Trade to give '*palo santo de guayacán*', a type of wood from the Americas with medicinal properties, to certain hospitals – for example, in 1531 to the plague hospital in Seville.[59] Such hospitals emerged to serve rich and poor alike, but increasingly in early modern Spain and the Americas there were specific hospitals for particular status groups.

The Crown saw that the welfare infrastructure of hospitals was extended to the New World. Early in the conquest, the Crown ordered viceroys, audiencias, and governors to establish hospitals.[60] The Crown was particularly keen to establish hospitals for the newly colonised indigenous population, and these institutions were intended as much to govern as to care. Amerindians themselves were expected to contribute to the cost of these welfare institutions and they were subject to a particular tax, the *tomín de hospital*, to fund the construction of indigenous hospitals. Ramos argues: 'thus in the New World changes were introduced which in Spain at the time would have been impractical or even inconceivable: that alms would come mainly out of the pockets of the poor'.[61] Thus the indigenous people were taxed in order to pay for welfare institutions which were also sites of colonial governance. The revenue sloshing through these colonial institutions attracted corruption as those charged with administering the hospitals often used them to supplement private wealth.[62] Indigenous people were not unaware of that such welfare institutions could be sites of corruption and control and they also tried to resist the construction of new hospitals or the payment of the *tomín* tax.

The Crown recognised the people of the Americas as subjects, and as such they could also petition the Crown for privileges and alms according to their status. In the 1542 New Laws of the Indies Charles ordered that Amerindians should petition directly on matters of justice, underlining the way in which this distribution served to reinforce the sovereign's position as the provider of justice in the imperial context. As with other imperial provisions, the Crown wanted to give the Amerindians access to justice, but in a way that was self-funding. Again, the Amerindians were taxed to pay for this imperial infrastructure that was meant to serve their needs. The *holpatan* tax was intended to support indigenous courts, and the *comunidades* tax was intended for community expenses.

When the Spanish imperial extended into the Americas, the landscape of status and the significance of place of origin became more complex. Status was no longer determined by socio-economic indicators of lordship and commoners. Proto-racial signifiers such as *negro/a*, *blanco/a*, *indio/a*, *mestizo/a* came to matter. All these people were subjects, and taxpayers, and used these categories when they made petitions to Crown regarding matters of justice and welfare. Amongst other things, Amerindians petitioned the Crown to complain about abuses of *encomienda* and *repartimiento*, to complain that they were being overtaxed, and to have their lordship status or lands recognised. Through these petitions for justice and welfare the unequal landscape of status was reinforced.

Conclusion

Sovereigns were obliged to provide justice and welfare in return for taxation. While the poor could not be left without basic necessities (or taxed into dire poverty), this distribution of justice and welfare could enforce the status inequalities that were hardened by particular taxation regimes. In Europe, nobles could claim mercies and privileges befitting their status. When the Spanish imperial state expanded to the New World, status inequalities within indigenous societies were recognised and upheld by the

Crown. As in Europe, indigenous nobles could claim certain privileges. The collision of the Old World and the New also forged new imperial inequalities. In the Old World in the sixteenth century the poor were already increasingly differentiated into categories of deserving and undeserving. With the collision of the Old World and the New, proto-racial categories which had already been important in the Old World added new layers to the imperial inequality nexus. Taxation and welfare helped code the imperial inequality relationship.

This chapter has focused on the reign of Charles V; his successor, Philip II, inherited an imperial state that was in many ways more politically stable but more fiscally volatile. Philip II engaged in both ambitious revenue raising and welfare reforms. By the reign of Philip II, rising economic inequality stretched historic status inequality at the same time as global expansion added new layers. Philip II issued his own poor laws to enshrine these inequalities, including, in 1568, forbidding Spanish vagabonds to live amongst Amerindians,[63] as Spaniards should not seem poor in relation to the Amerindians. Philip II also commissioned more royal hospitals to stabilise the landscape of inequality. While the structure of inequality changed as the imperial state expanded, taxation and welfare continued to be important instruments for the creation and maintenance of the Spanish imperial state.

Notes

1 Jane Burbank and Frederick Cooper, *Empires in World History and the Politics of Difference* (Princeton, NJ: Princeton University Press, 2010), p. 8.
2 *Ibid.*, p. 8.
3 J. H. Elliott coined the term 'composite monarchy'; see 'A Europe of composite monarchies', *Past & Present* 137 (1992), 48–71.
4 A. Domíngo Ortiz, *The Golden Age of Spain 1516–1659*, trans. J. Casey (London: Weidenfeld & Nicolson, 1971), pp. 108–9.
5 See Carla Rahn Phillips, *Ciudad Real, 1500–1750: Growth, Crisis and Readjustment in the Spanish Economy* (Cambridge, MA: Harvard University Press, 1979).
6 Geoffrey Parker, 'War and economic change: The economic costs of the Dutch', in Geoffrey Parker (ed.), *Spain and the Netherlands, 1559–1659: Ten Studies* (Glasgow, 1979), p. 188, cited in Dennis O Flynn, 'Fiscal crisis and the decline of Spain (Castile)', *Journal of Economic History* 42.1 (1982), 139–47, p. 145.
7 David Vassberg, *Land and Society in Golden Age Castile* (Cambridge: Cambridge University Press, 1984), p. 219.
8 For example, in the twelfth century, Alfonso VII conceded freedom and immunity from all tribute ('*liberas et immunes ab omni tributo*') to clergy of Toledo,

and the exemption of knights and military orders of Toledo from royal tax; see Tomás Muñoz y Romero (ed.), *Colección de fueros municipales y cartas pueblas de los reinos de Castilla, León, Corona de Aragón y Navarra* (Madrid: Imprenta de Don José María Alonso, 1847), pp. 370, 384–5.
9 See Helen Nader, *Liberty in Absolutist Spain: the Habsburg Sale of Towns, 1516–1700* (Baltimore, MD: Johns Hopkins University Press, 1990), p. 72.
10 Helen Nader has shown how this drove the desire to buy town status; see Nader, *Liberty in Absolutist Spain*, p. 194.
11 Nader, *Liberty in Absolutist Spain*, 78.
12 See J. B. Owens, '*By my absolute royal authority': Justice and the Castilian Commonwealth at the Beginning of the First Global Age* (Rochester, NY: University of Rochester Press; Woodbridge: Boydell & Brewer, 2005).
13 Nader, *Liberty in Absolutist Spain*, p. 195.
14 AGS, *Patronato Real*, leg. 7, fol. 158, Feb. 1518, cited in Auerlio Espinosa, *The Empire of the Cities: Emperor Charles V, the Comunero Revolt, and the Transformation of the Spanish System* (Leiden: Brill, 2008), p. 46.
15 *Colección de documentos inéditos para la historia de España* (CODOIN), 2: 334, 'juramento de Carlos', cited in Espinosa, *The Empire of the Cities*, p. 53.
16 *Cortes de los antiguos reinos de León y Castilla* (CLC), 4:260–3; Sandoval, *Historia del emperador*, 80:125; Juan Ginés de Sepúlveda, *Obras completas: Historia de Carlos V*, bilingual edition by E. Rodríguez Peregrina (Pozoblanco: Ayuntamiento de Pozoblanco, 1995; 1780), p. 39 [lib. 2, 8], cited in Espinosa, *The Empire of the Cities*, p. 53.
17 'Proposición leída el 9 de febrero por el señor don Pedro Ruiz de la Mota en las Cortes de Valladolid 1518', AGS, *Patronato Real*, Cortes, leg. 8, fol. 1, cited in Espinosa, *The Empire of the Cities*, p. 54.
18 For example, Petition 28, Sandoval, *Historia del emperador*, 80:130; CLC, 4, 1520 Cortes, cited in Espinosa, *The Empire of the Cities*, p. 54.
19 Sandoval, *Historia del emperador*, 80: c. 120–30, 1520 Cortes cited in Espinosa, The *Empire of the Cities*, p. 55.
20 Prudencio de Sandoval, *Historia del Emperador Carlos V, rey de España* (Madrid, P. Madoz y L. Sagasti, 1846), vol. II, p. 20.
21 'Capitulos de lo que ordenaban de pedir los de la junta', in Martín Fernández Navarrete, *Colección de documentos inéditos para la historia de España*, vol. 1 (Madrid, 1842), pp. 272–83; for the original document see AGS, PTR, LEG,3,DOC.137.
22 *Ibid*.
23 'Carta de un religiosos sobre estos movimientos', Sandoval, vol. II., pp. 105–16, 109.
24 Tavera to Charles, 28 July 1532, AGS, Estado, leg. 24, fol. 184. Aurelio Espinosa, 'The Spanish Reformation: Institutional reform, taxation, and the secularization of ecclesiastical properties under Charles V', *The Sixteenth Century Journal* 37.1 (2006), 3–24, p. 20.
25 *Ibid*., p. 9.
26 Espinosa, *The Empire of the Cities*, p. 113.

27 *Novísima recopilación de las leyes de España* (first printed 1805 and 1806) (Madrid: Boletín Oficial del Estado, 1993), Libro VII, titutlo XXXIX, Law I, 703.
28 *Novísima recopilación*, Libro VII, Law XIII of titutlo XXXIX.
29 Tamar Herzog, *Defining Nations, Immigrants and Citizens in Early Modern Spain and Spanish America* (New Haven, CT: Yale University Press, 2003).
30 Libro VII, Titulo XXXIX 'del Socorro y recogimiento de los pobres', law 1, *Novísima recopilación*.
31 Herzog, *Defining Nations*.
32 'Asiento hecho por el emperador Carlos V, ó sea por la emperatriz en su nombre, con el Marques del Valle sobre el descubrimiento y conquista de las islas y tierra firme del mar oceano', 27 Oct 1529, *Colección de documentos inéditos para la historia de España*, vol. 1 (Madrid: Academia de la Historia, 1848), pp. 108–10.
33 Hernán Cortés, First Letter from Mexico, in *Hernan Cortes: Letters from Mexico*, ed. and trans. Anthony Pagden (New Haven, CT: Yale University Press, 1986), pp. 3–46, p. 28.
34 Article 10, New Laws of the Indies, 1542, cited in Lesley Byrd Simpson, *The Encomienda in New Spain: The Beginning of Spanish Mexico* (Berkeley: University of California Press, 1950, ACLS Humanities E-Book XML edition 2008), p. 129.
35 Article 38, New Laws of the Indies, in Simpson, *The Encomienda in New Spain*, p. 131.
36 Articles 21 and 33, New Laws of the Indies, in Simpson, *The Encomienda in New Spain*, p. 130.
37 Cited in Simpson, *The Encomienda in New Spain*, p. 131.
38 Article 46, New Laws of the Indies, in Simpson, *The Encomienda in New Spain*, p. 131.
39 Murdo J. Macleod, 'Aspects of the internal economy of colonial Spanish America', in *The Cambridge History of Latin America* (Cambridge: Cambridge University Press, 1984), p. 225.
40 In 1501 Queen Isabel of Castile declared that the Amerindians were her subjects and vassals, and consequently could not be enslaved or treated differently from the subjects of Castile.
41 William B. Taylor, *Landlords and Peasants in Colonial Oaxaca* (Stanford, CA: Stanford University Press, 1972), pp. 26–7.
42 Taylor, *Landlords and Peasants*, pp. 4–5.
43 Susan Kellog reports that testamentary evidence indicates that indigenous people in Mexico City got steadily poorer, having fewer moveable goods to bequeath. See Susan Kellogg, *Law and the Transformation of Aztec Culture, 1500–1700* (Norman: University of Oklahoma Press, 1995), pp. 149–50.
44 Macleod, 'Aspects of the internal economy', p. 227.
45 Adrian Masters, 'The two, the one, the many, the none: Rethinking the republics of Spaniards and Indians in the sixteenth-century Spanish Indies', *The Americas* 78.1 (2001), 3–36, p. 29.
46 Taylor, *Landlords and Peasants*.

47 Taylor, *Landlords and Peasants*, note 4, p. 234.
48 Aristotle, *The Nichomachean Ethics*, trans. David Ross, revised with an introduction and notes by Lesley Brown (Oxford: Oxford University Press, 1980, paperback reprint 2009), p. 156.
49 Aristotle, *Nichomachean Ethics*, p. 156.
50 See Aurelio Espinosa, 'Merced', in Joel Mokyr (ed.), *The Oxford Encyclopedia of Economic History*, 5 vols (New York: Oxford University Press, 2003), vol. 3, pp. 485–6.
51 Adrian Masters, 'A thousand invisible architects: Vassals, the petition and response system, and the creation of Spanish Imperial Caste Legislation', *Hispanic American Historical Review* 98.3 (2018), 377–406, p. 382.
52 Macleod, 'Aspects of the internal economy', p. 223.
53 Archivo General de Indias (AGI), PATRONATO, 38, R. 1.
54 AGI, PATRONATO, 245, R. 4.
55 AGI, INDIFERENTE, 422, L. 15, F. 11R–11V.
56 MPM Constitution (1761) *Reglamento de la fundacion y establecimiento del Monte de Piedad que se instituye para socorro de las viudas de los oficiales militares* (Madrid: Imprenta D. Gabriel Ramírez), cited in Pablo Ortega-del-Cerro, 'The Spanish Monte Pío Militar: Institutional protection for the widows and other relatives of naval officers, 1730–1900', *Social Science History* 43 (2019), 813–33, p. 816.
57 AGI INDIFERENTE, 1961, L. 2, F. 99.
58 See Julia McClure, 'The charitable bonds of the Spanish Empire: The Casa de Contratación as an institution of charity', *New Global Studies* 12.2 (2018), 157–74.
59 AGI INDIFERENTE, 1961, L. 2, F. 88R–88V.
60 *Recopilación de leyes de los reinos de las Indias* [Compilation of the Laws of the Kingdoms of the Indies], 4 vols (Madrid: Cultura Hispánica, 1973), vol. 1: Tíitulo Cuarto, Ley Primera, cited in Gabriela Ramos, 'Indian hospitals and government in the colonial Andes', *Medical history* 57.2 (2013), 186–205, p. 190.
61 Ramos, 'Indian hospitals and government', p. 193.
62 *Ibid.*, p. 202.
63 'De los vagabundos y gitanos', *Recopilación de Leyes de las Indias* (Madrid: Impresor y Libero, 1841), Vol II, Book VII, tit. 4, Law I (Philip II, 1568, Felipe IV, 1628), p. 319.

7

Political economies of welfare of the Spanish Empire: Tax and charity for the Hospital de los Naturales of Potosí

Camille Sallé

Introduction

Who is obliged to finance welfare institutions and who can access poor relief services were economic and political issues to which early modern European states formulated various solutions. The operation of welfare systems and the role of charity in polities such as the Italian city-states or the British constitutional monarchy during the sixteenth and seventeenth centuries, a period of extensive debates about poor relief, are well known.[1] Recent research agendas invite us to explore, with different methodological options, the articulation between taxation and welfare arrangements in other kinds of polities, namely empires.[2] My contribution to this volume addresses these questions by focusing on the case of one hospital within the polycentric Spanish Empire and its associate tax regime, the *Hospital de Naturales* (Hospital of the Natives) of Potosí. This case provides good insights into how redistribution was designed in a hierarchised society in the early modern world.

Inequalities in the hierarchised old regime societies of early modern Europe were understood according to the idea of the naturalness of differences between individuals.[3] The mechanisms of redistribution embedded in charitable policies did not aim to transform the social order, but to align themselves with the principle of distributive justice.[4] For thinkers of the sixteenth and seventeenth centuries following the Scholastic tradition, distributive justice (*aequitas*) referred to the proper assignation of common goods by guaranteeing to each individual that which corresponded to their status.[5] Accordingly, authorities were willing to channel their charitable transactions by distinguishing between the receivers. Hospitals were one of the institutions mediating these charitable transactions across the early modern period.[6]

In the early modern Spanish Empire, charity, the protection of the poor, and especially the evangelisation and protection of Native American vassals were tools for the legitimation of the king's sovereignty.[7] Hospitals in the

New World, and especially the so-called 'royal hospitals', were one way of symbolising the relation of protection between the poor and the king, besides being a marker of Christian civilisation and providing the communities with spiritual and physical welfare.[8] During the decades after the conquest of the Inca Empire by the *conquistadores*, hospitals were funded by religious and civil authorities or individuals in the Spanish cities of the viceroyalty of Peru. From the 1570s, a set of reforms aimed to reinforce royal power against those of the *conquistadores* and the church. Hospitals were to be subsumed under the *Patronato Real* – the patronage of the king over the Church by papal agreement that allowed, at least in theory, the control of royal officials over religious institutions and their revenues. However, we still know little about how these hospitals were financed at that time. Who had to pay for charity in this corporate society structured by difference of status? By which channels were the resources necessary to secure the activities of an urban hospital to be extracted?

The mining city of Potosí (in present-day Bolivia) was a major site of extraction within the early modern Spanish Empire. It was also a longstanding site of attraction for a regional labour force from the viceroyalty of Peru. Because of the impact of its silver production for the Spanish monarchy and at global scale, it has been considered by various historians as a worthy case for considering the rise of global capitalism.[9] However, the welfare policies developed in such a context remain little studied. Whereas in Castile, during the sixteenth century, charitable institutions remained mainly financed by alms and loans, in 1575 the higher royal authority in Peru, the viceroy Francisco de Toledo (1569–81), established a new tax to support the *Hospital de Naturales* of Potosí, called the *medio peso del hospital*.[10] Thanks to an increasing number of studies, we have now a better understanding of how taxes worked in the colonial regime of the viceroyalty of Peru.[11] Depending on their status, Spanish, Afro-descendant, *mestizo*, or indigenous colonial subjects were subject to different levies, such as sales taxes and taxes on food (*alcabalas* and *sisa*), tithe, and tribute. Each one defined economic and social relations. Various historians have underlined that the relation between the king and this category of vassals was embedded in the tribute, which conveyed a 'colonial pact'.[12] At that time, for some jurists, the tribute represented the fair price that the native population had to pay for receiving the benefits of Spanish 'civilisation': evangelisation and security. Andeans had also to comply with other colonial obligations, such as labour services, but this depended on their rank, age, or gender. From 1575 to the 1630s, the *medio peso del hospital* intended for the Potosí hospital was another levy imposed upon the Andean workers in the mining city.

The sources by which to trace the history of this tax regime are heterogeneous, although, so far, we do not have the archives of the treasury which managed the tax, nor the hospital archive. We do, however, have access to legal texts, descriptions, and petitions of colonial subjects that allow us to sketch the political rationality of the viceroy's financial plan and its reception; the silences of the records, for example of the Royal Treasury accounts, also say something about the financial involvement of the agents of the Spanish Empire, in this case, of the king in the hospital's economy. However piecemeal this history is, it still provides good insights about how colonial taxation regimes were contested and negotiated by local populations, and contributes to our understanding of the historical relation between tax and welfare.

The first section of this chapter retraces the main features of the hospital's economy from its creation and describes the *medio peso* regime. The second section shows that this welfare policy was characterised by the plurality of the mechanisms of redistribution channelled by the very same institution. The third section discuss how the inscription of the principle of *aequitas* in this policy was challenged by the demographic dynamics of the early seventeenth century. The final section looks at some criticisms levelled both by Andeans and Spanish subjects, highlighting the controversial nature of this tax, and showing that during the seventeenth century tax was not the only way to finance welfare in the Spanish Empire.

A new tax for welfare: From private charity to the *medio peso del hospital*

The volatile demography of Potosí was characterised by the importance of its Andean population. Andeans flocked to the 4,000 metre altitude of Potosí on a voluntary or forced basis, in migrations, to work in the silver mines of the Cerro Rico.[13] Andean and transatlantic migrations turned this mining centre into one of the most populated human settlements of the viceroyalty. Estimated at 120,000 inhabitants in 1570, including the Euro-descendant and Afro-descendant population, this number rose to 160,000 in 1610, larger than Amsterdam (80,000), or London (130,000).[14] Whereas Lima, the capital of the viceroyalty, had at least two hospitals in the 1570s, one of *Indios* and one of *Españoles*, this was not the case in Potosí. The hospital of Vera Cruz, also designed as a '*hospital de los Naturales*' and administrated by the Municipal Council, was, from its creation in 1555 until 1609, the only hospital of the city.

The *Hospital de la Vera Cruz* originated from private charity. The necessary sums came from donations by Spaniards who rushed from various parts of the empire to the silver mountain of the Cerro Rico when Potosí was still no more than a mining settlement. The motivations of these benefactors were multiple. One reason may have been that because the hospital was designated as *'hospital de los Naturales'*, it was an adequate receptor for the Spaniards willing to align their charitable practices with the injunction to restitution. Restitution to the native Indians of the goods unjustly acquired during the conquest was promoted by the Dominicans and endorsed by royal officials.[15] Donations to hospitals, in their own terms, absolved Spaniards and helped them to escape royal justice. Thus, through this institution the Spanish miners performed a relation of charity with the Andean population who were the main agents of the discovery, extraction, and transformation of the silver.[16]

Soon after its foundation, the hospital became an object of negotiation between the *vecinos* (citizens) organised in *cabildo* (municipal council) and the king. Petitioning was a well-known practice of bargaining with the king for the corporate groups of the Spanish Empire and enabled them to build, from bottom up, the political space of the viceroyalty.[17] After the transformation of the settlement into an autonomous city, the Municipal Council sought to reclaim the patronage of the institution by putting forth the vecinos' agency in the foundation of the hospital, that is, their financial involvement. Meanwhile, the Municipality wrote petitions to the Council of the Indies repeatedly asking the king for subsidies to secure the resources of the hospital.[18] In spite of these municipal appeals, royal funding for the hospital remained ad hoc. For example, in 1563, the Royal Treasury delivered 600 pesos from the tributes of some *repartimientos* (a fiscal and administrative unit created by the colonial authorities), but the Royal Treasury's accounts did not register further regular subsidies the following years.[19] In the Spanish composite monarchy, economic capital and support were often given in exchange for political capital. In the case of Potosí's political economy of charity, the *vecinos*, through the evocation of their foundation of the hospital de los Naturales, could suggest that they were mediating the relation of protection between the king and his new Andean vassals, and could claim political power over the management of the hospital.

During the first decades of its existence, the hospital relied financially mainly on private donations. This economy was similar to many charitable institutions in Castile.[20] But this situation was also shaped by competition for financial resources between various institutions. In the viceroyalty of Peru, a part of the tithe was theoretically meant to be for the hospitals (*the noveno y medio*), according to the *Patronato Real*. Because the hospital of the neighbouring religious capital of La Plata secured this part of the ecclesiastical tax, Potosí's hospital had to rely on other sources of revenue. During the 1560s, the hospital possessed some land and some houses in the city, some rights to exploit mines in the Cerro, and had received various promises of donations.[21] In 1571, it gained a new source of income after obtaining plenary indulgences that were expected to promote donations.[22] Plans for the growth of the hospital were discussed by the Municipal Council, such as the building of a new room for Spanish patients and the recruitment of a Spanish female nurse, a surgeon, a barber, and a priest, which suggests the willingness to adapt the services to various categories of recipients of the growing city. At that time, the hospital seems to have suffered financial needs even if it is likely that the issue was rather the consistency of the rents. The main change in the charitable economy described above occurred in 1575, when in response to what was identified as a lack of secured funds, the viceroy Francisco de Toledo used his tax-raising powers to set up a new financial scheme for the hospital.

The government of the viceroy Francisco de Toledo (1569–81) was a turning point in the extractive economy of Potosí. Broadly, it marks the unprecedented involvement of the colonial state in the organisation of the tributary and labour system of the viceroyalty of Peru.[23] At the scale of the viceroyalty, Toledo promoted the process of *reducción*, the concentration of the indigenous population in colonial towns. The aim was to facilitate the levy of the tribute from men between eighteen and fifty years old of each *repartimiento de Indios*. Toledo then massively monetised the tribute, obliging indigenous people to sell their products or labour in exchange for money. One effect of this was to channel the labour force towards mining.[24] Meanwhile institutionalising this political and economic order, Toledo ordered that each tributary had to pay a *tomín* (one-eighth of a *peso*) reserved to the hospital de los Naturales of each *repartimiento*, collected by indigenous authorities *(caciques* and *alcaldes)*.[25] This type of taxation was not a common means to finance poor relief at that time in Castile.[26] It echoed, in the European debate about poor relief, the idea that communities should provide for their poor. This idea was put explicitly in the viceroy's ordinance to justify the new tax: 'It is fair *(justo)* that from them [the Natives] came the supply for the support of these hospitals, because in them they would be assisted and healed in their sicknesses'.[27]

However, in the case of Potosí, the viceroy ordered that not the *tomín* but the *medio peso del hospital* would be the means to provide for the city's *hospital de los Naturales*. The *medio peso del hospital* was, in theory, and like the tribute, a tax per capita of half a peso that had to be paid per year by the *mitayos*.[28] The *mita* was a compulsory paid-labour system with pre-Hispanic roots, which forced migration to Potosí of a percentage of the male indigenous tributaries of each *corregimientos* (provinces), the *mitayos*, for one year. These workers, accompanied by their families, came from a region that stretched some 800 miles north to south and 250 miles east to west between Cuzco and the southern border of present-day Bolivia. They were allocated to individual Spaniards who exploited the mines. The wages of these forced labourers were fixed at a rate below those paid to hired labourers. The Royal Treasury received an indirect profit from this system, as the royal fifth tax paid by silver producers was the main source of the increase of the royal income.[29] However, Potosí's economy did not solely rely on the mita but also on the voluntary labour of many Andean migrants who stayed in Potosí, on Andean women working for the silver production, in Spanish households or in the marketplace.[30] Scholars have shown the mita's profound consequences for the organisation of labour relations, the mining boom of Potosí, and on related migrations. It is also on this labour extraction system, and not on the tribute system per se, that the viceroy established the new tax regime for financing the welfare institution of the city.

The ordinance promulgated by the viceroy in Potosí in 1575 designed the hospital's administration, rights of access, and funding. However, it neither provides precise rates for the new tax nor a complete description of the tax regime, so we must sketch that from other sources. The ordinance encouraged private donations and the involvement of the Spanish vecinos by confirming the municipality's patronage. A *mayordomo* (administrator) named by the Municipal Council had to manage the hospital's finances. He was accountable to the municipality and to the royal official (*corregidor*). Deputies from the municipality were to visit the sick and to participate in the control of the institution. Toledo also allocated sixty *mitayos* to work in the mines as part of the remuneration of the physician he appointed – according to a commentator, the renting of these workers by the hospital had a value of 4,000 *pesos ensayados*.[31] The hospital also received some mitayos to work, for example, in the apothecary, in addition to the enslaved labour provided by Afro-descendants inside the hospital and on the field properties. As in the colonial convents, the charitable economy of this institution partly relied on forced labour.

The *medio peso* was allocated to the general expenses of the hospital, including the wages of the priest and surgeons. It was also supposed to finance the wages of the *alguaciles* (executive officers) who, in each parish, had to identify the sick and bring them to the hospital (24 pesos per year).[32] The *medio peso* was to be deposited in a treasury distinct from the Royal Treasury, called *Caja de Granos*, established to collect the tribute of the *mitayos* and another weekly tax, the *granos* (a monetary value). This treasury was under the custody of an accountant, the *Contador de Granos*. This accountant had to provide the *mayordomo* of the hospital with the sums due for the medio peso.[33] At the end, the mayordomo was the one who decided the allocation of these sums in the hospital's economy, although he was accountable for these expenses before the Municipal Council and representatives of the royal power. The *Contador de Granos* had interests in the successful collection of the granos as a stakeholder paid from them, but probably more indirect interest in the collect of the *medio peso*. However, the main agents to collect these taxes were likely to be the captains of *mita* and Andean chiefs (*principales*). The role of these Andean agents as mediator between the Andean community and the colonial power is well known. Established by Toledo to guarantee the delivery of the contingents of mitayos, the authority of the captains spread across various fiscal and administrative units; they were also in charge of collecting the granos. As tax collectors, these Andean chiefs mediated the relationship between taxpayers and the city's hospital. Thus, the tax regime of the medio peso relied on the structure of the mita obligation and its local agents.

In the context of an indebted royal Treasury, Toledo's scheme for funding the hospital aimed to relieve the king of any financial commitment, while maintaining the principle of charity towards the poor. During the following years, the records of the Real Treasury of Potosí did not register regular expenses in favour of the hospital.[34] It was this balance, avoiding the royal input, that the judge Matienzo praised few years later in a letter to the Council of Indies: 'among the noticeable things of this settlement [there is] a hospital that the viceroy let here done and provided for healing the Natives ... and here they are healed and cared as if they were very rich Spaniards ... without consuming the treasury of its Majesty'.[35] Once again, the justification of the tax relied on the idea that this kind of auto-financing was the fairest solution: as far as the hospital was established to cure the Andeans workers, they should provide for it. Thus, the *medio peso* tax regime was a local variation of a new way of financing welfare institution in the Spanish Empire, which was, however, related to existing colonial practices, imperial policy, and larger debates about how to provide for poor relief. Yet, because viceroy orders in the Spanish Empire were of a judicial nature and aimed to solve problems by applying often pre-existing norms (or understood as such), vassals could appeal his decision.[36]

The many categories of the beneficiaries and the plurality of redistributive mechanisms

Not all the thousands of *mitayos* who had to migrate to Potosí each year could benefit from health treatment in the hundred beds of the hospital, even though all of them had to pay. To legitimise the tax, Toledo planned an off-site service: the hospital's doctor, surgeons, and barbers would visit the sick in the *rancherias* (indigenous neighbourhoods circling the Spanish centre), and medicines from the hospital's apothecary would be provided to them in case of minor sickness or of lack of space in the hospital. Off-site relief was necessary, according to the viceroy's ordinance, to convert 'what they have to give' in their 'utility' and 'benefit'.[37]

The lack of space in the hospital was not the only cause that might delegitimise the tax imposed on the Andean workers. While the dedication of the hospital to the *'Indios Naturales'* was repeated throughout the text, many other colonial categories of population were also mentioned in it. Among the patients of the hospital were free and un-free Afro-descendants, Spaniards, and *'Indios de servicios'* or *yanaconas*.[38] The ordinance explained this diversity by means of a number of reasons: Spanish inhabitants turned towards the hospital to comply with their duty to cure the dependants of their household; thanks to the indulgences, the hospital was attractive to Spaniards who wished to die well. Above all, claimed the ordinance, it was the only hospital in the city for receiving charity and treatments: even if the hospital was mainly dedicated to the *'Indios'*, no one could be refused.[39]

It was this variety of colonial subjects that the legislator was to accord with specific economic rights and duties. The issue was thus to regulate the access of non-taxpayers to the premises. In response, the viceroy institutionalised a differentiated regime of access to the welfare services, according to different ways of paying for treatment. The aim proclaimed by the ordinance was to ensure the absence of prejudice for the 'true poor and sick who should be cured [in the hospital]' by making the others pay a fair price for their treatment.[40] Accordingly, Spanish masters were to pay for their dependants (Afro-descendant slaves and *indios de servicios*). The price was to be established by the *mayordomo*, the deputies from the municipality, and the physician. The same regime was expected from the Spaniards willing to enter the hospital if they did not willingly give the expected alms.

However, the identity of the 'true poor' was somewhat ambiguous and did not fit perfectly with either the category of *mitayos* or with that of 'Indio'. The colonial authorities acknowledged, to some extent, the complexity of the colonial society and the existence of poor Europeans. Among the patients admitted to the hospital were Andean women who were not necessarily working for a Spanish master.[41] Andean chiefs who were exempted from tribute and from labour obligations could benefit from its off-site services.[42] The ordinance also conceded that the '*negros* and *yanaconas* without masters', as well as 'those serving Spaniards so poor that they cannot afford them the cure', should be received in the hospital like the '*hatunrunas*', members of the Andean communities.[43] The ordinance only explicitly mentions the exemption of any payment for the 'numerous' 'Spaniards, *mestizos*, *negros*, or *mulatos* who would be known to be poor'. In the early modern period, being poor was a fluid condition mostly related to someone's inability to live in accord with what was expected from his status rather than based on a determinate amount of capital.[44]

The ordinance did not specify such criteria but entrusted the *mayordomo* and the deputies – meaning the Spanish members of the municipality – with the authority to allow the entrance of any 'Spaniard', 'mestizo', 'negro', or 'mulatto', and, when necessary, to recognise their condition of being 'poor' that permitted exemption from fees. It is likely that the distinction between these 'poor' people would reassert itself once in the hospital, whether by space, diet, or the gendered or ethnic category of the nurses looking after them. Instead, the 'Indios' were to be admitted without the intervention of the deputies. The subjects categorised as 'Indios' were still to be considered as the legitimate beneficiaries of the hospital's charity, epitomised by the lighter control that should be exerted on their admission. However, if the poor were not expected to pay for welfare services, the Andean members of the community were expected to contribute through taxation.

If we consider who had to pay, the access regime designed by the ordinance was structured around the principle of personal association, whether this meant belonging to the community or to the household. Thus, alongside the principle that 'Indians' as a group should pay for the welfare services planned for them coexisted the idea that the master should pay for his household. Both overlapped also with the mainstay that the rich, through the giving of alms, should pay for the poor. Therefore, the legislation designated various ways to participate in the charitable economy.[45]

Through the intervention of the representative of the royal power, general rules for the contribution of a part of the Andean population had been established through a compulsory tax. Yet, for another group of inhabitants of the city, the sums they gave in exchange for the services provided by the hospital were mainly referred to as 'alms' in the ordinance as well as in notarial documents, which means a voluntary and Christian gesture transforming these beneficiaries into benefactors. Institutionalising such differentiated modalities of contributing to the charitable economy, the viceroy's policy seemingly aimed not only at guaranteeing the health care of the entire population of Potosí – which he could hardly pretend to achieve – but at guaranteeing a differentiated access to spiritual and physical health care, in line with the principles of distributive justice (*aequitas*) and the preservation of social order.

The funding system institutionalised by Toledo, articulating fees and taxes, did not obliterate the requests to the king to provide other forms of funding. For example, in 1605 the municipality of Potosí made representations to the king concerning the necessity of a financial solution to support the poor and asked for the allocation of alms from the Royal Treasury, or of a rent on a *repartimiento*. This last option should be preferred, according to the municipality, because 'a *repartimiento de Indios* could not be given with more reason, since as much tribute they paid as much they help themselves'.⁴⁶ The funding by the Andean population of the poor relief system also coexisted with arrangements in which Spanish elites were willing to participate in the charitable economy. In 1619 the administration of the hospital officially shifted from the hands of the municipality to those of a brotherhood of twenty-four Spanish Potosínos, mainly powerful miners. Their initial donation of 6,330 pesos might have helped to repay certain debts and refund the hospital's capital. For the new members of the brotherhood, their voluntary contributions opened a door for bargaining for privileges with the king and likely contributed to their social capital.⁴⁷ The fraternity was then evoked as an ideal solution to stimulate donations by the Spanish elites.⁴⁸ As far as the *medio peso* policy was still applicable, the creation of this brotherhood illustrates the coexistence of voluntary and compulsory participation on which the colonial economy of welfare was based.

Taxpayers: An unequal distribution of the medio peso?

To what extent did the Andean *mitayos* participate in the funding of the hospital in this mixed economy of welfare? The absence of archives from the *Caja de Granos* and of the accounts of the hospital prevents us from precisely evaluating the incomes from the *medio peso*. At least during the sixteenth century, reports suggest substantial sums. In 1577, Matienzo wrote to the Council of the Indies that the annuity allocated by the viceroy was 6,000 pesos.⁴⁹ In 1585, the miner Capoche estimates at more than 6,600 pesos the value of the annuity brought to the hospital by the tax, less than half of the 14,000 pesos of the total income, of which 6,000 pesos were dedicated to the wages of the officials of the hospital.⁵⁰ Without further royal subsidies, the other part would presumably have been covered by income from loans, rents, sales of remedies, and alms. Thus, the Andean workers were, at least at that time, contributing considerably to the funding of the hospital's activities.

At an individual level, the economic burden of the *medio peso* seems to have been small. The *medio peso* would have counted for less than 1% of the wages a *mitayo* was expected to earn through his obligatory work, a relatively light burden.⁵¹ However, taking into account the expenses necessary to live in Potosí and to comply with the colonial obligations (including tribute, *granos*, and *medio peso*), researchers have shown that the wages of a *mitayo* would not have been enough.⁵² The *mitayo* would have to work as a 'free worker' on the labour market. But colonial obligations were also assumed collectively. Family, through the labour force of its other members, might have had its importance in securing subsistence. Furthermore, like the tribute, the *medio peso* was described as a per capita tax, but in practice it was to be collectively assumed under the responsibility of the Andean chiefs. We might look at the burden of the tax at this collective level.

In the decades following Toledo's intervention, the tax represented an increasing burden for the Andean communities. The plan of Toledo was said to correspond to an equitable repartition of the tax correlated to the population of each *repartimiento* sent to the *mita* at Potosí. The quota of mitayos was in theory correlated to the human resources of each *repartimiento*. In reality, the percentage of the population submitted to the *mita* varied between the regions. In the *mita* design of 1575, the contingent of mitayos was 17% of the tributaries of Charcas, 16% of the tributaries of La Paz, 15% of those from Cusco, and 13% from Canas y Canches.[53] Charcas, for example, which represented around 33% of the *mitayos* to be sent to Potosí between 1578 and 1610, would have been expected to contribute more to the economy of the hospital than the other regions (see Table 7.1).[54] In Toledo's scheme, because the tax of the *medio peso* was conditioned by the number of workers, the basis for its distribution was necessarily unequal among the community, in order to follow a principle of equity.

Were the communities that contributed the most to the hospital economy the ones that benefited the most from it? Both the lack of sources and the functioning of the system complicate the tracing and evaluation of redistributive fluxes. For example, health risk depended on the type of work performed in silver production, yet we do not know how it was distributed among the various Andean communities whose members were working in Potosí. We are just as ignorant of people's use of the hospital, which probably correlated to the distance of the *repartimiento* from Potosí and the possibility of returning easily back home. Moreover, demographic dynamics affected the concrete realisation of the *mita* system, and by extension the mechanisms of redistribution channelled by the *medio peso*.

A disconnection occurred between the *mita* quotas and the demographic trends of the Andean population. It is likely that the same discrepancies affected the *medio peso*, which would have increased the economic burden on the communities and possibly exaggerated the regional inequalities. As shown by Paula Zagalsky,[55] the obligation of the *mita* remained the same during the period 1578–1610, despite the demographic fall affecting the Andean population, caused by disease and migration. In the documentation consulted we do not find mentions of general revisions of the obligation of the *medio peso* until its suppression in the 1630s. While the real number of *mitayos* arriving in Potosí decreased, the practices correlated to the *mita* also evolved. From the beginning of the seventeenth century, many captains of *mita* delivered money to the miners instead of the quota of effective labour force (a commutative practice named '*Indios de plata*'). Communities used

Table 7.1 Estimation of the regional contribution to the medio peso (in pesos) from the mita contribution (1578–1610).

Year	Repartimientos de Charcas		Repartimientos de La Paz		Repartimientos de Cuzco		Repartimientos de Chucuito		Total mita	Total medio
	Mita gruesa	Medio peso	Mita gruesa	Medio peso	Mita gruesa	Medio peso	Mita gruesa	Medio peso		
1,578	4,471	22,355	3,197	15,985	3,422	1,711	2,364	1,182	13.454	6,727
1,585	4,465	22,325	3,197	15,985	3,323	16,615	2,364	1,182	13.340	66,745
1,599	4,481	22,405	3,137	15,685	3,403	17,015	2,364	1,182	13.384	66,925
1,610	4,471	22,355	3,137	15,685	3,376	1,688	2,364	1,182	13.348	6,674

various strategies to recover the amount necessary for the Indios de plata. For example, Andeans sold produce in Potosí or rented out pack animals. The success of these practices varied from one community to another.[56]

The payment of the tribute was expected to benefit from such complementary economic practices and from the labour of the free workers in the silver production process.[57] It is likely that similar strategies were used to pay the *medio peso*. In this regard, one must keep in mind the agency of the Andean lords, who might suffer incarceration and other sanctions but also had economic interests in Potosí. It raises the question of the degree and forms of coercion exerted on the Andean authorities to comply with this colonial obligation. We do not know for now how, in this context, the levy was concretely distributed and operated at the infra-community level, and what could have been the ability and strategies of the Andean chiefs to comply with this extraction. But we know one of the strategies they used to face this colonial obligation: to resort to royal justice to obtain a suppression of the tax.

Negotiations around the meaning and payment of the medio peso

A few years after Toledo's order, the tax system became an object of criticism. Using the well-studied channels of communication between the king and his subjects, both Spanish Potosínos and Andean chiefs contested the tax, participating thus in the political space of negotiation linking the ruler and the ruled. However, their criticisms originated from different interests and interpretations of the *medio peso*.

By 1576, some Andean subjects were petitioning the royal tribunal (*Audiencia*) of La Plata about this additional tax.[58] Facing the request for its suppression, the judges were divided between those who were willing to follow the viceroy's ordinance, and others who advised subtracting the *medio peso* from the tribute paid by the Andeans living in Potosí. In the following decades, the nature of the tax continued to be discussed, and, with it, the question of who should pay for welfare. If financed from the tribute, the *medio peso* would have been subtracted from the sum paid for the doctrine – probably giving rise to opposition by the clerics of the *repartimientos*. Alternatively, it could have been deducted from the part of the tribute dedicated to the king's earnings.[59] Instead, as a tax distinct from tribute, the medio peso was correlated by some colonial administrators to the cost of the workforce.

For being established alongside the pay increase ordered by Toledo, the *medio peso* would not have subtracted anything from the 'fair price' of the labour of the Andean workers.[60] But for some miners, it was considered as an additional wage cost. Two texts describing Potosí and written by Spanish agents of the mining economy illustrate the disagreements about the meaning and legitimacy of the tax among the Spaniards. According to the miner Capoche, the *medio peso* was, in the final analysis, financed by the miners – 'those using [the Indios], for having the obligation of healing them in their diseases' – because it was issued from the increase of the daily wages.[61] Capoche claimed that such a financing scheme was a kind of *sisa* (sales tax) imposed to the 'Republic', namely, to the Spaniards.[62] By contrast, according to the mines' inspector Garcia de Llanos, the *medio peso* was a tax on the person, not a tax on the daily wages of the *mitayos*. It was fair, stated Llanos, that the *tomines* del hospital were to be paid by all the *mitayos* of the *mita gruesa* (the total contingent), 'because all of them are bound by the need of being cured in it'.[63] Capoche's and Llanos's divergent interpretations illustrate the coexistence of various rationalities to justify the tax. If Llanos alluded to the principle of the use of the welfare amenity to claim that Andeans must pay, Capoche instead invoked the responsibilities attached to the profits extracted from the labour force. Yet, for many miners, it is likely that an annuity from a determined *repartimiento*, or even charity, might have appeared preferable to this tax linked to the labour system.

Andean chiefs too, in the name of their community, represented their interpretation of the tax and its (in)justice. In 1582, some of the Andean chiefs of the jurisdiction of Charcas – whose contribution to the *mita* and thus to the *medio peso* was around 33% – wrote a petition addressed to King Philip II in which they denounced many aspects of Toledo's policy.[64] They called for the king's benevolence and justice, asking for the suppression of the *medio peso* by representing themselves as 'very poor'. This mode of self-representation was quite a common strategy used by Andean subjects in their petition because it conveyed an appeal to the obligation for justice and protection.[65] Moreover, they also mobilised the principle correlating use of the hospital and tax payment. These Andean chiefs were mainly of the old nation of Charkas and Qaraqara, in competition for the captaincies with the Qullas (Cuzco region). They differentiated their communities from those of the northern provinces of the Collasuyo: 'In the hospital of the city of Potosí, we, the natives of this province of the Charcas, we do not have sick Indios, instead they [the sick] are the Spaniards, *mestizos*, *mulatos*, *negros*, *yanaconas*, and Spaniards' servants, the same the Collasuyos, and if some of us are sick, they would be very few.'[66] The way in which the petitioners distinguished themselves particularly demonstrates that the fiscal regime supporting the institution was one of differentiation, not only between the 'true poor' and the others, nor just between the colonial fiscal categories, but also between Andean communities. This contradicts the discourse of the colonial authorities claiming a generic category of '*naturales*' cured at the hospital.

Who the taxpayers were, what the nature of this tax was, and thus its justification, varied depending on the colonial subjects. But both Andean's authorities, masters of mines, and royal officials asked for its suppression, finally achieved in 1633. During the 1610s, the president of the Audiencia Diego de Portugal wrote various letters to the *Consejo de Indias* arguing against the subtraction of the *granos* and *medio peso* from the pockets of the *mitayos*, especially as their number was decreasing. Concerning the *medio peso*, the president declared that 'being nursed in the hospital of this city all the Spaniards who enter in it for free, and with more care and delight than the Indios, it costed them money from their own lands'.[67] During the following year the president, as he represented the usefulness of the *mitayos* for the service of the king and the 'public good', kept urging for measures that would be beneficial to 'the Real consciousness, good, conservation and relief of vassals so useful and miserable as these Indios'.[68] Yet, solving this issue without burdening the Royal Treasury and without decreasing the income of the hospital was a delicate matter.

The implementation of royal charitable policies was no different from other measures, revealing the polycentric and negotiated government of the empire. In 1618, a royal decree ordered that nothing should be subtracted from the daily payment of the 'Indios', and that their conservation and good treatment should be achieved by other means, but the royal decision was suspended by the viceroy de Esquilache (1614–21). Some ten years later, the royal official Don Pedro Andrade de Sotomayor was still arguing for the suppression of the tax, because, he wrote, the hospital had enough land estates thanks to donations by Spaniards.[69] In 1631 the viceroy finally recorded the suppression of the *medio peso*, making the regional authority (the president of the Audiencia) responsible for the implementation of a new arrangement. From that time to the end of the seventeenth century, the charitable economy of the hospital of Vera Cruz relied mainly on a mix of donations, capital investment, and endowments, like most Latin American religious institutions.

Conclusion

The *medio peso* tax was, for Potosí's hospital, a financial tool enacted by royal officials, responding to local demographic circumstances, relying on local agents and the labour organisation of the *mita*. But just as hospitals were not the only institution of welfare in the Spanish Empire, the idea of a tax-supported welfare system was not hegemonic. In Potosí, voluntary alms were preferred to tax, which was considered an extra labour cost by employers and as an illegitimate economic burden by Andean chiefs. This chapter has focused on demonstrating how taxpayers of the *medio peso* used at least one way to contest and negotiate the tax regime: the resort to royal justice. By doing that, they participated in the formation of welfare as an object of the political space of the Spanish Empire – that is, in the negotiations between ruler and ruled about the poor relief system and how it was to be paid for.

The history of the financial arrangements of Potosí's hospital could not be generalised to all the hospitals of the viceroyalty, even less of the empire. In Potosí's case, the institutionalisation of the principles of distributive justice did not pass by the creation of hospitals for specific social categories, as in Lima, but by defining rights of access and regimes of payment for welfare. This chapter has shown that in this hierarchised society, redistribution worked through multiple mechanisms, structured by gendered, geographical, and ethnic differences and criteria of belonging. However, despite its specificities, the solution imagined for financing Potosí's hospital was rather the enactment of principles debated elsewhere. Thus, the history of the tax regime of the *medio peso* is part of the history of the welfare system of the Spanish Empire. Broadly, this case stands against a linear narration about welfare. Against the model of evolution from civic and individual charity to a tax-supportive welfare system, it illustrates the coexistence of multiple mechanisms of redistribution, embedded in the very same institution.

Notes

1 Brian Pullan, *Poverty and Charity: Europe, Italy, Venice, 1400–1700* (Aldershot: Routledge, 1994); Thomas Max Safley, *The Reformation of Charity: The Secular and the Religious in Early Modern Poor Relief* (Boston, MA: Brill, 2003).
2 See introduction to this volume.
3 Francesca Trivellato, 'The moral economies of early modern Europe', *Humanity: An International Journal of Human Rights, Humanitarianism, and Development* 2 (2020), 193–201.
4 Giovanni Levi, 'Reciprocidad mediterránea', *Hispania* 60.204 (2000), 103–26.
5 Cecilia Font de Villanueva, 'The School of Salamanca: Some thoughts on the subject of justice', in Daniela F. Parisi and Stefano Solari (eds), *Humanism and Religion in the History of Economic Thought* (Rome: Franco Angeli, 2010), pp. 96–112.
6 Ole Peter Grell, Andrew Cunningham, and Jon Arrizabalaga (eds), *Health Care and Poor Relief in Counter-Reformation Europe* (New York: Routledge, 1999).

7 Julia McClure, 'Poverty and empire', in David Hitchcock and Julia McClure (eds), *The Routledge History of Poverty in Europe, c.1450–1800* (New York: Routledge, 2020).
8 Gabriela Ramos, 'Indian hospitals and government in the colonial Andes', *Medical History* 5.2 (2013), 186–205.
9 Jason Moore, '"This lofty mountain of silver could conquer the whole world": Potosí and the political ecology of underdevelopment, 1545–1800', *Journal of Philosophical Economics* 4.1 (2010), 58–103; Kris Lane, *Potosí: The Silver City That Changed the World* (Oakland, CA: California University Press, 2019).
10 Linda Martz, *Poverty and Welfare in Habsburg Spain: The Example of Toledo* (Cambridge: Cambridge University Press, 1983).
11 Karen B. Graubart, 'Taxation, obligation, and corporate identity in 16th-century Lima', in Emily A. Engel (ed.), *A Companion to Early Modern Lima* (Leiden: Brill, 2019), pp. 82–102; Sarah Albiez-Wieck and Raquel Gil Montero, 'The Emergence of colonial fiscal categorizations in Peru: Forasteros and Yanaconas Del Rey, sixteenth to nineteenth centuries', *Journal of Iberian and Latin American Studies* 1 (2020), 1–24; Raquel Gil Montero, 'El tributo andino reinterpretado: El caso del corregimiento de López', *European Review of Latin American and Caribbean Studies* 99 (2015), 69–88.
12 Tristán Platt, *Estado boliviano y ayllu andino: tierra y tributo en el norte de Potosí* (Lima: University of St Andrews, 1982).
13 It is a specificity of mining extraction in Peru to rely on a native labour force.
14 Peter John Bakewell, *Mineros de la Montaña Roja: el trabajo de los indios en Potosí; 1545–1650* (Madrid: Alianza, 1989).
15 Aliocha Maldavsky, 'Teología moral, restitución y sociedad colonial en los Andes en el siglo XVI', *Revista Portuguesa de Filosofia* 75.2 (2019), 1125–48.
16 The term 'miner' refers here to the individuals exploiting the mines, not those digging in them.
17 Jorge Díaz Ceballos, *Poder Compartido: Repúblicas Urbanas, Monarquía y Conversación En Castilla de Oro, 1508–1573* (Madrid: Marcial Pons, 2020); Alejandra Irigoin and Regina Grafe, 'Bargaining for absolutism: A Spanish path to nation-state and empire building', *Hispanic American Historical Review* 88.2 (2008), 173–209.
18 Archivo General de Indias [hereafter AGI], CHARCAS 32, La Villa Imperial de Potosí, 10-1-1563.
19 AGI, CONTADURUA 1801, fol. 50c.
20 Maria Luz Lopez Terrada, 'Las finanzas de una institución asistencial: la gestión económica del Hospital General de Valencia durante el siglo XVI', in *Ciudad y hospital en el Occidente europeo: 1300–1700* (Lleida: Milenio Publicaciones, 2014), pp. 263–58.
21 Archivo y Biblioteca Nacionales de Bolivia [hereafter ABNB], MNL 52-17, 1564; ABNB, MNL 52-17, 1570.
22 ABNB, MNL 52-17, 1571.
23 Manfredi Merluzzi, *Politica e governo den Nuovo Mondo: Francisco de Toledo viceré del Perù (1569–1581)* (Rome: Carocci, 2003); Jeremy Ravi Mumford,

Vertical Empire: The General Resettlement of Indians in the Colonial Andes (Durham, NC: Duke University Press, 2012).
24 Raquel Gil Montero and Paula C. Zagalsky, 'Colonial organization of mine labour in Charcas (present-day Bolivia) and its consequences (sixteenth to the seventeenth centuries)', *International Review of Social History* 61.24 (2016), 71–92.
25 'Ordenanzas generales para la vida en común de los pueblos de indios', Arequipa, 6 de noviembre de 1575, in Guillermo Lohmann Villena and María Justina Sarabia Viejo, *Francisco de Toledo. Disposiciones Gubernativas Para El Virreinato de Perú. T.II* (Seville, 1989).
26 Jonathan Barry and Colin Jones, *Medicine and Charity before the Welfare State* (Abingdon: Routledge, 1991).
27 'Ordenanzas generales para la vida en común de los pueblos de indios', p. 259.
28 'Ordonanza para el hospital de Potosí' (1575), in Villena and Sarabia Viejo, *Francisco de Toledo. T.II.*
29 Bakewell, *Mineros de la Montaña Roja*; Jeffrey A. Cole, *The Potosí Mita, 1573–1700: Compulsory Indian Labor in the Andes* (Stanford, CA: Stanford University Press, 1985).
30 Rossana Barragán, 'Working silver for the world: Mining labor and popular economy in colonial Potosí', *Hispanic American Historical Review* 9.2 (2017), 193–222; Jane E. Mangan, *Trading Roles: Gender, Ethnicity, and the Urban Economy in Colonial Potosí* (Durham, NC: Duke University Press, 2005).
31 Luis Capoche, *Relación general de la villa imperial de Potosí (1585)* (Madrid, 1959), 60r–v.
32 *Ibid.*
33 ABNB, CPLA 5.
34 John J. Te Paske *et al.*, *The Royal Treasuries of the Spanish Empire in America* 2,2 (Durham, NC: Duke University Press, 1982); completed with ponctual survey in AHP, Cajas Reales, Libros comunes.
35 AGI, CHARCAS 16, R.16, N.65, Carta del licenciado Juan de Matienzo, 1577-12-23, fol. 5r.
36 Tamar Herzog, 'Colonial law: Early modern normativity in Spanish America.', in Jörg Tellkamp (ed.), *A Companion to Early Modern Iberian Imperial Political and Social Thought* (Leiden: Brill, 2020), pp. 105–27.
37 *Ordonanza para el hospital de Potosí* (1575).
38 The *yanacona* had its origin in the pre-Hispanic period. Under the colonial regime it signified a kind of Andean servant detached from the *ayllu* and working for individuals, for the king, or for the Church. From 1566, they were obliged to pay tribute in cash to the Crown, but usually they did not pay at all.
39 *Ordonanza para el hospital de Potosí* (1575).
40 *Ibid.*
41 *Ibid.*
42 In the usual tribute system, a full tribute payer was a married couple. Nobles were exempted.
43 The *indios hatunrunas* was a member of an *ayllu* (Andean community).

44 Cynthia E. Milton, *The Many Meanings of Poverty: Colonialism, Social Compacts, and Assistance in Eighteenth-Century Ecuador* (Stanford, CA: Stanford University Press, 2007).
45 Sarah Albiez et al., *Ethnicity, Citizenship and Belonging: Practices, Theory and Spatial Dimensions* (Madrid: Iberoamericana, 2011).
46 AGI, CHARCAS 32, Ynstrucion de la villa de potossi para su majestad, 1605.
47 AGI, CHARCAS 55, 'el cabildo y hermandad del hospital de la Veracruz'.
48 AGI, CHARCAS 418, L.3,F.206v–207r.
49 AGI, CHARCAS 16, R.16,N.65, Carta del licenciado Juan de Matienzo, 1577-12-23.
50 Capoche, *Relación general de la villa imperial de Potosí*, 60r–v.
51 The daily wage of a mitayo established by Toledo in 1574–75 varied depending on the task: between 2.75 reales and 3.5 reales in the sixteenth century and between 3 and 4 reales during the seventeenth century.
52 Bakewell, *Mineros de la Montaña Roja*.
53 *Ibid*.
54 It is possible that the relation between the number of mitayos and the value of the medio peso by repartimiento slightly varied; yet, the number given by Capoche for the total of the mita gruesa and the total of the medio peso correspond. Numbers for the mita gruesa in Paula C. Zagalsky, 'La mita de potosí: una imposición colonial invariable en un contexto de múltiples transformaciones', *Chungará* 46.3 (2014), 375–95.
55 Zagalsky, 'La mita de potosí'.
56 Bakewell, *Mineros de la Montaña Roja*.
57 *Ibid*.
58 ABNB, LAACH5:287v-288, 27/10/1576.
59 The repartimientos of mita were mainly the Crown's repartimientos. Zagalsky, 'La mita de potosí'.
60 AGI, CHARCAS 17,R.1,N.8, 1590-03-05, Carta de la Audiencia de Charcas.
61 Capoche, *Relación general de la villa imperial de Potosí*, f.59v.
62 Capoche, *Relación general de la villa imperial de Potosí*, f.59v.
63 García de Llanos, *Diccionario y maneras de hablar que se usan en las minas y sus labores en los ingenios y beneficios de los metales (1609)* (Madrid, 2009), 130.
64 The petition is known as the 'Memorial de Charcas'.
65 Caroline Cunill, 'El indio miserable: nacimiento de la teoría legal en la América colonial del siglo XVI', *Cuadernos Inter. ca mbio sobre Centroamérica y el Caribe* 8.9 (2011), 229–48.
66 'Memorial de Charcas', in Thérèse Bouysse-Cassagne, Olivia Harris, and Tristan Platt, *Qaraqara-Charcas Mallku, Inka y Rey en la provincia de Charcas (siglos XV–XVII)* (Lima, 2015), p. 832.
67 AGI, CHARCAS 19, R.3, N. 72, 2/4/1613.
68 AGI, CHARCAS 19, R.6,N.119, 31/3/1616. AGI, CHARCAS 19, R.7, N.130, 30/5/1617.
69 AGI, CHARCAS 55, carta de Don Pedro Andrade de Sotomayor.

8

Poverty, health, and imperial wealth in early modern Scotland

Andrew Mackillop

Introduction

Ideas of poverty, inequality, and associated practices of public social welfare have historically provided countries with ways of demarcating who does and who does not belong to the nation. In this respect, the use in the twenty-first century of xenophobic discourses on 'health tourism' and 'welfare tourism' by populist governments is part of a much longer history.[1] The entangled nature of this intersection raises fundamental questions in a British context about the presumed dynamic between social welfare, the politics of citizenship, and the enduring legacies of empire. The United Kingdom's creation in 1948 of the National Health Service (NHS) followed immediately in the wake of decolonisation in South Asia. This timing embedded in British popular culture, over the succeeding decades, a sense that 'the cradle to grave' welfare state was a watershed moment, a powerful symbol of a new post-war consensus which distinguished Britain from its imperial past and indicated its socially inclusive and progressive future.[2] The old inequalities of empire were, it seems, to be replaced with a new emphasis on social and health equality. While this idealised image of post-war Britain's trajectory has met with cogent reappraisal, it remains deeply embedded in national self-perception and culture.[3]

The privileging of a 'national' story focused around the post-1945 moment and the apparent pivot away from empire has served to decouple questions of health and social inequalities from the history of British colonialism. Even the most insightful recent studies of the pervasive presence of empire in British culture tend to see developments such as the NHS as separate from the influence of Britain's colonial past.[4] Yet the relationship between these two dimensions of the country's experience stretches back centuries in ways that mean empire shaped attitudes to social and health inequalities just as surely as it did geopolitical, military, naval, or financial policies. The seemingly domestic character of institutions as diverse as churches, schools, asylums, and hospitals that worked to alleviate material poverty always contained powerful, if 'silent', influences derived from the country's colonialism.[5]

This chapter further historicises the long connection between empire, ideals of national well-being, and the related use of welfare provision to regulate social inequality. Using the example of early modern Scotland, it considers how anxieties over poverty, migration, and societal progress – or, to use the terminology of the time, 'improvement' – intertwined with the cultural politics of Britain's pre-1815 empire.[6] Despite its seminal significance to Scotland's post-union development, the multilayered nature of 'improvement' remains a noticeably understudied topic. As an ideology and a set of practices it aimed at ending national inequality within the Union by modernising Scotland's economy. It is for this reason that the phenomenon is rightly understood as a post-union variation of Scottish patriotism.[7] In practical terms the result was the implementation of new forms of agricultural and manufacturing production which radically altered the lives of the vast bulk of the population in a remarkably short period between c. 1740 and c. 1820. Besides its broad societal objectives, 'improvement' brought with it fundamental implications for the individual. Embedded in its assumptions was an emphasis on new modes of moral and social discipline as well as more productive forms of individual work ethics and collective labour.[8]

However, at precisely the same time as Scotland's propertied, political, religious, and civic leadership implemented these various transformations, the country became ever more immersed in Britain's worldwide empire. One way the tensions created by this intersection could be reconciled involved representing the new imperial influences as the means of delivering better public welfare and the amelioration of new forms of social inequality. Empire came to be projected as the means of developing national health and personal wealth even as it generated formidable new disparities across all aspects of Scottish society.

Why Scotland?

Early modern Scotland is a useful case study of these broader themes because of its distinctive trajectory within the British Union and Empire. Key aspects of its development during the long eighteenth century reveal deep ambiguities between contemporary understandings of domestic 'improvement' and overseas empire. As an initially impoverished (at least by reputation) and, later, rapidly developing province of the new Great Britain, imperial opportunities transformed the nature and pace of the country's 'improvement'.[9] While part of the wider British world and empire, the country was exposed to the effects of global colonialism in unique and intense ways. Participation in overseas expansion and exposure to the consequent returning influences evolved gradually from the early 1600s to early 1740s, before increasing sharply in the succeeding decades. Contemporary commentators asserted continually that the Empire offered the prospect of substantial material profits and wider societal 'improvement'.[10] At the same time, Scots of all social and geographic backgrounds became enthusiastic participants in, and supporters of, British overseas expansion.[11] However, as key regions developed rapidly through such connections, Scottish civic society grappled with how best to benefit from but also contain what many observers feared by the 1760s had become the Empire's excessive and destabilising domestic influence.

This climate of anxiety was evident across the whole of Britain and Ireland and was not unique to Scotland. Yet it expressed itself with a particular degree of intensity in a provincial society beset with doubts over social instability, mass migration, and the sustainability of national 'improvement'.[12] Faced with the positive attraction of capital accumulation via empire and the negative repulsion of socio-cultural upheaval, post-union Scotland was at the forefront of wider British cultural strategies designed to absorb returning overseas influences. One of the most high-profile means of achieving this integration of empire involved conspicuous medical, educational, and social philanthropy by those associated with potentially destructive forms of overseas wealth. In this way, any threat to civic and national health was turned into a form of virtuous support by transforming empire into the means of promoting social improvement as well as individual and collective health. Again, it should be stressed that this cultural tactic was common to Britain and Ireland, as the donations to schools and hospitals by the Bristol-based slave trafficker, Edward Colston, demonstrates.[13] Yet long-eighteenth-century Scotland's relative economic underdevelopment and its disproportionate engagement with Britain's overseas empire meant that the deployment of colonial wealth in the regulation of social inequalities had a significant and still only partially understood impact. The country's experience provides a window into the cultural strategies which aligned individual and collective conceptions of poverty, health, and national wealth with empire through the conspicuous use of colonial profits in the social welfare sector.

Empire and national poverty: Cause or solution?

To understand why the domestic influence of empire inspired such an ambivalent socio-cultural response, it is important to grasp the enduring extent of anxiety in post-union Scotland over the progress of 'improvement'.[14]

For much of the seventeenth and eighteenth century the country was an international byword in poverty. At no time was this sense of a poor nation getting poorer more evident than on the eve of the kingdom's union with England and Wales in 1707. Destitution seemed to be everywhere – at home and in the country's prospects abroad. A sequence of four famines between 1695 and 1699 induced mass mortality and a surge in migration to Ireland. Taking advantage of yet another round of land sequestration in the aftermath of the failed Jacobite rising in Ireland, perhaps as many as 20,000 Scots arrived in Ulster in just two years between 1696 and 1698.[15]

The palpable sense, by the 1690s, of the need to combat social impoverishment and national enfeeblement resulted in what was by European standards a late effort to become a colonial power in the Atlantic world.[16] Empire was envisaged as an antidote to both individual material poverty and the failing health of the Scottish body politick.[17] The scale of financial losses during the attempt to establish a colony at Darien did not rob Scotland of as much of its venture capital as is often believed. But the project's failure did compound a climate of crisis which was exploited by those seeking a unionist solution with England.[18] Scotland's experience in the 1690s and 1700s is an object lesson in how perceptions of poverty, fragile national health, and international inequality generated hopes of empire as a solution, leading in turn to colonial ventures that deepened societal impoverishment and ultimately contributed to the loss of sovereignty.

The relationship between failed Scottish empire and successful British union is well known.[19] Far less well appreciated are the complex uncertainties that emerged in the succeeding century regarding imperialism's capacity to ensure national 'improvement' without exacerbating existing social inequalities. It often seemed to long-eighteenth-century contemporaries that Scottish society was overcompensating for its earlier exclusion from, or partial participation in, English imperialism. While the free movement of people and goods was enabled by the 1707 Union, it took a further generation or so before the country experienced an intense and comprehensive immersion in an empire spanning both the Atlantic and Asia hemispheres.[20] There emerged a range of interactions with the former English empire which encompassed all of Scotland's regions and the entirety of its social order, from landless Lowlanders and Highlanders to Glasgow 'tobacco lords' and state-service gentry and aristocracy.[21] This immersion in overseas empire was profound and exposed a still relatively undercapitalised and provincial society to the full force of early modern globalisation in a compressed timeline. In the far north, Orcadian communities developed a mutual dependency with the Hudson's Bay Company (HBC). The supply of labour to the fur-trading organisation was wholly disproportionate. By the early 1800s, 79% of the servants employed at the corporation's forts in British North America were Orcadians.[22] The HBC–Orkney connection is a telling historical example of how global empire often worked through and, in the process, entrenched older regional and local patterns of itinerant labour.[23]

Meanwhile, beginning in the late 1740s and continuing through until the Napoleonic wars, the Scottish Highlands developed another niche, empire-aligned economy, again based on the supply of labour. In this instance, it was soldiers for the British Army. Despite having no more than 2% of Britain's population, the region supplied approximately 10–12% of all regular forces in North America during the Seven Years War (1756–63).[24] While imperial service facilitated the rehabilitation of a despised and marginalised cultural and linguistic minority, this mode of interaction came at the cost of confirming stereotypes of the Scot as a poor economic migrant.[25] Images such as the 1775 'Scotch Butchery' depicted Highland soldiers as unthinking dependents of the British state willing to erase political liberties and civilised norms in order to alleviate their own material impoverishment. In their efforts to use empire as a means of addressing their own economic inequality, Scottish soldiers were stereotyped as imposing the political equivalent on North American colonists.[26]

Heavy involvement in North America not only perpetuated older, negative stereotypes of underdeveloped, unequal Scotland, it raised increasingly uncomfortable questions about the nature of progress and its limitations. Where empire ought to have generated positive commercial and human connections it seemed equally capable of creating alarming new inequalities both in the colonies and at 'home'. Rather than sustainable economic 'improvement', commentators fretted at the demographic consequences for Scotland's small population base. By the early 1770s this anxiety found expression in the notion of entire rural communities being swept up into 'A Dance called America'.[27] The rhetoric is telling: this was a 'rage' or 'mania' for migration which infected the body politick, drawing off human resources (still seen as vital to national well-being) to the 'unimproved' frontiers of North America. Such fears were understandable. Between 1763 and 1775, perhaps as many as 15,000 people left the Scottish Highlands for the colonies of settlement. Despite its limited demographic base, the region supplied 18% of all British migrants to North America during these years.[28] The implications were stark: was the development of empire to be at the cost of underdeveloping Scotland? Were the much-vaunted overseas connections as much threat to national vitality and progress as an unalloyed solution? One reason why colonial wealth became aligned so conspicuously with the enhancement of health and social infrastructure in Scotland in this period was precisely to counter the emerging and negative connotations associated with excessive involvement in empire.

Mass migration also exposed in new ways the stark inequalities of Scotland's social and propertied order. The surge in population mobility after 1763 cast the landlord elite in an unflattering light, with their manipulation of rising prices in the arable and pastoral economies driving a set of steep estate rental increases. Private proprietary power rather than productive market development seemed to spark deep social instability and the drain of a key national resource. By the 1760s and 1770s the country's landed elite faced public condemnation for their rapacious rent policies and for seeking enhanced revenues from their tenantry without having first managed the necessary agrarian improvements. As one pamphlet noted, it seemed that the modern maxim of economy was simply a means 'to rob people of their comforts'.[29] Accused of oppression and short-sighted rental policies, the landed classes were the subject of as much critical appraisal as empire by the early 1770s.

By the second half of the eighteenth century it seemed to many observers that Scotland was rooted in a cycle of extremes, see-sawing from delayed involvement in empire to excessive and highly unstable overinvolvement. It is precisely this pattern which gives the example of Scottish society a wider resonance when considering the historic relationship between imperialism and the management of inequalities. The Union settlement did not banish the older questions of national impoverishment or provide easy answers to how these challenges could be addressed in a sustainable and 'virtuous' way. It simply reconfigured and globalised them. A sense of brittle angst among the political, economic, and intellectual elite over the progress of 'improvement' was compounded by an awareness that opinion in England still viewed Scotland as a poverty-stricken backwater.[30] The perception was so persistent that it explains why Scots are at the centre of one of the most powerful images produced in the early modern British and Irish Isles relating to nativist fear of the poor economic migrant. Richard Newton's 1796 satirical print 'A Flight of Scotchmen' captures the deeply embedded assumptions that linked Scotland, poverty, and empire with the stereotype of the migrant as an intrusive, socially destabilising, and potentially destructive 'other'.[31] As both the putative cure of old inequalities and the cause of equally alarming new social instabilities, empire needed to be repackaged as a force for civic improvement, social welfare, and individual health and well-being.

Empire as corruption: Scottish society and the nabob

Almost one hundred years after its inception, therefore, the Union remained beset with cultural ambivalences that often expressed themselves through inter-related themes of poverty and a reliance on economic migration. As in the earlier age of famine and Darien, dependency on empire seemed a double-edged sword. Deep anxieties persisted over whether imperialism could ever be a panacea for ongoing socio-economic underdevelopment. In that context, Scotland became a crucible where the realities of new forms of inequality and migration, and persistent fears over the unstable character of economic progress, collided with the increasing arrival home of imperial personnel and their colonial wealth. Nowhere was this ambivalence more acute than in attitudes to individuals returning from the United English East India Company's (EIC) service between *c.* 1750 and *c.* 1820. Known in contemporary terms as 'nabobs', these administrators, merchants, mariners, financiers, soldiers, and medical personnel faced serious cultural disquiet and suspicion. They became metaphors for wider societal insecurities over the Empire's capacity to induce political and social instability and unwanted cultural change at home as well as abroad. More than any other group associated with overseas colonialism, including planters and merchants active in the transatlantic enslavement-based economies, nabobs seemed to personify the Empire's unwelcome transformative power, be it in relation to commodities, social hierarchies, or the character of individuals and whole peoples.[32] Hardening ideas around race and colour contributed to this negative assessment: had young men in the East India Company's service departed for Asia as 'White', 'Europeans', 'Britons', and 'Scots' but returned as corrupted, and corrupting, 'Orientalised' 'Others?'.[33] The cultural angst surrounding the figure of the nabob spoke to deep-seated, ongoing fears of emigration's destabilising effects, the tenuousness of individual and national health and wealth, and society's limited capacity to control the forces of modern change. These anxieties were simply the layering of an explicitly imperial dimension onto pre-existing suspicions of economic migrants and their capacity to destabilise society while attempting to alleviate their own material inequalities.

This phenomenon was common to all of Britain and Ireland, as the controversy around Robert Clive's actions and the impeachment of Warren Hastings indicate. The 'nabob' controversy lasted from *c.* 1750 to *c.* 1790 before the French Revolution and new forms of economic production and social unrest displaced it as a central concern in British cultural and political life.[34] Yet, as with so many other aspects of post-union Scotland's links with British imperialism, these issues played out with a distinctive intensity north of the border. While involvement in the East India Company had been limited before *c.* 1720, Scots began moving in larger numbers to Asia under the corporation's auspices from the 1740s. This trend meant that Glasgow's expansion in the tobacco trade found a less spectacular parallel in the eastern half of the Empire. The pattern of disproportionate involvement evident in other colonial-related sectors such as the army and the Hudson's Bay Company became increasingly apparent in Asia by the 1760s. With only around 12% of Britain and Ireland's population, Scots nonetheless secured around 20% of the Company's elite civil offices by the 1790s and 20–23% of the thousands of army officer posts created between c. 1750 and c. 1815.[35] In addition, by the 1790s Scots commanded 28% of all Europe-to-Asia voyages undertaken by the Company's fleet, a top-heavy presence at the upper echelons of a key branch of world trade.[36]

The notable profile of Scots in the British colonial presence in Asia extended into the rapidly expanding 'country trades'. This was the term used for intra-Asian commerce rather than the transhemispheric import–export business between Europe and Asia that until 1813 lay under the monopoly of the East India Company. Here, too, Scots were present in greater numbers than their small share of population in Britain and Ireland would warrant. A list from 1778 of British and Irish individuals involved in the country trades in Madras (Chennai) showed that 24% were Scots: by 1810 it was 30%. In Calcutta (Kolkata) in 1804 the ratio was 20%.[37] All these profiles were significantly higher than the country's decidedly marginal share of population back in the British and Irish Isles.

These patterns of participation inevitably shaped the extent and character of the returning connection. In a Scottish society perennially sensitive to the still fragile nature of its national 'improvement' and imbued with a strong imperative to emulate the affluence of England, the prospect of substantial profits from Asia ought to have sparked a positive reaction. In some key respects, though, it did not. The ambivalence over whether empire could enrich the body politick and alleviate destabilising inequalities found a lightning rod in the anxiety over the impact of nabobs arriving back north of the border. This they did in increasing numbers by the mid- to later 1750s. A 'List of Scotsmen who in our time have acquired good fortunes in E. Indies & returned their fortunes to Scotland' drawn up in 1760 already had forty-five individuals.[38] Typical among them was the Calcutta-based country trader Archibald Stirling: after returning to Scotland in 1748 with at least £18,000, he acquired the estates of Cawdor in Lanarkshire and Keir in Perthshire.[39] In transferring his colonial profits to the culturally prestigious medium of landed wealth, Stirling conformed to a broader and significant pattern of embedding and domesticating empire.

The intrusion of imperial capital into Scottish society and politics intensified between the 1760s and 1780s. Conspicuously corrupt electioneering in Perth in 1768 and in Stirling in 1774, where it was reported that the nabob Sir Archibald Campbell of Inverneil spent the colossal sum of £17,000, began to look like prophecy fulfilment.[40] The same phenomenon was evident in England, but perceptions of how resilient each society might be in the face of these imperial influences were very different. The overpowering presence of 'Oriental luxury' and 'corruption' seemed at its most intense in a small country insufficiently robust in its material and societal development to absorb such external pressures. Scotland seemed stuck in an unvirtuous circle, needing empire to improve, yet peculiarly vulnerable to the new inequalities of wealth and unequal power generated by the Empire. The disquiet over whether nabob influence would work to 'improve' or 'corrupt' Scotland was understandable. If migration to the western hemisphere of the Empire seemed to drain Scotland of its people – a key national resource – the Asia half seemed to facilitate the emergence of an unaccountable propertied and political elite. To many contemporaries, the already highly unrepresentative franchise in Scotland was hijacked by the eighteenth-century equivalent of imperial 'dark money', amplifying pre-existing inequalities in access to political rights and liberties in the process. By the 1790s, 13% of English and Welsh seats were held by individuals with links to the East India Company: in Scotland it was 28%. During these decades the Scottish political elite were far more 'imperial' than their English, Welsh, and even Anglo-Irish counterparts.

Trends in the landed sector compounded the sense of a society increasingly overexposed to returning imperial influence and capital. With noticeably smaller urban, manufacturing, financial, and consumption sectors than England, Scotland's rural order was understood to be absolutely central to the country's prospects of improvement. Analysis of estate purchases by those with empire connections confirms the disproportionate impact on Scotland. Following the likes of Archibald Stirling of Cawdor and Keir, Scottish acreage was acquired by returnees at a higher per capita rate than that of England.[41] While Glasgow tobacco lords and sugar merchants acquired approximately 145 estates in west central Scotland, Asia-derived wealth spread out through a much less regionally concentrated pattern of purchasing. In this way, East India Company military commanders, merchants, civil servants, doctors, and maritime captains became landowners all over Scotland.[42] In doing so, all these new owners became important local political and economic leaders who were expected to manage the material enhancement of their communities.

Reconciling empire and improvement: Colonial profits and welfare philanthropy

The cultural strategies used by returnees to reinsert themselves and their money into 'home' society demonstrate an acute awareness of the hostility that could be provoked through association with certain forms of empire and empire wealth. Sojourners were sensitive to the nabob's reputation for excessive luxury, for deploying morally dubious wealth in ways that destabilised land markets and inflated commodity prices while inducing a climate of uncertainty over sustainable societal development.[43] Their responses show an astute, if decidedly calculated, awareness of the need to make their wealth appear virtuous, civically enhancing, and aligned with the objectives of patriotic improvement. Imperial profits had to be seen to help individuals and their material circumstances while bettering the overall health of the national body politick. This cultural imperative to show that empire could produce sustainable improvement and less inequality drove strategies of conspicuous investment in hospital provision, educational resources, and poor relief. Again, it is important not to exceptionalise Scotland in this respect. All over Britain, Ireland, and other European societies, charity and philanthropy were closely linked to efforts at legitimising empire.[44] To these cultural priorities were added new economic attitudes towards labour productivity. Hospital building, the alleviation of poverty, and the preservation of individual health was designed to better equip populations for a more developed, commercial economy. Such objectives were especially attractive to those seeking to reintegrate themselves and their overseas wealth.[45]

The process manifested itself in different ways but can be traced all over Scotland. Because of the country's lower levels of material affluence compared with English localities, a little money could go a long way. A good example of this is the £5 donation by William Fraser to his home parish of Petty in Inverness-shire. William served in the East India Company from 1685 to 1704 and died in London in 1715. His allocation of £5, as well as a further £50 for a local school, are an early indicator of the cultural politics of laundering imperial fortunes through conspicuous philanthropy. Set against the vast profits made through British colonialism in this period, £5 can seem almost meaningless. However, Petty was typical of the poor, sparsely populated rural communities that characterised most of Scotland in this period: in 1792, its total annual collection for poor relief amounted to £6.[46] Fraser's donation over three quarters of a century earlier was, in that context, transformative. The capacity for wealth made in India to substantively impact local communities can be traced in the parish of Lairg in Sutherland. In 1803 Captain Hugh Mackay of the Company's Madras army, the son of the parish minister, was killed at the Battle of Assaye. In his will he left the considerable sum of £500 for the purposes of poor relief. The scale and significance of this injection of imperial profits was highlighted in the Statistical Account in 1845, which stressed how the £25 per annum arising from the interest on the original sum was considerably larger than the £12 raised annually by congregation collections.[47] A review of wills registered at Calcutta, Madras, and Bombay and the noting of bequests in the Statistical Account confirms a further twenty-eight similar examples beside those of Petty and Lairg, stretching across the entire country from Lerwick in the Shetlands to Morebattle in Roxburgh.[48]

Such injections of external wealth were, of course, exercises in socially conservative displays of paternalism. As noted in an important study of the philanthropic strategies of genteel English families with connections to slavery, the purpose of charity was 'the maintenance of the balance of inequality'.[49] While soliciting donations for a new hospital in Inverness in 1799, its advocate argued that the civic project would inculcate 'gratitude' among the lower classes.[50] The 'trickle-down' economics of imperial philanthropy were about securing acceptance for the new forms of wealth and inequality made possible by heavy involvement in colonial ventures. In this sense, the objective of such charity was not the removal of material impoverishment but rather a politics of conspicuously alleviating inequality in order to embed new wealth. This tactic induced a more confident tone among Scotland's landed, clerical, mercantile, and burgh elite that the new forms of inequality and poverty created by changes in the economy would not spiral into resentment, alienation, and political or physical resistance. The more immediate aim, of course, was to enhance the reputation and status of the individual donor. Yet this self-interested agenda did not mean such bequests were insignificant in local terms. William Wordie was from St Ninian's parish, which encompassed the important regional centre of Stirling. When he died as a successful country trader in Calcutta in 1786 he left the substantial sum of £1,000 to his native parish for the purposes of poor relief. Precisely as he intended, his actions entered local memory. In a statistical survey of the parish, the minister noted that, despite an influx of poor from surrounding rural districts, the provision of relief was highly effective. In his explanation for this local success, Wordie's will was highlighted as a contributing factor.[51] The same association with civic virtue, rather than any connotation of nabob wealth, similarly characterised the remembrance of Fraser and Mackay's donations.

The cultural dynamics of domesticating empire through charity involved remaining sensitive to ongoing ambivalent attitudes to migration and the question of whether empire aided or hindered improvement. This concern partly explains why donors often insisted their contributions be linked to civic infrastructure and educational institutions designed to enhance labour productivity and economic modernisation. In this way, any residual suspicions associated with money from Asia were effaced through the ability of overseas profits to expand the potential for local wealth. In 1774 the East Indiaman commander, Captain John Ramsay, left the substantial sum of £200 to the poor of his native Dundee. Even though the town was the fourth largest in Scotland, this was still a donation that substantially augmented its poor relief capacity. The precise stipulations of his will show the intricate associations between alleviating poverty and encouraging productivity. Elderly brewers and merchant seamen were to be supported while a number of poor young men and boys by the name of Ramsay were to be trained in these particular trades. Poor relief and economic improvement blended seamlessly, not least by indicating that an economically active and productive working life would secure social care in later old age. Additional donations to a local school offering free provision and to the Edinburgh society for the advancement of science underlines the applied and highly instrumentalised concept of charity underpinning Ramsay's objectives.[52] The same alignment of welfare towards those who had been, or might in the future be, economically productive explains why the Madras-based mariner David Wilson left one tenth of his wealth in 1738 to the hospital for decayed merchants in Stirling.[53] John Mather's Madras will of 1807 similarly aligned wealth to economically enabling education by assigning bursaries for young men from his home parish in Aberdeenshire.[54] All across urban Scotland returnees deployed their wealth in this way, so as to underscore the positive benefits of certain forms of human mobility within the British Empire. At the same time, their civic philanthropy reinforced social discipline by privileging modes of education and welfare that were accessible only to those willing to accept the new economic order and its related hierarchies and inequalities. Typical in this respect is the grant of £2,000 in the 1819 will of the Calcutta-based merchant John Maclachlan, for the establishment in Glasgow of a 'free school' for the children of poor Highlanders. Built on John Street in telling proximity to another of the city's 'useful' educational centres, The Andersonian Institute, it taught over 200 boys and girls reading, writing, arithmetic, English grammar, and geography by the 1840s. This was exactly the sort of practical curriculum needed to meet the city's burgeoning need for literate and numerate labour.[55]

The likes of Ramsay, Wilson, and Maclachlan were part of a structural intersection between empire and social welfare in early modern Scottish and British society, the scale and legacies of which have yet to be fully excavated and understood. Because emigration was widely perceived to be a symptom of Scotland's underdevelopment, many successful migrants felt the imperative to alleviate poverty by encouraging civic and economic improvement. In 1799, the Highland town of Inverness began a global subscription campaign to support the building of a state-of-the-art infirmary. Expatriates in London were mobilised and sought out donations from across the entire empire. The financial returns are testimony to the way emigration, empire, and ideas of civic health were realigned into a positive rather than negative dynamic. In just three Caribbean colonies, 151 people with connections to the Highlands and Islands donated £1,374; in Canada, the fur trading company of Messrs McTavish and Co. in Montreal secured sixty-five donations totalling £402.[56]

These philanthropic tactics show how understandings of the migrant and of empire were undergoing a crucial transformation. No longer lost to their home society, the imperial sojourner remained connected to it and indeed could be an active member of the community, contributing to its 'improvement' from a distance. In this way, any uncertainties regarding the Empire's capacity to facilitate the health and wealth of the nation (in both an individual and wider civic sense) were erased. Even the most violent and coercive aspects of colonial expansion were now conducive to improvement. On 17 August 1799 Provost Inglis of Inverness wrote to the town's agent in London thanking him for the £288 received from India (which included a donation from Parsi merchants in Bombay). Inglis emphasised the positive resonance between charity, violence, and empire, adding: 'We hope after a successful campaign against Tippo our countrymen in Bombay who have not taken the opportunity to subscribe will think of their poor countrymen at home and that from your friends in Bengal and Madras you will have communications …'[57] Through subsequent subscription efforts, twenty-three Scottish officers and ordinary soldiers in Highland regiments stationed in India advanced a further £677. In all, at least £2,741 (the conservative 'real price' equivalent in 2020 of £246,500) of the overall costs of the infirmary came from overseas.[58]

The diasporic subscription model used in the case of Inverness was not the only way of using ideas of 'patriotic wealth' to link empire with local improvements in health and welfare provision. Such investment also took the form of large-scale donations which enabled the construction of impressive civic projects. The Bombay shipping entrepreneur John Forbes from Strathdon left £10,000 in his last will and testament for such purposes. This single grant constituted 76% of the entire costs of Aberdeen's new asylum constructed in 1819.[59] Similarly, the substantial fortune of the East India Company surgeon James Crichton formed the basis of the royal asylum constructed in Dumfries in 1838, a development understood by contemporaries as marking a major advancement in regional provision.[60]

One last example, albeit perhaps the most conspicuous, indicates how the alignment between empire, migration, and the advancement of health and social provision could have a locally transformative and enduring impact. Between 1810 and 1820, the Company surgeon Dr Alexander Gray and senior Company officer Major-General Andrew Anderson each left over £10,000 to their home town of Elgin. The results transformed the burgh's townscape, leaving it in some ways as one of the most 'imperial spaces' anywhere in the United Kingdom. Colonial wealth financed the construction of what are still two of the most impressive public buildings in a regionally significant urban centre.[61] Gray's hospital (one of the NHS's most important hospitals in the north of Scotland) would cater to physical health. Meanwhile, Anderson's Institution would tend to the old and educate the young in ways conducive to future personal moral virtue, wider economic productivity, and the alleviation of material inequalities.

In such buildings was the confluence in ideals of virtuous empire, civically minded migration, and socially productive wealth made manifest for all to see. It was certainly the intention of their founders, and the other colonial philanthropists discussed here, that the correct conclusion to be drawn was that empire, health, and wealth (both individual and societal) were one and the same thing.

Conclusion

How the northern part of the British Union negotiated issues of empire, returning migrants, wealth accumulation, resultant inequalities, and social planning in the eighteenth and early nineteenth centuries might not at first glance appear to have many contemporary resonances. Yet debates over how countries best provide for the social, educational, and health needs of their populations, and who is to be counted as entitled to such provision, are a conspicuous feature of many democracies in the twenty-first century. Across Europe and in the post-Brexit United Kingdom, 'welfare chauvinism' has blended increasing distrust of free movement of peoples with more restrictive definitions of citizenship and belonging.[62]

Surprisingly similar questions dogged Scottish society in the age of union and empire. Emigration was widely seen as an enduring badge of the country's poverty and its lack of sustained and sustainable improvement. The figure of the migrant carried connotations of economic opportunism and social disruption that would be instantly recognisable in many of the anti-immigrant discourses used by modern populist and right-wing movements. In the eighteenth century, cultural fears over empire were such that these negative associations compassed even high-ranking individuals from Scotland or elsewhere in Britain and Ireland who had ventured to Asia and returned home with new wealth and enhanced influence. These nabobs were acutely conscious of the connotations attributed to them. Countering the belief that they carried the 'vices' of Asia – excessive luxury, authoritarianism, morally tainted wealth, and cultural corruption – back with them involved a policy of civic reintegration through high-profile health and social welfare philanthropy. Scottish society's expanding need for better educational and welfare provision provided the ideal means of displaying moral virtue and social responsibility, and of confirming that the returned migrant belonged to and was a valued part of their community.

A key lesson to be drawn from the historic example of post-union Scotland is that idealised notions of health and social provision and equality of citizenship have always combined with anxieties over the effect of overseas influences. Be it East India Company nabobs in the eighteenth century or the 'economic migrant' in the twenty-first century, the 'alien' 'other' has served to determine the boundaries of belonging and the limits of equality. Perceptions of empire involved a profoundly ambiguous set of connotations that held out the promise of alleviating material inequality but did so in ways which seemed to generate new versions of the very social phenomenon it was supposed to cure. It is also the case that the politics of health and welfare have been a way of reinscribing and defending the boundaries of Britishness for centuries before the creation of the NHS. In the age of empire and 'improvement', those returning from Asia supported new hospitals, asylums, and modes of education that enhanced labour productivity while ameliorating the worst of the emerging inequalities produced by the new economic order. They did so as a conspicuous means of reintegration, of demonstrating they were part of society rather than an alien threat to it. The phenomenon occurred over the entire country, from rural areas like Sutherland, important regional centres like Inverness, Elgin, Aberdeen, Dundee, Stirling, and Dumfries to Glasgow, the country's new commercial metropolis. Human mobility in an imperial context now carried clear connotations of progress, wealth, social development, and civic responsibility. The migrant arriving back from overseas was a positive rather than negative phenomenon. The contrast with populistic politics in the twenty-first century, where questions of contributing to and accessing health and welfare systems are used to exclude immigrants and stigmatise other minorities, is striking.

Notes

1 Michael Blauberger and Susanne K. Schmidt, 'Welfare migration? Free movement of EU citizens and access to social benefits', *Research and Politics* 1.3 (2014), 1–7.
2 John Darwin, *The Empire Project: The Rise and Fall of the British World System 1830–1970* (Cambridge: Cambridge University Press, 2009), pp. 560, 580; Christopher Harvie, 'The moment of British nationalism, 1939–1970', *The Political Quarterly* 71.3 (2000), 328–40.
3 David Edgerton, *Warfare State: Britain, 1920–1970* (Cambridge: Cambridge University Press, 2006), pp. 60–6.

4 Sathnam Sanghera, *Empireland: How Imperialism Has Shaped Modern Britain* (London: Viking, 2021), 105–6.
5 Kate Donington, *The Bonds of Family: Slavery, Commerce and Culture in the British Atlantic World* (Manchester: Manchester University Press, 2020), pp. 254–6.
6 Catherine Hall and Sonya Rose, 'Introduction: Being at home with the empire', in Catherine Hall and Sonya O. Rose (eds), *At Home with the Empire: Metropolitan Culture and the Imperial World* (Cambridge: Cambridge University Press, 2006), pp. 13–14.
7 C. A. Bayly, *Imperial Meridian: The British Empire and the World, 1780–1830* (London: Longman, 1989), pp. 121–4.
8 T. M. Devine, *The Transformation of Rural Society: Social Change and the Agrarian Economy, 1660–1815* (Edinburgh: Edinburgh University Press, 1994), pp. 13–21, 134–61.
9 Eric Richards, 'Scotland and the uses of the Atlantic empire', in Bernard Bailyn and Philip D. Morgan (eds), *Strangers within the Realm: Cultural Margins of the First British Empire* (Chapel Hill, NC and London: University of North Carolina Press, 1991), pp. 67–114; T. M. Devine, 'The spoils of empire', in T. M. Devine (ed.), *Scotland and the Union, 1707–2000* (Edinburgh: Edinburgh University Press, 2008), pp. 91–108.
10 *The Scots Magazine* 27 (Edinburgh: A. Murray and J. Cochran, 1765), p. 134; John Campbell, *A political survey of Britain* … vols I–II (London: Richardson & Urquhart, 1774), vol. I, pp. 222–3.
11 T. M. Devine, *Scotland's Empire, 1600–1815* (London: Penguin, 2003), pp. 320–46; John M. MacKenzie and T. M. Devine, 'Introduction', in John M. MacKenzie and T. M. Devine (eds), *The Oxford History of the British Empire: Scotland and the British Empire* (Oxford: Oxford University Press, 2011), pp. 1–19.
12 John Dwyer and Alexander Murdoch, 'Paradigms and politics: Manners, morals and the rise of Henry Dundas', in J. Dwyer, A. Murdoch, and R. Mason (eds), *New Perspectives on the Politics and Culture of Early Modern Scotland* (Edinburgh: John Donald, 1982), pp. 216–39.
13 Saima Nasar, 'Remembering Edward Colston: Histories of slavery, memory, and black globality', *Women's History Review* 29.7 (2020), 1218–25.
14 Colin Kidd, 'North Britishness and the nature of eighteenth-century British patriotisms', *The Historical Journal* 39.2 (1996), 367–70.
15 Karen Cullen, *Famine in Scotland: The 'Ill Years' of the 1690s* (Edinburgh: Edinburgh University Press, 2010), pp. 123–88.
16 Douglas Watt, *The Price of Scotland: Darien, Union and the Wealth of Nation* (Edinburgh: Luath, 2014), pp. 214–17.
17 David Armitage, 'The Scottish vision of empire: Intellectual origins of the Darien venture', in John Robertson (ed.), *A Union for Empire: Political Thought and the British Union of 1707* (Cambridge: Cambridge University Press, 1995), pp. 97–118.
18 Christopher Whatley, *The Union and the Scots* (Edinburgh: Edinburgh University Press, 2006), pp. 139–57; Andrew Mackillop, 'A union for empire?

Scotland, the English East India Company and the British Union', *The Scottish Historical Review*, 87.2 (2008), 116–34.
19 Whatley, *The Scots and the Union*, pp. 251–7.
20 Douglas Hamilton, 'Scotland and the eighteenth-century empire', in T. M. Devine and Jenny Wormald (eds), *The Oxford Handbook of Modern Scottish History* (Oxford: Oxford University Press, 2012), pp. 424–6.
21 T. M. Devine, *The Glasgow Tobacco Lords: A Study of the Tobacco Merchants of Glasgow and Their Trading Activities, c. 1740–90* (Edinburgh: Edinburgh University Press, 1990), pp. 55–102; A. Mackillop, 'Subsidy state or drawback province': Scotland and the British fiscal-military complex', in Aaron Graham and Patrick Walsh (eds), *British Fiscal Military States, 1660–1783* (London: Routledge, 2016), pp. 187–99.
22 Suzanne Rigg, *Men of Spirit and Enterprise: Scots and Orkneymen in the Hudson's Bay Company, 1780–1821* (Edinburgh: John Donald, 2011), p. 17.
23 Jelle van Lottum and Jan Luiten van Zanden, 'Labour productivity and human capital in the European maritime sector of the eighteenth century', *Explorations in Economic History* 53 (2014), 90–8.
24 Matthew P. Dziennik, *The Fatal Land: War, Empire and the Highland Soldier in British America* (New Haven, CT and London: Yale University Press, 2015), pp. 53–71.
25 Linda Colley, *Britons: Forging the Nation, 1707–1832* (London: Pimlico, 2003), pp. 105–31.
26 'The Scotch Butchery', London, 1775, available at https://www.britishmuseum.org/collection/object/P_1868-0808-4532 (last accessed 23 March 2022).
27 James Hunter, *The Making of the Crofting Community* (Edinburgh: Birlinn, 2018), p. 36.
28 T. C. Smout, N. C. Landsman, and T. M. Devine, 'Scottish emigration in the seventeenth and eighteenth centuries', in N. Canny (ed.), *Europeans on the Move: Studies in European Migration, 1500–1800* (Oxford: Clarendon Press, 1994), pp. 101–2.
29 *A candid enquiry into the causes of the late and the intended migrations from Scotland. In a letter to J_____ R_____ Esq; Lanark-shire* (Glasgow: P. Tait, 1774), pp. 6–27; *The Present Conduct of the Chieftains and Proprietors of lands in the Highlands of Scotland* (Edinburgh: n.p., 1773), pp. 4–12.
30 K. M. Brown and A. Kennedy, '"Their Maxim is Vestigia nulla restrorsum": Scottish return migration and capital repatriations from England, 1603–c.1760', *Journal of Social History* 52.1 (2018), 1–25; Paul Langford, 'South Britons' reception of North Britons, 1707–1820', in T. C. Smout (ed.), *Anglo-Scottish Relations, 1600–1900* (Oxford: Oxford University Press, 2005), pp. 143–69.
31 British Museum, Richard Newton, 'A Flight of Scotchmen' (London: William Holland, 1798), available at https://www.britishmuseum.org/collection/object/P_2001-0520-22 (last accessed 23 March 2022).
32 Philip Lawson and Jim Philips, '"Our Execrable Banditti": Perceptions of nabobs in mid-eighteenth century Britain', *Albion* 16.3 (1984), 226–40; Tillman

W. Nechtman, *Nabobs: Empire and Identity in Eighteenth-Century Britain* (Cambridge: Cambridge University Press, 2010), pp. 81–139.

33 Nicholas B. Dirks, *The Scandal of Empire: India and the Creation of Imperial Britain* (London: Harvard University Press, 2006), pp. 26–189.

34 A. Mackillop, 'The Highlands and the returning nabob: Sir Hector Munro of Novar, 1770–1807', in Marjory Harper (ed.), *Emigrant Homecomings: The Return Movement of Emigrants, 1600–2000* (Manchester: Manchester University Press, 2005), pp. 233–61; Nechtman, *Nabobs*, pp. 11–15, 88–95.

35 George K. McGilvary, *East India Patronage and the British State: The Scottish Elite and Politics in the Eighteenth Century* (London: I. B. Tauris, 2011), pp. 48–229; T. M. Devine and Angela McCarthy, 'Introduction: The Scottish experience in Asia, c.1700 to the present: Settlers and sojourners', in T. M. Devine and Angela McCarthy (eds), *The Scottish Experience in Asia, c.1700 to the Present: Settlers and Sojourners* (London: Palgrave Macmillan, 2017), pp. 1–21.

36 H. V. Bowen, *The Business of Empire: The East India Company and Imperial Britain, 1756–1833* (Cambridge: Cambridge University Press, 2006), p. 273.

37 British Library, Asia, Pacific and Africa Collections, India Office Records [hereafter IOR], O/5/30, fos. 7–15, 130–34, 198–206, 210–13; O/5/26: 'List of Private Trade Europeans resident Calcutta, 13 November 1804.'

38 National Records of Scotland [hereafter NRS], GD345/1166/4/152. I am grateful to Dr David Brown of the NRS for supplying this reference.

39 IOR, B/66, p. 469; Glasgow City Archive [hereafter GCA], T-SK 11/2/16–20, 24, 32, 37; T-SK 15/11, pp. 8–11.

40 *The Scots Magazine* 29 (Edinburgh: A. Murray and J. Cochran, 1767), pp. 665–9; *The Scots Magazine* 36 (Edinburgh: A. Murray and J. Cochran, 1774), pp. 555–8.

41 Stephanie Barczewski, *Country Houses and the British Empire, 1700–1930* (Manchester: Manchester University Press, 2014), pp. 128–33; Stephanie Barczewski, 'Scottish landed-estate purchases, empire and union, 1700–1900', in Stephanie Barczewski and Martin Farr (eds), *The MacKenzie Moment and Imperial History: Essays in Honour of Professor John MacKenzie* (Cham: Palgrave Macmillan, 2019), pp. 181–2.

42 T. M. Devine, 'The colonial trades and industrial investment in Scotland, c. 1700–1815', *The Economic History Review* 29.1 (1976), 1–13; Mackillop, 'The Highlands and the returning nabob', pp. 233–61.

43 Sir John Sinclair, The Statistical Account of Scotland, available at https://statacscot.edina.ac.uk:443/link/osa-vol9-p51-parish-forfar-logie_pert (last accessed 23 March 2022).

44 Colley, *Britons*, pp. 55–60; Donington, *The Bonds of Family*, pp. 254–6.

45 Kathleen Wilson, *The Sense of the People: Politics, Culture and Imperialism in England, 1715–1785* (Cambridge: Cambridge University Press, 1998), pp. 73–9.

46 The National Archives, Kew [hereafter TNA], PROB 11/549, pp. 211–13; Sir John Sinclair, The Statistical Account of Scotland, available at https://statac

cscot.edina.ac.uk:443/link/osa-vol3-p31-parish-inverness-pettie (last accessed 23 March 2022).
47 IOR, L/AG/34/29/203, pp. 88–95; Sir John Sinclair, The Statistical Account of Scotland, available at https://stataccscot.edina.ac.uk:443/link/nsa-vol15-p60-parish-sutherland-lairg (last accessed 23 March 2022).
48 IOR, L/AG/34/29/22, pp. 537–41; L/AG/34/29/209, pp. 1–6; L/AG/34/29/185 [1780], pp. 164–5; L/AG/34/29/205 [1806], pp. 36–9; L/AG/34/29/341 [1788], pp. 108–9; L/AG/34/29/201, LAG/34/29/187 [1786], pp. 117–19, 128–30; L/AG/34/29/6 [1786], 1; L/AG/34/29/7 [1792], 21, 47; L/AG/34/29/9/5; IOR, P/416/90, pp. 24–5; TNA, PROB 11/1058: pp. 273–4; PROB 11/549, pp. 211–13; PROB 11/672, pp. 173–4; PROB 11/630, pp. 119–21; NRS, CC/3/3/12, pp. 72–86; The Statistical Accounts of Scotland, 1791–1845, available at https://stataccscot.edina.ac.uk/static/statacc/dist/home (last accessed 23 March 2022).
49 Donington, *The Bonds of Family*, p. 254.
50 Highland Archive Centre, Inverness [hereafter HAC], Royal Northern Infirmary Records: HHB/1/1/1: Inverness 10 May 1799 to Alexander Fraser, London.
51 IOR, L/AG/34/29/5 [1786] 1; Sir John Sinclair, The Statistical Account of Scotland, available at https://stataccscot.edina.ac.uk:443/link/osa-vol18-p401-parish-stirling-st_ninians (last accessed 23 March 2022).
52 NRS, CC/3/3/12, pp. 72–86.
53 *Records of Ft St George: Copies of Wills, Probates and Letters of Administration, Mayor's Court of Madraspatam, 1735–44, Vol. I* (Madras: Government Press, 1936), p. 21.
54 J. Gordon. The New Statistical Account of Scotland, available at https://stataccscot.edina.ac.uk:443/link/nsa-vol12-p340-parish-aberdeen-fyvie (last accessed 23 March 2022).
55 National Library of Scotland [hereafter NLS], EMS.b.1.57. J. and D. Nichol, 'A Plan of Glasgow' (Glasgow: F. Orr & Sons, 1844); *Minutes of the Committee of Council on Education; with Appendices*, vol. II (London: W. Clowes & Sons, 1844), p. 337; GCA, Registers of Seisins (1781–1820), Barony of Glasgow, [1409]: 17 Nov. 1832. I am grateful to Dr Stephen Mullen, University of Glasgow, for drawing this and related sasines to my attention.
56 HAC, HHB/1/2/1, pp. 5–10.
57 HAC, HHB/1/1/1: Inverness, 17 August 1799: Inglis to Alexander Fraser, Lincoln's Inn.
58 HAC, HHB/1/2/1, pp. 4–5. The modern estimate is drawn from the Measuring Worth calculator, available at https://www.measuringworth.com/calculators/ukcompare/relativevalue.php (last accessed 23 March 2022).
59 TNA, PROB 11/1651, pp. 99–104; J. Gordon. The New Statistical Account of Scotland, available at https://stataccscot.edina.ac.uk:443/link/nsa-vol12-p92-parish-aberdeen-aberdeen (last accessed 23 March 2022).
60 J. Gordon. The New Statistical Account of Scotland, available at https://stataccscot.edina.ac.uk:443/link/nsa-vol4-p15-parish-dumfries-dumfries (last accessed 23 March 2022).

61 NRS, SC26/38/1/101–113: Elgin, 14 December 1824; NLS, EMS.s.759: Robert Ray, 'Plan of the Burgh of Elgin from actual survey' (Edinburgh: Leith & Smith, 1838).
62 Anders Ejrnæs and Bent Greve, 'Populism, welfare chauvinism and hostility towards immigrants', in Bent Greve (ed.), *Welfare, Populism and Welfare Chauvinism* (Bristol: Policy Press, 2019), pp. 138–50.

9

Compromise and adaptation in colonial taxation: Political-economic governance and inequality in Indonesia

Maarten Manse

Between 1870 and 1920, the colonial tax system in Indonesia was radically reformed. The Dutch colonial state that occupied most of the archipelago between 1815 and 1945 abolished old and introduced new forms of taxation. Dutch colonial civil servants envisioned a full-fledged, standardised tax state, in which all subjects were to pay their taxes 'equally, to capacity, fairly and in accordance with standards of modern bureaucracy and governance'.[1] Tax policy became seen as a pivotal instrument to answer questions typical to twentieth-century 'civilisational' or 'ethical' colonialism about inequality, welfare redistribution, and social development – issues about which Dutch officials grew increasingly obsessed in order to harness and legitimise the idea of 'benign' and just colonial governance. Yet, often the political and economic structures that had been built in the nineteenth century to support colonial authority rarely matched the fiscal ambitions of the twentieth. This chapter shows that, as a result, officials had to constantly compromise and adapt their standards to the realities of governance on the ground. Consequently, practices of taxation barely reflected underlying ideologies, leading to the continuation of already established political, economic, and fiscal inequalities within the colony.

Before 1870, Dutch colonial fiscal policy was characterised by coerced labour, tributes, and duties that had their origins in allegedly indigenous 'pseudo-feudal' patterns of agricultural production, land tenure, and social organisation. By 1870, these were no longer deemed suitable to underpin the colonial state. Instead, taxes had to be equally redistributed and were to serve the common and shared interests of colonised societies across the Indonesian archipelago. Convinced as they were of the disciplinary, moralising, and modernising power of taxes, Dutch colonial civil servants believed taxation would foster governance, in which the *raison d'état* of states served the wealth, benefit, and productivity of populations, by supposedly tying colonised societies to the state, optimising popular productivity and welfare, and transforming colonial subjects into governable persons.[2] Thereby, they claimed to enhance processes of capital accumulation, economic growth, unification, centralisation, public involvement, and bureaucratisation characteristic of modern tax states and essential to elevate indigenous society from the depths of feudalism to European standards of capitalism and political, fiscal, and cultural modernity.[3]

Yet, while the 'will to improve' of 'ethical colonialism' has been demonstrated to motivate much of Dutch imperial ambitions,[4] how various modes of modern 'fiscal governmentality' were worked out in practice in the field of colonial empire and what its consequences were for the actual improvement of fiscal equality and equity has remained neglected in historiography. Indeed, colonial Indonesia remained characterised by exploitation, overtaxation of specific indigenous populations, and economic inequality and injustice until long after 1920.[5] Colonial states were generally reluctant to 'place the burden of imperial expansion on the backs of metropolitan taxpayers', and their taxes were rooted not in legitimacy but coercion, increasing the fiscal burden on indigenous populations while minimising state responsibility.[6] Ninety per cent of export taxes in the Dutch East Indies, for instance, was levied from agricultural production by indigenous people, and, around 1931, only half of the colonial state's expenditures were devoted to its own upkeep.[7]

Thus, there seem to have been structural tensions between Dutch colonial ambitions and practices. Tracing the experiences of both statesmen and subjects through the archives of local colonial officials, this chapter demonstrates that the roots of these tensions are found in the ways in which taxation was locally organised. An important aspect, the chapter shows, was that officials were dependent on the nature of local political organisation and cooperation with local elites, which reinforced existent and introduced new forms of political and economic inequality in Indonesia.

The first section explores how the Dutch attempted to transform their exploitative regimes of coerced labour into a coherent and unified system of monetary taxes. The second section analyses how, in order to make this system work, taxes were regrafted into the same local principles of indirect rule and social organisation and practices of negotiation as before, thereby hampering any potential for actual standardisation or unification.

Taxation on paper

After the demise of the Dutch East India Company at the end of the eighteenth century, the Dutch continued on a track of mercantilist and enlightened imperialism but focused primarily on their colonies in Indonesia, more specifically the island of Java and the Moluccas. A devastating war in Java (1825–30) in response to the reformist and experimental policies of the early architects of the colonial state rendered the island devastated and the treasury empty. The Dutch subsequently opted for a policy of capitalist exploitation based on the monopolisation of trade in cash crops produced by coerced labour. Such 'cultivation systems' were implemented in Java in 1830 and in West Sumatra in 1848, while in the Moluccas, such a system had already existed since the mid-seventeenth century. These schemes shaped much of the colonial-political and economic constitution of Indonesia up until about 1900.

Taxing land and labour

In Java, the most densely populated island of Indonesia, peasants traditionally performed services for and paid small tributes to their landlords and rulers in complex systems of taxation, redistribution, and reciprocity. The colonial state monopolised these systems by awarding local rulers from Java's landed aristocracies and village elites, with whom the Dutch had had long-established relations before 1800, positions within its bureaucracy in exchange for their cooperation in its regimes of taxation, coerced cultivation, and construction work.[8] These elevated classes of local elites, together with higher noblemen and other economic and political intermediaries (such as Chinese entrepreneurs), were appointed to govern districts and manage cash-crop plantations in exchange for profit shares, while the Dutch state imposed a monopoly on the export of cash crops to the Netherlands. This way the Dutch exported around 178 million guilders' worth of cash crops between 1840 and 1860 from Java to the Netherlands. The total of colonial profits (*batig slot*) comprised an estimated 20% to even 52% of total Dutch national government income (see Figures 9.1 and 9.2).[9] Colonial profits were used in the Netherlands to invest in infrastructural projects and putting off the introduction of income taxes until the 1890s.[10] This way, Javanese peasants contributed large shares to the Dutch national state budget (see Figure 9.1), creating new inequalities within the Dutch kingdom between colonial and metropolitan subjects.

In Java, the colonial tax system became based on land and labour. Land was taxed under the *land rent*, which taxed yield based on the value of land. It was imposed by the British governor, T. S. Raffles, in 1811. From its imposition until its final revisions in the twentieth century, levying it was hampered by lack of information. The absence of a proper cadastral system and laws and guidelines made the land rent system vulnerable to haggling and corruption. Its revenue was structurally negotiated among the colonial administration and village elites (usually wealthy, landowning peasants) who shared in its profits and were entitled to services from the same taxpayers.[11] Landowning peasants had more bargaining power than

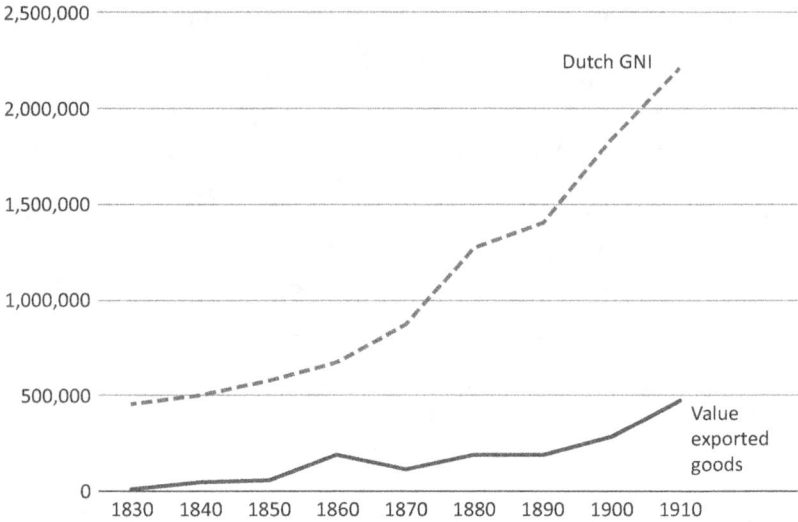

Figure 9.1 Value of exported goods from Java to the Netherlands compared to Dutch gross national income in fl. (guilders) 1,000, 1830–1910.

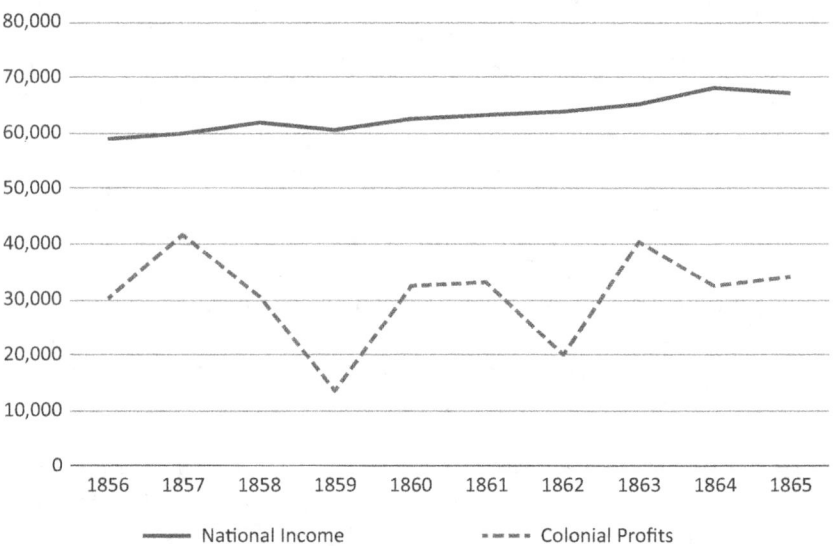

Figure 9.2 Total colonial profits vs. Dutch gross national income (including colonial profits), 1856–65.

landless peasants as their concentrated wealth provided them with access to political power. Consequently, a disproportionally large share of the tax burden landed on the shoulders of the weakest. As explained further below, by enforcing the political capacity of these richer, landholding peasants, the Dutch contributed to further political and economic differentiation by enhancing already existing forms of inequality.[12]

Though the land rent contributed significantly to the colonial treasury, its value was still surpassed by that of coerced labour around 1930.[13] Apart from coerced cultivation, peasants were expected to perform unpaid 'corvée services' – mandatory duties, traditionally performed by people to their landlords, village chiefs, and rulers, usually as a condition for land tenure. These services were worked around by the state over the course of the nineteenth century into elaborate systems of labour exploitation. They comprised a range of works, varying from the construction and maintenance of roads and government buildings to delivering mail and patrolling villages at night. Levied at both provincial and village level, they were of central importance to the functioning, but also the self-legitimisation, of the colonial state, grafted by underlying discursive discourses about indigenous economic mentality.[14] Corvée services were claimed to have disciplinary power to promote labour ethics, cure 'innate laziness', and provide the 'tutelary guidance' necessary to uplift indigenous society to higher standards of development.

Coerced labour had a profound impact on Java's economy. This impact must not be sought simply in terms of exploitation and underdevelopment,[15] as more recent research has demonstrated that Java's economy in fact grew and became more resilient during the nineteenth century.[16] Rather, its consequences were felt through the organisation of village life, as the operation of coerced labour regimes reshaped social hierarchies. Village chiefs received positions of hereditary succession, which they used to expand their political capital at the cost of other, less fortunate peasants. As a result, the possibilities for social mobility of the lower classes of people declined.[17]

Under the growing influence of liberalism at home, coerced labour became increasingly seen as the remnant of 'Javanese feudalism', unbefitting a modern colonial empire, which ideally was based on wage labour, private capital accumulation, and income tax payment. Moreover, the colonial state's focus on Java meant that the tax burden was imposed primarily on Javanese peasants. Subject to corvée and cultivation services as well as land rent, the Javanese were the most highly taxed population group in Indonesia (see Table 9.1). Extraction outside of Java took place in different forms (such as import and export duties or direct export of resources) than direct charges of tax or labour extraction from the (much sparser) indigenous

Table 9.1 Head and land tax revenue levied on Java and the 'Outer Territories' in fl. (guilders), 1870–1920.

	Head tax revenue in fl. (guilders)	Land tax revenue in fl. (guilders)
1870	1,005,000	36,000
1880	1,616,000	173,000
1890	4,613,000	178,000
1900	4,871,000	142,000
1910	7,350,000	206,000
1920	14,993,000	549,000

population. From around 1850 heated criticism of the monopolisation of trade fused with this liberal-moral concern about the well-being of Java's peasants and its resultant inequality in the tax burden, and gave new impetus to calls for reform.[18] In the 1860s the Dutch parliament called for gradually diminishing the use of coerced labour. The monopoly on export of cash crops was abolished in 1870. From 1900 onward, liberal rhetoric got intertwined with humanitarian principles of ethical colonialism that stimulated the gradual deconstruction and replacement of forced labour regimes with monetary income taxes.

Monetary taxation

Colonial tax policy underwent several major changes around the turn of the twentieth century. This was motivated by the rapid Dutch colonial expansion in Indonesia in the late nineteenth century as well as the concern about the well-being of Java's peasantry discussed above, supported by the strong developmental undertones of civilisational-ethical colonialism, and the accordant rising costs of these developments (see Figure 9.3) in tandem with nascent financial autonomy of the colony from the motherland. The combination of these developments required more sophisticated forms of extraction to keep up the appearance of just fiscal policy and redistribution of the burden of empire. As the empire accelerated, expanded, and professionalised, its administrators claimed to seek to improve the welfare of its subjects, but the tax system still reflected earlier modes of capitalist extraction. Hence, the accumulated corvée systems had to be revised to make 'all contribute not in labour, but money'.[19]

In 1854, it was stipulated that all corvée services had to be 'gradually abolished' and replaced with monetary taxes, by allowing people to structurally 'buy' or 'pay off' their labour services in exchange for a small amount of 'head tax' which would then fund the public works

Political-economic governance in Indonesia 183

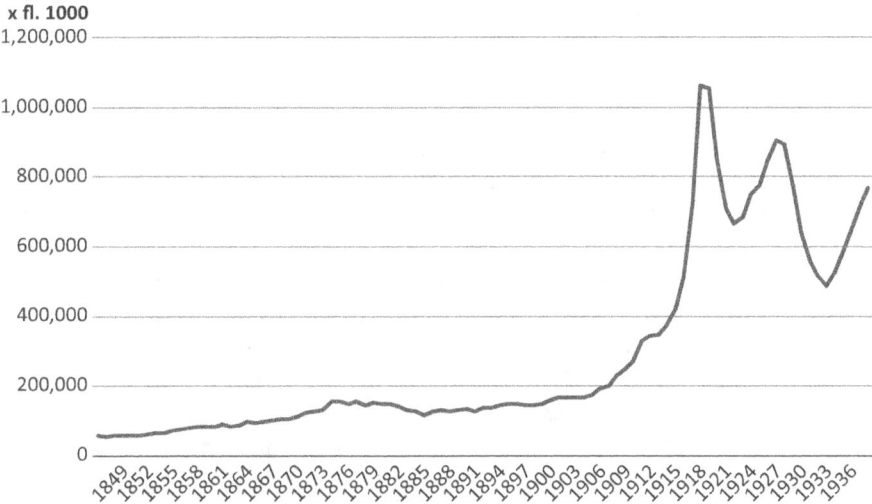

Figure 9.3 Government spending in the Dutch East Indies in fl. (guilders) 1,000, 1848–1938.

previously carried out in coerced labour.[20] Thus, head taxes could theoretically only be levied from people liable to corvée. Yet in practice, many others were also assessed by indigenous civil servants, who 'attempted to seek the favour of their Dutch superiors' by maximising tax revenues.[21] A first centrally levied head tax was imposed in Java in 1882 to replace the personal corvée services performed by peasants to the Javanese aristocracy.[22]

However, the footings on which the various corvée regulations were organised were at the time still largely unknown. In 1889 the government ordered a comprehensive investigation into the principles of Java's corvée labour regime. Such investigations rather 'produced' than 'disclosed' facts, enabling the state to further verify and legitimise its claims over Java's agricultural labour reserve,[23] to demonstrate 'the state's right to power through its will to the production of truth'.[24] In many provinces, it was determined that landholding was the crucial factor determining taxability while only in some parts of Java was this the case and only under very specific conditions.[25] This encouraged chiefs to award landless peasants small plots of land to demand more taxes and services, sometimes for their own private purposes.[26] Meanwhile, the circular increase in labour demand and the absence of proper fiscal institutes to carry out state activities encouraged chiefs to keep claiming the labour power of subjects in order to fulfil the increasing demands of the state rather than to enforce the imposition of monetary taxes. Only richer peasants were able to 'buy off' their services, while poorer, landless peasants, the labour reserve of Java, were pushed into a position of 'pseudo-landholding' and taxability without acquiring the means to carry their burden.[27]

Monetary taxation required a full reinvention of the political constitution of society and abolition of old rights and privileges, which was not in the interest of indigenous officials, who were still crucial to the operation of the local colonial administration. Many colonial officials turned a blind eye to the continuation of personal services by their indigenous counterparts.[28] As a result, while the average amount of labour services levied per capita decreased roughly by half between 1880 and 1920, by 1929 about 11.4 million individuals in Indonesia (about a quarter of the total indigenous population) still performed some kind of coerced services.[29] Labour exploitation remained a crucial element of Dutch colonialism.

Until the 1870s, Europeans, as well as indigenous people within the colonial state outside of Java, paid virtually no direct tax. The coerced labour and cash crop systems generated sufficient revenue to carry the burden of governance, while outside of Java it was in no position to demand tax payments until later in the nineteenth century. In an attempt to alleviate some of the burden imposed upon Javanese peasants, a range of income and property taxes for other population groups was introduced between 1878 and 1920, albeit only after much protest.[30] Moderation in tax assessments was advised to prevent friction, especially in the case of 'Foreign Orientals' (Asian people from outside of Indonesia, who formed a separate socio-legal category next to 'Europeans' and 'indigenous people'), many of whom were crucial to the functioning of local economies as intermediaries.[31] Minister of Colonies P. P. van Bosse advised in 1878 to 'keep tax revenues below expectations for the first few years, and let the principles of the new taxes sink in' rather than 'causing serious difficulties and resistance because of fiscal narrow-mindedness'.[32] Such doctrines of moderation were commonly applied to stimulate gradual adaptation and stable compliance. Hence, tax rates remained rather low: a maximum of 2% over annual income, 4% over property in the tax system for Europeans and 'Foreign Orientals'.[33]

Between 1880 and 1915, these taxes were reformed several times and exported to all regions conquered by the Dutch between 1870 and 1920, until gradually most of Indonesia was covered by the colonial tax regime. In 1908, a series of income and 'company taxes' for indigenous people was imposed and merged with the income tax system of 'Foreign Orientals' in 1914, at a rate of 40 cents for every 10 guilders of income for the coming year, based on income assessments of the preceding year.[34] These income taxes aimed to subject all indigenous people across the archipelago to the same standards of extraction and governance. Taxpayers were inscribed in tax registers which subjected them, at least on paper, to a place of residence, an individual source of income (usually a plot of land), and a fixed social position. These were confirmed on tax bills that were awarded after the assessment, which also functioned as proof of identification.[35]

These taxes were intended to monetise, standardise, and uniformise tax payment, but in particular the income taxation of indigenous peoples (over 95% of the total population in 1910)[36] remained diversified into a mixture of income (or company), head, and land taxes.[37] The average assessment per capita diverged widely, from 0.42 guilders in Timor to 4.35 guilders in East Sumatra (see Table 9.2), corresponding to welfare differences among these regions. Tax collection was problematised in many parts of Indonesia by lack of money, local corruption, and poor administrative capacity, adding to the inequality of the burden between regions where taxes were successfully levied, and regions where that was not the case.[38]

Furthermore, the state's bureaucratic categories rarely aligned with local patterns of social organisation. In the highlands of West Sumatra, for instance, property and income were not held or earned individually, but communally. Land was owned by families or lineages as a whole and inherited in the female line.[39] This suited colonial systems of coerced production (introduced in West Sumatra in the 1840s), which were

Table 9.2 Average direct tax assessments per capita in the 'Outer Territories', in fl. (guilders), around 1913.

Province			
Directly ruled territories		'Self-governing' territories	
Timor	0.42	Aceh	0.54
Tapanuli	0.49	East Sumatra	0.72
West Borneo	0.68	Bali and Lombok	0.77
West Sumatra	0.885	Riau	0.86
Bali and Lombok	0.93	South and East Borneo	0.96
Jambi	0.97	Timor	0.99
Ternate	1.16	West Borneo	1.09
South and East Borneo	1.17	Ambon	1.14
Menado	1.185	Ternate	1.32
Riau	1.32	Menado	1.53
Bengkulu	1.41		
Aceh	1.43		
Ambon	1.58		
Lampung	1.62		
Palembang	2.22		
East Sumatra	4.35		

indifferent to who owned land under which circumstances, as long as they were used for cash crop production.[40] However, this way, coffee cultivation became 'the only source of welfare being taxed'.[41] To monetary income taxation, the system of shared property and matrilineal inheritance posed various problems. The Dutch feared that, since they could not pass on property, men lacked stimulus to develop proper work ethics to accumulate capital, income, or property required for personal taxation.[42] In Dutch colonial patriarchal notions of society, men supposedly held both political power and authority over property, and hence were taxable persons who supposedly diffused their tax burden by employing the labour power of their women and children. But in West Sumatra (male) political leaders held no authority over taxable income or property, and were untaxable. In 1908, the Dutch, radically, decided to appoint the male family representatives as the taxable persons nonetheless, and designated the family lands as taxable and executable objects.[43] This generated much popular resentment, which finally culminated in anti-colonial revolt.[44] The rebellion was suppressed, but the tensions the Dutch brought into society were never permanently resolved and levels of tax compliance remained low.[45]

Towards unification

In 1920, the income tax systems of indigenous people and 'Foreign Orientals' were merged with that of Europeans into a unified income tax.[46] By that time, the purpose of colonial taxation and governance had been fully recast into the terms of colonial governance. Crucial to this project was the standardisation and equalisation of taxpayers. The colonial state imposed upon itself the moral duty to govern the entire archipelago in a uniform and equal manner to demonstrate strong, legitimate, and 'benevolent' rule. By making the separate and dispersed peoples of Indonesia share in the burden of colonial administration equitably, it would supposedly automatically transform them into a unified class of taxpaying, obedient subject-citizens.[47] Thus, monetary taxes became used to collectivise and standardise subjects and unify and reform the colony at large. They replaced labour services as the disciplinary tools to extirpate what the state considered social deviance (such as communalism, nomadism, or statelessness), and stimulate 'productive behaviour' and settlement to create taxable sedentary peasantries everywhere and keep increasingly bigger masses of people under control.

However, while officials envisioned a centralised and uniform population of settled subjects that operated in the same political legal-fiscal sphere, the colony remained crossed by numerous differences. Social differentiation

Political-economic governance in Indonesia   187

between European and other socio-legal classes remained unbridgeable in practice. Wages and incomes of many coolies, craftsmen, or day labourers were in fact so low that the majority of the indigenous population was virtually untaxable.[48] In 1906, the Director of Finance reported that 93% of the indigenous population earned less than 150 guilders annually, while around 1925, still only 25% of the indigenous population in the archipelago was reported to earn above the minimal taxable income of 120 guilders per year.[49] The unified income tax of 1920 supposedly taxed these incomes within the same regime as European incomes of up to 120,000 guilders.[50] It was hence considered very unwieldy.[51] The manpower and administrative capacity of the state was too low to tax all these different incomes properly and equitably, let alone to resolve the huge income and welfare differences among the various sociolegal groups and ethnicities in the archipelago. The chief administrator of Bali sighed in 1919:

> Every year, when going into the *desa* ... I see hundreds of poorly dressed Balinese sitting around me, all listening unmoved to their assessments of 1.50 to 2 guilders ... Even if I knew their incomes, where would I find the time to assess 25,000 people and calculate their assessments?[52]

To many officials, the unification remained an 'achievement on paper', politically motivated in the spirit of uplifting and integrating the indigenous populations into a unified colonial society that existed only in the minds of colonial theorists in The Hague.[53]

Tax in practice

So, what remained of the Dutch colonial state's towering ambitions of social engineering and tax reform if we look at how it was implemented in the period of roughly 1870–1920? The practice of taxation, this section demonstrates, was dependent on unpredictable realities of governance which further curtailed the potentially redistributive power of taxation and made colonial society less equal.

Indirect rule and local political power

A crucial factor that explains both the successes as well as the limitations of Dutch colonial rule and tax collection is its perpetual reliance on local elites. During the era of coerced cultivation, the organisation of labour, taxation, and administration was outsourced to village elites and local aristocracies, as a classic example of indirect rule. These elites ensured the state of their loyal cooperation in exchange for shares in production output, profits, land,

and labour. During the conversion of the political economy into monetary tax systems around 1900, these shares and renumerations were transformed into 'collectors' wages' of (usually) 8%.

As a result, tax reforms, rather than being imposed from the heights of bureaucracy, worked through the local knowledge, social organisation, and practices of these regional elites and the desires of targeted populations. This entailed the integration of local knowledge systems as well as customary strategies of negotiation and deference using specific forms of patrimonial bureaucracy, which had been the cornerstone of rule and extraction, and would remain so in the colonial era. The latter is not illogical, as local systems of governance and taxation were more adaptive, fluent, flexible, and dynamic and provided better answers to local challenges than the 'alien' principles of European statecraft. And who to administer these better than the people and chiefs already present? Hence, around 1928, an overwhelming 90% of the colonial civil servants were of Indonesian descent,[54] and collected taxes under the auspices of the colonial 'Department of Interior Administration', which coordinated all matters of governance throughout the archipelago.

This had a profound impact upon power relations in Indonesian village life. In Java, for instance, village leaders, originally elected representatives and arbiters in matters of customary law, became authoritarian rulers who, granted hereditary succession, accumulated increasing wealth and power and started claiming much larger shares of tax revenue, land, and labour than they were entitled to.[55] These village elites gained increasing influence over the essential intelligence (land surveys, population censuses) that informed tax assessments as well as the coordination of taxation. This resulted in high levels of economic differentiation and erosion of a healthy tax base of wealthy individuals.[56] In pre-colonial Java, the tax burden had to be carefully outbalanced, as peasants could opt to run away and pledge loyalty to a different lord or bargain for better terms elsewhere, resulting in possible loss of essential labour power and rendering rulers constrained by the potential mobility of their followers.[57] But increasingly supported by the political and military power provided since the imposition of the cultivation system, village chiefs in Java became better able to retain and trace their followers, thereby exerting much greater control over extraction from their people.[58] Indeed, indirect rule 'required only a minimal state apparatus', but also increasingly empowered local elites who 'had an interest in withholding resources and knowledge from the centre'.[59] Across Indonesia, the ambiguous role of village chiefs as government tax collectors and village representatives started prompting chiefs to navigate between the government's, the village's, and their own interests, of course often favouring the latter.[60]

This became a serious problem on the island of Ambon. Here, the Dutch had maintained a monopoly on spice trade since the seventeenth century, overseen by a class of indigenous *raja* (village rulers) who shared in its profits.[61] When the monopoly collapsed in the nineteenth century, these raja lost their primary source of income. After the full abolition of the spice monopoly in 1865, they were no longer able to fund the expensive lifestyles to which they had become accustomed. A group of raja wrote to the Dutch governor general, asking for a raise of their monthly stipends.[62] Some reportedly even lacked means to buy the appropriate regal outfits they were entitled to and expected to wear ceremonially, and had to borrow suits for formal occasions from richer colleagues or European officials.[63] Their prestige as rich, powerful, local spice lords crumbled rapidly and they started experiencing difficulties in enforcing their rights and entitlements to income, land, and labour. This caused political crisis and instigated the kind of problematic 'corrupted' or 'despotic' behaviour that the ethical policy was supposed to prevent. The head tax that the Dutch imposed as an alternative to the raja's previous labour entitlements were poorly paid and offered insufficient revenue, and the Dutch refused to contribute from the central colonial treasury.[64]

As a result, many raja resorted to acquiring 'unlawful income', by obfuscating tax money. One of them forced his subjects to sell their cloves to him at prices considerably below the market value to his own benefit and illegitimately demanded formally abolished forms of services, but for political reasons the Dutch had little choice but to keep supporting him.[65] Forced to keep up the appearance of the powerful prestigious lords they had once been, without being offered support or durable alternatives to previous entitlements, the raja felt driven to destitution and criminal behaviour. Meanwhile, nationalist parties jumped into the power vacuum rendered by the raja, mobilising villagers for mass support against the state and encouraging them to not pay their taxes but party contributions instead.[66] After the transition towards monetary taxes, the colonial state no longer required nor accommodated the use of authoritarian intermediating rulers. Interestingly, this partially reduced the kind of political inequality that had emerged between elites and commoners under the spice monopoly. The abolition of services curtailed the sway the raja had had over the labour economy.[67] But by discarding their power, the legitimacy of the state itself, in the eyes of the people interwoven with the position of the raja, became disputed. Therefore, repairing the inequalities imposed under coerced cultivation systems led to a potential undermining of state power. Hence, the state had a vested interest in maintaining inequality, although in Ambon it was no longer fully able to do so.

Resilience and resistance

Continued reliance on local ruling elites rendered much of the ambition to use taxation as a disciplinary, equalising, and civilising instrument unfulfilled. To impose modern taxes, officials relied on rather unmodern principles and ruling techniques provided by the societies they governed. Indeed, even in 'the age of bureaucracy', 'European empires were often a-modern, or de-modernising in their governing practices'.[68] This only contributed to the fiscal inequality that colonial officials attempted to reduce.

Equally important were the evasive ways in which the state dealt with resilience. Regions where taxation was challenging had a higher chance of remaining exempted. A fascinating example of this is the island of Seram, geographically located close to Ambon, but socio-politically rather different. The mountainous interiors of Seram were inhabited by a collection of disunified ethnic groups or tribes. Contrary to the Ambonese and Javanese, they lived not in larger structures of state-societies based on organised cultivation (and accordant forms of taxation and governance), but in disparate, mobile communities. They were largely non-monotheistic and practised head-hunting. Therefore, the Alfurs can be recognised as an insular example of the kind of mountainous and peripheral people who understood 'the art of not being governed' – the deliberate strategies of avoiding fixed village settlement, centralised agriculture, record keeping, and administration to keep the intrusion or development of states at bay and remain unknown, unmapped, unregistered, and, hence, untaxed.[69] Because of these topographical and socio-cultural conditions and the absence of larger kingdoms, empires, resources, or other economic attractions, Seram was left untouched (except for its coastal regions, which were subjected to colonial governance and taxes) while Ambon was subjected to colonial rule in the seventeenth and eighteenth centuries. By the later nineteenth century, however, the Dutch urge to claim, unify, and command the entire Indonesian archipelago under Dutch imperial rule brought forth a new effort to violently conquer the island's interiors in order to include, 'civilise', and 'tranquilise' the island's population. After a series of difficult and gruelling military campaigns to gain some minimal territorial control, the Dutch introduced a regime of coerced labour duties and head taxes, concepts entirely alien to the island's inhabitants. To enable the levying of taxes there, the Dutch set up a similar network of indirect rule as elsewhere, appointing headmen of clans as, indeed, raja, a title that did not exist on Seram prior to colonisation.[70] The new 'chiefs' were dressed up in suits and paraphernalia, and were expected to levy head taxes and labour services in return for the standard enumerations and 8% collectors' wage.[71]

However, these chiefs had not the kind of absolute authority that Java's village chiefs or Ambon's raja had historically accumulated. Rather than territorial rulers making claims on people's wealth, they were clan chiefs safeguarding spiritual and political order among the tribes. They continuously bargained with their subjects, who in turn ignored the new joint administration of elevated chiefs and the Dutch state as much as they could and 'escaped' their designated villages on a regular basis to evade registration and tax assessment.[72] Forced settlement, a typical Dutch strategy in 'stateless spaces', and construction of roads were experienced as such a restriction of freedom that many refused to be registered or reveal their names and took off into the forests.[73] The colonial army intervened to bring them back, but with limited effect as many took off again the moment the army had left.[74] Some people even constructed 'fake', provisional houses on the beach which they only inhabited during the government's inspection visits, to keep up the appearance of 'village inhabitancy'.[75] Only under the structural implicit threat of military violence were the Dutch able to enforce such village inhabitancy and payment of taxes. Thus, rather than actively improving or reforming the way people lived their lives, the state sought to minimise opposition and resistance to maintain the pretence of order, peace, and tranquillity. The ability of subjects on Seram to evade, resist, and deflect the state suggests that on-the-spot colonial power was far more limited than the state claimed. As a result, taxes were levied successfully only in regions where the state was on reasonably good terms with local elites, such as Java. Hence, the distribution of the tax burden depended much on the interaction between the state and its middlemen.

Thereby, differentiation in the political power of the colonial state immediately impacted the level of fiscal equality in particular regions as well as throughout the archipelago. Dependent on the divergent functioning of local intermediating elites and the local disposition and behaviour of subjected populations, the colonial bureaucracy levied its taxes largely only in name. Much of the tax system was outsourced to these intermediaries who often levied them on their own terms. This rendered an eroded and immature tax base to the post-colonial Indonesian state upon independence in 1945.[76] Lack of 'clearly delineated plans for the establishment of efficient extractive structures' undercut the state's towering governmental ambitions of social reform, improvement of justice, and fiscal unification.[77] By 1925, 80% of income tax was still only collected in Java.[78] Adaptation and compromise to local realities of capable mediating elites and popular resilience made the colonial tax system heavily diversified and unequal.

Conclusion: Colonial inequality within

Taxation in colonial Indonesia took place in a field of tension between questions of public finance and governance, which were frequently at odds with each other. Taxes were designed and wielded as governmental tools to transform and standardise subjects. The imposition of monetary head and income taxes was essential to replace the pseudo-feudal systems of nineteenth-century colonial labour exploitation with monetary taxes as aligned to aspirations of 'ethical', developmental colonialism. This entailed tying the archipelago together under a centralised, unified system of direct income taxes under high bureaucratic standards, to redistribute the tax burden more fairly among the inhabitants of the colony and increase fiscal equality.

However, to both fiscally unify and equitably reach into the pockets of subjects in a state crossed by numerous geographical, ethnic, social, and economic divisions was an impossible task in a colonial society that was fundamentally unequal and unfair. Moreover, reorganising the tax system required a complete reorganisation of the political-economic foundations on which the colonial state was grafted, informed heavily by local social organisation revolving around labour duties, personal privileges, and patrimonial forms of rule. Considering the limited capacity of the colonial bureaucracy and its weak institutional infrastructure both prior to and during the rapid imperial expansion of the Dutch colonial state over the archipelago, such a reorganisation was untimely and unrealistic. Hence, the Dutch continued governing through such local mechanisms using the local elites already present. But while outsourcing the tax system to cherry-picked headmen made the operation of the tax system more cost-efficient, it also prevented the emergence of a transparent and just bureaucracy. For many local chiefs, tax levying became a difficult balancing act between the demands of the state and the expectations of their populations. Often, levying taxes in informal ways was a whole lot easier than observing the decrees and bureaucratic guidelines of the government. However, power, both formal and informal, was unevenly distributed. As a result, the imposition of monetary taxes, intended to increase equality, only enabled further political inequality.

Conditioned by these local challenges, the colonial tax systems in Java, Sumatra, and the Moluccas differed radically. The downward mobility of elites in Ambon supported gradual political and fiscal equalisation of formally differentiated social classes, and the resilience of populations in inaccessible places like Seram or the difficulties posed by the social conditions in West Sumatra obstructed taxation, while in Java, relatively smooth cooperation with increasingly corrupted village elites enabled previously impossible levels of tax levying. Given these various pragmatic differences and the roots of political inequality, the methods, rates, and burden of taxation remained dissipated and disunified, and the amount of tax paid and ways in which subjects experienced the tax regime depended on when and where they lived. As a result, fiscal inequality grew, as the ever-expanding colony was funded by taxes still largely paid by small portions of the colonised population. The root cause of this development is found in the compromises of local officials and the resulting discrepancies within the local organisation of the colonial state.

Notes

1 As put by Director of Finances F. A. Liefrinck in 1910, in Arsip Nasional Republik Indonesia [National Archives of Indonesia; ANRI], General Secretariat Archives [Algemeene Seceratie; AS], 'Grote Bundel' [GB] TGA 10649, herein: Director of Finance to Governor General, 4–7-1910.
2 See for instance J. Kielstra and C. Lulofs, 'Verplichte Diensten of Geldelijke Heffingen?', *Tijdschrift voor het Binnenlandsch Bestuur* 46 (1914), 28–44.
3 The colonial economist J. H. Boeke, for instance, explained indigenous poverty from 'backward, primitive methods [...] of organisation [...] pre-capitalist conceptions of labour and helplessness in regards to the demands of a money-economy'. J. H. Boeke, 'Tropisch-Koloniale Staathuishoudkunde: Het Probleem' (PhD thesis, Amsterdam: UvA, Debussy, 1910). See also O. R. E. Brunner, *De Unificatie van het Belastingstelsel in Ned.-Indië* (Weltevreden: Kenanga, 1928), pp. 22–4; W. Frijling, 'De Algemeene Belasting op de Bedrijfs- en Andere Inkomsten', *Koloniaal Tijdschrift* 4 (1915), 44.
4 T. M. Li, *The Will to Improve: Governmentality, Development, and the Practice of Politics* (Durham, NC: Duke University Press, 2007); E. Locher-Scholten, *Ethiek in Fragmenten: Vijf Studies over Koloniaal Denken en Doen Van Nederlanders in de Indonesische Archipel, 1877–1942* (Utrecht: Hes, 1981).
5 A. Booth, 'The burden of taxation in colonial Indonesia in the twentieth century,' *Journal of Southeast Asian Studies* 11.1 (1980), 94; A. Booth, *Economic Change in Modern Indonesia: Colonial and Post-Colonial Comparisons* (Cambridge: Cambridge University Press, 2016), pp. 104–10.
6 E. Frankema and A. Booth, 'Fiscal capacity and the colonial state: Lessons from a comparative perspective,' in E. Frankema and A. Booth (eds), *Fiscal Capacity and the Colonial State in Asia and Africa, 1850–1960: Studies in Economic History* (Cambridge: Cambridge University Press, 2019), pp. 11–13.
7 A. J. Vandenbosch, *The Dutch East Indies: Its Government, Problems and Politics* (Berkeley: University of California Press, 1942), p. 172; A. Booth, *Colonial Legacies: Economic and Social Development in East and Southeast Asia* (Honolulu: University of Hawai'i Press, 2007), pp. 241–66.
8 M. R. Manse, 'Promise, pretence and pragmatism: Governance and taxation in colonial Indonesia, 1870–1940' (PhD thesis, Leiden University, 2021), pp. 157–66.

9 C. Fasseur, 'Kultuurstelsel en Koloniale Baten: De Nederlandse Exploitatie van Java 1840–1860' (PhD thesis, Leiden University, 1975), p. 20; J. de Jong, *Van Batig Slot naar Ereschuld: De Discussie over de Financiële Verhouding tussen Nederland en Indië en de Hervorming van de Nederlandse Koloniale Politiek, 1860–1900* ('s-Gravenhage: SDU, 1989), pp. 9, 39–41.
10 De Jong, *Van Batig Slot naar Ereschuld*, p. 42.
11 W. R. Hugenholtz, 'Landrentebelasting op Java, 1812–1920' (PhD thesis, Leiden University, 2008), pp. 39–40.
12 R. E. Elson, *Village Java under the Cultivation System, 1830–1870* (Sydney: Allen & Unwin, 1994), pp. 203–5; J. Breman, *The Village in Java and the Early-Colonial State* (Rotterdam: CASP, Faculty of Social Sciences, Erasmus University, 1980).
13 A. Booth, 'Towards a modern fiscal state in Southeast Asia, c. 1900–60', in E. Frankema and A. Booth (eds), *Fiscal Capacity and the Colonial State in Asia and Africa, 1850–1960: Studies in Economic History* (Cambridge: Cambridge University Press, 2019), p. 49.
14 S. H. Alatas, *The Myth of the Lazy Native: A Study of the Image of the Malays, Filipinos and Javanese from the 16th to the 20th Century and Its Function in the Ideology of Colonial Capitalism* (London: Frank Cass, 1977); F.A. Noor, *The Discursive Construction of Southeast Asia in 19th Century Colonial-Capitalist Discourse* (Amsterdam: Amsterdam University Press, 2016).
15 C. Geertz, *Agricultural Involution: The Process of Ecological Change in Indonesia* (Berkeley: University of California Press, 1963).
16 Elson, *Village Java*.
17 Ong Hok Ham, 'Pajak Dalam Perspektif Sejarah', *Prisma* 14.4 (1985), 81; J. Breman, *Control of Land and Labour in Colonial Java: A Case Study of Agrarian Crisis and Reform in the Region of Cirebon During the First Decades of the 20th Century* (Leiden and Dordrecht: Foris, 1983), p. 6; Hugenholtz, 'Landrentebelasting op Java', pp. 24–5.
18 See for instance W. R. van Hoëvell, 'Schets van een Ethisch Program', *Tijdschrift voor Nederlandsch Indië* I (1849).
19 Nationaal Archief [National Archives of the Netherlands; NA], Archief Ministerie van Koloniën: Openbaar Verbaalarchief [Ministry of Colonies, public minutes; MinKol OV) [2.10.36.04] inv. nr. 44, Verbaal [Vb.] 6–3–1907, nr. 27, Director of Finance to Governor General, 14–12–1905.
20 RR 1854, art. 57, in NA MinKol 1850–1900 3196, Vb. 13–5–1879 n3. See also C. F. Schoch, *De Heerendiensten op Java en Madura Volgens het Regeerings-Reglement van 1854* ('s-Gravenhage: Van Stockum, 1891), p. 1. From 1905 onward, peasants were allowed to 'buy off' collectively. F. Fokkens, *De Afschaffing der Laatste Heerendiensten op Java* (Baarn: Hollandia, 1914), p. 16.
21 F. Fokkens, *Eindresumé van het bij Besluit van den Gouverneur-Generaal van Nederlandsch-Indië van 24 Juli 1888 N°8 Bevolen Onderzoek naar de Verplichte Diensten der Inlandsche Bevolking op Java en Madoera (Gouvernementslanden)* (2 vols, Batavia: Smits, 1901–02), I, part 1, p. 18.

22 Staatsblad van Nederlandsch-Indië ('s-Gravenhage: Schinkel; Batavia: Landsdrukkerij, 1816–1948) [Stbl.] 1882 n136 and 137.
23 Fokkens, *Eindresumé*.
24 A. L. Stoler, *Along the Archival Grain: Epistemic Anxieties and Colonial Common Sense* (Princeton, NJ: Princeton University Press, 2009), pp. 29–31.
25 Manse, 'Promise, pretence and pragmatism', pp. 173–85.
26 J. M. van Vleuten, 'Invloed van Heerediensten en Hoofden op het Grondbezit', *Tijdschrift voor Nederlandsch-Indië* 1.1 (1872), 299; 'Belasting in Arbeid en Belasting in Geld op Java', *De Gids* 36 (1872), 230; Schoch, *De Heerendiensten*, pp. 3–4; Elson, *Village Java*, p. 91.
27 Breman, *Control of Land and Labour*, pp. 9–13, 20; Elson, *Village Java*, pp. 119–20, 205–6.
28 NA MinKol 1850–1900 3241, Vb. 16–10–1879 n2, herein: Vb.
29 ANRI, Departement van het Binnenlands Bestuur [Department of Interior Administration; DepBB] 586, herein: DepBB, 18–1–1929: 'Statistiekkaart'.
30 De Jong, *Van Batig Slot naar Ereschuld*, pp. 145–9.
31 ANRI AS Besluit [decision] 30–12–1878 nr.1, herein: 'Besluit Invoering van de personele belasting en het patentrecht.'
32 NA MinKol 1850–1900 3162 Vb. 12–30–1878 n1, herein: Minister of Colonies [MinKol] to Governor General [GG], 8–11–1878.
33 Stbl. 1878 n86, 87, 349, and 350.
34 Stbl. 1914 n130.
35 Manse, 'Promise, pretence and pragmatism', p. 95.
36 P. Boomgaard and A. J. Gooszen, *Changing Economy in Indonesia: A Selection of Statistical Source Material from the Early 19th Century up to 1940*. Vol. 11: *Population Trends 1795–1942* (Amsterdam: Royal Tropical Institute, 1991), p. 10.
37 J. Roest, 'Vergelijkend overzicht van de Buitenbezittingen van de inlandsche bevolking geheven directe belastingen over 1913', *Tijdschrift voor het Binnenlandsch Bestuur* 48 (1913), 518–29.
38 J. W. Meijer Ranneft and W. Huender, *Onderzoek naar den Belastingdruk op de Inlandsche Bevolking* (Weltevreden: Landsdrukkerij, 1926), pp. 146–59; Commissie tot Herziening van het Belastingstelsel in Nederlandsch-Indië, *Vierde Verslag van de Commissie tot Herziening van het Belastingstelsel in Nederlandsch-Indië* (Weltevreden: 's Landsdrukkerij, 1925), p. 37.
39 Taxes were levied based on the size of families, and usually only levied over export and trade. E. E. Graves, *The Minangkabau Response to Dutch Colonial Rule in the Nineteenth Century* (Ithaca, NY: Cornell University Modern Indonesia Project, 1981), pp. 6, 55–8; J. S. Kahn, *Constituting the Minangkabau: Peasants, Culture and Modernity in Colonial Indonesia* (Providence: Berg, 1993), p. 164.
40 Kahn, *Constituting the Minangkabau*, p. 123.
41 ANRI AS GB MGS 4233, herein: MGS 24–9–1904: GovSWK to GG, 18–7–1901, p. 20.
42 F. A. Heckler, *Voorstellen Betreffende de Invoering van Directe Belastingen in het Gouvernement Sumatra's Westkust*, 3 vols (Batavia: 1905–06), vol. I, pp. 64–82.

43 Stbl. 1908 n93; Heckler, *Voorstellen*, vol. II, pp. 19–24.
44 R. Amran, *Sumatra Barat: Pemberontakan Pajak 1908* (Jakarta: Gita Karya Geka, 1988).
45 Manse, 'Promise, pretence and pragmatism', pp. 246–53.
46 Stbl. 1920 n678.
47 Brunner, *De Unificatie*, pp. 12–14.
48 Daily wages for coolies and day labourers on sugar plantations in Java were around ƒ0.30–0.50 in 1870–90 to about ƒ2 for skilled craftsmen in 1920. By comparison, coolies working in tin mines on the island of Bangka (east of Sumatra) earned around ƒ0.44 daily in 1932. Until around 1930, such wages barely covered the costs of living. N. Dros, *Changing Economy in Indonesia: A Selection of Statistical Source Material from the Early 19th Century up to 1940. Vol. 13: Wages 1820–1940* (Amsterdam: Royal Tropical Institute, 1992), pp. 11–12, 20–32, 42–4, 121–41, 150, 550–60, 569–71.
49 ANRI Department of Finances 355, herein: Director of Finances, 1–5–1906: nota; Departement van Landbouw, Nijverheid en Handel, *Mededelingen van het Centraal Kantoor voor de Statistiek. No. 69 Eenige Bijzonderheden Betreffende het Aantal Aangeslagenen in de Inkomstenbelasting, 1925* (Batavia: Landsdrukkerij, 1925), pp. 3–4.
50 Stbl. 1920 n678.
51 Brunner, *De Unificatie*, pp. 7–8, 20–2, 35.
52 ANRI AS Besluit 17-3-1920, n742-743, herein: *Controleur* of Badung to the Assistent-Resident of South Bali, 17-12-1919.
53 C. Lulofs, 'Belastingpolitiek in de Buitenbezittingen', *Tijdschrift voor het Binnenlandsch Bestuur* 43 (1912), 74–94.
54 Vandenbosch, *The Dutch East Indies*, p. 71.
55 R. Van Niel, 'The effect of export cultivations in nineteenth-century Java,' *Modern Asian Studies* 15.1 (1981), 43–4; Breman, *The Village in Java*, pp. 20–1.
56 Booth, *Colonial Legacies*, pp. 12–15, 112–17, 197–8.
57 Breman, *Control of Land and Labour*, p. 18; M. van Rossum, 'Desertion', in M. van Rossum, K. Hofmeester, and M. van der Linden (eds), *Handbook Global History of Work* (Berlin and Boston, MA: De Gruyter Oldenbourg, 2017), pp. 515–16.
58 Elson, *Village Java*, p. 17; Ong, 'Pajak', p. 74.
59 J. C. Scott, *Seeing Like a State: How Certain Schemes to Improve the Human Condition Have Failed* (New Haven, CT: Yale University Press, 1998), p. 77.
60 Meijer Ranneft and Huender, *Onderzoek naar den Belastingdruk*, p. 145.
61 G. Knaap, *Kruidnagelen en Christenen: De Verenigde Oost-Indische Compagnie en de Bevolking van Ambon 1656–1696* (Leiden: KITLV Uitgeverij, 2004), pp. 181–4, 327–8.
62 ANRI AS GB MGS 4263, herein: MGS, 22-6-1903: 33 *raja* of Ambon to GG, 16-8-1902, 'rekestanden'.
63 *Ibid.*, Res. Ambon to GG, 7-7-1902.
64 ANRI AS GB MGS 4263, herein: Besluit 26-8-1864 n32: GovMol to GG, 30-5-1864; Besluit 15-3-1865 n7, GovMol to GG, 27-12-1864; MGS

22-6-1903: 'Nota betr. request der regenten van Ambon gehouden verzoek bij wijze van tractement een geldelijke tegemoetkoming te verlenen, Controleur J. van Lier.'
65 R. Chauvel, *Nationalists, Soldiers and Separatists: The Ambonese Islands from Colonialism to Revolt, 1880–1950* (Leiden: KITLV Press, 1990), pp. 89–94.
66 Chauvel, *Nationalists*, pp. 116–19.
67 *Ibid.*, Res. Ambon, 18-1-1881.
68 P. Crooks and T. H. Parsons, 'Empires, bureaucracy and the paradox of power', in P. Crooks and T. H. Parsons (eds), *Empires and Bureaucracy in World History: From Late Antiquity to the Twentieth Century* (Cambridge: Cambridge University Press, 2016), p. 20.
69 J. C. Scott, *The Art of Not Being Governed: An Anarchist History of Upland Southeast Asia* (New Haven, CT: Yale University Press, 2009), pp. 9, 81–9, 229–30.
70 R. F. Ellen, 'On the contemporary uses of colonial history and the legitimation of political status in archipelagic southeast Seram', *Journal of Southeast Asian Studies* 28.1 (1997), 78–102.
71 NA MinKol 1901–1953 OV 244, Vb. 6-6-1904 n3, Res. Abmon to GG, 13-11-1903: Nota betr. de organisatie van bestuur van het eiland Ceram en andere gedeelten van het gewest Amboina, Extract Besluit GG, 1-1-1904; Res. Ambon to GG, 2-9-1903.
72 NA MinKol 1901–1953 OV 1230, Vb. 14-8-1914 n41, herein: Res. Ambon to GG, 12-1-1914. See also W. Manuhutu, 'Pacificatie in Praktijk: De Expansie van het Nederlands Gezag op Ceram. 1900–1942', in J. van Goor (ed.), *Imperialisme in de Marge: De Afronding van Nederlands-Indië* (Utrecht: Hes, 1985), pp. 298–9.
73 M. C. Boulan-Smit, 'We, of the banyan tree: Traditions of origin of the Alune of West Seram' (PhD thesis, Australian National University, 1998), pp. 53–6.
74 NA MinKol 1901–1953 1230 Vb. 14-8-1914 n41, herein: Res. Ambon to GG, 12-1-1914.
75 Manuhutu, 'Pacificatie in Praktijk', pp. 277–8, 295; M. R. Manse, 'From headhunting to head taxes: Colonial fiscal policy and violence on Seram, ca. 1860–1920', *Bijdragen tot de Taal-, Land- en Volkenkunde* 177.4 (2021), 1–35.
76 A. Booth, 'The evolution of fiscal policy and the role of government in the colonial economy', in A. Booth, W. J. O'Malley, and A. Weidemann (eds), *Indonesian Economic History in the Dutch Colonial Era* (New Haven, CT: Yale University Southeast Asia Studies, 1990), pp. 239–42.
77 Frankema and Booth, 'Fiscal capacity', p. 14.
78 Booth, 'The evolution of fiscal policy', p. 4.

10

Imperial revenue and national welfare: The case of Britain

Gurminder K. Bhambra

Introduction[1]

The British state emerged through an Act of Union between the Kingdoms of England and Scotland in 1707. The long-standing personal union of the Kingdom of England with the Kingdom of Ireland was later formalised through the 1800 Anglo-Irish Act of Union following the brutal repression of the 1798 Irish rebellion. Whereas Ireland had been 'a separate, albeit dependent, kingdom within a wider British composite state', it was now formally integrated into the United Kingdom of Great Britain and Ireland.[2] This also incorporated Ireland into the broader project of British empire in complex ways.

The composite nature of the British state is part of the reason why a simple presentation of a *national* history is not possible; its national histories are several. Another reason is the broader colonial entanglements that come to constitute the British state. By the late eighteenth century – in the aftermath of the loss of the Thirteen Colonies of the United States – the Home Office and Foreign Office were established as distinct administrative units within the British state. Responsibility for the remaining colonies was initially located within the Home Office; that is, under the remit of domestic, and not of foreign, affairs.[3]

All this is to say that the territorial boundaries of the British state, as well as its organisational structure, have never been congruent with what many see as the imagined nation; and, at times, the imaginary of the state has also extended to include territories beyond the island or islands. In a similar way, the populations that inhabit the variety of territories encompassed within the British state have been differentially included in understandings of national identity. My concern in this chapter is with how we have come to a national framing of the state and its political community in the present, notwithstanding the wider relationships that have historically defined it.[4]

In brief, my argument is that the British state was an imperial state with a national project at its heart. The imperial state was constituted, in part, through 'relations of extraction'[5] – to use Martin Daunton's resonant phrase for taxation – while the national project comes into being through 'relations of redistribution', or welfare. The asymmetry between these relations, I argue, calls into question the dominant conceptualisations within social science of issues of distributive justice and welfare, both historically and in the present.

Relations of extraction

The 'relations of extraction' – or taxation – that bind together rulers and ruled are central to the social contract deemed, from Locke onwards, to be at the heart of the modern state.[6] The idea that citizens and their property were to be protected and, in their turn, they provided financial support to the state to do so through taxes – and that the levels of both were to be determined through some form of deliberation, usually via a legislative assembly – has come to be commonplace. As the authors of a call for a new fiscal sociology set out: 'Taxes formalize our obligations to each other. They define the inequalities we accept and those that we collectively seek to redress.'[7] Martin, Mehrotra, and Prasad go on to argue further that taxation is crucial in the development of the 'imagined community' of the nation to the extent that it 'enmeshes us in the web of generalized reciprocity'.[8]

A focus on taxation – and the distributed returns to citizens of that taxation – then, clarifies the nature of the state, its limits and its boundaries. While taxation was initially seen to be a significant factor in the state's ability to wage war, by the mid-twentieth century it became more extensively bound up with its execution of domestic issues of welfare. This can be seen in the shift from Charles Tilly's pithy statement that, in the early modern period, 'war made the state and the state made war'[9] to the claim by Richard Titmuss that, by the mid-twentieth century, we can see how modern war had had a profound influence on social policy as demonstrated by the emergence of the welfare state.[10] What is at issue is what sort of state was made by imperial wars and whose welfare did those wars secure.

Income tax had first been raised in Britain in 1798 to cover the costs of its wars with revolutionary France. After the end of these wars in 1815, however, it was discontinued as a consequence of strong public opposition to it. Income tax was not reintroduced in Britain until the mid-nineteenth century: first, as a temporary measure by Peel in 1842, before coming to be an established part of the social contract of the state through Gladstone's reforms in 1853. These also brought Ireland into the income tax regime following the earlier Act of Union that established the United Kingdom of Great Britain and Ireland. During this period, and through to the end of the nineteenth century, the 'fiscal constitution' of the state – with its emphasis on a judicious balance of taxes and taxpayer consent – has been regarded as being remarkably successful by historians of British taxation.[11]

One such historian, Martin Daunton, argues that the tax system was designed 'to be carefully balanced to ensure proportionality ... to be a means of integration and not conflict';[12] as such, 'no group or interest felt it was unduly burdened' by taxation.[13] In this way, the British state is seen to have established a high level of trust in the central state and fellow taxpayers. But, as Douglas Kanter argues, one of the problems with this narrative is that the UK was not just 'British' but also included Ireland, and 'Irish fiscal policy fits uneasily into this account'.[14] At the very outset of reintroducing income tax into the British state, Peel omitted Ireland from any obligation to pay due to a concern with exacerbating opposition to the Act of Union. However, when the famine occurred in 1845, there was then resistance to the provision of relief by central government due to the Irish being deemed to have not paid their share of taxation.

The grants that were provided for famine relief were converted to loans, which accrued interest, increasing 'the total sum owed by some 75 per cent'.[15] Later negotiations around the partial remission of these consolidated annuities turned on the requirement to bring Ireland into the income tax regime. There was a belief among many in Ireland that not only should famine relief have been a moral responsibility of the central government, but that the new regime of taxation would generate a surplus that would be used to reduce taxes in the rest of Britain; that is, as Kanter argues, that the poorer periphery would subsidise tax breaks at the wealthier centre.[16]

The consensus on taxation that Daunton otherwise represents as a feature of the British state, then, did not exist in Ireland where the debate on fiscal policy – in particular arguments about overtaxation – remained a strong feature in movements for Home Rule from the mid-nineteenth century onwards. Such debates find their parallel, Kanter suggests, within the wider empire, where arguments about economic justice intersect with those of social entitlement in movements of colonial opposition. This was particularly the case in India, as Christopher Bayly, among others, has also suggested.[17]

One of the key expenses of the state, for which income tax was initially raised, was war. However, over the nineteenth century the military costs of the British state were largely exported to the wider empire and specifically to India. As Bayly notes, both through indirect means of 'tribute' as well as 'directly through the overseas use of the Indian Army', the company-state sustained the domestic military-fiscal machine.[18] The Indian peasant, he goes on to argue, 'bore a heavy part of the costs of Britain's world role which the British people were not prepared to bear'.[19] The standard idea of the 'nation-at-arms', then, should actually be understood as the empire-at-arms, as both personnel for the army and the costs of war through colonial taxation were increasingly borne by the wider empire. This reduced the claims of the British state on the national economy to below the levels of the eighteenth century and eased the burdens of domestic taxation. It also removed any requirement for national military conscription and allowed 'the domestic state to disarm and "civilianize" itself'.[20]

One consequence of this was that while continental Europe was convulsed in revolutions in 1848, Britain, in contrast, saw the demise of equivalent struggles, such as Chartism. One explanation for this, as Daunton suggests, is that the rhetoric of equity and the generally low levels of domestic taxation 'meant that the working class was assimilated to the state rather than viewing it as coercive or exploitative'.[21] Similarly, Miles Taylor argues that 'by displacing the tax burden from metropole to periphery' and generally facilitating an improvement in living conditions, working-class discontent in Britain during this period was eased.[22] However, while there was no fiscal revolt in Britain, Taylor notes that there was an eruption of serious discontent across the empire: with riots and rebellions in 'Ceylon, the Ionian Islands and the Orange River' together with fiscal crises across the wider empire, including in the Caribbean.[23] A major uprising was temporarily averted in the Punjab, but not stayed. The subsequent events of 1857 were precipitated by factors that had mitigated against such disturbances domestically – primarily a sense of an unfair burden of taxation.

During the latter half of the nineteenth century, within Britain, there was a single rate of income tax imposed upon the domestic population. Those earning below £160 – which was four times the national average wage of around £40 in 1900 – received a full abatement and did not pay any income tax. Those earning up to £400 'were granted an abatement of £160, which fell to £70 on incomes between £600 and £700'.[24] In 1909, a supertax was introduced on large incomes, over £5,000 – the salary of a high court judge or the Chancellor of the Exchequer – and 'a tax-free allowance of £10 was introduced for children under 16'.[25] The abatements together with the tax-free allowances for children meant that *the working class and much of the middle class did not pay any income tax at all until the First World War.*

Considerations around the proper balance of taxation operated somewhat differently in the Empire. The East India Company, after the defeat of the local rulers at the Battle of Plassey in 1757, had, in 1765, obtained the right to collect taxes in the Provinces of Bengal, Bihar, and Orissa. The Company initially maintained the structures of the existing taxation regime, with land revenue forming the bulk of its taxation income, but this was diversified over time to include new taxes such as the salt tax and the opium tax.[26] An income tax was explicitly implemented after the British Crown took over direct rule a century later.

The Indian Income Tax of 1860 was closely modelled on the British version, except, as the Governor of Madras Charles Trevelyan noted, while the financial system was transplanted to India, 'a basic requirement of that system, representation of taxpayers, was wanting'.[27] There was an exemption for those earning less than Rs. 200 a year, but there was no system of abatement such that tax was paid on the whole income once it reached the taxable minimum. There was also no allowance for children. The average income at the time was around Rs. 20–27, which meant that the exemption limit was at eight to ten times the national average. The exemption limit was raised to Rs. 1,000 by 1903, which, at the time, was over twenty times the average income of Rs. 45. This led to some within Britain arguing that India was lightly taxed. However, by examining the revenue raised in taxation as a proportion of national income, Dadabhai Naoroji demonstrated clearly that India bore the heavier burden.[28] Further, if land revenue was considered as a form of taxation rather than rent, which many argued that it should be, then the recognised tax burden would have significantly increased.

There were a series of full exemptions from income tax. However, these all fell 'on the side of government servants, pensioners, ... foreign shipping concerns, tea agents, and the holders of sterling debt rather than in favour of the general taxpayers'.[29] Further, as Shankar Pagar sets out, no tax was deducted from the salaries of employees of the India Office in London despite those salaries being paid out of Indian revenues – this included the Secretary of State for India whose £5,000 salary would have put him amongst the highest earners in the entire empire.[30] While there is much to discuss about the forms and rates of taxation, the central issue for my purposes here is the following, paraphrased from Naoroji: not only was India more heavily taxed than England, but there was another additional circumstance: the whole of British taxation returned entirely to the people themselves from whom it was raised, but that which was obtained out of India did not all return to them.[31]

As George Wingate wrote in 1859 and whom Naoroji quotes:

> Taxes spent in the country from which they are raised, are totally different in their effect from taxes raised in one country and spent in another. In the former case, the taxes collected from the population at large ... are again returned to the industrious classes. ... But the case is wholly different when the taxes are not spent in the country from which they are raised. In this case, they constitute no mere transfer of a portion of the national income from one set of citizens to another, but an absolute loss and extinction of the whole amount withdrawn from the taxed country.[32]

To put it in anachronistic, Keynesian, terms, the 'multiplier' has its effects elsewhere while the extraction depresses activity locally.

What we see through this discussion is (a) that Britain established domestic legitimacy and quiescence through imperial revenue; and (b) that that imperial revenue included the taxes extracted from a colonised population. In the following section, I go on to discuss the 'relations of redistribution' more explicitly in terms of their construction as welfare and examine the extent to which 'the web of generalized reciprocity' applied to all those under British rule.

Relations of redistribution

Scholars of distributive justice, such as Michael Walzer, argue that redistribution presupposes a bounded world.[33] Collective solidarity relies on an understanding of 'us', as insiders, as opposed to 'them', as strangers. Such a demarcation determines who ought to be seen as the legitimate beneficiary of the distribution of collective goods and social entitlements. This is a widespread and commonplace understanding of welfare systems which are understood to pool and redistribute wealth raised through taxation for the benefit of the members of the political community. While the necessity of boundaries to the possibility of just distribution is regarded as self-evident, what is rarely considered is where the resources that are to be redistributed come from. Further, and relatedly, there is little discussion of what the entitlements are of those broader constituencies who have contributed to the building up of those collective resources, but who are under the rule of the political community without being seen to be part of it.

The community constituted through the relations of political extraction is much more extensive than that which comes into being through the relations of redistribution. This raises the further question of the nature of the arguments to establish a legitimacy of using the resources extracted from the imperial community and redistributing them solely to the national community. The provision of welfare in Britain in the eighteenth and nineteenth centuries occurred through a 'mixed moral economy' of limited state interventions supplemented by the work of voluntary organisations, friendly societies, and private charitable activity.[34] The low burden of domestic taxation, made possible through the imperial relations of extraction, meant that, until the twentieth century, the state had less involvement in the direct provision of national welfare. For example, as Pat Thane notes, at the end of the nineteenth century it is estimated that more money was transferred to the poor through charities in London alone than was expended nationally via the Poor Laws.[35]

While much is written about how charities were organised, who benefited from them, and the relations of deference they created, there is remarkably little systematic work on where the money that was disbursed through philanthropic initiatives came from. There is a separate literature on the extent of money brought back to Britain from empire, but the connections between the two are rarely made. The salaries paid to those working for the East India Company, for example, were exceedingly high and regardless of rank all employees received an annual pension of £1,000 so long as they had completed between 25 and 35 years of service. In addition, there were various allowances – not to mention the private investments (or loot, as William Dalrymple has called it) – which meant that they were able to retire well on their return to Britain.

The 'nabobs', as returning East India Company employees were known, were recognised as part of Britain's growing philanthropic community. As Tillman Nechtman notes, for example, '[n]ewspaper subscriptions show that Company employees were substantial donors to charities';[36] but scholarship on the relationship between charity and welfare rarely acknowledges this association with imperial wealth. An exception to this is the chapter by Andrew Mackillop, in this volume, which makes a more substantial connection between the circulation of imperial wealth and charitable initiatives within early modern Scotland. Mackillop sets out how wealth made in the Empire was deployed to secure status back at home through charitable activities such as contributing to the poor relief of a parish, funding hospitals and infirmaries, and donating to institutions of learning. Further, he shows how an imagined community of belonging was often mobilised to elicit charitable donations from members across empire for national welfare projects.

The situation was somewhat different in terms of charitable initiatives in relation to issues of colonial welfare. As Andrea Major argues, 'British philanthropic interest in the subcontinent tended to be more concerned with its moral rather than its material condition.'[37] This was despite the fact that across the period of British rule – from the East India Company onwards – India faced a series of devastating famines and periods of food scarcity. One of the most intense periods of famine and scarcity was from 1860 to 1910 – coinciding with the implementation of the income tax in India. During this period, it is estimated that over 14 million people died of starvation; they died in the context of grain being exported by rail from the famine regions and taxes continuing to be collected even in the worst affected areas.

While environmental factors, such as the failure of the monsoon, contributed to food shortages in specific areas, these shortages were never absolute. As Ajit Ghose argues, in the latter half of the nineteenth century India was a food-surplus country; the issue was that '[e]xports of foodgrains were taking place even in years when thousands, or perhaps millions, were dying of starvation'.[38] The maintenance of exports was a consequence of what were presented as colonial laissez-faire policies which prevented officials from interfering in the natural operation of free trade. These policies did not, however, prevent them from collecting tax from an impoverished population; tax in such circumstances was coercive and in breach of the voluntarism otherwise inscribed in the idea of laissez-faire. Famines were products of colonial public policy.

Decisions on famine policy, as Kate Currie notes, reflected broader policy struggles 'over the efficacy or otherwise of state intervention ... within the spheres of the market and taxation'.[39] Deliberations by British civil servants in India tended to go along the following lines: around 80% of the people dying from starvation come from the labouring classes and do not earn sufficient to pay taxes; to keep them alive through famine relief would stretch the wage funds of the taxpaying population and lead to a further increase in the population at the lowest levels; this would put further pressure on the food supply and lead to further famines; such a course of action would demoralise the population and increased debt together with taxation would be more fatal to the country than famine itself.[40] Public finance trumped public health in such considerations; especially as any measures to avert deaths in the colony would have had an impact on imperial finances and the preferred activities that this income was to support – that is, celebrations in India to proclaim Victoria Empress of India and preparations for the war with Afghanistan funded by Indian taxes.[41]

Discussions about whether Indian subjects were entitled to any relief from the government occurred in the context of earlier arguments about the Poor Laws in Britain and Ireland. Apparently, the encouragement of idleness in the local population, as a consequence of providing any material relief in times of food shortages, had to be avoided as a priority. In addition, there were increasing discussions about overpopulation and famines were regarded as one way in which such concerns could be addressed. Perhaps more pertinently, the case against famine relief was made in the fear that if the arguments for such relief at such times were accepted, then that would lead to arguments for the permanent maintenance of the Indian poor – that is, for their inclusion within the generalised web of reciprocity. The 1880 Famine Commission, for example, set out the following: 'The doctrine that in time of famine the poor are entitled to demand relief ... would probably lead to the doctrine that they are entitled to such relief at all times, and thus the foundation would be laid of a system of general poor relief, which we cannot contemplate without serious apprehension.'[42]

This was at a time when general poor relief was provided as a legal right to the destitute poor in Britain – whether deserving or undeserving.[43] While provisions made through the Poor Laws were not regarded as particularly generous, they were deemed, as Boyer argues, to be 'enough to ensure that unemployed workers and their families could subsist in good health'.[44] Further, Lorie Charlesworth argues that had Poor Law entitlements in England and Wales not been protected as legal rights, then the level of relief would have been as little as it had been in Ireland in the 1840s. During the Irish famine, she argues, the British government and its Irish administration were permitted, as a consequence of the limited poor law structures introduced into Ireland, 'to legally abdicate responsibility for preventing deaths by starvation'.[45] Mike Davis similarly draws the links between Ireland and India, stating that in both contexts they were turned into laboratories for utilitarianism, 'where millions of lives were wagered against dogmatic faith in omnipotent markets'.[46]

As such, not only was there not a general commitment to the alleviation of poverty in India, but even calls for the mitigation of the worst effects of famine were denied as they could potentially lead to calls for a more general entitlement. One of the few dissenting voices in such discussions by British officials in India was that of James Caird, who 'drew attention to the fact that India spent on famine relief less than two per cent of what Britain spent annually in relieving the poor' at home.[47] As a final note, the Famine Fund that was started after the 1880 Famine Commission had recommended that extra taxation should be imposed on the Indian population for the purpose of raising money that could then be stored up for the specific purpose of providing relief in the case of future famines. This fund was maintained at around £1 million annually, but when there was need to call on it in relation to a subsequent famine, the money was found not to be available, having been expended on the Afghan war among other non-famine-related activities.[48]

The relations of extraction – both political and economic – explicitly bound India into the British polity and were implicated in its general conditions of immiseration. There was little acceptance, however, that these relations generated 'a web of reciprocity' in terms of equivalent relations of redistribution. Indeed, actions were taken specifically to limit any reciprocity arising motivated out of private philanthropy or individual charitable concern. Classical liberal theory may have enunciated a principle of voluntarism applied to the recognition of the distress of others and eschewed what it regarded as compulsion in the provision of relief. However, in the case of the recognition of the distress suffered by subjects of empire, voluntarism was strongly dissuaded under accusations that it would undermine the Government of India.[49] The issues of asymmetry were to become even starker across the twentieth century, highlighting further what Desmond King calls the illiberalism of the liberal state.[50]

Imperial revenue and national welfare

The balance that Daunton argued had been so central to the deliberations and domestic activities of the British state in the nineteenth century came to be significantly disrupted by the wars of the subsequent one. The burden of taxation increased during the period of the First World War as 'the heavy interest payments to holders of the national debt came into conflict with demands for increased expenditure on education, health and housing'.[51] Military conscription was brought in in 1916 and the level of income tax exemption was cut from £160 to £130, which drew many more people into the payment of income tax. Within a couple of years, however, the number of taxpayers was reduced again 'by raising the tax-free allowance for children and extending it to wives'.[52] It was with an eye to this particular history of balance that, in the immediate aftermath of the First World War, there were a number of debates among welfare economists about the feasibility of setting up a system of national welfare to be funded through taxation.

One such economist was Arthur Bowley, who sought to ascertain the amount of money that could be taken from the rich and added to the wages of the poor such that it would both alleviate poverty and not be an undue burden on the rich. In making his calculations, Bowley determined the national income, which was made up of the total income of people within the United Kingdom as well as income received from abroad, deducted the amount that would be necessary for running the government and then divided the remainder by the population of the UK.[53] The national dividend, then, that was to provide the economic basis for welfare provision was, as Pigou writes, 'the objective income of the community, including, *of course, income derived from abroad*'.[54] The national dividend was explicitly an imperial dividend distributed nationally.

As Richard Temple had noted in his earlier presentation of the 'General Statistics of the British Empire', of the £203 million at the disposal of the British state for general government, £89 million came from the UK, £74 million from India, and £40 million from territories and colonies in the rest of empire.[55] Over half the money at the disposal of the government at Westminster came from the labour, resources, and taxes of those within empire and beyond the national state. The taxes and resources of colonised subjects were taken into account when making calculations about the feasibility of national welfare provision in the metropole (i.e., in terms of calculating the size of the national fund) without ever taking them – colonised subjects – into account as the recipients of the distribution of that fund – not even in the most extreme cases of famine and starvation.

It goes without saying that these resources were then also used to fund such schemes as they came into being in the twentieth century, just as they had been used to fund the infrastructure of the state over the previous two centuries. Indeed, no less a figure than Winston Churchill, as Chancellor of the Exchequer, stated the following:

> The income which we derive each year from commission and services rendered to foreign countries is over £65 million. In addition, we have a steady revenue from foreign investments of close on £300 million a year ... That is the explanation of the source from which we are able to defray social services at a level incomparably higher than that of any European country ... These resources from overseas constitute the keystone ... of our economic position.[56]

This statement was in response to an interjection by Ellen Wilkinson MP in the House of Commons claiming that the post-war sacrifices that Churchill was calling to be made were 'class sacrifices, not national sacrifices'. As Churchill sets out, while there were disparities among the classes in Britain, all classes benefited from overseas resources, especially as these were used to defray the costs of social services. Radical arguments about class were countered by conservative claims about the nation, but each was belied by the colonies and empire – and their 'classes' – that underlay both claims. This common erasure comes to be central to the development of politics oriented to the welfare state.[57]

It was the shared experience of 'total war', that, according to Asa Briggs among others, 'forced politicians to consider the "community" as a whole' and to deploy communal resources 'to abate poverty and to assist those in distress'.[58] Warfare and welfare, then, were conjoined in bringing together the idea of citizens as a nation. This was reinforced through the processes by way of which material resources 'were distributed and redistributed within national boundaries'.[59] As such, the national frame can be regarded as explicitly coming into being in terms of determining the population to whom recompense was to be made in the aftermath of two devastating wars in the context of a growing national electorate able to lobby for such demands.

However, not only were the wars fought by the British Empire, and not simply the British nation, but they were also significantly funded by that wider population through increased taxation. The 'small wars' of empire across the nineteenth century had been almost entirely fought and funded by India, as mentioned earlier; and Indian troops were also used in the Crimean War and African soldiers in the Boer War. During the First World War, over one million Indian soldiers served overseas and over two million fought for the Allies in the Second World War, where India's contribution 'roughly equalled that of South Africa, Canada, New Zealand, and other Commonwealth territories put together'.[60]

In addition, as Anita Singh sets out, India was 'a financial reservoir for imperial defence'.[61] During both wars, the Home Charges that India paid to Britain for colonial rule were dramatically increased, as was expenditure on the military. After the First World War, India provided a coerced gift to Britain of £100 million to aid the war effort and Britain's debt to India of £55 million was unilaterally erased through currency manipulation. During the Second World War, alongside the increase in military expenditure attributed to the Indian budget, India further supported the British war effort through a series of 'forced loans' that provided goods and services to the British in return for 'I.O.U.s', that is, sterling balances. As Aditya Mukherjee states, the rapid expansion of the currency – together with the fact that nothing returned to India for the goods and services provided – 'led to severe shortages and runaway inflation' in India.[62]

In earlier discussions about how the war was to be funded, Keynes had argued that one option was to let prices rise more than real wages. This would redistribute incomes away from wages to profits, which could then be taxed in order to pay for the war. Such a scheme, however, would disproportionately hurt the poorest classes and in order to ensure domestic working-class support it was disregarded in favour of a system of graded taxation.[63] However, the scheme which was regarded as too regressive for implementation in Britain was, as Utsa Patnaik argues, implemented in India upon 'a colonised population with one-thirtieth of the per head income' and which, in 1943, led to the deaths of over 3 million civilians in the Bengal famine.[64] This was a consequence of public policy decisions made in Britain which again valued national lives differently to the lives of those in the colonies.

Britain, in contrast, was able to contain inflationary pressures at home and was also able to develop and implement welfare policies – policies, which, as Noel Whiteside argues, had as their objective 'to protect the whole population – but particularly the working population – from the consequences of the conflict'.[65] Specifically, there was a concern to redistribute national income through cost-of-living subsidies as well as providing other social services. How this was to be paid for, however, was a real issue given that in the immediate post-war period 'the Labour government faced enormous economic difficulties' including a 'lack of raw materials, productive capacity and financial resources'.[66] The balance of payments crisis of 1947–48 further exacerbated these issues.

Britain emerged from the Second World War owing more than £3 billion to her creditors while also being committed to the construction of the welfare state.[67] How this was to be managed was how Britain had always managed its domestic responsibilities – by turning to the Empire. There were two primary ways by which Britain did this: first, it ran down the amount it owed to India and Pakistan after independence; and second, it subordinated the economies of its remaining colonies to its national concerns. In other words, the imperial dividend continued after the end of empire and was integral to the construction of the post-war welfare state.

By the end of 1945, Britain owed India £1.3 billion, 'a third of the total built up by Britain ... [and] almost one-fifth of Britain's net receipts from the United States under Lend-Lease'.[68] From the outset, British officials sought to write down the balances owed, given that they could not unilaterally write them off, even though this had initially been attempted (and had actually been done after the First World War). Marcelo de Paiva Abreu sets out the many ways by which Britain managed what was called 'concealed cancellation': the lower rates of interests on the loans obtained by Britain from India, higher pension charges including liability for all pensions of civil and military personnel working in India prior to independence, and, perhaps most importantly, the devaluation of sterling in 1949, which occurred without a gold clause such as that which had protected creditors like Argentina and Brazil.[69] Officially, there was a cancellation of around a third of outstanding Indian balances, although this figure is considered a serious underestimation, all things considered.[70]

In addition to cancelling a significant amount of its debt to India, Allister Hinds argues that Britain also harnessed colonial resources from its remaining empire and aligned colonial fiscal and monetary policy to the needs of its own national economy. As he sets out, 'Malaya was the most valuable of Britain's dollar earning colonies' – with its exports of rubber and tin – closely followed by the Gold Coast, to become Ghana, and Nigeria.[71] The dollars earned by these countries, through sale of their raw products, were put into a 'dollar pool' controlled by Britain. The dollar-earning capacity of the colonies that remained under Britain's control was central to Britain's domestic recovery. In this way, as David Fieldhouse argues, British colonies were made to tie up funds that they might have otherwise used for their own development 'in order to give Britain cheap credit' and 'to subsidize Britain's post-war standard of living'.[72]

While the British government maintained a 'benevolent rhetoric of economic development' towards its remaining colonies, the reality, as Fieldhouse argues, was rather one of 'economic exploitation'.[73] From 1946 to 1951, for example, 'the colonies were lent or given some £40 million' through the Colonial Development and Welfare Acts and, at the same time, were required 'to lend or tie up in London about £250 million'.[74] The colonies were thus used 'to protect the British consumer from the high social price which continental countries were then paying for their post-war reconstruction' and were unable to use their own funds to pay for development at home.[75] Britain's policies were condemned by a variety of figures and the Nigerian newspaper *West African Pilot* ran an editorial stating: 'Colonial socialism is aimed at developing the resources to expand the production of foodstuffs and raw materials which Britain needs badly to carry out her socialism at home.'[76] As such, the health of the sterling area in the post-war period can be seen to have been 'central to the [possibility of] success of the Government's domestic programme'.[77]

The development of the British welfare state in the post-war period, then, depended on the writing down of the debt that Britain owed to newly independent India and Pakistan, appropriating the dollar-earnings of its remaining colonies, and subordinating the economic development requirements of those colonies to its own needs. The economic health of the British state relied on these relations of economic and political subordination and yet there is almost no discussion of them in the literature discussing the emergence of the domestic welfare state.

Conclusion

As John Hills argued, in an altogether different context but useful for my purposes here: 'the redistributive effect of the welfare state cannot be judged just by looking at who benefits from it ... One also has to look at who pays for it through the tax system and in other ways.'[78] Once we consider the state to have been an imperial state and not just a national state, we come to understand the deeper inequalities that the welfare state represents that we have not yet systematically thought about, let alone come to terms with how we might provide reparation. The relations of extraction of the British state constituted it as an imperial state; its relations of redistribution exemplified the national project at its heart. The asymmetry here is reproduced within mainstream social science every time the nation-state is taken as the unit of analysis and not the wider empire, or imperial state. The injustice embodied in that asymmetry is central to arguments about the legitimacy of the white working class and is reproduced in discourses and practices that privilege national citizens over others.[79]

The historical provenance of the material resources available to be redistributed was broader than the nation; it was imperial. Yet, the imperial community is neither acknowledged in terms of the contributions it has made to the resources appropriated by the state, nor is it regarded as a legitimate beneficiary of the distribution of those collective resources. There were both direct and indirect benefits to the domestic population of taxation within the wider empire. The direct benefits resulted from the simple accrual of additional wealth and resources for domestic purposes, including the reduction in the domestic tax burden of the national population and increased social services available to them. The indirect benefits involved the compounded loss suffered by the colonised populations and the global patterns of inequality that continue through to the present.[80] The end of empire did not bring an end to the legacies of its social structures, including their modes of legitimation.

My call here is for a better social science, located in a more adequate understanding of the shared histories that have configured our present, in order to find more expansive and generous solutions to the problems that face us. That 'us' must be inclusive of those currently presented as 'other' and outside the web of reciprocity in which obligations are recognised – both historically and contemporaneously. The imperial relations of extraction maintained the standard of living of the national population at the expense not only of the livelihoods of colonial subjects, but often their very lives. The recurrence of famine throughout the period of British rule was a consequence of colonial policies of extraction for which there was no mitigation and no consideration that there ought to be any mitigation through systematic welfare provision to these taxpayers. While it may have been the metropolitan bourgeoise that explicitly exploited colonised populations, as Aditya Mukherjee argues, 'metropolitan society as a whole benefit[ed] at the cost of the entire colonial people'.[81]

There is an urgent need for us to reconsider the broader, shared histories of the polity undivided as central to the future possibilities of the welfare state. This will involve a reconfiguration of our disciplines, what I have elsewhere called epistemological justice, as well as justice through material reparations.

Notes

1. This chapter is a slightly shortened version of 'Relations of extraction, relations of redistribution: Empire, nation, and the construction of the British welfare state', *British Journal of Sociology* (2021).
2. Patrick A. Walsh, 'The fiscal state in Ireland: 1691–1769', *The Historical Journal* 56.3 (2013), 632.
3. J. C. Sainty, 'Introduction', *Office-Holders in Modern Britain: Home Office Officials 1782–1870* (London: Athlone Press, 1975).
4. Gurminder K. Bhambra, 'Comparative historical sociology and the state: Problems of method', *Cultural Sociology* 10.3 (2016), 335–51.
5. Martin Daunton, 'How to pay for the war: State, society and taxation in Britain, 1917–24', *The English Historical Review* 111.443 (1996), 882–919.

6 Gurminder K. Bhambra and John Holmwood, *Colonialism and Modern Social Theory* (Cambridge: Polity, 2021).
7 Isaac William Martin, Ajay K. Mehrotra, and Monica Prasad, 'The thunder of history: The origins and development of the new fiscal sociology', in Isaac William Martin, Ajay K. Mehrotra, and Monica Prasad (eds), *The New Fiscal Sociology: Taxation in Comparative and Historical Perspective* (New York: Cambridge University Press, 2009), p. 1.
8 Martin, Mehrotra, and Prasad, 'The thunder of history', p. 3.
9 Charles Tilly, *The Formation of National States in Western Europe* (Princeton, NJ: Princeton University Press, 1975), p. 42.
10 Richard M. Titmuss, *Essays on 'The Welfare State'* (London: Allen & Unwin, 1958); see also Michael Mann, *The Sources of Social Power*, vol. 3 (Cambridge: Cambridge University Press, 2012).
11 Douglas Kanter, 'The politics of Irish taxation, 1842–53', *The English Historical Review* 127.528 (2012), 1121–55.
12 Martin Daunton, 'Payment and participation: Welfare and state-formation in Britain 1900–1951', *Past & Present* 150 (1996), 173.
13 Daunton, 'How to pay for the war', p. 885.
14 Kanter, 'The politics of Irish taxation', p. 1123.
15 *Ibid.*, p. 1139.
16 *Ibid.*, p. 1151.
17 Christopher A. Bayly, 'Ireland, India and the Empire: 1780–1914', *Transactions of the Royal Historical Society* 10 (2000), 377–97.
18 Christopher A. Bayly, 'Returning the British to South Asian history: The limits of colonial hegemony', *South Asia: Journal of South Asian Studies* 17.2 (1994), 15.
19 Bayly, 'Returning the British to South Asian history', p. 16.
20 *Ibid.*, p. 18.
21 Daunton, 'How to pay for the war', p. 885.
22 Miles Taylor, 'The 1848 revolutions and the British Empire', *Past & Present* 166 (2000), 158.
23 Taylor, 'The 1848 revolutions and the British Empire', p. 152.
24 Daunton, 'Payment and participation', p. 176.
25 *Ibid.*, pp. 176–7.
26 John F. Richards, 'Imperial finance under the East India Company, 1762–1859', in Durba Ghosh and Dane Kennedy (eds), *Decentring Empire: Britain, India and the Transcolonial World* (London: Sangam Books, 2006).
27 Sabyasachi Bhattacharya, *The Financial Foundations of the British Raj: Ideas and Interests in the Reconstruction of Indian Public Finance 1858–1872*, rev. edn (Hyderabad: Orient Longman, 2005), p. 52.
28 Dadabhai Naoroji, *Poverty and un-British Rule in India* (London: Swan Sonnenschein & Co., 1901).
29 Shankar Madhav Pagar, *The Indian Income Tax: Its History, Theory, and Practice* (Forgotten Books, 2012 [1920]), p. 98.
30 Pagar, *The Indian Income Tax*, p. 187.

31 Naoroji, *Poverty and un-British Rule*, p. 314.
32 *Ibid.*, pp. 57–8.
33 Michael Walzer, *Spheres of Justice* (New York: Basic Books, 1983).
34 Paul Johnson, 'Risk, redistribution and social welfare in Britain from the Poor Law to Beveridge', in Martin Daunton (ed.), *Charity, Self-Interest and Welfare in the English Past* (London: UCL Press, 1996).
35 Pat Thane, *Foundations of the Welfare State*, 2nd edn (Harlow: Pearson Education, 1996).
36 Tillman W. Nechtman, 'A jewel in the crown? Indian wealth in domestic Britain in the late eighteenth century', *Eighteenth-Century Studies* 41.1 (2007), 76.
37 Andrea Major, 'British humanitarian political economy and famine in India, 1838–1842', *Journal of British Studies* 59.2 (2020), 230.
38 Ajit K. Ghose, 'Food supply and starvation: A study of famines with reference to the Indian sub-continent', *Oxford Economic Papers*, New Series, 34.2 (1982), 378.
39 Kate Currie, 'British colonial policy and famines: Some effects and implications of 'free trade' in the Bombay, Bengal and Madras Presidencies, 1860–1900', *South Asia: Journal of South Asian Studies* 14.2 (1991), 26–7.
40 S. Ambirajan, 'Malthusian population theory and Indian famine policy in the nineteenth century', *Population Studies* 30.1 (1976), 5–14.
41 Mike Davis, *Late Victorian Holocausts: El Niño Famines and the Making of the Third World* (London: Verso, 2002).
42 Quoted in Davis, *Late Victorian Holocausts*, p. 33.
43 Robbie Shilliam, *Race and the Undeserving Poor: From Abolition to Brexit* (London: Agenda Publishing, 2018).
44 George R. Boyer, 'The evolution of unemployment relief in Great Britain', *Journal of Interdisciplinary History* 34.3 (204), 432.
45 Lorie Charlesworth, *Welfare's Forgotten Past: A Socio-Legal History of the Poor Law* (Abingdon: Routledge, 2010), p. 179.
46 Davis, *Late Victorian Holocausts*, p. 31.
47 Ambirajan, 'Malthusian population theory', p. 11.
48 Davis, *Late Victorian Holocausts*.
49 Currie, 'British colonial policy', p. 33.
50 Desmond King, *In the Name of Liberalism: Illiberal Social Policy in the USA and Britain* (Oxford: Oxford University Press, 1999).
51 Daunton, 'How to pay for the war', p. 884.
52 *Ibid.*, p. 889.
53 Arthur L. Bowley. *The Division of the Product of Industry: An Analysis of National Income Before the War* (Oxford: Clarendon Press, 1919).
54 Arthur C. Pigou, *The Economics of Welfare* (London: Macmillan, 1929), p. 31, my emphasis.
55 Richard Temple, 'The general statistics of the British Empire', *Journal of the Statistical Society of London* 47.3 (1884), 468–84.
56 Winston Churchill, 'Gold Standakd [*sic*] and Cost of Living', Hansard, HC Deb 15 April 1929 vol 227 cc34–6, available at: https://api.parliament.

uk/historic-hansard/commons/1929/apr/15/gold-standakd-and-cost-of-living#S5CV0227P0_19290415_HOC_148 (last accessed 24 March 2022).
57 Denise Noble, 'Decolonizing Britain and domesticating women: Race, gender, and women's work in post-1945 British decolonial and metropolitan liberal reform discourses', *Meridians: Feminism, Race, Transnationalism* 13.1 (2015), 53–77.
58 Asa Briggs, 'The welfare state in historical perspective', *European Journal of Sociology* 2.2 (1961), 226, 228.
59 Mann, *Sources of Social Power*, p. 463.
60 Anita Singh, 'Imperial defence and the transfer of power in India, 1946–1947', *The International History Review* 4.4 (1982), 569.
61 Singh, 'Imperial defence and the transfer of power', p. 569.
62 Aditya Mukherjee, 'Indo-British finance: The controversy over India's sterling balances, 1939–1947', *Studies in History* 6.2 (1990), 231.
63 Utsa Patnaik, 'Revisiting the "drain", or transfer from India to Britain in the context of global diffusion of capitalism', in Shubhra Chakrabarti and Utsa Patnaik (eds), *Agrarian and Other Histories: Essays for Binay Bhushan Chaudhuri* (New Delhi: Tulika Books, 2017), pp. 206–7.
64 Patnaik, 'Revisiting the "drain"', p. 208.
65 Noel Whiteside, 'Creating the welfare state in Britain, 1945–1960', *Journal of Social Policy* 25.1 (1996), 87.
66 Whiteside, 'Creating the welfare state in Britain', p. 86.
67 C. C. S. Newton, 'The sterling crisis of 1947 and the British response to the Marshall Plan', *The Economic History Review* 37.3 (1984), 391–408.
68 Aditya Balasubramanian and Srinath Raghavan, 'Present at the creation: India, the global economy, and the Bretton Woods conference', *Journal of World History* 29.1 (2018), 82.
69 Marcelo de Paiva Abreu, 'Britain as a debtor: Indian sterling balances, 1940–53', *The Economic History Review* 70.2 (2017), 586–604.
70 Balasubramanian and Raghavan, 'Present at the creation'.
71 Allister E. Hinds, 'Sterling and decolonization in the British Empire, 1945–1958', *Social and Economic Studies* 48.4 (1999), 107.
72 D. K. Fieldhouse, 'The Labour governments and the Empire-Commonwealth, 1945–51', in Ritchie Ovendale (ed.), *The Foreign Policy of the British Labour Governments, 1945–1951* (Leicester: Leicester University Press, 1984), p. 96.
73 Fieldhouse, 'The Labour governments and the Empire-Commonwealth', p. 95.
74 *Ibid.*, p. 98.
75 *Ibid.*, p. 99.
76 Quoted in Allister E. Hinds, 'Sterling and imperial policy, 1945–1951', *Journal of Imperial and Commonwealth History* 15.2 (1987), 160.
77 Newton, 'The sterling crisis', p. 392.
78 John Hills, 'Funding the welfare state', *Oxford Review of Economic Policy* 11.3 (1995), 33.
79 Shilliam, *Race and the Undeserving Poor*.

80 Gurminder K. Bhambra, 'Colonial global economy: Towards a theoretical reorientation of political economy,' *Review of International Political Economy* 28.2 (2021), 307–22.
81 Aditya Mukherjee, 'Empire: How colonial India made modern Britain', *Economic and Political Weekly* 45.50 (2010), 76.

Part III

Post-colonial legacies

11

Making investor states: Haitian foreign debt and neocolonial economic governance in nineteenth-century France

Alexia Yates

In 1825, France officially recognised the independence of its former colony Saint-Domingue (now Haiti), more than two decades after the struggles of enslaved Haitians had made that independence a fait accompli.[1] Official recognition came with conditions, including payment of an indemnity of 150 million francs by Haiti to dispossessed French colonists and the establishment of a privileged tax regime for French trade with the island. These were significant concessions, agreed by Haitian president Jean-Pierre Boyer within sight of a French naval squadron threatening blockade. The indemnity represented roughly three years' worth of Haiti's total annual production at the time, while the reduction of customs duties on French trade would have reduced public revenues by up to 50%.[2] But the payment aimed to perform work beyond the narrowly economic. Interpreted variously by contemporaries as an act of purchase (of national sovereignty, of enslaved property, of territory) or as a compensation (to expropriated proprietors), it was a transaction that held out the promise of resolving relations between contracting parties, with the exchange of money ending mutual obligations.[3] As historian Mary Lewis has written of Haiti's 'long decolonization', the indemnity might be seen as an effort to 'decolonize the colonists' themselves, by providing closure and new directions for their formerly imperial lives.[4] Yet this closure remained elusive. Haiti was forced to borrow 30 million francs on the French market to honour the first annual instalment of the indemnity, and as early as 1826, the island's resources proved insufficient for the millions of francs in annual payments required to service both the indemnity and the loan.[5] Rather than a terminus, the indemnity was the starting point of a debt relationship that extended and shaped Franco-Haitian economic (and political) relations for decades.

The modes of economic governance through which European empires were organised in the nineteenth century were diverse. As contributions to this volume show, the accumulation and redistribution of resources from colonised territories required the mobilisation of bureaucracies, legitimising discourses, and state violence. Economist Thomas Piketty estimates that in the years before its independence, 70% of the output of Saint-Domingue was realised as profit to French planters and slaveholders, who represented just over 5% of the island's population. In 1790, these amounts added about 3% to France's national income.[6] The work of extracting profit from Haiti continued after independence, though it could not do so on the same terms. Franco-Haitian economic relations offer a distinct perspective on how these imperial structures were reconfigured into post- or neo-colonial arrangements.

Financial control mechanisms, formal and informal, were central to the model of imperium that France pursued as a supplement to its territorial occupations in the nineteenth century. This chapter approaches the 1825 Haitian loan as one such mechanism, helping to make up the financial institutions that composed a new age of global capital and empire in the nineteenth century. As historian David Todd observes, issuing this loan on the French market helped inaugurate one of the most important (and distinctive) trends of French financial practice: an enthusiasm for investment in foreign public debt.[7] This enthusiasm was shared by government officials, who viewed French capital as a vector of national influence abroad, and by the investing public that this official sanction helped foster. The bonds of foreign states arguably acted as imperialising agents.[8] They not only enhanced the control of capital-rich over capital-poor states. As they moved into the mattresses, drawers, and safe deposit boxes of a growing investing class, they also helped make hierarchised global relations meaningful, in an immediate way, to the life chances of ordinary individuals, and trained their owners in ways of contemplating debtor states and their citizens that supported imperial extraction.

The indemnity and welfare payments that the French state orchestrated for former colonists developed institutional and imaginative space for the expression of nostalgic post-colonial identities. These were identities with significant economic consequences. This chapter places the 1825 loan – the other side of the indemnity – in a similar frame, asking what bondholders thought they were doing when they opted to buy a portion of Haiti's debt and how their decisions illuminate practices and understanding of post-colonial financial extraction.[9] In ways less calculable than percentages of gross domestic product (GDP), the loan had important impact on the dispositions and institutions of France's capital-exporting classes. Mobilisation around the outstanding debts of foreign states – debts which were the direct translation of colonial property relations – was a school in which investors, the public, and politicians debated and discovered the means of informal empire and neocolonial relations, practising modes of reasoning and persuasion that thickened the web of legal and cultural arguments for extraterritorial financial exploitation. Investors in Haiti's foreign debt worked across the nineteenth century to align French national interests with those of the investing class – to create an investor state that would defend the rights of its foreign investors and impose obligations on borrowing countries. The developmental discourse that often cloaked these demands applied as much to investment's putative contribution to Haitian development as to its significance for French economic growth. This chapter, then, contributes to this volume's efforts to put the emergence of nation-states in Europe and the colonised world in the same frame, and adds a consideration of private actors as important parties to the institutional arrangements composing the economic life of the imperial nation-state.

French extraction in the nineteenth century

The combination of indemnity and loan that formed Haiti's notorious 'double debt' started at 156 million francs (excluding interest) and was purely extractive, generating no capital for public investment.[10] When rolled into the loans that Haiti contracted at the end of the century – partially in order to complete paying the original 1825 obligation – payments to French citizens and companies averaged about 5% of the country's annual GDP in the six decades leading up to the Great War, at which point Haiti's financial difficulties provided pretence for the country's occupation by American forces.[11] In France, these transfers involved shifting notations between accounts in the ledgers of the state bank, the Caisse des Dépôts et Consignations, while in Haiti, exports of specie and goods under the eyes of an aggrieved populace became sufficiently difficult that ships were loaded secretly in order to avoid riots.

Haitian payments to France were relatively small in French terms, representing between 2% and 1% of its annual GDP over the century. But for Haiti the costs of servicing the debt were significant, swallowing at times as much as half of public expenditure. When debt costs are combined with military expenses – a military maintained, in significant part, on the basis of justified fear of French invasion – payments relating to Haiti's postcolonial status consumed between 40% and 80% of annual state spending across the nineteenth century.[12] The debt put tremendous pressure on public revenues. To meet its obligations, the Haitian government adopted measures such as exceptional land taxes and the sale of public properties, as well as a coercive labour regime – a *code rural* (1826) that aimed to increase agricultural exports by tying workers to the land, and which included aggressive campaigns against independent communities of small-scale producers. The depletion of specie also provoked the introduction of a paper currency, commencing a long period of monetary instability.

The debt aggravated long-standing conflicts between the rent-seeking Haitian elite and a peasantry inclined towards autonomous production and the destruction of the plantation economy. Moreover, as debt repayment exported public revenues to Europe, Haiti's elites acted similarly, storing their extracted wealth abroad rather than reinvesting, a key factor in what historian Johnhenry Gonzalez describes as a 'self-reinforcing cycle of counterinstitutionality'.[13]

In France, the benefits of thus financialising Haiti's independence did not accrue to the state straightforwardly. What was paid of the indemnity went to former colonists themselves, and the structure and payment schedule was such that most of the 25,838 recognised claimants received very small sums, distributed over a long period.[14] While the amount may in principle have been comparable to that expended in the British abolition of slavery – a liquidity infusion that contributed directly to that country's industrialisation in the nineteenth century – the ultimate disbursements were considerably lower.[15] Contemporary critics suspected that the financial arrangements, which lacked any government guarantee, were intended to benefit France's banking interests, as well as to shore up the standing of the country's elite (whose members were well represented among the Saint-Domingue planter class) and the fortunes of its creditors (the large merchant houses that supported indebted plantations in the former colony).[16] Certainly, bankers were well informed on the prospect of the Haitian settlement, and government insistence that the loan be contracted by French banks, on the French market, demonstrated an intention to subsidise the country's financial sector.[17] The Haitian indemnity was part of other restorative economic measures – most importantly, an indemnity decreed in the same month in favour of émigré metropolitan landholders whose properties had been lost in the Revolution – which observers subsequently considered together as 'key elements of reestablishing general affluence, the Treasury's wealth, state credit, and public security', enriching France 'in the billions through the rapid rise in the capital value of its securities and all its real estate assets'.[18]

The 1825 loan was auctioned in Paris on behalf of the Haitian state by the house of C. Ternaux, J. Gandolphe, et Cie. in November 1825. The official announcement advised that the *président du conseil*, the Comte de Villèle, selected a loan repayment schedule that would avoid Haiti needing to introduce any new taxes, and that would take advantage of the country's growing prosperity.[19] The 30 million francs was divided into 30,000 bonds of 1,000 francs, each entitled to 6% interest (60 francs/year), and 1,200 bonds would be retired annually over twenty-five years, paying down the principal. By these arrangements, Haiti would need to dedicate 3 million francs to loan payments in the first year, set for 1827. Ternaux's father, the industrialist

Louis-Guillaume Ternaux, penned a promotional brochure for the loan, affirming that such amounts were not only well within Haiti's existing capacities, but that the country's future development – aided by the removal of 'the French government's frequently threatening attitude, which has long kept Haitians in a state of fear detrimental to the spirit of enterprise' – would make this and future loans easy to service.[20] Haiti intended to sell the bonds to a banking house for no less than 900 francs (intermediaries make their profits on the gap between the price they pay for a bond and the price for which they sell it), but a banking consortium of Laffitte et Cie., Rothschild frères, and other intermediaries won the contract for 800 francs per bond.[21] (One of the key members of this consortium was the Syndicate of Receivers General, a grouping of state tax officials directed by Villèle, testament to the state's interest in the issuance.) Haiti received 24 million of the 30 million it would owe, raising the effective interest to 7.5%.

Haiti sought to reduce the indemnity within months of conceding to the 1825 Ordinance, and payments faltered nearly immediately. After contracting and distributing the proceeds of the loan in 1825–27, Haiti needed to renegotiate terms of payment, reaching a new agreement in 1828, but was still unable to resume regular service of either the indemnity or the loan. In 1838, the amount of the remaining indemnity was cut in half (and the loan revised in 1839, reducing interest and amounts repayable) and payments resumed, but a hiatus was necessary again from 1843 to 1848, during civil war in Haiti. The terms of the renegotiations that followed in 1847/48 were such that loan interest payments continued to be in abeyance through the early 1850s, requiring a new agreement in 1854.[22] Payments of interest and principal were steadier from this point, though interrupted in 1867–69, before the loan was paid off in 1883.

These unequal economic relations were both violent and imperial in character. The country's national 'assets' provided security for its debts: the products of its public domains (for the loan) and seemingly its very independence (for the indemnity). As an 1831 legal consultation observed, the 1825 agreement meant that, *in extremis*, 'the only reparation to which France can lay claim is that of retaking Saint-Domingue'.[23] Haitians rejected the idea that their country's sovereignty was a dependent variable, and decoupling the question of its political standing from its financial and commercial relations occupied Haiti's politicians for the next fifteen years. This was seemingly accomplished by the separate political and economic treaties achieved in 1838.[24] Yet the framework for France–Haiti negotiations was infused with a presumed fungibility of Haiti's political independence and by the violence such vulnerability necessarily implied. Government ministers repeated seemingly irrepressible statements on their 'lack of interest' in revisiting Haiti's independence, but in the same breath mused on what forms of coercion the government might pursue in order to exact compliance.[25]

Explicitly imperial analogies permeated official exchanges, as when in 1831 the French consul to Haiti, Gaspard Mollien, chastised Boyer in the midst of difficult negotiations, responding to the President's gesticulations by asking, 'Mr. President, are you trying to make out like the dey of Algiers?'[26] Mollien was referring to the 'fan affair' or 'fly whisk incident', in which the dey of Algiers striking a French diplomat with a fly swatter in 1827 became a pretence for blockading, and later invading, the Ottoman province. Territorial claims were advanced in different forms, from anonymous pamphlets suggesting the establishment of free ports under French control in Haiti, to banker and deputy Jacques Laffitte reminding legislators that one of the most effective measures Haiti could take to improve its financial situation would be to open property ownership and business permissions to foreigners.[27] Moreover, the violence implied in repeated calls for replacing 'ministerial cowardice' with 'energetic measures' was frequently tangible.[28] While the Minister of Finance teased legislators in 1832 that they surely wouldn't demand that he 'turn up in front of Haiti with a warship' in order to exact payments, in fact naval deployments – in 1825, 1828, 1838, 1852, and 1854 – punctuated renegotiations of economic affairs.[29]

Practising extraction

An estimated 2,000 to 3,000 French capitalists purchased bonds entitling them to biannual interest payments from Haiti's national revenues.[30] We can glean something of how these individuals may have assessed their investment by first exploring the conditions of its issuance. In some ways, the Haitian loan was received as another in a slew of foreign loan ventures, arriving in the midst of a frothy and eroding market for Latin American securities – a context that former planter and negotiator of the indemnity agreement, Charles Esmangart, described as 'a loan mania'.[31] French journalists compared the loan favourably to Mexico's or Columbia's and weighed up its chances of success against a Spanish loan issued at the same time. But its distinct political significance was never far from view. Oppositional newspaper *Le Courrier* wrote in October 1825 that, 'In a few days, Paris, which didn't want anything to do with lending to the King of Spain, will give millions to Boyer. Who would have said it forty years ago? Things that were unthinkable in 1785 are completely straightforward today, much to the horror of a few people who don't want to advance with their century.'[32] Ternaux's promotional brochure was emblazoned with 'profits to benefit the Greeks', aligning the Haitian venture with other independence struggles, and was addressed to the Duc de La Rochefoucault-Liancourt, with whom Ternaux worked in the Société de la Morale Chrétienne, a major source of anti-slavery activism in the early nineteenth century.[33] In the first volume of the Saint-Simonian journal *Le Producteur*, a long article praised the loan as 'without question the most characteristic fact of our current moment', illuminating 'the reconciliation of the white and Black races'.[34]

Ternaux and Laffitte were both shareholders in *Le Producteur*, which links such purportedly humanitarian impulses closely to the marketing of the loan. Certainly, some bondholders would later defend their entitlements as virtuous when contrasted to the immoral and illegitimate claims of former slaveholders.[35] Liberal discourse in favour of the venture reasoned that the loan would 'admit' Haiti to the 'general association' of industrial peoples, where it could 'share with its former masters the advantages of public credit'.[36] Yet the extent and durability of any such ethical rationales are questionable; certainly, they coexisted easily with financial priorities. One of the loan's core selling points was always its link to the indemnity and to former colonists, its mission to 'heal still painful wounds, and reinstate fortunes [of dispossessed planters] engulfed in the shipwrecks of time'.[37] Bypassing the country itself, the loan's contribution to the new state was to be institutional and symbolic, bringing clarity and security to Haiti's political standing, from which productivity and growth would ostensibly follow.

In contrast to most countries involved in this early debt bubble, Haiti occupied a prominent and familiar (which is not to say better understood) place in the French economic imaginary.[38] Potent invented traditions of the island's fecundity may have acted powerfully on the minds of those who invested; certainly, they informed bitter accusations against the Haitian government when it proved an uncompliant debtor. Yet ideas about Haiti's wealth grew considerably more complex in the decades that followed its independence. Historian Yun Kyoung Kwon has shown that during the Restoration (1815–1830), Haiti was a touchstone in debates between royalists and liberals about the legacy of the French Revolution and the future of France's colonial empire. The press frequently surveyed 'the situation of Haiti', with conservatives and pro-slavery groups offering accounts that emphasised confusion and economic deterioration as the offspring of both republicanism and abolition, while liberals countered with favourable assessments of Haiti's growing population.[39] In discussions of the loan, one does not have to go far to find scepticism, even mockery, of the idea of Haitian affluence. 'They told us,' the daily *La Quotidienne* wrote in early November 1825, 'that the Haitian republic was rich, powerful, and strong, and look, it can't manage to borrow money, not event at *ten percent*.'[40] This is especially the case for racist arguments regarding the ostensibly meagre productive capacities of its free Black citizens.[41] Already in 1826, on the occasion of the first annual drawing of bonds from the loan, the daily *Le Constitutionnel* thought it scandalous that government ministers were not declaiming the obvious truth of Haiti's poverty to the public.[42] Accurate information on the country's public finances was scant, but seemingly less important to those who nevertheless invested than other ways of 'knowing' the country and trusting to the loan's enforcement.

Initial investors were certainly both well off and well connected – despite presenting themselves as 'small capitalists' or 'family men, with no experience of speculation, who took part in this loan on public trust'.[43] The first bondholder association, formed in 1830, contained members of the banking syndicate that had participated in the loan and was headed by Lieutenant General Louis Lemoine, who served in the Revolutionary and Napoleonic wars. The security's rapid decline in value – from an initial 840 francs in November 1825 to 700 francs by 1827, to 195 in 1848 – meant that bondholders became a more varied group as time went on.[44] For instance, lower prices likely granted access and influence to Jean-Pierre Vaur, sometimes referred to as Baron Vaur, a French trader in Port-au-Prince who attached himself to the loan negotiation process in the 1830s and emerged as one of its largest bondholders and most active organisers in the second half of the 1840s.[45] Records of the investors participating in the association in the early 1850s show that nearly half of its 550 members owned fewer than five bonds, and some bondholders, such as a widow named Lalleux in 1877 (see Figure 11.1), penned letters exhibiting credible economic distress. Yet the most active members of these committees remained former bankers and brokers, and few of their members were likely as modest as petitioning discourse portrayed. Even a former military serviceman (and assiduous petitioner) named Laurent, who explained that without the income of his Haitian bonds he would be unable to leave the Hôtel des Invalides 'where one freezes with the cold', reported that the savings he had tied up in the affair amounted to the hefty sum of 20,000 francs.[46]

The nature of their agreement – a contract with a foreign sovereign, immune from any foreign legal jurisdiction – meant that bondholders dissatisfied with Haiti's behaviour had to seek political routes of redress. They formed associations in order to negotiate collectively with the Haitian government, taking an active role in the settlements of 1838 and 1848.[47] In both instances, bondholders obtained the assistance of French diplomatic agents, successfully adding specific conditions for loan repayments onto new agreements for the indemnity. The process was not easy. The standard government view in both France and Britain (the two most important capital-exporting nations) was that the private affairs of international capitalists were just that, private, and without necessary implication for matters of government. As an internal historical note on the loan and indemnity

Haitian foreign debt and nineteenth-century France 227

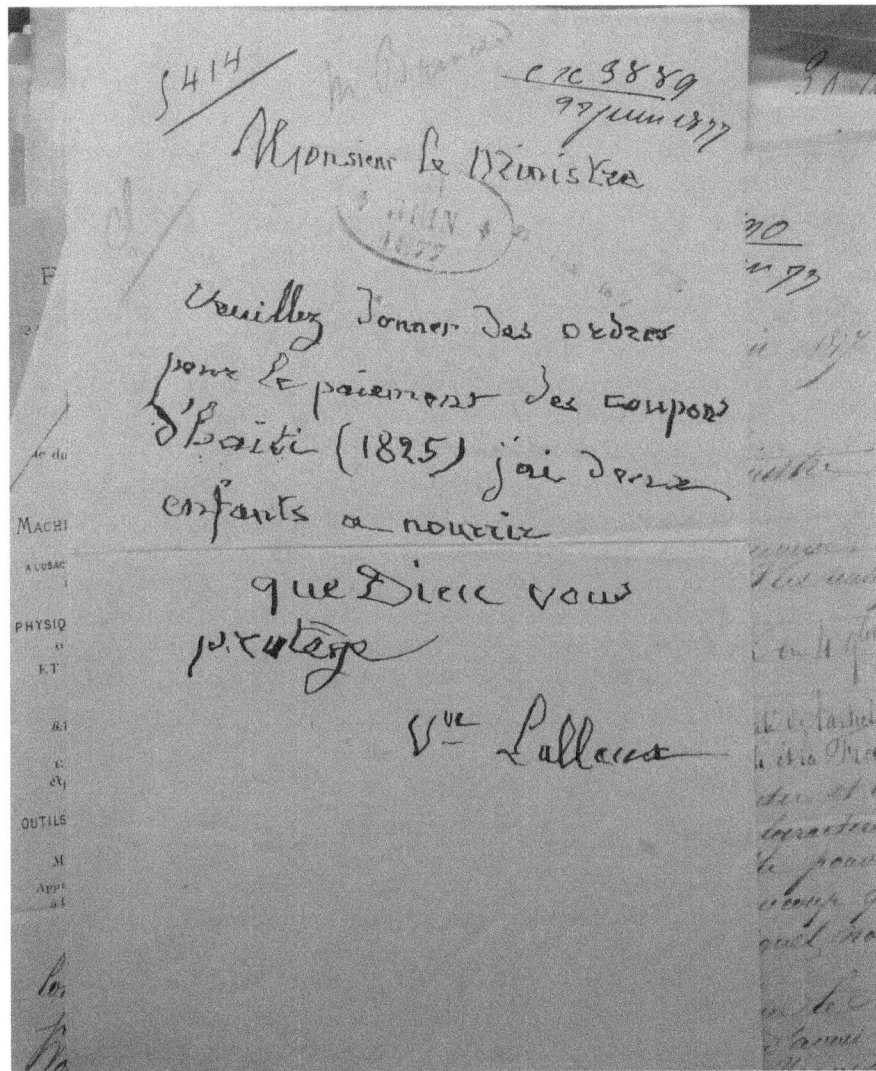

Figure 11.1 Letter signed Veuve Lalleux, *c.* 27 June 1877. It reads: '*Monsieur le Ministre*, Would you order the payment of the coupons of the Haiti (1825) loan I have two children to feed. God protect you.'

negotiations for the Ministry of Foreign Affairs summarised in 1845, 'Can one seriously contend that the French government should turn the lucky or unlucky outcomes of banking affairs into a question of international politics?'[48] In the Chamber of Deputies just a year earlier, François Guizot, the Minister of Foreign Affairs, made a formal statement that the government viewed the loan and indemnity as distinct agreements, and acknowledged no particular responsibility for the former.[49] To press their claims upon the government, then, bondholders cleaved to the notion of the 'double debt', which, in their usage, was not merely a description of the compounding obligations confronting Haiti, but a way of affecting the unification and politicisation, in the eyes of the French state, of Haiti's creditors.

Singly and in organised groups, for decades bondholders kept up a steady stream of letters and petitions to members of the government in which they rearticulated their rights as creditors, their perceptions of Haiti's behaviour, and their views on the responsibilities of the French state in their regard. Arguments centred on a few key points. First, that the Haitian state *could* pay, but would not; the government was a bad faith debtor rather than an impoverished one. Second, that the loan was sufficiently 'national' – insofar as it was linked to the 1825 Ordinance, promoted by the government, and supported by its institutions, like the Caisse des Dépôts et Consignations – that the French state owed creditors political intervention, if not a financial guarantee. Third, that bondholders deserved as much protection as indemnity holders, given that the loan 'simply substituted one group of French citizens for another, in their relations to the Haitian government', as one 1846 petition to the Chamber of Deputies put it. 'If you consider the circumstances that prompted them to make the loan, namely: the urging of the government and the political interests that prompted this invitation,' the petition continued, bondholders 'enjoy even more rights to their government's protection'.[50]

Bondholder mobilisation on this matter was helping to formulate a growing 'common sense' around the conditions and purpose of international finance and public debt that emerged in capital-rich countries in the first half of the nineteenth century.[51] Bondholders attached a kind of political, civilising purpose to public debt itself. As an 1845 petition suggested, fulfilling the terms of the loan would help 'reestablish and consolidate order in this Republic, agitated so cruelly and for so long by revolutionary anarchy'.[52] Not only would Haiti be seen as a reliable counterparty by the credit-giving nations that increasingly composed the globe as a financialised space, but working to pay its debt would also foster what bondholders called 'improving' investment in Haiti's local production and trade: from taxing *tafia*, 'the drink of the people', to setting up state monopolies in mahogany, to establishing concessions for tobacco cultivation and sale, there was no shortage of revenue-generating possibilities, so long as the Haitian government 'values its honour' and 'takes pride in paying'.[53] For a former colony excluded on racial and political grounds from the international community of civilised nations, the stakes of this uplift were especially high. One group of bondholders took it upon themselves to explain the situation directly to the Haitian envoys in Paris in the 1840s, reminding them of the burden that fell on their shoulders, as free Black people and people of colour, to summon the self-regard necessary to equal and surpass Europe's distinguishing institutions – chiefly, commitments to contracts. Failure threatened both (Black) humanity and sovereignty: 'Without respect, what is a man? What is a People? What is a Government? [...] have you reflected on how far your existence as a free and independent Government might fundamentally depend on the exactness with which you keep your commitments [...].' The consequences were unavoidable, for the natural laws of debt demanded that creditors 'gnawed at by despair' can never 'let their debtor sleep peacefully'.[54] Debt unfulfilled plunged both lender and borrower into a state of nature. Insofar as Haiti's sovereignty and freedom could be claimed as an extension of French civilisation (a common liberal position at the time), disregard for the sanctity of a financial contract also risked admitting the failure of France's cultural and political *rayonnement*. Even if not all bondholders subscribed to the view of one petitioner in 1851, who stressed the imperial ambitions motivating investors who 'came to the aid of the agenda of the minister at that time, an agenda whose goal was to return the former colony to the King's authority', the politics of international debt maintained a coercive hierarchy and dependence between the former metropole and colony.[55]

Indeed, the intensity of the criticism and bitterness to which creditors subjected the Haitian state certainly owed something to what they viewed as a perverse post-colonial power reversal. A spate of petitions in the early 1850s referred with shock and dismay to the lavish coronation ceremony of the new Emperor Soulouque, 'all paid for by money that he's stealing from bondholders' and about which 'we can do nothing but complain'.[56] Another sent on the same day observed bitterly that 'Haiti's bad faith is blatant, it's laughing at its creditors and goes so far as to claim that France would receive a poor welcome from its army, if it had the front to ask for what it owes to French creditors'.[57] (Soulouque was a touchstone for racist criticism of Haitian society and politics in the mid-nineteenth century, and publications like Cham's famous graphic album *Soulouque et sa cour* in 1850 no doubt mobilised bondholders as it did many others in their antipathy and fascination with Haiti.[58]) Read alongside letters expressing more explicitly racialised worldviews, the resonance and insinuations of this discourse take on particular weight. In 1834, for example, an investor named

Boullange complained of having to endure 'a handful of blacks who've pompously called themselves a Republic' showing up 'the weakness and impotence of the French ministry'; another petition expressed disgust that 'a black man, swimming in luxury and opulence, dared to make a show of spending a million francs on fancy furniture, while in France his creditors were dying of hunger and calling for divine justice!'[59]

The strength of feeling this relationship could evoke was reinforced by the processes of actualising bondholder advocacy. For some of these bondholders, like Laurent referenced above, mobilisation over this issue took up decades of their lives and consumed volumes of intellectual and emotional space.[60] Advocacy meant organising, meeting with other bondholders, publishing tracts, and pursuing restitution against French bankers and agents in court. For many, it was a process of self-actualisation, of adding oneself, collectively, to larger processes – even asserting the rights of ordinary individuals to political participation. Commenting in 1852 on the poor response they received from France's Consul General to Haiti, Maxime Raybaud, a group of bondholders complained that he 'is piqued that shopkeepers, smallholders, mere civil servants with small appointments dare to involve themselves in international affairs, dare to get engaged in interpreting diplomatic conventions, dare, as part of these arrangements, to demand their execution'.[61] Investors came together in meetings at the Stock Exchange, and payments and petitions issued from the domestic confines of Jean-Pierre Vaur's home. Interests were diverse and differently understood. Bondholder groups split in 1851 – a splinter group declared the existing association 'more Haitian than French' – resulting in a tumultuous meeting at the Exchange, with investors 'accusing one another of their incompetence, their failings, their poor plans of action; from the perspective of public morality, it was a scandalous meeting'.[62] An ordinary bondholder then found themselves with at least two possibilities for collective representation, each presenting different narratives of interests with which a prospective adherent could align.

One episode captures the extent to which advocacy was a situated, emotional, and personal endeavour. In September 1853, a delegation of three bondholders – Caron, Chappey, and Jances, representing the minority association of bondholders – visited Eugène Séguy-Villevaleix, chargé d'affaires for the Haitian legation in Paris, to discuss ongoing payments of back interest. Writing afterwards to the Minister of Foreign Affairs, the bondholders recounted a terse exchange in which their questions and concerns were repeatedly rebuffed, until tensions bubbled over and Villevaleix reportedly declared, 'I have no desire to discuss this with you, sirs, as almost all bondholders are in Bad Faith.' This alleged invective – recorded with underlines and capitalisation – moved the visitors to cry out with indignation:

What's that? Bondholders are in <u>bad faith</u>! Those who are still waiting for 18 out of 25 years of interest payments? Those who have been repeatedly deluded and misled by deceitful promises! Those from whom, now that you've already taken fifty million, you want to make off with the last guarantees on their securities!!! We'll tell you something, Monsieur de Villevaleix, it isn't the bondholders who are acting in <u>bad faith</u>; it's the Haitian government and all its agents that are acting <u>with the most exceptional bad faith</u> against us!

With this outburst, Villevaleix reportedly threatened to throw them out, and 'his family, his servants ran out to calm things down.' The bondholders refused to leave, saying that they would bring the matter to their government, prompting Villevaleix's 'scornful' reply: 'your government will never do anything for you, and <u>lets my government do what it likes!!!</u>' This finally compelled the bondholders to decamp, 'nearly ashamed at seeing our government so arrogantly disdained by agents of the feeble Haitian Empire!!!'[63]

The bondholders' tale is not a strictly reliable account, but its mode of narration and the general context of the encounter capture the extent to which the matters of the Haitian loan could be deeply personal affairs. A diplomatic agent is confronted in his residence, family near at hand, while the bondholders' anger is visible on the page, scratched with exclamation points and multiple underlines (see Figure 11.2). Contempt overflows their descriptions of Séguy-Villevaleix, reduced to a personification of arrogance. These embellished accounts aimed to both accentuate the alleged depths of Haitian duplicity and provoke mortification among the government recipients. The charge of 'bad faith' was not simply the conventional accusation of a creditor against a recalcitrant debtor. It was imbued with a sense of intrinsic incapacity and unreliability, linked to a series of characterisations of Haitian behaviour that faulted the country for failing to adhere to the standards of a civilised society.[64]

The familiarity and intimacy of the lingering imperial relationship, as well as the racist aspects of its inequities, help explain why, in comparison with bondholder campaigning around other contemporary foreign loans such as the Spanish or Portuguese debts, Haitian bondholders are notable in their support for the use of violence in enforcing creditor demands. Certainly the country's sovereignty appeared malleable, as suggestions for installing French customs agents to survey receipts or retaking cities such as Môle-Saint-Nicolas implied.[65] Calls for 'energetic' measures ('a severe and forceful ultimatum', the new bondholder committee demanded in 1853) were scarcely veiled urgings for more direct interventions.[66] When a petition in 1852 offered 'a last cry of desperation, and invoked *ultima ratio regum* [a resort to arms], the final argument of governments', it showed that recourse to military violence was often a desired eventuality.[67] And when the 1848 agreement between Haiti and its creditors came to an end in

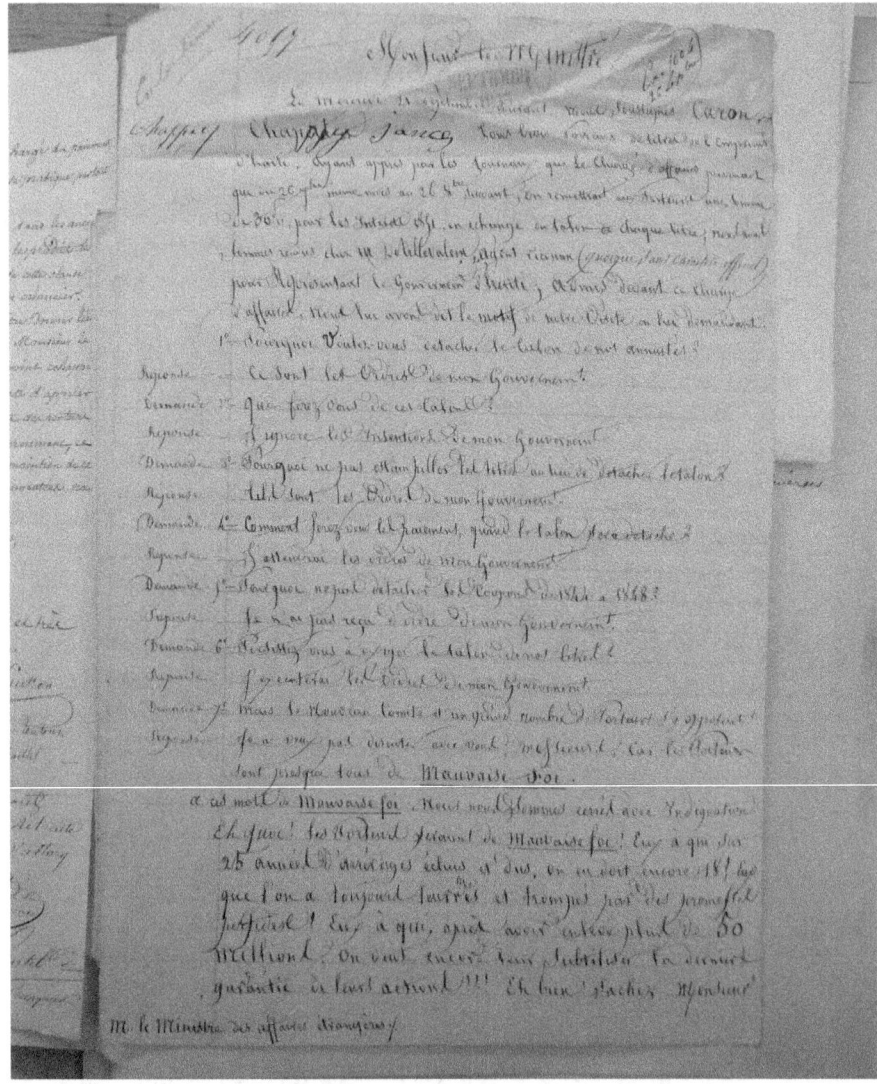

Figure 11.2 Petition from bondholders Chappey, Caron, and Jances, September 1853. Source: FR-MAE Centre des archives diplomatiques de La Courneuve 752SUP 312.

the early 1850s, the French state finally responded in line with bondholder demands. Diplomatic officials and a naval detachment were deployed to Haiti in 1854 to reach a new deal on the country's loan obligations. In March, Rear-Admiral Duquesne presented himself in Port-au-Prince with the frigate *Iphigénie*, the brig *Méléagre*, and the aviso steamer *Ardent*, under orders from the Minister of the Navy and Colonies to get definitive terms for repayment. The convoy left with £60,000 sterling to put towards back payments to French creditors, 'saluting' the Haitian colours with twenty-one cannon shots as it went.[68]

When one of the leading members of the Haitian bondholders committee, Antoine Guitton, described the loan in a popular investment manual that he published under the pseudonym A. G. de Méhiclet in 1858, he praised the decisiveness of this armed intervention. In contrast to 'the weakness of earlier governments', France's Napoleon III had ensured that 'the Haitian government knows now very well that it cannot suspend this last agreement without consequence'.[69] The result was 'the most favourable transformation in the situation of bondholders', with the security placed 'on a regular and most reassuring footing'.[70] Here at last was the enforcement and assurance on which investors had likely counted from the start of the venture. From 1854, payments were managed and the loan supervised by the French state.[71] Public subsidy secured private profit; prices were healthy throughout the loans remaining years, and annual drawings continued to reimburse bonds at their full face value (with only slight interruption in the 1860s), achieving complete repayment the 1880s.

Conclusion

The Haitian debt was one of the very first foreign loans on the French market. The amounts at stake in this transfer of capital were relatively small, from a French perspective. Much of it, in practice, went unrealised. But as Guitton's career as a popular investment authority shows, for example, the loan ran through the heart of how French savers learned to engage in global investment. If we turn to a social history of this loan in the French context, we begin to discern ways in which international debt might school its participants in modes of argument and understanding, as well as modes of political engagement, that both constituted and reflected France's informal, financial empire in the nineteenth century. Certainly, not every investor dedicated great thought to these particular securities. (Though it is worth reflecting that in 1852, at least 520 people – of which 63 owned only one bond, and so were engaged for only modest sums – came in person or via a representative to validate their membership in the association.) But in working to get at the meaning of the Haitian loan in the eyes of its creditors, we open a much wider frame onto practices and positionalities that helped transform and maintain imperial relations.

The particularity of the Haitian loan also places racism and imperial violence at the core of the dispositions of dominance and demands for state intervention that characterised mobilisation around international investment. As the independence debt lingered across the century, unevenly distributed and enforced, it provided renewable grist for dreams of national and imperial grandeur. Plans for retrieving expropriated plantations grew dim as time passed, but the claims of Haiti's creditors were evergreen, multiplying as bonds changed hands and especially once Haiti undertook new borrowing from the 1870s. These claims survived through numerous revolutions and regime changes, in both Haiti and France. Part of this durability is explained by how property as a legal institution is encoded in capitalism. But this chapter suggests that another part lies with the ways that international investment and debt enforcement can become part of ordinary people's everyday lives, composing a habitus of imperial extraction, fostered by state support.

Notes

1 *Loi et ordonnances relatives à la république d'Haïti et aux indemnités stipulées en faveur des anciens colons de Saint-Domingue* (Paris: Imprimerie de Mme Veuve Agasse, 1826). On the complexity of this agreement, see Jean-François Brière, 'La France et la reconnaissance de l'indépendance haïtienne: Le débat sur l'ordonnance de 1825', *French Colonial History* 5 (2004), 125–38; and for contemporary perspective, B. Vendryes, *De l'indemnité de Saint-Domingue, considérée sous le rapport du droit des gens, du droit public des français et de la dignité nationale* (Paris: n.p., 1839).

2 Simon Henochsberg, 'Public debt and slavery: The case of Haiti (1760–1915)' (MA thesis, Paris School of Economics, 2016), available at http://piketty.pse.ens.fr/files/Henochsberg2016.pdf (last accessed 24 March 2022); Victor Bulmer-Thomas, *The Economic History of the Caribbean since the Napoleonic Wars* (Cambridge: Cambridge University Press, 2012), chapter 7; Frédérique Beauvois, 'Monnayer l'incalculable? L'indemnité de Saint-Domingue, entre approximations et bricolage,' *Revue historique* 3.655 (2010), 609–36.

3 Frédérique Beauvois, 'L'indemnité de Saint-Domingue: "Dette d'indépendance", ou "rançon de l'esclavage"?' *French Colonial History* 30 (2009), 109–24. On the role of Haitian negotiators in the shift from political to financial closure, see Friedemann Pestel, 'The impossible *Ancien Régime colonial*: Postcolonial Haiti and the perils of the French restoration', *Journal of Modern European History* 15.2 (2017), 261–79.

4 Mary Dewhurst Lewis, 'Legacies of French slave-ownership or the long decolonization of Saint-Domingue', *History Workshop Journal* 83 (2017), 151–75, 167.
5 Bondholders received interest payments in 1827 and 1828, but these funds (nearly 5 million francs) came from the French government, via the banking consortium that floated the loan. They were added to Haiti's debt, and repaid by further borrowing in 1835. See Thomas Madiou, *Histoire d'Haïti: t.7, 1827–1843* (Port-au-Prince: Editions Henri Deschamps, 1988 [1847]), pp. 159–60.
6 Thomas Piketty, *Capital and Ideology*, trans. Arthur Goldhammer (Cambridge, MA: Harvard University Press, 2020), pp. 218, 276.
7 David Todd, *A Velvet Empire: French Informal Imperialism in the Nineteenth Century* (Princeton, NJ: Princeton University Press, 2020); David Todd and Alexia Yates, 'Public debt and democratic statecraft in nineteenth-century France', in Nicolas Barreyre and Nicolas Delalande (eds), *A World of Public Debts: A Political History* (Basingstoke: Palgrave Macmillan, 2020), pp. 79–106.
8 In this respect, they can be seen as another manifestation of empire that spares taxpayer expense, a topic explored by Madeline Woker in this volume.
9 Deborah Cohen asks similar questions of British foreign investment in 'Love and money in the informal empire: The British in Argentina, 1830 to 1930', *Past & Present* 245.1 (2019), 79–115.
10 François Blancpain, *Un siècle de relations financières entre Haïti et la France (1825–1922)* (Paris: L'Harmattan, 2001); Jean-François Brière, *Haïti et la France, 1804–1848. Le rêve brisé* (Paris: Karthala, 2008); Gusti-Klara Gaillard-Pourchet, 'Haïti-France. Permanences, évolutions et incidences d'une pratique de relations inégales au XIXe siècle', *La Révolution française* 16 (2019), doi: 10.4000/lrf.2844. See also Romuald Le Pelletier de Saint-Rémy, *Saint-Domingue. Etude et solution nouvelle de la question haïtienne* (Paris: A. Bertrand, 1846), vol. 2, pp. 110–55. See Paul Gilbert's contribution on post-colonial Britain in this volume for a discussion of the boundaries between colonial investment and development aid.
11 Henochsberg, 'Public debt and slavery', p. 57.
12 Bulmer-Thomas, *Economic History*, p. 185.
13 Johnhenry Gonzalez, *Maroon Nation: A History of Revolutionary Haiti* (New Haven, CT: Yale University Press, 2019), p. 33.
14 The 1838 revision to the indemnity effectively cut the debt from 120 million (150 million minus the 30 million paid instalment) to 60 million francs, and the payment period extended from five to thirty years. When combined with increasing numbers of beneficiaries as descendants proliferated, roughly a third of indemnity-holders received between 1 and 7 francs a year, two thirds between 15 and 250 francs, with a few larger payments. See Beauvois, 'Monnayer l'incalculable?', and the ongoing research of historians responsible for the slavery, indemnity, and compensation database 'Repairs': https://esclavage-indemnites.fr/public/ [last accessed 24 July 2022].
15 Catherine Hall, Nicholas Draper, Keith McClelland, Katie Donington, and Rachel Lang, *Legacies of British Slave-ownership: Colonial Slavery and*

the Formation of Victorian Britain (Cambridge: Cambridge University Press, 2014).
16 Benoît Joachim, 'L'indemnité coloniale de Saint-Domingue et la question des rapatriés', *Revue historique* 246.2 (1971), 359–36.
17 Todd, *Velvet Empire*, pp. 250–2.
18 Gaston d'Audiffret, 'Rapport sur le projet de loi relatif à la répartition des sommes versées par le gouvernement d'Haïti, 7 février 1840', in *Système financier de la France*, 3rd edn (Paris: Dupont, 1863), vol. 4, pp. 409–27, 414.
19 'Emprunt d'Haïti', *Gazette nationale ou Moniteur universel*, 13 October 1825, p. 1406.
20 Louis-Guillaume Ternaux, *Considérations sur l'emprunt d'Haïti* (Paris: n.p., 1825), p. 23.
21 *Gazette nationale ou Moniteur universel*, 12 November 1825, p. 1521.
22 *Précis historique des faits relatifs à l'emprunt d'Haïti [...] publié par le Comité* (Paris: Guiraudet et Jouaust, 1849); *Un mot sur la situation de l'Emprunt d'Haïti [...] publié par le Comité* (Paris: Guiraudet et Jouaust, 1852).
23 Joseph Remy, *Consultation de M. Remy, jurisconsulte, pour les porteurs d'annuités de l'emprunt d'Haïti et pour les colons* (Paris: Dupont et Lagnionie, 1831), p. 15.
24 Conditions for the loan payment were added in 1839. See Blancpain, *Un siècle de relations financières*, pp. 69–75.
25 Minister of Foreign Affairs, Duc de Broglie, Chambre des Députés, séance du 29 décembre, *Journal des débats*, 30 December 1832.
26 Madiou, *Histoire d'Haïti*, t.7, p. 95. Mollien had become well known as an explorer of Senegal before joining the French foreign service. See Jean-François Brière, 'Du Sénégal aux Antilles: Gaspard-Théodore Mollien en Haïti, 1825–1831', *French Colonial History* 8 (2007), 71–9.
27 For territorial demands – specifically, the Samana peninsula – see *La Vérité sur Haïti, ses deux emprunts…Par un Subrécargue* (Paris: Moreau, 1828) and Ministère des Affaires Etrangères [hereafter MAE] 752SUP 312, Anon. *Note relative aux créances françaises sur Haïti* (s.d. [1846]). Laffitte's comments in Chambre des députés, 3 juin 1837, *Gazette nationale ou Moniteur universel*, 4 June 1837, p. 1411.
28 Chambre des députés, 3 juin 1837, *Gazette nationale ou Moniteur universel*, 4 June 1837, p. 1411.
29 Chambre des députés, séance du 29 décembre, *Journal des débats*, 30 December 1832.
30 This estimate from Jean-François Brière, 'L'Emprunt de 1825 dans la dette de l'indépendance haïtienne envers la France', *Journal of Haitian Studies* 12.2 (2006), 126–34, p. 129. By the 1850s, bondholder groups claimed to represent approximately 800 bondholders.
31 Charles Esmangart, *Nouvel avis aux colons de Saint-Domingue sur le paiement de l'indemnité* (Paris: Dezauche, 1836), p. 42.
32 *Le Courrier*, 29 October 1825.

33 Lawrence Jennings, *French Anti-slavery: The Movement for the Abolition of Slavery in France, 1802–1848* (Cambridge: Cambridge University Press, 2000).
34 'Emprunt d'Haïti', *Le Producteur* 1 (1825), 44–50.
35 Laurent, *La Vérité sur l'emprunt perçu par le gouvernement français pour le compte de la république d'Haïti* (Paris: A.T. Breton, 1842).
36 'Emprunt d'Haïti', *Le Producteur*, pp. 45, 46.
37 Ternaux, *Considérations*, p. 7.
38 Marc Flandreau and Juan Flores, 'Bonds and brands: Foundations of sovereign debt markets, 1820–1830', *Journal of Economic History* 69.3 (2009), 646–84. This bubble was, in any event, an affair of well capitalised (and well informed) investors: Giorgio Fodor, 'The boom that never was? Latin American loans in London, 1822–1825', Universit' Degli Studi di Trento, Economics Department, Discussion Paper no. 5, (2002).
39 Yun Kyoung Kwon, 'When Parisian liberals spoke for Haiti: French anti-slavery discourses on Haiti under the Restoration, 1814–1830', *Atlantic Studies* 8.3 (2011), 317–41, p. 322.
40 Reported in *Le Courrier*, 6 November 1825.
41 Pamphlets like the anonymous *La Vérité sur Haïti, ses deux emprunts, etc.* (Paris: Imprimerie Moreau, 1828) attributed fantasies of Haitian wealth to efforts by financiers to push the loan and despaired of the potential for agriculture organized by free Blacks. The productivity of free versus enslaved labour, and the capacity of Blacks to engage effectively as wage workers, was a key point of contention in economic and abolitionist debates; see Caroline Oudin-Bastide and Philippe Steiner, *Calculation and Morality: The Costs of Slavery and the Value of Emancipation in French Antilles* (New York: Oxford University Press, 2019); Naomi J. Andrews, 'How should slaves disappear?': Defending slavery in France, 1834–1848', *Slavery and Abolition* 41.3 (2020), 643–68.
42 *Le Constitutionnel*, 4 October 1826.
43 *Emprunt d'Haïti, Réclamation des porteurs d'annuités, 31 octobre 1831* (Paris: Setier, s.d.), 7; MAE 752SUP 312, Lettre de Boullange, Palais Royal, au Ministère des Affaires Etrangères, 16 octobre 1834.
44 Brière, 'L'Emprunt de 1825', p. 129. The bonds later made notable gains: 315 francs in 1852, 640 francs in 1859, 500 francs in 1872. See *Cours authentique Bourse de Paris*, 21 May 1852, 17 August 1859, 23 August 1872.
45 Madiou describes Vaur in 1833 as 'having as much self-importance as if he'd been an official diplomatic agent'; Madiou, *Histoire d'Haïti*, t.7, p. 207. An 1851 list of members of Vaur's committee records him as owning between 420 and 483 bonds (he signed three times) out of the 11,670 in circulation. (This total was disputed by rival bondholder groups.) See MAE 752SUP 312. On Vaur, see his 1835 dossier for the Légion d'Honneur: Archives Nationales LH/2680/11.
46 MAE 752SUP 312, Lettre de Laurent au Ministère des Affaires Etrangères, 24 novembre 1844.

47 On bondholder associations, see Marc Flandreau, 'Collective action clauses before they had airplanes: Bondholder committees and the London Stock Exchange in the 19th Century (1827–1868)', Graduate Institute of International and Development Studies Working Paper, No. 01/2013.
48 MAE 752SUP 312, Bureau d'Amérique et des Indes, Politique, Note, février 1845.
49 *Gazette Nationale ou Moniteur Universel*, 2 June 1844, p. 1593.
50 MAE 752SUP 312, Pétition à la Chambre des Députés, 15 février 1846. Emphasis original.
51 Juan Luis Simal, 'National credit and the international financial market: The Spanish debt and its foreign bondholders, 1820–1834', *Journal of Iberian and Latin American Studies* 25.3 (2019), 381–402; Juan Pan-Montojo, 'State credit and foreign debt in the early nineteenth-century: Contradictory representations of a renovated scenario', *Journal of Iberian and Latin American Studies* 25.3 (2019), 361–80; Barreyre and Delalande (eds), *A World of Public Debts*, part 1.
52 MAE 752SUP 312, Pétition, Comité de l'emprunt au MAE, 14 juin 1845.
53 MAE 752SUP 312, J. Devillers à Messieurs les envoyés du Gouvernement d'Haïti, s.d. [1840s].
54 MAE 752SUP 312, J. Devillers à Messieurs les envoyés du Gouvernement d'Haïti, s.d. [1840s].
55 MAE 752SUP 312, Pétition de Breton à Monsieur le Président Louis-Napoléon, 1 février 1851.
56 MAE 752SUP 312, Lettre signé Exter au Président de la République Française, 15 décembre 1851.
57 MAE 752SUP 312, Lettre signé Busson au Prince Louis-Napoléon Bonaparte, 15 décembre 1851.
58 Cham, *Soulouque et sa cour par Cham* (Paris: Charivari, 1850). On Soulouque's significance in Britain at the same time, see Jack Webb, *Haiti in the British Imagination: Imperial Worlds, 1847–1915* (Liverpool: Liverpool University Press, 2021), chapter 1.
59 MAE 752SUP 312, Boullange au MAE, 16 octobre 1834 ; Breton à Monsieur le Président, 1 février 1851.
60 For some bondholders, mobilisation was professional; at least two of the largest holders of Haiti's bonds, bankers named Dubourg and Sarrans the elder, were also members of the bondholder committee for Spanish public debt.
61 MAE 752SUP 312, copie d'une lettre de Picard au Ministre des Affaires Etrangères, Drouyn de Lhuys, 22 décembre 1852. Emphasis original.
62 MAE 752SUP 312, Pétition du Nouveau Comité à l'Empereur, 21 janvier 1853; Lettre de Guérin et. al. au MAE, 9 février 1852.
63 MAE 752SUP 312, Lettre de Caron, Chappey, et Jances au Ministre des Affaires Etrangères, septembre 1853.
64 On standards of 'civilisation' and Haitian recognition, see Julia Gaffield, 'The racialization of international law after the Haitian Revolution: The Holy See and national sovereignty', *American Historical Review* 125.3 (2020), 841–68.
65 MAE 752SUP 312, *Note relative aux créances françaises*.

66 MAE 752SUP 312, Nouveau comité au MAE, 12 avril 1853.
67 MAE 752SUP 312, Nouveau comité (55 signataires) au Président de la République Française, septembre 1852.
68 MAE 752SUP 312, Newspaper clipping, 8 April 1854.
69 G. de Mériclet, *Nouveau tableau de la Bourse de Paris*, 4th edn (Paris: E. Dentu, 1858), pp. 169–70.
70 A. G. de Mériclet, *La Bourse de Paris*, 2nd edn (Paris: E. Dentu, 1857), p. 153.
71 'Décret impérial portant promulgation de la convention relative au remboursement de l'emprunt de 1825, conclue entre la France et Haïti le 1er octobre 1854', *Moniteur universel*, 25 December 1854.

12

The lure of the welfare state following decolonisation in Kenya

Lyla Latif

Introduction

Alongside the local, including religious, forms of taxation that existed in the territories that came to be colonised by Europeans,[1] imperial authorities often also imposed their own fiscal order upon colonial populations. This was aimed at paying for the administrative costs of the colony.[2] Colonial tax systems were created to respond to the fiscal realities of the colonies. Governing a colony was costly and British bureaucrats encouraged their colonial administration officers to find ways of paying for their local expenses without help from the British treasury. From an economic perspective, requiring colonies to pay for their own expenses was an effective means of limiting the metropole's spending on the Empire. Therefore, the colonies needed to collect sufficient revenue to pay for local administration. This was indeed a great challenge since there was substantial variance in the level of economic development, economic opportunities, and the costs of governing the colonies.

The colonial administration would not be able to collect much in revenue from the hunter and gatherer communities, nomads, fishermen, and farmers who made up the colonised population of East Africa, for example. Instead, revenue would be mobilised from establishing an export industry and trade taxes. To achieve this goal, an economic system modelled on a labour force was therefore necessary. Consequently, the tax system of colonised territories was designed to support colonial capitalism and 'to create new opportunities for financing the colonial state'.[3]

In its Kenya colony, a tax system was established to generate local contributions to the costs of British colonial governance. Since the focus was on meeting colonial expenditure needs, minimal amounts were put towards local public services.[4] This marked the narrative that would resonate for years to come on the disconnect between the tax system and its usefulness for establishing a welfare colonial state. One of the fundamental principles of British colonial rule was that colonial states had to be financially self-sustaining.⁵ Consequently, the implementation and expansion of colonial taxes was based on a principle which did not resonate with distributive justice that supported spending on social welfare. The colonial administrators did not treat taxation and welfare as a reciprocal relationship as it is commonly understood, but as antithetical. Such a conceptualisation of the tax system was later inherited at independence.

The chapter also argues that historical inequalities in the design of the tax system have been buffered against subsequent change by the post-colonial states because of the imperial vision set out through the Organisation for Economic Co-operation and Development (OECD) of keeping former colonies subordinate to European political and economic needs. The post-colonial focus on revenue mobilisation in order to finance domestic economic growth put pressure on the newly independent state to identify its own sources of revenue, failing which it would resort to borrowing from its previous colonisers. The debt conditions shaped the ordering of a domestic economy dependent on international financial institutions of the OECD that were heavily inclined towards revenue extraction and capital flight. Effectively, the colonial tax model that prioritised a fiscal system based on supporting the (global) economic market over welfare was thus entrenched. Taxation continues to be viewed as the fiscal tool to support private sector growth and foreign direct investment upon which welfare would be contingent.

By focusing on Kenya, the chapter discusses how the post-colonial state continues to serve the interests of British and OECD capital. In maintaining the capitalist status quo, the Kenyan tax system continues to inhibit redistribution towards welfare. To explain this further, the chapter starts by describing the colonial history of Kenya, explaining how fiscal issues were addressed and whether the colonial tax system fostered the vision of developing a welfare system for its colony. It finds that the way in which people were taxed and governed in colonial Kenya was part of a conscious strategy to structure inequalities through the distribution of revenue away from financing welfare. It also finds that the colonial vision of a fiscal system set against the provision of welfare was continued by the subsequent independent government of Kenya.

Part III of this volume, on post-colonial legacies, focuses on the lasting legacies of imperial inequalities created through unequal taxation regimes and the manipulation of notions of welfare. This chapter sets out how the Kenyan nation was not able to decolonise from the economic and fiscal inequalities created by the British Empire after political independence and how a new form of fiscal imperial relations emerged that prevented Kenya from financing its own welfare state. While domestic tax systems should have the ability to evolve independently, post-colonial tax systems evolve in relation to pressures from outside.⁶ Even today, normative tax regimes in post-colonial states are shaped by the former colonising powers' social, economic, and political structuration and this creates power asymmetries and inequalities.⁷ Consequently, post-colonial fiscal regimes continue to resonate with their historical past.⁸

The colonial fiscal history of Kenya

The disconnect between a fiscal system and welfare provision is usually engineered through a capitalist market. Historically, the fiscal governance of colonial territories focused on extracting revenue to finance colonial economics, fostering structures that would serve capitalism. Therefore, colonial capitalism is a way of understanding the role of colonialism in enabling the development of tax systems that imprinted capitalist development in colonial territories. Colonial capitalism also explains the processes by which international structures ensured the capitalist imprint was inherited by post-colonial African states.

Colonial capitalism operating though the exercise of coercive power and by the desire to profit through exploitation created economic arrangements that cast a colonised population to the social margins to become peripheral subjects of capitalism and divided them from each other in the name of economic well-being. This was done by granting differential privileges to workers and non-workers, to individuals and to corporations, to local firms and foreign firms. The tax system facilitated such differentiation, whereby white settlers and foreigners were granted tax privileges on their income and profits while the income and profits earned by locals was subject to the hut, poll, and land taxes imposed by the colonial administration. Additional local rates were imposed by the Local Native Councils constituted by the area chiefs to finance local community needs, such as building local schools.⁹ Through this approach, in the context of Kenya, indigenous or native people were forced into labour on various white settler farms to earn an income based on which they could afford to pay their hut or poll taxes.¹⁰

Similarly, resources extracted from its Kenya colony through taxation were directed to Great Britain, instead of the revenue being redistributed to local development. In fact, local development, such as building schools and dispensaries, was subjected to the political vision of *'majimboism'* (devolution) by which the colonial government engaged local native chiefs to convince their population to contribute towards their collective development needs. These local native chiefs were then brought within the colonial legal system and vested with political power to mobilise local funds for local development needs. This laid down the foundation of an asymmetrical legal and tax system.[11]

In the context of colonial Kenya, political and economic asymmetry is observed in placing the native population as subjects of capitalism to serve the economic interests of the Empire through the imposition of taxation. These people had become wage labourers in order to meet the colonial state's demand for taxes. The legal and fiscal structures that were created under the 1921 Income Tax Ordinance to support such extraction of income also defined the economic ordering of society. The native population were put in a position of shouldering the burden of taxation without being granted commensurate access to political and economic power. They were also confronted with additional revenue demands from colonial officials, such as paying the land, income, and ad valorem taxes while at the same time continuing to pay the colonially imposed hut and poll taxes.[12] There is an influential strand of literature that stresses the intimate link between colonial repression, tax extraction, and institutions designed for the fiscal exploitation of native colonial populations.[13] This literature reveals how inequality was embedded in designing taxation. Subsequently, the historic colonial inequalities made it harder for post-colonial states to decolonise from tax-based inequalities.

During the period of colonial rule in Kenya the imperial power's coercion-intensive approach to taxation was secured through its colonial office. Such coercion was based on the threat of violence and sanctions against those who failed to pay the tax.[14] The colonial administration put in place processes of establishing political authority, legal systems, and international relations which were clearly designed to protect the imperial fiscal system which was made up of interest groups and organised coalitions, such as the Colonist Association created to dispossess the native population of their land.[15] As a result, the tax system, which was based upon stratified revenue extraction that mainly focused on Africans as taxpayers, was protected from reorganisation.

Colonised states seeking independence, as part of the negotiations for decolonisation, were forced to preserve this system.[16] They implicitly accepted the idea that the legal ideology and norms informing state formation and the wider political and fiscal system had already been defined and systems put in place within which they were to fit. Within this framework, independence meant constraints on the possibilities of the subordinated people as a nation. The problem with an acquired post-colonial tax system meant that independent states would remain passive players in a system actively created by and for groups in power.[17] This generality also extended to the fiscal structure of post-colonial states and constrained the development of a post-colonial welfare state.

The origin of this antagonistic relationship lay in the role of the colonial legal order that established property rules and prioritised imported capital, which motivated class antagonism and created economic classes. In doing so, British rule in Kenya established its preferred modus operandi, and its engineered social structuring reinforced this vision. The colonial administration sought only the economic security of its metropolitan legal order and taxation system that was in place to govern domestic affairs and international relations.[18] The underlying objective of doing so was to extract revenue from its colonies. Relatedly, therefore, the tax regime was symptomatic of the political authority and the interest groups it protected. Connectedly, the post-colonial tax regime was also symptomatic of its former colonial authority's fiscal history.

While colonised states gained independence, internationally they remained within the single power system represented by the former colonial powers constituted as the OECD, World Bank, and International Monetary Fund (IMF), giving the illusion of facilitating socio-economic welfare.[19] The colonial administration, during the native population's pursuit for independence, took the existing political and legal relations, 'reconstituted them in terms of imperatives and then gave them back to the people as their own'.[20] In establishing this domestic architecture for self-rule, the colonial administration also ensured it kept its hegemonic influences intact and buttressed from change within independent Kenya. Thus, while Kenya was recognised at the international level as a sovereign state in political spaces, it remained constrained by the legal orders established by the dominant groups and external players such as the OECD, World Bank, and IMF. Hence, the long colonial interaction between the Kenyan people and their former coloniser evolved in relation to pressures from these institutions.[21] Thus, the independent state of Kenya became subject to a legal system established upon norms drawn out of the vision of the international institutions.[22] At an international level, the relationship between Kenya and Britain could be seen as more of an imposition affected by power differentials rather than an interactional process. Consequently, the post-colonial independent state of Kenya was not truly post-colonial, its tax system remained largely similar to its colonial tax system, and this continued to replicate colonial inequalities.

The British colonial tax regime's post-colonial transition was supposed to be premised upon the delivery of what would become an independent welfare state,[23] but instead, the newly independent government of Kenya continued the application of its colonial tax regime, preventing its reform. The post-colonial Kenyan tax regime was reconstituted along the coercion-intensive colonial approach to taxation, which was incompatible with establishing a welfare state. This trend continues to be reflected in both domestic and cross-border tax policies and law. Even today, domestic tax policy and double taxation agreements setting out preferential tax rates for foreigners and providing them with various tax incentives continue to reveal an antagonistic relationship between economic and social classes within and across the border.[24] This follows the antinomy between the colonial administration and the conception of a welfare state that independent Kenya sought to move towards.

As the labour reserve economy of the British Empire, the sole purpose of the Kenyan tax system had been to extract revenue with which to recover colonial expenditure on development[25] and to ensure the subordination of labourers to the market structure.[26] The difficulty with changing the nation's colonially inspired tax system in the present is associated with the capacity of the state to repay the debts associated with structural adjustment plans. Further, there are considerations around the economic performance required to effectively implement policies associated with permitting the nation-state to access international markets.[27] To explain this, I now turn to examine the move to independence in order to show how the fiscal Kenyan state formalised its assimilation with the economic market developed around asymmetrical power relations, leading to a diversion from forming a welfare state.

The move to independence

If one is to construct a model of the British colonial vision for its Kenya colony, it would resemble a model of a capitalistic commercial enterprise. Large tracts of arable land were made available for white settlers as incentives for inward migration and investment, and mandatory hut taxes were imposed that forced the native population to work for the settlers.[28] The local taxes that were collected were used to remunerate civil servants and to finance infrastructure. Mainly, local tax was redistributed to the main hub of colonial administration, Nairobi.[29] Rural areas where the natives largely resided missed out on the redistributive effects of taxation. Clearly, the economic and social fragmentation between the colonial administration, the settlers, and natives shows a change in the way power and privilege were distributed through legal means.[30] Invariably, the legal order and tax system that existed created social structuring engineered around inequalities, and the asymmetrical power relations between settlers and the native population were treated as the defining feature of the colonial legal system and taxation policy. Thus, taxation became a form of control. Key tax terms, such as the hut tax, implied this control and power relation.

Changes in legal and social understandings were prompted by returning native veterans from the First World War who questioned the colonial administration's commitment to provide them with equal treatment in fiscal allocations, social services, and access to land and political posts.[31] This suggests that the natives were beginning to demand from the colonisers a transition from the extractive colonial administration protecting individual rights to a modern welfare-based colony.[32] The colonial administration, intent on placating the growing dissent, passed an ordinance to vest the Local Native Council with the power to impose local community taxes with which to provide local public goods and services.[33] This was a strategic move by the colonial administration to push the burden of providing social services onto local communities, who were to be taxed by the Local Native Councils as a form of domestic resource mobilisation for financing their local needs.[34] This was the colonial form of social production through local community-based taxation. Implicit in the creation of this new tax order lay the interests of maintaining the existing modes of social hierarchy. Colonial imposition of tax was not directed towards the benefit of the native population. Consequently, the additional local tax imposed by the Local Native Councils came to be seen as an unequal burden or obligation, and as something that had no commensurate benefits or guarantees. The tax raised hardly sufficed to construct and equip local health clinics and schools.[35]

In pursuit of their collective ideology the native population then formed, for example, the Kavirondo Taxpayers Association, to push the colonial administration towards a modern welfare-based colony.[36] This was the onset of a native-conceptualised tax system shaping the beginning of redistributive practices based on the provision of social services and social welfare as part of their broader vision of African socialism. They took an interactional approach by forming an association to advance their demands and sought political support through their African representative to the colonial Legislative Council to table and discuss how the colonial budget was to be apportioned.[37] The argument advanced by the colonial administration was embedded in the idea of devolution that granted the indigenous population local autonomy to seek out local ways to address their needs. This was the Empire's effort to find a legal system for its Kenyan colony that would only communicate the concepts of order that the British wanted to enforce. A welfare model did not resonate with the colonial ideological position. This led to native people defining their problems differently. Instead of continuing the interactional approach with the colonial administration, they opted for self-rule and ousting the British from what had become known as the 'Kenya colony'.

Formal political independence for Kenya from British colonial rule was achieved in 1963.[38] Yet upon its departure, the British colonial administration did not leave behind a fully fledged and viable nation capable of forming a welfare state. This is because state building was neither the original intention nor the primary objective of the colonial power.[39] Theirs aim was simply to create an administrative framework conducive to peace, submission through order, and the extraction of resources.[40] The administrative framework so established later provided the justification for economic exploitation and political domination of the newly independent Kenyan state.[41] This culminated in the formulation of a written constitution, negotiated at Lancaster House in the United Kingdom, as a pre-condition for the independence of Kenya.

The Independence Constitution that was negotiated was based on the existing colonial legal order and fiscal system. Hence, the Kenyan economy continued, even after independence, to be controlled and directed by its former colonial ruler.[42] Thus, being the outpost, as it was, of imperially conceived international monopoly capitalism, the Kenyan economy could not help but respond to the demands of metropolitan markets.[43] As a result, Kenya's fiscal approach was based on its conceptualisation as a state participating within the existing economic order as opposed to intervening into this order.

Independence thus meant the ability to make laws within the country but not the power to change the structure of the economy, the international taxation system, or the pattern of trade with the outside world. The private sector and private investment from both domestic and external sources were given a privileged critical role to play in the development of the country. Contrary to the claims made to the citizens by the newly independent government to set the country on a social welfare model pursued through an equitable tax and redistributive policy, the government instead promoted free enterprise and foreign investment, permitting investors to export their entire profits without assessment for domestic taxation.[44] This approach to tax, effectively at play today, embedded inequality within the tax regime so that the country appeared as a vulnerable entity open to the 'scramble for tax'. The vulnerability in the form of tax base erosion subsequently resulted in the removal of the provision of social services from the centre of the government's fiscal obligation to its taxpayers. This implied social engineering of the development of the post-colonial Kenyan state is the direct consequence of the colonial tax model.

This predisposed Kenya to a particular pattern of economic development reminiscent of its colonial history – where the burden of taxation fell on the citizens whereas the benefits from domestic resource extraction that were accrued were guaranteed for foreign investors. This attitude towards tax extraction to meet the demands of the privileged class continues to resonate even today despite the fiscal principles established in the 2010 Constitution of Kenya that require the provision of equitable development as part of the government's fiscal obligation.

The relationship between tax and development as construed under article 201 (b) (iii) of the 2010 Constitution of Kenya and article 10 (2) which binds the government to specific principles of tax governance (human rights, equality, good governance, accountability, and sustainable development) have not yet been implemented as part of the nation's tax legislation, which remains rigidly path dependent.[45] The constitutionally entrenched norms have not resulted in the political will and subsequent legal rules to reorganise the colonial tax model. In fact, the constitution seems to have mastered the art of both initiating change and preventing it. Article 2 (6) of the Constitution provides that 'any treaty or convention ratified by Kenya shall form part of the law of Kenya under this Constitution'. Going by this, the rules governing both domestic and international taxation, which have largely been devised by former imperial states to benefit their own economic and business purposes, have been codified as treaties and conventions that article 6 seeks to introduce as part of Kenyan law. The negotiation of these treaties resulted in an antagonistic relationship at the international level that overlooks post-colonial African perspectives in the creation of tax norms. As such, at the domestic level, institutional pressures from outside that dictate a country's participation within the global economic and financial order force African governments to disconnect their tax regimes from contributing to social change through welfare. As a result, most of the redistributive spending is directed towards facilitating economic growth, leaving social services and welfare conditional upon the delivery of a sustainable future economy.[46]

Clearly, the colonial tax model reproduced by the independent government had the effect of ensuring that the British colonial legacy based on local extraction without commensurate social benefits remained intact. Even the locally proposed post-colonial fiscal model based on African socialism, discussed below, prepared by the independent government reiterated the colonial approach to disconnect tax from development. Such approaches subsequently eroded the confidence of the ruled in the fiscal behaviour of the Kenyan state and its handling of resources placed in its trust that generate revenue towards the goal of forming a welfare state. Consequently, taxation came to be seen as an unequal burden to the state, and as a remission with no commensurate benefits or guarantees for Kenyan citizens. It came to be viewed as the evolution of a new form of coercion-intensive Leviathan stripped of its colonial image and repackaged as a post-colonial, native-led, revenue-extractive state.

The post-colonial fiscal state and its relationship to its colonial past

The independent Kenyan state inherited the legal system and tax design already put in place by the old Empire. The new government based its tax philosophy around Adam Smith's maxims of taxation,[47] which were stated in Sessional Paper No. 10 of 1965, 'African Socialism and its Application to Planning in Kenya'.[48] This sessional paper set out the blueprint on which the independence government organised itself. The phenomena of public finance in the paper were based on the idea that while social services and welfare are necessary and tax must be redistributed for their achievement, economic rights take precedence over social services and welfare – a significant departure from the original native vision of African socialism.

The paper argued that the provision of social services and welfare would depend on the availability of funds. It tied the mobilisation of such funds to the economy and thereby observed that adopting a liberal, free-market model would help sustain the new economy which would subsequently transit into a welfare state. This confirmation in the paper was a subtle statement resonating with the colonial approach on removing the provision of social services and welfare from the centre of government's fiscal obligation to its taxpayers. It belied the struggle towards independence, which was based on self-rule, equality, non-discrimination, access to social services and welfare, land use, and economic participation. African socialism, the catchphrase promoting the lure of a welfare state itself, turned oxymoronic.

Relatedly, the colonial Income Tax Ordinance of 1920 was enacted as legislation after independence. This meant the continuation of the asymmetrical taxation power relationships that were clearly designed to protect interest groups and preserve the autonomy of private foreign enterprise. Thus, a large chunk of the tax burden fell upon individuals on whom were imposed direct and indirect taxes, while corporations were given tax exemptions and incentives.[49] A further asymmetrical relationship is observed in the suspension of the country's domestic tax statute where cross-border taxation of foreign resident persons or corporations is concerned. Local tax laws and rules would not apply where a double tax treaty arrangement existed based on which an individual or corporation, the subject of tax, was a foreign resident whose income accrued from Kenya. Tax would be subject to the treaty rules, which favoured the resident state over the source state. In this way, the double tax treaty regime denied the domestic state (being the source state) its jurisdiction to tax. This is an example of the old Empire reconstituting its inequalities in the post-colonial era.

Recent scholarship, commentaries, high-level reports, and policy briefs have extensively described and discussed how double tax treaties erode the tax base of many developing countries.[50] In enacting the 1920 Tax Ordinance into law, the Kenyan government implicitly accepted the idea that the taxation ideology and norms of the wider political system had already been defined and systems put in place within which they were to fit, despite the inequality and power asymmetries. Kenya would remain a passive player in a tax system actively created by and for groups in power. The independent state became subject to the command model of law affected by power differentials rather than an interactional process. This had the effect of ensuring that the British colonial legacy remained intact and buttressed from reorganisation in order to protect British interests.

The impact of such asymmetrical power relations and inequalities continue to be deeply felt within Kenya's tax system, such that taxation is seen as an unequal burden or obligation to the state, and as a remission that has no commensurate benefits or guarantees for Kenyan citizens. It comes as a repackaged institution where the former colonial order replaced by the Kenyan state establishes a fiscal relationship that treats individuals according to class and economic structures, thereby continuing the power asymmetries and inequalities. The system based on individual taxpayers' contribution to tax (direct and indirect taxation), as opposed to taxing business profits, has resulted in a system that is unable to mobilise adequate sources of revenue to finance social services or progress towards welfare. The limited tax collection arises from a limited tax base. The majority of Kenyans are employed in the informal sector and fall within the exempt threshold for tax.[51]

The administrative framework so established provided the justification for economic exploitation and political domination of the newly independent Kenyan state. Relatedly, the formulation of a written constitution, negotiated at Lancaster House as a pre-condition for the independence of Kenya, thwarted the country's real development from using its indigenous roots, directed by its own local needs.[52] Thus, even after independence, the Kenyan economy continued to be controlled and directed by its former colonial ruler. Kenya had the power to make laws in the country but not to change the structure of the economy the British chose for it, nor the power to alter the pattern of trade with the outside world nor its tax design. This effectively restricted the government from establishing a welfare state. The Sessional Paper No. 10 of 1965 reveals this problem.[53] The sessional paper attempted to build a society on the basis of African socialism offering the possibility of creating a welfare state; unfortunately, it only skirted around the edge of conceptualising welfare, without offering much insight.

Instead, the sessional paper explained the policy of the government that followed colonial undertones of an economic ordering based on prioritising economic development over the provision of social welfare. The paper was based on the encouragement of development mainly through private enterprise (mimicking colonial capitalist ideology). It emphasised that in order to develop and sustain the system, there had to be a continuing injection of imported capital and skill (giving preference to foreign influences). The role of the public sector was primarily to facilitate and encourage the growth of domestic capitalism (a system disconnected from welfare). The public sector was intended to provide the necessary economic infrastructure, capital, and, where needed, social overheads.[54]

This imagined attraction of maintaining the colonial-inspired economic system at the expense of conceptualising African socialism and modelling their state along indigenous governance that promoted social welfare was strong enough to encourage African leaders to maintain the evolving system. Hence, the importance of free enterprise and the sanctity of private property became significant for the emerging Kenyan elites. Its undertones were evident during the 1960 Constitutional Conference at Lancaster House. The constitution worked out the appropriate institutions – economic, political, and constitutional – that Kenya was to adopt to retain the colonial system at independence. Thus, a laissez-faire capitalist society was created without an obligation to provide social welfare.

Such were the social engineering measures undertaken by the colonial administration. The institutions that maintained the capitalist system, such as the Employers Trade Union and foreign-owned financial institutions (Barclays Bank, Standard Chartered), were not attacked by the Kenyan leaders. Instead, they defended private property, promoted free markets, allocated taxes to economic outputs at the expense of social services and welfare, and appealed for more foreign investment and technical expertise. During the 1960 Conference, the Kenyan government affirmed to the financial and banking circles in London that the future Kenyan government would not dismantle the economy, and that it would adopt capitalism as its economic model.[55] Assurances were given that the independent government of Kenya would recognise the country's dependence on foreign investment and would take measures to ensure its security by producing a tax stratum with privileges for private enterprise.

Before Kenya became independent, a report prepared by the International Bank for Reconstruction and Development (IBRD), titled *The Economic Development of Kenya*, reinforced all the principles and objectives the independent government would abide by.[56] Key among them was the insistence not to deviate from a capitalist economy to one based on socialist ideologies. The government detailed their acceptance of the IBRD report in their document titled *The Observation*, endorsing the view that private investment from both domestic and external sources had a critical role to play in the development of Kenya and affirming the government's commitment to create conditions and services designed to encourage private foreign investment.[57] A welfare state was therefore seen as one that would not be commensurate with the retention of a capitalist-based economy in the newly independent state. Accordingly, the tax regime directed its redistributive effects away from the provision of social services and welfare and towards establishing parastatals and state corporations focused on facilitating agriculture and husbandry for export.

All this later contradicted the notion of African socialism that the government promised its people as the welfare governance model. Instead, African socialism was explained along the lines of creating a politically stable and just society based on equal opportunities and human dignity. Welfare or the provision of social services seemed to have been removed from the explanation. African socialism was initially conceptualised as the basis for overturning colonial inequalities during the colonial administration.[58] It was envisaged as the golden goose that would lead the country towards a welfare system where social security, education, and health care would be the government's top priorities.

However, since their version of African socialism was not defined and set out concisely, the independent government crafted a model that promised the lure of a welfare state as the next iteration that would follow the strong economy which only capitalism could deliver. Clarifications on the kind of African socialism to be adopted were made by the politicians. It was not to take the form of nationalisation.[59] It was to be adapted to African traditions: communal and egalitarian but adapted to modern circumstances given the colonial legacy and the impact of colonial capitalism on traditional African society.[60] Hence, the system of governance and the economic model had to be modified to reflect these realities.

Thus, the sessional paper set out to achieve three strategies. First, to reform the inherited colonial economy by establishing a mixed economy, one in which the role of private enterprise and that of government are complementary to each other. Second, to Africanise the entire economy, creating state corporations to be wholly owned and financed, or substantially subsidised, by the state. Third, to ensure that foreign investment continued to be attracted to and retained within Kenya.[61] The paper argued that without economic growth none of the three strategies propounded would be achieved. It also argued that a focus on the provision of social services and welfare would undermine economic growth. It reiterated reliance on the tax base of the country, seen as the citizens, and it affirmed privilege for private enterprise in the form of tax cuts to cajole their capital towards the Kenyan economy. This effectively pushed the burden of tax to the citizen, analogous to the colonial imposition of tax on the native population.

Consequently, the role of the individual, and in particular their economic activities, were central to the achievement of the three strategies. The paper did not prescribe the type of political system Kenya should adopt as part of its strategies. Since the inherited economic structure was left intact and it was based on colonial capitalism, it followed that capitalism continued to be the economic foundation of the political system in Kenya. It is quite puzzling why the paper on African socialism was referred to and defended as socialist when its ideology was patently capitalist. The lure of a welfare state lay in the contrast between the noun and verb of African socialism.

The sessional paper placed a great emphasis on economic growth. Any impediments to the economic growth of Kenya were to be avoided. Redistributing taxes towards the provision of social services and welfare would compromise this economic model and hence the paper made it imperative to focus the fiscal obligations of the state on absolute economic growth. Provision of social services and welfare therefore became conditional upon the success of the economic model. This in effect meant avoiding any tampering with the present economic system, even if the economic system was based on a power hierarchy where Kenya was at the bottom of the pyramid when it came to negotiating trade and tax norms and rules, while its former coloniser remained at the apex.

The economic system closely interacts with the domestic taxation system and the power hierarchies can be seen through the cross-border approach to taxation. The fact that international business taxation rules were earlier set by the OECD and introduced as part of the domestic framework without the recipient African state having an opportunity to formulate these rules confirms the colonial legacy based on extraction of sources of revenue,[62] thereby continuing to embed inequalities into the fiscal regime of the postcolonial state. The choice of tax rules being determined based on residence rather than source is an example. Though these rules have changed over time, mentioning them here only serves to emphasise the points made on power asymmetries.

The private sector and private investment from both domestic and external sources were given a critical role to play in the development of the country. Contrary to the claims made to citizens by the newly independent government about setting the country on a social welfare model, the government instead promoted free enterprise and foreign investment, permitting investors to export their entire profits without assessment for domestic taxation. This has inevitably predisposed Kenya to a particular pattern of economic development – where the burden of taxation falls on the citizens whereas the benefits from domestic resource extraction that were accrued are guaranteed for foreign investors. As a result, the cycle of inequality and power asymmetries continue as a result of hierarchies of authority that exist at the international level within which Kenya remains hardly equal.

Conclusion

This chapter discussed the origin of the fiscal Kenyan state and explained how the legal order and tax system adopted by the independent government had the effect of ensuring that the British colonial legacy based on revenue extraction and a privileged tax stratum remained intact and protected from reorganisation. It explained how this subsequently eroded the confidence of the ruled in the fiscal behaviour of the Kenyan state in detracting away from forming a welfare state.

Taxation, catapulting the start of the modern post-colonial Kenyan state, was seen as an unequal burden or obligation to the state, and as a remission that has no commensurate benefits or guarantees for Kenyan citizens. It came as a repackaged catallactic institution where the former colonial administration, replaced by the Kenyan state, established a fiscal relationship that treated individuals according to class and economic structures, thereby continuing the power asymmetries and inequalities and luring away the dream of a welfare state.

Thus, as argued throughout this chapter, British colonial laws remain connected with the post-colonial Kenyan state, reproducing power asymmetries and inequalities (now through international institutions). The imperial-led contouring of the independent Kenyan state ensured that the British colonial legacy would remain intact. The underlying objective of doing so was to entrench the imperial power as a rentier state continuing to extract revenue from its former colonies. The post-colonial tax regime became the tool with which to achieve this vision.

The British colonial tax regime's post-colonial transition was supposed to be premised upon the delivery of what would become an independent welfare state, but instead, the newly independent government of Kenya was required to respond to the demands of metropolitan markets. In so doing, Kenya had to commit to continue the application of its colonial economic ordering, buttressing it from modification. This implied that Kenya's tax system would also be reconstituted along the coercion-intensive colonial approach to taxation, which is incompatible with a welfare state.

Notes

1. Roland Oliver, *The Cambridge History of Africa*, vol. 3: *c. 1050 to c. 1600* (Cambridge: Cambridge University Press, 1977); B. A. Ogot, *General History of Africa: Africa from the Sixteenth to the Eighteenth Century* (New York: UNESCO, 1992).
2. Leigh A. Gardner, *Taxing Colonial Africa: The Political Economy of British Imperialism* (Oxford: Oxford University Press, 2012).
3. Ewout Frankema and Anne Booth, *Fiscal Capacity and the Colonial State in Asia and Africa, c. 1850–1960* (Cambridge: Cambridge University Press, 2020), p. 4.
4. Gardner, *Taxing Colonial Africa*.
5. Facundo Alvaredo, Denis Cogneau, and Thomas Piketty, 'Income inequality under colonial rule: Evidence from French Algeria, Cameroon, Tunisia and Vietnam and comparisons with British colonies 1920–1960', *Journal of Development Economics* 152 (2021).
6. Okanga Okanga and Lyla A. Latif, 'Tax vulnerabilities in Africa: Revisiting inclusivity in global tax governance', *African Journal of International Economic Law* 1.2 (2021).
7. Bruce Berman, *Control & Crisis in Colonial Kenya: The Dialectic of Domination* (Nairobi: East African Educational Publishers, 1999).
8. Joseph Schumpeter, 'The economics and sociology of capitalism: The crisis of the tax state', in Jurgen G. Backhaus (ed.), *Navies and State Formation* (Berlin: LIT Verlag, 2012).
9. George Ndege, *Health, State, and Society in Kenya* (Rochester, NY: University Rochester Press, 2001).
10. Yash P. Ghai and J. P. W. B. McAuslan, *Public Law and Political Change in Kenya: A Study of the Legal Framework of Government from Colonial Times to the Present* (Oxford University Press, 1970).
11. David Leonard, *African Successes: Four Public Managers of Kenyan Rural Development* (Berkeley: University of California Press, 1991).
12. Attiya Waris, 'Taxation without principles: A historical analysis of the Kenyan taxation system', *Kenya Law Review* 1 (2007), 274–304.
13. Gurminder K. Bhambra, 'Colonial global economy: Towards a theoretical reorientation of political economy', *Review of International Political Economy* 28.2 (2021); Madeline Woker, *Empire of Inequality: The Politics of Taxation in the French Colonial Empire, 1900–1950* (New York: Columbia University Press, 2021); Goran Therborn, *Inequality and the Labyrinths of Democracy* (London: Verso, 2020); Hiroyuki Hino, Arnim Langer, John Lonsdate, and Frances Stewart, *From Divided Pasts to Cohesive Futures: Reflections on Africa* (Cambridge: Cambridge University Press, 2019); Andrew Smith and Chris Jeppesen, *Britain, France and the Decolonisation of Africa: Future Imperfect?* (London: UCL Press, 2017); Alessandro Stanziani, 'Scales of inequality: Nation, region, empire', *Annales* 70.1 (2015), 99–109.
14. Peter Karari, 'Modus operandi of oppressing the 'savages': The Kenyan British colonial experience,' *Peace and Conflict Studies* 25.1 (2018).

15 E. S. Atieno-Odhiambo, 'The colonial government, the settlers and the "trust" principle in Kenya 1939', *Transafrican Journal of History* 2.2 (1972), 94–113.
16 Ahmed Mohiddin, *African Socialism in Two Countries* (London: Croom Helm, 1981).
17 Tatah Mentah, *The State in Africa: An Analysis of Impacts of Historical Trajectories of Global Capitalist Expansion and Domination in the Continent* (Cameroon: African Books Collective, 2010).
18 June Starr and Jane F. Collier, *History and Power in the Study of Law: New Directions in Legal Anthropology* (Ithaca, NY: Cornell University Press, 1989).
19 Asad Ismi, *Impoverishing a Continent: The World Bank and the IMF in Africa* (Canadian Centre for Policy Alternatives, 2004).
20 Peter Fitzpatrick, 'Is it simple to be a Marxist in legal anthropology?' *Modern Law Review* 48.4 (1985), 472–85, p. 479.
21 Tatah Mentah, *The State in Africa: An Analysis of Impacts of Historical Trajectories of Global Capitalist Expansion and Domination in the Continent* (Langaa RPCIG, 2010).
22 Robert Kidder, 'Towards an integrated theory of imposed law', in Sandra Burman and Barbara Harrell-Bond (eds), *The Imposition of Law* (New York: Academic Press, 1979), pp. 289–306.
23 Kenya African National Union, *The KANU Manifesto for Independence, Social Democracy and Stability* (Nairobi: KANU Publication, 1960).
24 Bruno Martorano, 'Taxation and inequality in developing countries: Lessons from the recent experience of Latin America', *Journal of International Development* 30.2 (2018), 256–73, doi: 10.1002/jid.3350; Alex Cobham and Petr Janský, *Estimating Illicit Financial Flows: A Critical Guide to the Data, Methodologies, and Findings* (Oxford and New York: Oxford University Press, 2020).
25 Daniel Kunzler, 'The influence of colonialism and donors on social policies in Kenya and Tanzania', in Carina Schmitt, *From Colonialism to International Aid: Global Dynamics of Social Policy* (Cham: Palgrave Macmillan, 2020).
26 Mohiddin, *African Socialism in Two Countries*.
27 Mohiddin, *African Socialism in Two Countries*; Lyla Latif, 'Centralised revenue redistribution as a potential cause of internal conflict in Kenya', *Modern Africa: Politics, History and Society* 4.1 (2016), 91–105.
28 Lewis H. Gann and Peter Duignan, *The Rulers of British Africa, 1870–1914* (London: Croom Helm, 1978); Robert Maxon, *Struggle for Kenya: The Loss and Reassertion of Imperial Initiative, 1912–1923* (Madison, NJ: Farleigh Dickinson University Press, 1973).
29 Ndege, *Health, State, and Society in Kenya*.
30 Daron Acemoglu, Simon Johnson, and James A. Robinson, 'The colonial origins of comparative development: An empirical investigation', *American Economic Review* 91 (2001), 1369–1401.
31 Maxon, *Struggle for Kenya*.
32 Ndege, *Health, State, and Society in Kenya*.
33 Kenya National Archives, Nairobi, *Minutes of the Proceedings of the Legislative Council* (14 May 1923).

34 Stephen Constantine, *The Making of British Colonial Development Policy, 1914–1940* (London: Frank Cass, 1984); Latif, 'Centralised revenue redistribution as a potential cause of internal conflict in Kenya'.
35 Ndege, *Health, State, and Society in Kenya*.
36 Charles Oyaya and Nana Poku, *The Making of the Constitution of Kenya: A Century of Struggle and the Future of Constitutionalism* (London: Routledge, 2018).
37 Abdalla Bujra, *Democratic Transition in Kenya: The Struggle from Liberal to Social Democracy* (Nairobi: African Centre for Economic Growth, 2005).
38 Ghai and McAuslan, *Public Law and Political Change in Kenya*.
39 Ann Beck, *A History of the British Medical Administration of East Africa, 1900–1950* (Cambridge: MA: Harvard University Press, 1970).
40 Caroline Elkins, *Britain's Gulag: The Brutal End of Empire in Kenya* (London: Pimlico, 2005).
41 Mohiddin, *African Socialism in Two Countries*.
42 Rok Ajulu, *Post-Colonial Kenya: The Rise of an Authoritarian and Predatory State* (London: Taylor & Francis, 2021).
43 Walter Rodney, *How Europe Underdeveloped Africa* (Pambazuka Press, 1972).
44 Government of Kenya, 'Sessional Paper No. 1 of 1963, Observations on the Report of an Economic Survey Mission for the International Bank for Reconstruction and Development' (Nairobi: Government Printer, 1963).
45 Government of Kenya, Constitution of Kenya, 2010 (Nairobi: Government Printer, 2010).
46 Mark Robinson, 'Aid, democracy and political conditionality in sub-Saharan Africa', in Oliver Morrissey and Frances Stewart (eds), *Economic and Political Reform in Developing Countries* (London: Palgrave Macmillan, 1995), pp. 81–96; Jonathan Glennie, *The Trouble with Aid: Why Less Could Mean More for Africa* (London: Zed Books, 2010); Latif, 'Centralised revenue redistribution as a potential cause of internal conflict in Kenya'.
47 (1) Taxes should be levied in proportion to property. (2) Taxes should be certain and not arbitrary. (3) A tax should be convenient to pay. (4) A tax should be economical to administer, for both the taxpayer and the state.
48 Government of Kenya, 'Sessional Paper No. 10 of 1965: African Socialism and Its Application to Planning in Kenya' (Nairobi: Government Printer, 1965).
49 Lyla Latif, 'Changing the tax architecture' (East Africa Tax and Governance Network, 2019).
50 See generally the websites of the Tax Justice Network, Tax Justice Network-Africa, African Forum for Debt and Development (AFRODAD), Independent Commission for the Reform of International Corporate Taxation (ICRICT), International Centre for Tax and Development (ICTD), Committee of Fiscal Studies (University of Nairobi), United Nations Economic Commission for Africa (UNECA), and the Economic Development in Africa Report 2020 by UNCTAD.

51 Angella Katee Ndaka, 'Informal sector and taxation in Kenya: Causes and effects', *International Journal of Law, Humanities & Social Science* 1.4 (2017), 77–86.
52 Mohiddin, *African Socialism in Two Countries*.
53 Government of Kenya, 'Sessional Paper No. 10 of 1965: African Socialism and Its Application to Planning in Kenya'.
54 *Ibid.*
55 *East African Standard*, 26 September 1960.
56 International Bank for Reconstruction and Development, *The Economic Development of Kenya* (Baltimore, MA: John Hopkins University Press, 1963).
57 Government of Kenya, 'Sessional Paper No. 1 of 1963, Observations on the Report of an Economic Survey Mission for the International Bank for Reconstruction and Development' (Nairobi: Government Printer, 1963).
58 Joel D. Barkan, *Beyond Capitalism vs. Socialism in Kenya & Tanzania* (London: Lynne Rienner, 1994).
59 Tom Mboya, *Freedom and After* (London: André Deutsch, 1963).
60 Mohiddin, *African Socialism in Two Countries*.
61 Government of Kenya, 'Sessional Paper No. 10 of 1965: African Socialism and Its Application to Planning in Kenya'.
62 Joan Apuun Atim, 'The double taxation architecture conceptualised Under Section 41 (5) of the Income Tax Act; Chapter 470, Laws of Kenya', *Financing for Development* 1.2 (2020), 146–65.

13

From capitation taxes to tax havens: British fiscal policies in a colonial island world

Gregory Rawlings

Taxation was never imposed in a uniform, consistent, or non-discriminatory form in the British Empire despite early twentieth-century metropolitan ideals that it should be. Instead, taxation mirrored the inequalities of colonial rule. Tax obligations, requirements, and assessments varied between categorisations of persons and their properties, which corresponded to segregated and hierarchical systems of colonial governance throughout empire. 'Natives' and settlers seldom paid the same taxes. And yet in 1922 the 'Inter-departmental Committee on Income Tax in the Colonies not possessing responsible government' released its report to the British parliament.[1] The committee proposed a 'model ordinance' that could be applied throughout the British Empire to raise local income tax. The model ordinance covered specified clauses, itemising a comprehensive approach to taxation in the colonial world. This included methods of assessment, provisions for deductibility, depreciation, exemptions, residence and non-residence, and relief from double taxation. What was striking about the report was not so much what it covered, which was almost all forms of economic activity 'as not to allow any substantial amount of income to escape the tax', but what it omitted.[2] The report and the model tax ordinance took conceptions and assumptions about income as they applied in the United Kingdom and other industrialised countries at the time and recommended imposing them throughout the empire. Although the committee claimed to acknowledge 'the great diversity of Colonial conditions and requirements', these were entirely absent in the model tax ordinance.[3] As the committee emphasised, 'the easiest and most expeditious means of securing that degree of uniformity which is generally admitted to be desirable will be for the officers responsible for the preparation of the Colonial Income Tax legislation to take a single model as the basis on which to work'.[4]

Yet the colonies that this tax template were aimed at were not uniform. Taxation, like other forms of economic governance across empire, were demarcated between hierarchies of persons, places, and properties.

Despite the committee's acknowledgement of colonial diversity, nowhere did its report document the substantive character of imperial pluralities, organised and experienced on the basis of class, race, and gender, and their inequalities, segregations, demarcations, subversions, and acts of colonial violence. Nowhere did the discourse of fiscal rectitude and standardised rules and regulations anticipate that just five years after the report was released to parliament, sixty indigenous Solomon Islanders would be massacred by British militia as a result of a dispute over tax while another six were hanged (some in front of their children); while in the New Hebrides (Vanuatu) attempts to impose capitation taxes (also known as poll, or head, taxes) were periodically abandoned as a result of protest and resistance.[5] This was not the kind of 'diversity' in 'Colonial conditions and requirements' that the committee probably had in mind when it developed its model tax ordinance for the British Empire.

This chapter explores fiscal practices and policies in two neighbouring territories in the Pacific: the Anglo-French Condominium of the New Hebrides (which became Vanuatu in 1980) and the British Solomon Islands Protectorate (BSIP). While both territories were closely connected at administrative levels, they developed contrasting fiscal regimes due to the specifics of their constitutional conditions. By 1950, Solomon Islands had a tax system in place that resembled the model ordinance first proposed for the colonies in 1922. Although there was a continuing distinction between 'native' and 'non-native' taxes and taxpayers, this was increasingly being dismantled as Solomon Islanders took up employment in the public and private sectors. By 1957 Solomon Islands had double taxation agreements (DTAs) with the United Kingdom, Sweden, Denmark, and Norway.[6] By contrast, the New Hebrides did not even have income tax in 1957, let alone a series of DTAs with other countries. When Solomon Islands became independent in 1978, it had a full, internationally recognisable tax system. When the New Hebrides achieved independence as Vanuatu in 1980, it did so as an internationally renowned tax haven, with a revenue base dependent on excise and customs duties and clear inequalities between wealthy expatriates and settlers who paid no income tax and an indigenous majority who continued to pay a range of indirect taxes as they had in the colonial period.

The emergence of tax havens, or offshore finance centres, in locations such as Vanuatu have their origins in imperial inequalities that were fostered in environments of diverse colonial experiences, encounters, and policies. Fiscal policy has been characterised by continuity and rupture between colonial and post-colonial orders, leading to further international inequalities in taxation which have been evident in the first two decades of the twenty-first century. In a 2019 review of offshore activity for the

International Monetary Fund (IMF), Nicholas Shaxson reported that between US$500 billion and US$600 billion is 'lost' in 'corporate' taxes every year because of tax haven use.[7] These are funds that could have been allocated to education, health care, and housing but are unavailable because of offshoring. In her ground-breaking analysis of tax havens, decolonisation, and capital mobility, Vanessa Ogle has observed that '[D]ecolonization, conceived in economic and financial terms', 'marked a transitory period during which old capital was in part removed, and during and after which new capital had to be mobilised to arrive in the form of official aid and private investment alike'.[8] It is ironic, then, that some US$200 billion is lost in tax revenue to 'low-income' countries every year, more than the US$150 billion that is spent on foreign aid.[9] Shaxson has reported that a total of US$2.6 trillion in US corporate funds (from the 'American Fortune 500 companies') is kept offshore, part of a total of US$36 trillion invested in tax havens worldwide.[10]

However, not all post-colonial (and remaining colonies) island states have become offshore finance centres facilitating these tax losses. Due to policies pursued in the colonial era, Solomon Islands, to the north of Vanuatu, never became a tax haven. Yet the post-colonial fiscal state that was bequeathed to Solomon Islands by the United Kingdom at independence in 1978 has struggled to fund essential services. Instead it has turned to its abundant natural resources – timber, fish, dolphins (destined for the international zoo trade), and minerals such as bauxite – which are exploited on an unsustainable and environmentally devastating scale, fuelling industrial and post-industrial production far from the archipelago's shores.[11] These trends – a tax haven geared towards an international clientele profiting from abstracted finance in and through Vanuatu, and a taxing state that has turned to the substantive extraction of its environmental resources as a renewed source of revenue in Solomon Islands – reflect post-colonial legacies from earlier imperial inequalities that emerged in the mid- to late nineteenth century, consolidated in twentieth-century projects of colonial governance, which were followed by fraught histories of decolonisation. This chapter explores these imperial fiscal orders and their associated inequalities (invariably punctuated by episodic acts of colonial violence and brutality). They have been fundamental in the production of new post-colonial legacies and inequalities that have become central challenges in the twenty-first century, representing a continuity of earlier orders rather than the abrupt ruptures, changes, and reconfigured sovereignties that decolonisation might have once promised.

Fiscal contexts: Colonial expansions in Oceania

From the mid-nineteenth through to the early twentieth centuries, France, Germany, and the United Kingdom pursued colonial claims in the Western Pacific (see Figure 13.1). France annexed New Caledonia as a penal colony in 1853. Convicts, which included political prisoners from French colonies elsewhere and participants in the failed Paris Commune, mingled with free settlers who established cattle ranches, together with mining companies attracted to New Caledonia by some of the largest deposits of nickel in the world. After a series of wars and conflicts throughout the second half of the nineteenth century and into the early twentieth century, the indigenous Melanesian Kanaks were largely dispossessed of their lands and territories and forced into small reservations in the least hospitable areas of the main island of Grande Terre. To the east of New Caledonia, the United Kingdom annexed Fiji in 1875. In 1893 the United Kingdom, after lobbying by Charles Woodford, an adventurer and naturalist from Kent who had had some administrative experience in Fiji, established a protectorate over Solomon Islands.

Both British and French interests converged to the south of Solomon Islands and northeast of New Caledonia in the New Hebrides. Both powers had settlers in the archipelago, had recruited labourers for plantations and mines in Australia, Fiji, and New Caledonia, and were involved in the production of copra,[12] cotton, and cocoa, and the harvesting of marine resources such as bêche-de-mer (trepang or sea cucumbers) and

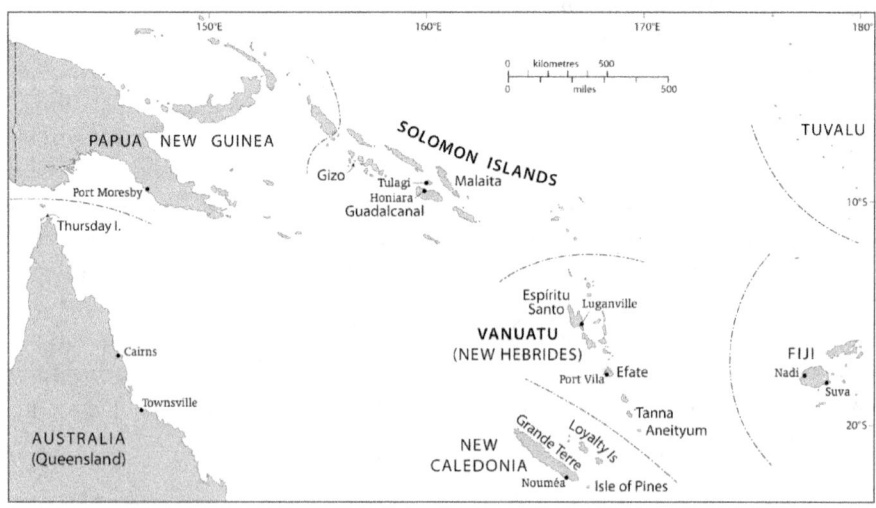

Figure 13.1 The Western Pacific.

pearl and trocas shell. As a result of intersecting British and French interests in the New Hebrides, and in the spirit of the *Entente Cordiale*, neither country could annex the archipelago outright. Throughout the nineteenth century, British and French commercial activity and settlement in the New Hebrides occurred in the absence of political organisation. In 1878 the New Hebrides was recognised as independent, despite the absence of a local sovereign government.[13] In 1887 a joint Anglo-French naval commission was established to provide limited government services to settlers in the group.

Neither France nor the United Kingdom was able to annex the New Hebrides but recognised that they both had increasing numbers of settlers in the archipelago who had important links with Australia and New Caledonia. Both British and French colonists had acquired vast tracts of land for themselves in dubious circumstances. As a result of largely unregulated settlement, France and the United Kingdom decided to share control of the New Hebrides and in 1906 declared a Condominium over the archipelago. Initially organised by a convention, the Condominium was upgraded by a revised protocol in 1914.

The Condominium agreement provided separate jurisdiction over British and French citizens in the archipelago. Foreigners had one month to opt (and were thus referred to as *optants*) between British or French law or the resident commissioners would decide for them. British and French citizens and their optants were collectively referred to as *ressortissants*. The indigenous majority were ineligible for *ressortissance*, and were instead left stateless while simultaneously controlled by France and the United Kingdom. British settlers were governed under English common law. French settlers were governed by French civil law. Agreements and disputes between France and the United Kingdom together with shared public services (such as the postal service) were placed under the jurisdiction of the Condominium, which provided a third tier of government. Indigenous New Hebrideans were subject to four legal systems – British, French, Condominium, and 'Native' – without enjoying the rights of citizenship anywhere. France and the United Kingdom established their own schools, civil services, hospitals, police forces, courts, immigration procedures, currencies, and tax systems which operated contemporaneously. Apart from the two national governments, the Condominium also had its own government, and local councils and chiefs provided a fourth in rural areas. Government services were invariably duplicated, occasionally triplicated, and at the most provided fourfold.

Thus, by 1906 three different colonial territories bordered one another. The Solomon Islands and New Caledonia were outright British and French territories respectively, governed exclusively by France and the United

Kingdom. The New Hebrides, however, was a sui generis territory governed by both France and the United Kingdom. This had profound implications for the organisation of colonial taxation and ensured that one territory became an orthodox taxing state (Solomon Islands), while the other became a tax haven (Vanuatu).

Fiscal organisation

The protocol by which France and the United Kingdom governed the New Hebrides included provisions for raising taxes. Article 5(2) of the Protocol covered Financial Provisions, asserting that '[T]he expenses of the joint services, with the exception of the expenses of the police force and the personal emoluments of the service of the administrative districts, shall be defrayed out of local taxes, to be imposed by the High Commissioners jointly, the receipts from fines and from the postal service, and all other revenue of a joint character.'[14] While the protocol did not specify that France and the United Kingdom could impose their own taxes in the Condominium, article 5(1) left this possibility open with the provision that 'Each of the two Signatory Powers shall defray the expense of its own administration in the Group.'[15] Before the Second World War, most colonial administrations were required to fund administration through local taxes, rather than rely on grants-in-aid from metropolitan treasuries. In the New Hebrides, however, the protocol required each signatory state to directly provide half the Condominium deficit if local revenue was unable to cover public expenditure.

To earn local revenue both France and the United Kingdom had to agree on common taxation measures. These agreements were concluded via joint regulations, which allowed the two Resident Commissioners to govern the New Hebrides as a whole, while continuing to exercise separate jurisdiction over their own *ressortissants*. Measures including taxation were based on negotiations between the two powers, that could last for decades. In the meantime, they could impose their own taxes on their own citizens, although the British residency tended to avoid this in favour of a joint approach with their French colleagues.

In 1934 the French governor of New Caledonia, Bernard Siadous, arrived in the New Hebridean capital of Port Vila to discuss with the British resident commissioner, George Andrew Joy, the auditing of Condominium accounts, the French copra tax, telecommunications, the Joint Court, and a proposal to increase taxation. British officials wanted to fund a joint Condominium administration by levying local taxes that would apply to British, French, and indigenous residents in the archipelago.

The United Kingdom had avoided imposing taxes on its own *ressortissants* in the archipelago over and above those that were already levied by the Condominium, namely excise and customs duties on exports and imports, which were largely paid by settlers and indirectly by Indigenous New Hebridean consumers who purchased goods from trade stores, particularly those living close to the towns of Port Vila and Luganville on the island of Espíritu Santo. By contrast, the French government focused on funding its own national administration in the New Hebrides. Taxes, particularly on turnover in specific sectors, were imposed on French settlers under the direction of the colonial government of New Caledonia. During the 1930s, France sought to extend its taxes to the Condominium as a whole, which the United Kingdom's administration rejected as the imposition of French taxation on British nationals. Governor Siadous countered that these new taxes would provide a single source of revenue for the joint Condominium administration.

The French government had, by 1934, managed to tax copra produced by French *ressortissants* as if it had been 'handled' by British or indigenous growers.[16] British officials objected to this. In his meetings with Siadous, Resident Commissioner Joy emphasised that the tax was unfair, 'contrary to the terms of the Protocol of 1914', was 'bad policy' and 'jeopardised' the cordial relations between French and British settlers.[17] Given the Great Depression, Joy continued that the copra tax 'conveyed the painful impression to British settlers that France was hostile to their interests and blind to their economic sufferings in a time of crisis'.[18] What Joy did not mention to Siadous, but that he thought lawyers in the Ministry of Colonies in Paris might have discovered, was that what he was 'really requesting on behalf of the British settler is that France should give a free market to British copra'.[19] The governor 'assured' Joy that he would lobby the 'French Government' to abolish the tax, which affected 3,700 tons of copra that was 'produced' by British settlers or purchased from indigenous New Hebrideans (who were also significant copra producers).

Other taxes considered for review (and possible increase) were customs and excise, the main way the Condominium earned its revenue. Both Joy and Siadous considered raising and reducing some of these taxes per item. Taxes on flour and rice remained unchanged, and the excise on 'petrol and paraffin' was reduced to 1d 'per gallon'.[20] 'The French' regarded these 'as necessaries on the grounds that paraffin is the poor man's means of artificial illumination and petrol essential to all settlers for maintaining maritime communication throughout the Group'.[21]

Violence and taxation

Protracted negotiations such as those between Joy and Siadous characterised joint British and French rule in the New Hebrides. To the north in Solomon Islands, however, British colonial officials were unimpeded by such requirements. The protectorate was administered as a unitary British colony. In 1896 and 1897, Woodford, who had been appointed to administer Solomon Islands when it became a British protectorate in 1893, advised the Colonial Office that the archipelago would be fiscally self-supporting from local taxation and the development of a copra plantation-based economy.[22] While the New Hebrides and Solomon Islands both had copra-based commercial economies, the latter could not rely on grants-in-aid to fill any deficit as the former could. A capitation tax was paid by European settlers in Solomon Islands until 1909 ('abolished in 1907–1908') and thereafter replaced with indirect customs duties and excise taxes.[23] As Clive Moore illustrates in his urban history of Solomon Islands' first capital at Tulagi, 'License fees and capitation taxes were levied and exports of tropical products such as copra, ivory nuts, bêche-de-mer and peal shell, green snail and turtle shell, rattan cane, coffee and orchids were also taxed.'[24] In 1921 and 1923, a capitation tax was imposed on indigenous Solomon Islander men aged between 16 and 60 years.

These taxes were levied to pay for the colonial state, and they provoked widespread resistance and discontent that was met with violence on an imperial scale. On 4 October 1927, a party of fifteen tax collectors arrived at Gwee'abe in the Kwaio region of Sinalagu Harbour on Malaita, one of the largest islands in Solomon Islands. The Kwaio people had resisted ever-encroaching colonial intrusion into their lands, territories, coastlines, and waters. Not only were the tax collectors demanding revenue, but they also insisted that the Kwaio surrender their firearms to government representatives. As the tax-collecting vessel, the *Auki*, lay anchored just offshore, tensions between the two groups increased rapidly. At first the Kwaio leader, Basiana, appeared to pay his tax. William R. Bell, the district officer leading the government party, recorded receipt in the account's paid ledger. However, at that point Basiana took a concealed rifle and struck Bell on the head with the gun's barrel, killing him in the ensuing attack. Fighting then erupted between the assembled Kwaio men, resulting in the deaths of all fifteen tax collectors including their British leaders, Bell and cadet officer Kenneth Lillies.

When news of the attack on the party of British tax collectors and their Solomon Islander crew made it back to Tulagi, the colonial government immediately made preparations for retaliation. A militia was formed comprising British settlers and members of the Solomon Islands constabulary. The Australian navy was recruited to join a fleet of government ships (including private vessels that sailed under government mandate) which proceeded towards Kwaio territory at Malaita in mid-October 1927.[25] On landing, troops were told to 'shoot any native on sight'.[26] A massacre followed. Some sixty people, quite unconnected with the attack on the tax collectors, were killed by BSIP forces while others died while fleeing the fighting, including children.

To stop the indiscriminate killing and further loss of life, Basiana and four of his supporters surrendered. Some 198 Kwaio men were taken to prison in Tulagi where 173 contracted dysentery, leading to the deaths of thirty prisoners in 1928 and 1929.[27] Of the seventy-one Kwaio men prosecuted at Tulagi, fifty-one were 'acquitted'.[28] Six men, including Basiana were executed, while a further seventeen were sentenced to terms ranging from three years to life imprisonment.[29] Basiana's two sons, 'Abaeata Anifelo (aged 14) and Laefiwane (aged 7), were forced to watch their father's execution.[30] As Moore observes, 'Understandably, the terrible memory remained with them all of their lives and they remembered their father, about to climb to the gallows platform, putting an ancestral curse on Tulagi.'[31] Tulagi was destroyed in fighting between Japanese and Allied forces fourteen years later and would never re-emerge as the Solomon Islands' capital after the Second World War.[32] As Moore has reflected, '[T]he Kwaio massacre and its aftermath were the largest and most severe random punishment ever meted out by British authorities in the Pacific.'[33] For the 'Kwaio people', the massacre and its origins in disputes over taxation 'have never been forgotten or forgiven'.[34]

Capitation taxes in the New Hebrides

In the New Hebrides, violence was associated with disputes over land and labour, homicide, and retaliation, rather than taxation as it was with the Kwaio in Solomon Islands. In 1927, the British and French resident commissioners issued a joint regulation to provide for a 'Native Capitation Tax', which was implemented inconsistently and unevenly throughout the archipelago.[35] Variable poll taxes were designed to be levied on the four districts that the New Hebrides were divided into – 'Southern, Central 1, Central 2 and Northern'.[36] Each region had two district officers – one British and one French – who were responsible for each power's *ressortissants* and could impose their own definitions of 'native law' on indigenous communities. They were also responsible for collecting local taxes. District agents made efforts to convince local populations that taxes were collected for their benefit and the provision of services in the islands. They were informed that taxes, both direct and indirect, were levied (or collection was planned, even if those plans were then cancelled), to pay for the Native Advocate (who lobbied on behalf of the indigenous population), fund the island courts, and prevent the spread of hookworm and yaws.[37] Four years before his meeting with Governor Siadous, Resident Commissioner Joy had to emphasise that 'the facilities for hospital treatment at Vila and Tanna, both hospitals being partially subsidised by the Government', and largely operated by the Christian missions, were together with 'the important fact that the commerce of the Southern and Central islands' had 'financially benefited the majority of the natives'.[38] In order to take censuses of individual islands for the purposes of tax collection, James Nicol, the British district agent on Tanna, informed Joy that he had 'told the Natives that the tax is primarily to pay for the services of the Native Advocate, caveats perhaps surveys etc. Any safeguard to their land usually appeals to them'.[39]

Even so, indigenous New Hebrideans were not particularly enthusiastic about the tax. On the island of Aneityum, twenty-one residents were exempted in 1930/31 out of a total eligible population of eighty-nine (1931) to ninety-four (1930).[40] Indigenous leaders in the Southern District recommended that taxes be exempted until after December 1931. The BDA was informed that volcanic activity and a cyclone had destroyed coconut plantations, resulting in a shortfall of copra. District Agent Nicol was somewhat sceptical of these claims, advising Resident Commissioner Joy that 'The Bush natives are, as usual, pleading poverty. These natives do a considerable trade in pigs, kava and tobacco, and they are also owners of cattle ... they suffered far less from the hurricane than the sea coast natives.'[41] While he sympathised with the damage to the latter's coconut plantations, he added, 'Cotton could be grown where coconuts would not bear fruit.'[42] However, in his correspondence with the British resident commissioner in Vila, Nicol identified a matter which went to one of the core features of the Condominium and its siloed exclusions and inclusions. Because indigenous New Hebrideans were stateless, births, deaths, and marriages went unrecorded for decades. Yet for Nicol, these statistics were vital if the capitation tax were to be successful. He recommended that 'some definite scheme for the registration of births and deaths, should be evolved as both will be necessary in time for the capitation tax'.[43] However, due to the requirement to negotiate anything that pertained to the Condominium with France, this did not occur until 1974, forty-four years after Nicol made this recommendation. In September 1930 the proposed tax collection in the Southern District was cancelled.

In 1934 the French administration complained that residents of Ifira island, located in Port Vila Harbour, were refusing to work for the

Condominium.⁴⁴ As virtually no one in the archipelago was paying direct taxes at this stage, the French resident commissioner proposed introducing compulsory labour in lieu of capitation tax paid in sterling or francs, the two official currencies in the New Hebrides at the time. The British resident commissioner rejected this outright as unjust and unfair:

> There is no direct taxation of the European and Asiastic population of Vila and if direct taxation is to be imposed on the natives it is the view of His Majesty's Government that in the absence of a special reason it could only be justified by applying the proceeds to native welfare such, for example, as education. You probably know that in Vila and all through the Group there is a price for commodities purchased by Europeans and a price for the same commodities purchased by the natives. The latter price is considerably higher. I consider it a most pernicious and unjust system and I direct attention to it here only to show that if the natives benefit from their proximity to Vila, the European commercial element also benefit from the proximity of the natives. If the natives are to be singled out for direct taxation we must justify its application. I find it difficult to give any substantial reasons for applying such a tax.⁴⁵

In rejecting the imposition of compulsory work in lieu of capitation tax payments, the British resident commissioner invoked the Draft Convention Concerning Forced or Compulsory Labour agreed at Geneva in 1930. Joy attached a copy in both English and French for the benefit of his French counterpart. He then added, 'His Majesty's Government have adopted the Convention with certain reservations and I think you will find that the French Government have acted similarly. Articles 1, 2, and 9, bear on the matter now under discussion. The general idea of the Convention is the complete suppression of compulsory labour. *In view of the attitude of our two Governments to the Convention we could hardly commence the adoption of compulsory labour in the New Hebrides.*'⁴⁶

More than a decade later, in 1946, French and British officials briefly considered introducing a capitation tax payable by everyone living in the Condominium, including indigenous New Hebrideans and British and French citizens and *ressortissants*, and thus remove its discriminatory features. However, the French administration withdrew their support of this initiative, reporting to their British counterparts that they 'had been frightened by having recently learnt of a protest which the Santo planters were sending to the French Colonial Office against recent insignificant increases in indirect taxation and he [Monsieur Fourcade, a French administration official] was not prepared to consider anything in the nature of a capitation tax'.⁴⁷ Some twelve or thirteen years later, the capitation tax at the Condominium level had fallen into disuse.⁴⁸ Although capitation taxes were abandoned by the central Condominium government in Port Vila, they were levied at variable rates by local government councils that were introduced from the 1950s through to the 1970s.[49] Taxation and its discontents, protests, and compliance had become part of divergent fiscal orders in New Hebrides and would set the stage for financing decolonisation in the decades following the Second World War.

Fiscal decolonisation: Funding independent states

In the 1960s and 1970s, the United Kingdom started moving its territories in the Pacific towards independence. France, by contrast, actively resisted decolonisation of its territories in the region, namely French Polynesia (Tahiti), New Caledonia, Wallis & Futuna, and their interests in the New Hebrides Condominium, for strategic, economic, and political reasons.[50]

The British administration Solomon Islands, which had faced episodic and highly organised opposition to colonial rule since the Kwaio massacre, gradually began to transfer powers of self-government in 1960 and 1967 when Legislative and Executive Councils were established and opened to indigenous Solomon Islanders. These replaced the settlers' Advisory Council which had first met in 1921.[51] In 1970, a constitution was adopted that provided for a Governing Council comprising the British High Commissioner (reclassified as Governor in 1974), nine appointed members, and seventeen popularly elected members, the majority Solomon Islanders.[52] In 1974, another constitution was introduced which further democratised the political system.[53] Political parties representing Solomon Islanders campaigned for the 1974 elections, which included the new position of Chief Minister. In 1976, the United Kingdom granted full internal self-government to Solomon Islands, appointing Sir Colin Allan, who had just coordinated the independence of the Seychelles, as Governor. In 1976, Allan became the last British governor of Solomon Islands and, like the Seychelles, negotiated its full independence which was achieved in 1978.

These constitutional advances, which gradually devolved power to Solomon Islands, beginning in 1950 with amendments covering the composition of the Advisory Council, eventually leading to independence in 1978, corresponded to changes in colonial taxation. The tax base was broadened considerably between 1944 and 1965. In preparing for post-war reconstruction,[54] British colonial authorities decided to retain capitation taxes, but they could not be imposed to coerce men to work on plantations to pay them.[55] Instead, rates, collection, and expenditure were devolved to local government councils. In some islands, no taxes were paid at all.[56]

In 1956, '[T]he Income Tax (Amendment) Regulation' was passed in Solomon Islands, effective from 1957.[57] Because the majority of Solomon

Islanders were engaged in subsistence agriculture, horticulture, and fisheries and did not earn regular salaries or wages over and above those required to meet local government poll taxes, there was generally no income to tax. However, British colonial authorities were unsure of the accuracy of these observations. They thus set about surveying economic sectors in the archipelago to identify potential sources of taxable income that indigenous Solomon Islanders participated in from 'Copra', 'Shell Fishing', 'Retail Trading', rent, 'Services', 'Salaries and Wages', and 'Products of Domestic Agriculture'.[58] The foundations for a standardised fiscal system had been established. Although the majority of Solomon Islanders were exempt from income tax because they had little or no income, civil servants, urban employees, British planters and merchants, expatriate businesses, and large multinational companies such as Levers and Burns Philp, paid tax on income and profits. As civil service positions were localised during decolonisation and Solomon Islanders were gradually recruited into the private sector in the 1960s and 1970s, an increasing number of indigenous income earners were taxed on salaries and wages. In 1965, a new income tax bill was passed into law, taking effect in 1966.[59] This provided for 'incentives' such as 'tax-holidays for new industries',[60] an increasingly important (though controversial) mechanism for decolonising states to attract foreign direct investment. By the time Solomon Islands became independent in 1978 it had an established tax system commensurate with notions and assumptions of fiscal modernity. The principle of income tax was clearly established even if most of the population still did not pay it because they were not earning regular salaries and wages. Those that were in the cash economy, and companies making profits, provided an important source of revenue for the new independent state. This was a significant contrast with its neighbour to the south, the New Hebrides. When it achieved independence as Vanuatu in 1980, it would have no income tax at all.

In 1963, the British administration in the New Hebrides proposed introducing income tax in the Condominium.[61] The French administration objected to these tax proposals outright, suggesting they would 'be premature' and be difficult to 'control', calculate, and collect.[62] The tax base would be narrow (due to the majority of population engaged in subsistence economic production, consumption, and exchange) and that 'in effect' the French authorities suggested that income tax would 'be collectable only on salaries of civil servants'.[63] Although the French residency in Port Vila agreed to examine the introduction of an income tax, from 1963 to 1970 there were no substantive initiatives to do so apart from vague French interest at some unspecified time in the future. Negotiations between the British and French residency and discussions in the settler and expatriate dominated the Advisory Council, which had been established in 1958, focused on budgetary constraints (the lack of money) and relatively minor amendments to indirect taxes such as customs and excise duties and business licence fees.

At the same time, capitation taxes reappeared with the introduction of local government councils in 1957, even though they had been abandoned at a Condominium level. In 1972, a 'Local Council' was established covering the southern area of the island of Pentecost.[64] An anthropologist conducting ethnographic research in the non-Christian, traditionalist village of Bunlap in South Pentecost at the time, Margaret Jolly, reported that there was widespread alarm at the capitation taxes, set at AU$2 for each 'man' and 50 cents for each 'woman' who agreed to local council authority.[65] Jolly observed that '[E]ven these small amounts were adjudged by the traditional people to be too high. This is not an unfair claim given that their per-capita cash income was often little more than a few dollars.'[66]

While indigenous New Hebrideans living in newly formed local area councils struggled to pay resurrected capitation taxes, British and French *ressortissants* continued to earn tax-free incomes. The lack of income taxes in the New Hebrides had not gone unnoticed in the world's money markets, where regulatory lacunae and pressure on the post-Second World War Bretton Woods system based on the gold standard and fixed exchange rates had led to exponential growth in internationally available US dollars for cross-border deposit and investment. This Eurodollar market (currencies traded and deposited outside their countries of origin) increased from some '[US]$7 billion in 1963 to about [US]$91 billion by the end of 1972'.[67] In 1967, a British law firm attuned to these developments opened a branch in Port Vila which led to a the 'rapid growth in the number of incorporated companies'.[68] A major Australian bank, the ANZ, followed shortly after in 1970.

To provide regulatory certainty for companies incorporating in the New Hebrides, and in response to the lack of progress in introducing an income tax, the British residency decided to convert the archipelago into a fully fledged offshore finance centre. With direct competency over its national corporate law, and no need to consult with their French counterparts, the British residency enacted Queens Regulations covering banks, banking, companies, and trust companies in 1970 and 1971.[69] Combined with the complete absence of direct taxation, these regulations provided the legal framework for companies, banks, and trusts to relocate to the New Hebrides. The archipelago's capital, Port Vila, boomed as a result. Expatriate lawyers, accountants, and bankers relocated to the new tax haven in large numbers, with Vila's population tripling between 1972 and 1974, witnessing a surge in new construction, skyrocketing land prices, and the expansion of auxiliary sectors in tourism and hospitality as new restaurants, boutiques, hotels, resorts, duty-free emporia, supermarkets, nightclubs, and cafes were opened to cater to the new financial services sector.[70]

The formation of an official tax haven in the New Hebrides was mirrored by an indigenous political awakening. In 1971, the New Hebrides National Party was formed, renamed as the Vanua'aku Pati in 1977, to represent indigenous political aspirations for independence. The undemocratic Advisory Council was replaced with a Representative Assembly in 1975, but the presence of appointed members led to electoral boycotts, protests, and divisions between largely English-educated advocates for independence and pro-French parties who either wanted to delay decolonisation, establish a francophone state, or partition the archipelago into separate countries. Secessionist efforts in the northern New Hebrides to establish a pro-French breakaway state were ended with the arrival of Papua New Guinean troops shortly after independence as the Republic of Vanuatu on 30 July 1980, which both France and the United Kingdom officiated over.

Despite the turbulent transition to independence, the offshore finance centre in the New Hebrides flourished. In its campaign for independence, the Vanua'aku Pati had specific policies for the tax haven.[71] It observed that companies incorporated in the New Hebrides mainly conducted their businesses outside of the archipelago, internationally. The party did not 'formally oppose this' but also felt that the 'benefits' were not 'being channelled effectively to the people'.[72] Further legislation was needed, particularly where it intersected with associated sectors in 'tourism and foreign investment' which had to be 'very strictly controlled'.[73] However, the country's first President, George Kalkoa (Ati George Sokomanu), concluded by asserting that 'the tax haven will be retained'.[74]

Conclusion

Colonialism has structured contemporary fiscal orders and possibilities for taxation and its avoidance. In assessing the emergence of offshore finance in the twentieth century, Vanessa Ogle has conceptualised tax havens as representing a global form of archipelagic capitalism.[75] She has observed that '[A]n archipelago-like landscape of distinct legal spaces – sometimes carved out within a national territory, sometimes located in smaller territorial units on the margins of more sizable states, sometimes hosted in city-states – re-created some of the unevenness that had characterised the nineteenth century world of empire.'[76] In assessing the emergence of archipelagic capitalism, of fiscal lacunae and tax-free oases located in island worlds and alpine valleys, Ogle argues that it is necessary to move analyses beyond orthodox assumptions dependent on ruptures and schisms, between regulated finance and deregulated globalisation, that occurred in the 1970s and instead unpackage earlier eras of colonial rule.[77] As she observes, 'retrieving the history of archipelago capitalism thus means reopening the history of the period between the 1920s and the 1980s in order to rethink the role of the state and the nation-state and to question the current historiographic obsession with the 1970s as a moment of discontinuity and sharp caesura'.[78]

The contrasting fiscal systems that emerged in the Pacific, in Solomon Islands and Vanuatu, each offering their own versions of 'archipelagic capitalism', have their origins at the outset of colonial rule. In the British Solomon Islands Protectorate, the United Kingdom assumed colonial control relatively late in the demarcation of global empire, at a time when the principle of taxing income, persons, and business turnover and profits was well established. Imposing a fiscal system with the violence of imperial orders invariably associated with land alienation and European control resulted in the consolidation of a plantation economy whereby capital was bound up in substantive production. The economy of the substantive, in the form of agriculture and plantation production, was fundamental in the colonisation of the New Hebrides as well. However, in the New Hebrides power was shared between France and the United Kingdom. Neither could agree on a comprehensive tax policy. As a result, direct taxation never eventuated in either the New Hebrides or its independent successor state, Vanuatu. In the late 1960s, law firms and banks discovered that the New Hebrides provided an 'imperial fiscal frontier' that Ogle has suggested for other British jurisdictions, from which 'taxable income' could be concealed on a global scale.[79] With independence in 1980, the stage for the New Hebrides's conversion into an offshore finance centre as Vanuatu, with the inherent inequalities between indigenous persons of the place and wealthy transnational tax exiles, had been set. In the meantime, Solomon Islands, with its taxation policies set against the body politic backdrop of violence and resistance, was instead fiscally organised with the orthodox metrics of a conventional taxing state to fund its decolonisation and independence as a sovereign country. Both Solomon Islands and Vanuatu have, however, remained implicated and embedded in projects of local and global capital accumulation in ways that synthesise the tax-conscious economies of money and finance with economies of the substantive and their investments in island worlds and their resources.

Acknowledgements

I would like to thank Judy Bennett and Margaret Jolly for reading an earlier draft of this chapter and providing incisive feedback and commentary on it. I would also like to acknowledge and thank Les O'Neill for preparing the map of the Western Pacific at Figure 13.1.

Notes

1 Report of the Inter-departmental Committee on Income Tax in the Colonies not possessing responsible government, Cmd 1788, December 1922, Western Pacific High Commission [hereafter WPHC] 16/II/137/4/4, Western Pacific Archives [hereafter WPA], MSS & Archives 2003/1, Special Collections, University of Auckland Libraries and Learning Services [hereafter cited as WPHC].
2 *Ibid.*, p. 5.
3 *Ibid.*, p. 5.
4 *Ibid.*, p. 5.
5 Roger M. Keesing and Peter Corris, *Lighting Meets the West Wind: The Malaita Massacre* (Melbourne: Oxford University Press, 1980); Johnson, Tanna to the Acting Resident Commissioner, Port Vila, October 30, 1946, New Hebrides British Service [hereafter NHBS] 4/II/48/7, WPA, MSS & Archives 2003/1, Special Collections, University of Auckland Libraries and Learning Services [hereafter cited as NHBS].
6 *Income Tax Act Cap. 123 Including Subsidiary Legislation.* Part XIV Administration 115. Continuation in force of double taxation agreements, Honiara, Government of Solomon Islands, available at http://www.ird.gov.sb/Resource.aspx?ID=107 (last accessed 25 March 2022).
7 Nicholas Shaxson, 'Tackling tax havens', *Finance and Development* 56 (2019), available at https://www.imf.org/external/pubs/ft/fandd/2019/09/tackling-global-tax-havens-shaxson.htm (last accessed 25 March 2022).
8 Vanessa Ogle, 'Funk money: The end of empires, the expansion of tax havens, and decolonization as an economic and financial event', *Past & Present* 249.1 (2020), 233.
9 Shaxson, 'Tackling tax havens'.
10 *Ibid.*
11 Mike Puia and Zahiyd Namo, '"They failed us": How mining and logging devastated a Pacific island in a decade', *The Guardian*, 30 May 2021, available at https://www.theguardian.com/world/2021/may/31/they-failed-us-how-mining-and-logging-devastated-a-pacific-island-in-a-decade (last accessed 25 March 2022). Nick Evershed, Andy Ball, Josh Nicholas, Ben Doherty, Kate Lyons, and Ben Sanders, 'Pacific plunder: The extraction of valuable resources from across the Pacific has made companies billions but comes at a sometimes catastrophic

cost', *The Guardian*, 31 May 2021, available at https://www.theguardian.com/world/ng-interactive/2021/may/31/pacific-plunder-this-is-who-profits-from-the-mass-extraction-of-the-regions-natural-resources-interactive (last accessed 25 March 2022).
12 Copra is desiccated and dried coconut flesh and was the primary plantation agricultural crop in both New Hebrides and Solomon Islands during the colonial period. Copra was a vital ingredient in food processing, cosmetics, and soaps in the nineteenth and early to mid-twentieth century. While it has largely been replaced in food processing by palm oil, it continues to be produced, although it no longer commands the relatively high (though fluctuating) market prices that it did up until the end of the 1970s.
13 Exchange of Notes Arrangement between Great Britain and France, respecting the Independence of the New Hebrides Group [1878] PITSE 1 (18 January 1878), Arrangement between Great Britain and France, Respecting the Independence of the New Hebrides Group, available at http://www.paclii.org/pits/en/treaty_database/1878/1.html (last accessed 25 March 2022).
14 Protocol respecting the New Hebrides, signed at London on 6 August 1914, by representatives of the British and French governments (ratifications exchanged at London, 18 March 1922).
15 *Ibid.*
16 Ken Buckley and Kris Klugman, *'The Australian Presence in the Pacific': Burns Philp, 1914–1946* (Sydney: George Allen & Unwin, 1983), p. 322.
17 British Resident Commissioner [hereafter BRC], Port Vila, to the High Commissioner for the New Hebrides, Suva, 26 August 1934, NHBS 1/I/251/34.
18 *Ibid.*
19 *Ibid.*
20 *Ibid.*
21 *Ibid.*
22 Clive Moore, *Tulagi: Pacific Outpost of British Empire* (Canberra: ANU Press, 2019).
23 Judith A. Bennett, *Wealth of the Solomons: A History of a Pacific Archipelago, 1800–1978* (Honolulu: University of Hawai'i Press, 1987), p. 433.
24 Moore, *Tulagi*, p. 80. As Judy Bennett has pointed out, though, this was 'standard' practice 'across much of the colonial Pacific along with duties on imports'. The region was 'not a free trade area unlike' the colony of New South Wales prior to Australian federation in 1901 (Judy Bennett, communication with author, 24 February 2021).
25 Greg Swinden, '"The Natives appear restless tonight": HMAS *Adelaide* and the punitive expedition to Malaita in 1927', in David Stevens (ed.), *Maritime Power in the Twentieth Century: The Australian Experience* (St Leonards, Sydney: Allen & Unwin, 1998), pp. 54–67.
26 Moore, *Tulagi*, p. 239.
27 Keesing and Corris, *Lighting Meets the West Wind*, p. 184.
28 *Ibid.*, p. 186.
29 *Ibid.*, p. 186.

30 *Ibid.*, p. 187; Moore, *Tulagi*, p. 368.
31 Moore, *Tulagi*, p. 368.
32 Tulagi was located on and occupied most of the land area of a small island by the same name. As Judy Bennett has remarked, there was '[N]o room for expansion ... even before the war there was talk of moving but [the] depression scuttled that' (Judy Bennett, communication with author, 24 February 2021).
33 Moore, *Tulagi*, p. 243.
34 *Ibid.*
35 Joint Regulation Number 6 of 1927: New Hebrides Native Capitation Tax, Discriminatory Native Legislation, NHBS4/II/81/1/5; Pacific Manuscripts Bureau (PMB), Joint Regulations of the New Hebrides: A Consolidated Edition of the Joint Regulations in Force on 18 October 1973, Prepared Under the Authority of the Resident Commissioners, Vols 1–3, Port Vila, PMB Doc. 445, Australian National University (ANU), Canberra; Margaret Jolly, *Women of the Place: Kastom Colonialism and Gender in Vanuatu* (New York: Harwood Academic Publishers, 1994), pp. 50–1.
36 Linden Mander, 'The New Hebrides Condominium', *Pacific Historical Review* 13 (1944), 158.
37 BRC, Port Vila to British District Agent [hereafter BDA] Tanna, 11 April 1930, NHBS 1/I/193/30.
38 *Ibid.* The emphasis on the provision of health care reflected the ways 'medical infrastructures were ... closely intertwined with the Condominium and the British and French Residencies'. Alexandra Widmer, 'Native medical practitioners, temporality, and nascent biomedical citizenship in New Hebrides', *Political and Legal Anthropology Review* 30, s1 (2010), 63.
39 BDA, Tanna to BRC, Port Vila, 27 March 1930, NHBS 1/I/193/30.
40 Census of Aneityum December 1931, Native Capitation Tax, Island of Aneityum, NHBS 1/I/193/30.
41 BDA, Tanna, to BRC, Port Vila, 27 March 1930, NHBS 1/I/193/30.
42 *Ibid.*
43 *Ibid.*
44 French Resident Commissioner, Port Vila [hereafter FRC] to BRC, Port Vila, 3 May 1934, NHBS1/I/151/34.
45 BRC, Port Vila, to FRC, Port Vila, 14 May 1934, NHBS1/I/151/34. Charging indigenous New Hebrideans 'as much as four times the price' for goods compared to Europeans was widespread amongst 'traders and merchants' at the time (Judy Bennett, communication with author, 21 February 2021).
46 *Ibid.*, emphasis added.
47 Note, 28 January 1947, NHBS4/II/48/7.
48 Discriminatory Native Legislation, NHBS4/II/81/1/5.
49 Margaret Jolly, 'Birds and banyans of South Pentecost: Kastom in anti-colonial struggle', *Mankind* 13.4 (1982), 338–56; Ralph R. Premdas, 'Vanuatu: The evolution of the administrative and political context of decentralization', *Public Administration and Development*, 4.3 (1984), 231–48.

50 Helen Gardner and Christopher Waters, 'Decolonisation in Melanesia', *Journal of Pacific History* 48.2 (2013), 113–21.
51 Bennett, *Wealth of the Solomons*, p. 162.
52 *Ibid.*, p. 320.
53 Clive Moore, 'Indigenous Participation in Constitutional Development: Case Study of the Solomon Islands Constitutional Review Committees of the 1960s and 1970s', *Journal of Pacific History*, 48.2 (2013), 167.
54 Heavy fighting between Japanese and US and Allied forces occurred in Solomon Islands during the Second World War. Judith A. Bennett, *Natives and Exotics: World War II and Environment in the Southern Pacific* (Honolulu: University of Hawai'i Press).
55 Ian C. Campbell, '"To Not Reinstate the Past": Wartime optimism and planning for the British Solomon Islands Protectorate', *Journal of Pacific History* 42.1 (2007), 66.
56 Taxation in Solomon Islands, *Solomon Islands Historical Encyclopaedia, 1893–1978*, available at https://www.solomonencyclopaedia.net/biogs/E0003 07b.htm (last accessed 25 March 2022).
57 *Ibid.*
58 P. M. Smith, Hampstead, London to Acting Accountant General, Honiara, Solomon Islands, 16 September 1958, WPHC 11/II/137/4/13.
59 Taxation in Solomon Islands, *Solomon Islands Historical Encyclopaedia*.
60 *Ibid.*
61 Note on Fiscal Policy', n.d., circa 1963, NHBS1/I/357/6/Part 3.
62 *Ibid.*
63 *Ibid.*
64 Jolly, 'Birds and banyans', p. 350.
65 *Ibid*, p. 351.
66 *Ibid.*, p. 351.
67 Sol Picciotto, 'Offshore: the state as legal fiction', in Mark P. Hampton and Jason P. Abbott (eds), *Offshore Finance Centres and Tax Havens: The Rise of Global Capital* (Basingstoke: Palgrave, 1999), p. 58.
68 'The investment industry in the New Hebrides', report for the Department of Prime Minister and Cabinet, NAA A 1838/366, A840/13/3, Part One, Ref. No. 70/6973, 25 August 1972, National Archives of Australia, Canberra.
69 Gregory Rawlings, 'Laws, liquidity and Eurobonds: The making of the Vanuatu tax haven', *Journal of Pacific History* 39.3 (2004), 330.
70 *Ibid.*, p. 327.
71 Walter Lini, *Beyond Pandemonium: From the New Hebrides to Vanuatu* (Wellington, New Zealand and Suva, Fiji: Asia Pacific Books and the Institute of Pacific Studies of the University of the South Pacific, 1980), p. 34.
72 *Ibid.*
73 *Ibid.*
74 *Ibid.* The tax haven had become economically significant by 1980, particularly in its contribution to local employment, urban infrastructure, and incentivising foreign direct investment. The new government wanted this to continue.

For discussion, see Gregory Rawlings, 'Villages, islands and tax havens: The global/local implications of a financial entrepôt in Vanuatu', *Canberra Anthropology* 22.2 (1999), 37–50; Rawlings, 'Laws, liquidity and Eurobonds', pp. 325–41.
75 Vanessa Ogle, 'Archipelago capitalism: Tax havens, offshore money, and the state, 1950s–1970s', *American Historical Review* 122.5 (2017), 1431–58.
76 *Ibid.*, p. 1432.
77 *Ibid.*, p. 1434.
78 *Ibid.*, p. 1434.
79 Ogle, 'Funk money', p. 233.

14

Imperial extraction and 'tax havens'

Alex Cobham

Introduction

Taxation was an important feature of European colonisation and extraction. In the context of post-colonial legacies which this section addresses, a major legacy of that period is that tax remains central to the extractive processes of economic and financial globalisation that have replaced formal empire. The global inequalities in taxing rights extant today are directly related to the economic governance of previous European empires. Tax-raising powers played a significant part in the development and funding of administrative control over colonies, whether formally in the hands of imperial governors, or held indirectly through local figures of authority or corporate agents of empire of which the East India Company is the most well known. At the same time as these, and a range of other processes of resource extraction, the imposition of taxation by illegitimate (colonial) authorities took a toll on the social contract between states and citizens. This created a deeper barrier to the subsequent legitimacy of post-independence states, including corrosive effects on tax morale. The damage to effective political representation may ultimately have been greater than that caused by direct resource extraction.[1]

The more recent era of globalisation has been characterised by a growing complexity of international economic and financial linkages, and the emergence of a new form of imperial extraction. That imperial extraction extends both to resources and, critically, also to the rights of states to tax. This new form of extraction relies on networks of dependent territories, above all those of the United Kingdom, which have been facilitated to establish themselves as financial hubs. This has involved the continuing political and legal support of the imperial power. At the same time, however, it has allowed the commercialisation of each jurisdiction's sovereignty, through legislative cooperation with international professional services firms intended to attract disproportionate volumes (on paper at least) of global trade and investment flows.[2]

Two major effects are apparent. First, the network of dependent territories underpins the maintenance of the City of London as a global financial centre.[3] Dirtier money is cleaned in the network of dependent territories, allowing the centre to present a *relatively* transparent and well-regulated front for large volumes of capital, including much illicitly extracted from former colonies. Taken together, the UK's network is, by multiple measures, the largest single actor in the provision of financial secrecy and of services for profit shifting.

This dominance in turn has contributed to the continuation of the City's role as a leading international financial centre, and (until now?) of the UK's disproportionate geopolitical influence. But not without cost. The UK and many dependent territories have been characterised as facing a 'finance curse'.[4] Similarly to the rent-seeking, corruption, and crowding out of more productive investment that can generate a natural resource 'curse', excess growth of the financial sector can lead to unnecessarily weak economic performance and the corrosive decay of governance and political representation. But whereas the resource curse is limited by the value of the resources available to a country, and can be mitigated by political and institutional responses, the finance curse is endogenous: the degree of excess growth depends in large part upon the willingness and ability of the (domestic) political system to put policymaking at the disposal of the (often largely international) financial sector.

In smaller jurisdictions such as Jersey or the British Virgin Islands, the dependence on finance can grow so far that it becomes *the* dominant force in politics – and that can foster a deeply embedded corruption. The need to respond to international 'competition' through successive reforms and (de)regulation, or yet lower taxation, can quickly become inescapable, even to the detriment of domestic political concerns. The cost to local populations of the 'tax haven' development path may be high.

The second effect is to deprive former colonies and other countries of their taxing and resource rights. The UK network facilitates the hiding of undeclared offshore assets and income streams, through the provision of financial secrecy including anonymous ownership vehicles. This generates not only personal tax evasion but wider criminality and corruption, including the illicit removal of state assets; and the same network also facilitates the profit shifting of multinational companies, which in effect nullifies the taxing rights of host countries, to the benefit of shareholders who are disproportionately found in the elites of Organisation for Economic Co-operation and Development (OECD) countries.

Estimates indicate that the UK network is also the largest single actor responsible for the worldwide loss of revenues to both individual and corporate tax abuse.[5] The same analysis, and a range of others,[6] show that lower-income countries lose disproportionately larger shares of their current tax revenues due to such cross-border tax abuse. That is, former colonies suffer a greater loss of their taxing rights than do the (former) imperial powers.

This deprives countries of substantial revenues and weakens their ability to curb inequalities through redistribution. There is also likely to be deeper political damage due to the importance of tax in underpinning the effectiveness and legitimacy of states, and to the strength of systems of political representation.

The dependent territories of OECD countries are often the subject of finger pointing in discourse about the threat of 'tax havens'. But these jurisdictions sit at the junction of the two effects described here, and may bear costs of both: the finance curse that stems from 'winning' and the erosion of taxing rights that results from 'losing'.

In this chapter I address, first, the role of taxation in the development of the state, with reference to both the immediate damage done by empire and the ongoing costs imposed by illicit financial flows that depend on financial secrecy. Second, I summarise the evidence on the dominance of the UK network in cross-border tax abuse worldwide, and the scale of direct damage caused. Third, I explore the role of the UK's dependent territories and a possible parallel to tax farmers of empire, and the challenges of their post-imperial context in international politics. With growing global commitment to curb the scale of tax abuse, I consider the potential implications of this analysis for linking UK responsibility for reparations with the need for a 'Plan B' for alternative development paths for the UK's dependent territories.

Taxation and statehood

The contributions of effective taxation can be summarised in the 'four Rs' of tax.[7] Revenue is crucial to states' ability to provide public services, from health, education, and infrastructure to effective administration and the rule of law. Redistribution is crucial to contain or eradicate both horizontal and vertical inequalities. Less obvious may be the role of taxation in re-pricing – ensuring that the true public costs and benefits of social goods (like education) and ills (such as tobacco consumption and carbon dioxide emission) are reflected in market prices.

Arguably, the most important result of tax, however, is too often overlooked: political representation. Prolonged reliance on revenues from natural resources or foreign aid tends to undermine channels of responsive government, giving rise to corruption and broader failures of accountability.

The act of paying tax provides an important accountability link between states and citizens, underpinning the social contract.[8] Empirical studies indicate that the higher the share of tax in government spending – that is, the more reliant any given government expenditure is upon funding from citizens – the stronger the process of improving governance and representation. Direct taxes (those on income, profits, assets, and capital gains) may play a particularly important role.[9]

The accountability relationship behind strengthening governance does not play out evenly. Studies for the Brazilian government showed that in the early 2000s, households earning less than twice the minimum wage paid almost half of their incomes in tax; but the great majority of that took the form of indirect taxes on consumption.[10] The highest earning households, those receiving more than thirty times the minimum wage, paid only around a quarter of their income in tax, split more or less evenly between direct and indirect taxes. It was the highest earning households who felt a sense of 'tax citizenship' – that government was spending *their* money, and that they had a right to hold government to account.

The accountability relationship also varies across states. Within Europe, for example, decades of research into tax morale and compliance find that both institutional quality and the strength of democratic governance are significant determinants.[11] Progress is typically marked after the end of undemocratic regimes (e.g. Franco's dictatorship in Spain), but differences in tax morale between countries can be persistent – for example, those between former members of the Soviet Union and other central and eastern European countries. Given the evidence on effective taxation driving democratic governance, as well as the reverse, and the strong role of social norms rather than narrow economic maximisation, slow progress is perhaps inevitable.

Consider the case of newly independent countries exiting from European imperial control. Notwithstanding any specific tax policies implemented in colonies, or the degree to which resources were extracted purely for the benefit of the imperial power, it seems inevitable that the expectations of state legitimacy, institutional quality, and democratic governance would be at rock bottom upon independence – albeit with a possibility of building strongly on the positive sentiment of that achievement by a new, genuinely national government.

On top of this, and as demonstrated by many of the contributions to this volume, the tax policies pursued in colonies are likely to have exacerbated rather than dampened these effects. First, tax farming was widely used – by empires throughout history and around the world, including the Babylonian Empire,[12] the early Roman republic,[13] and the Ottoman Empire[14] – as a broadly reliable way of subcontracting the administrative work necessary to collect revenues from a population. One side effect of tax farming may be to separate the revenue-raising process from any positive contribution of the state in taxpayers' lives, and therefore potentially to reduce the perceived legitimacy of the process. Where the British Empire gave tax farming rights to private charter companies, such as the East India Company, it seems unlikely that this would have improved perceptions of the legitimacy of the process or of the colonising state itself (to the extent this was distinct in any case from the companies in question).

Second, and aside from whether the revenues might be used for the benefit of the population, the forms of taxation chosen were typically antagonistic to the idea of fairly shared contributions. While taxation was an important feature of European colonisation and extraction – the colonial 'drain' – it has largely not been central to research on imperial legacies.[15]

Tax was used in multiple ways both by British imperial administrations, including in quite different periods and regions of the world, and not necessarily with great success, and by British charter companies which relied heavily, again in a range of ways, upon their delegated powers to tax. Contemporary comparative statistics confirm the range of direct and indirect taxes in use and suggest important differences – including those between producer countries (tending to use trade and other indirect taxes when exports are substantial, and relying more on direct taxes otherwise), and 'node' jurisdictions (which may map to the later 'tax havens', and where trade taxes tend to be most prominent).[16]

The proposals of the Secretary of State for the Colonies, the third Earl Grey, led to the 1852 introduction in the Gold Coast protectorate (now Ghana) of a poll tax of one shilling for every person, including children, with a view – at least initially – to use the revenues to provide local services. The imposition, and lack of visible benefits (more than a third of the revenue being needed to cover the immediate costs of raising it, and most of the rest going to salaries), led to riots in 1854 and 1857, and with revenues falling sharply the tax was finally eliminated in 1864.[17] Decades later, by which time the Gold Coast had become a formal colony, the distrust remained profound. As the 1884 Blue Book stated, 'no means exist whereby a census could be taken of the Gold Coast settlements, the natives of which are suspicious of their numbers being counted, having, perhaps a lively recollection of the old days when the poll tax was in force'.[18]

As the end of formal British empire drew closer, the British imperial administration of the Solomon Islands imposed a poll tax as late as 1921, on males aged 16 to 60. Here there seems never even to have been the intention to provide public services, the tax being introduced instead directly with a view to covering the administration's own costs and, per resident commissioner Charles Workman, to 'act incidentally as an incentive to recruiting' for the emerging copra industry.[19]

The role of the East India Company as a direct collector of tax revenues in parts of India may be the most well known example. The key element of the approach was to use the revenues raised to pay for the commodities purchased from Indian traders – so that these were, in effect, provided to the Company at zero cost for export.[20] Lesser known examples suggest tax may have been important also for later charter companies that pursued otherwise opposite economic strategies. The British North Borneo Company, for example, was granted a charter as late as 1881, and expressly forbidden there from operating as a monopoly trader. The company's revenues – and shareholders' returns – arose instead from taxes (including on the sale of opium), customs duties (including on the major export business, tobacco), and from sales of the land under their control.[21]

The importance of tax in state building continued to be largely overlooked in 'development' policy thinking for decades afterwards, albeit in quite a different way. A relative dearth of attention to tax, generally, had left the path clear by the 1980s for some of the most simplistic and destructive policy recommendations to become baked into what has been labelled 'the tax consensus', which for many years formed the basis of advice given around the world by the International Monetary Fund (IMF) and other multilateral and bilateral aid donors.[22] John Williamson's famous identification of a broader 'Washington Consensus' included tax reform as the third of ten elements, 'about whose proper deployment Washington [or rather, its political and technocratic elites] can muster a reasonable degree of consensus'.[23]

The Consensus is often seen unfairly as summarising a 'neoliberal' worldview that has been uniformly imposed on lower-income countries. Williamson intended to describe the contours of policy views as he saw them, and the tax discussion makes this especially clear:

> Increased tax revenues are the alternative to decreased public expenditures as a remedy for a fiscal deficit. Most of political Washington regards them as an inferior alternative. Much of technocratic Washington (with the exception of the right-wing think tanks) finds political Washington's aversion to tax increases irresponsible and incomprehensible. Despite this contrast in attitudes toward the merits of increasing tax revenue, there is a very wide consensus about the most desirable method of raising whatever level of tax revenue is judged to be needed. The principle is that the tax base should be broad and marginal tax rates should be moderate.[24]

The 'tax consensus' – related to, but more developed than, Williamson's sketch – was first identified in specific terms in chapters of a 2004

UNU-WIDER book which provided a more detailed critique.[25] The key components that have become dominant in the recommendations to IMF client countries are these:

- first, to aim for *neutrality* of the tax system;
- second, to pursue redistributive goals (if any) via expenditure not taxation; and
- third, to achieve revenues of the order of 15–20% of GDP (although revenues in high-income OECD countries typically 30% or 40%).[26]

Tax neutrality, that the tax system should not distort production or consumption decisions, leads in practice to lower pressure on direct taxation, to trade liberalisation in the interests of efficiency, and to much greater emphasis on sales taxes to provide revenues.

The underlying ideology is that economic growth should be seen as the main aim of policy, and that taxes are an obstacle. The key assumption implicit is that an economy without taxes would deliver an efficient outcome, and so it is thought to follow that taxes should create as few distortions as possible. But of course, this assumption does not hold. In the real world, removing all government intervention would deliver chaos rather than some imagined high-growth equilibrium.

The importance of tax in state building and redistribution is entirely absent from the analysis, leaving only an Economics 101 model of the most basic microeconomic interactions. Once this extreme assumption is relaxed, it follows that (distortionary) taxation may be efficiency-enhancing, so that even a policymaker fixated on economic growth rather than sustainable human development could not support the main policy recommendations of the tax consensus in this regard.

The decision not to use tax for redistribution relies on the assumption that governments have at their disposal a full range of instruments, not least the option to make direct cash transfers to households. Non-progressive taxation can in theory be combined with this to generate the equivalent effects of a progressive tax, for example on incomes. But if governments do not have the capacity or simply the level of revenue necessary to make such transfers, then the tax consensus requires giving up most of their power to reduce inequality, for no clear benefit in return.

The most dangerous assumption is a hidden one, and returns to the question of statehood. The tax consensus is effectively predicated on the view that government is the basis for the solution to an optimal taxation problem, in which the outcomes concern revenues, redistribution, and perhaps re-pricing, in light of some typically implicit aim of human well-being. Policymakers and their advisers need only think of the right tax tools to deliver their preferred outcomes (or the preferred outcomes of their citizens).

In practice, however, government is itself an *outcome* of taxation. Both the extent of effective political representation, and the level of corruption, may be associated with the long-term reliance on tax as a source of revenue. A long history of sustained, legitimate representative government may mean that, for the medium term, the state can be treated as exogenous. But even in Western Europe, the difference in attitudes to tax and to state legitimacy is marked, according not least to the relative historical proximity of periods of dictatorship. For lower-income countries that may have long histories of illegitimate colonial rule, and potentially also more recent undemocratic governance, it is unsustainable to treat the state as exogenous in an optimal tax problem.

The tax consensus is oblivious to this, and as such should be considered as not fit for purpose – not in general, not in lower-income countries in particular, and perhaps most clearly, not for countries with a legacy of empire that potentially includes low levels of tax compliance and/or of institutional quality and governance. The obstacles to effective taxation and statehood stemming from imperial legacies, however, extend further – into the core features of the current period of globalisation.

In 2015, the world recognised tax as the primary means of implementation for the United Nations (UN) Sustainable Development Goals (target 17.1) and adopted a common goal to reduce illicit financial flows (target 16.4). Illicit financial flows are cross-border flows motivated by the laundering of the proceeds of crime, by grand corruption, the abuse of market regulations, or by corporate or individual tax abuse. They have two common features. One is that they are, necessarily, hidden: they depend upon financial secrecy to achieve their goal, typically through the use of anonymous legal vehicles and financial asset classes, and jurisdictions that provide these and do not require transparency or offer international administrative cooperation.

The second common feature of illicit flows is their effect: in general, across the range of types, illicit financial flows reduce both the resources available to states (the funds held, or revenues due), and the effectiveness and legitimacy of states to use their funds for the broader benefit of the population. Poorer, less well governed states are the result of illicit flows. And while a persistent 'development' narrative has labelled lower-income countries (typically former colonies) as corrupt, the jurisdictions that facilitate illicit financial flows overwhelmingly enjoy higher per capita incomes – and are typically either OECD member countries or their dependent territories. Of these, the UK and its network is by far the most important actor.

The UK's 'offshore' network

In the years following the Second World War, the end of empire and the concomitant departure of colonial officials, settlers and businessmen from the colonial world cascaded from site to site. From Asia to North Africa, sub-Saharan Africa, the Caribbean and elsewhere, Europeans gradually and reluctantly ceded power ... [D]ecolonization, it is argued here, created a money panic of sorts, leading to a withdrawal of funds by individuals, private companies and mixed, public–private enterprises ... a significant share of funds was moved to an emerging system of offshore tax havens. Low-tax jurisdictions offering opportunities to avoid and evade taxation in countries with regular higher tax rates were not new at this point, but, owing to the influx of funds from the imperial and colonial world, expanded significantly during the years of decolonization. In these decades, savvy lawyers and bankers discovered Switzerland, Liechtenstein, Luxembourg, the British Channel Islands and, for the United States, the Bahamas and Bermuda, for the purpose of registering companies and trusts, or just depositing funds in bank accounts in order to benefit from zero or very low tax rates.

Vanessa Ogle, 'Funk money', 2020, pp. 6–7.[27]

[I]t is no coincidence that the City of London, once the capital of the greatest empire the world has known, is the center of the most important part of the global offshore system ... accounting for about half the world's secrecy jurisdictions. This is a layered hub-and-spoke array of tax havens ... which mostly emerged from the ashes of the British empire.

Nicholas Shaxson, *Treasure Islands*, 2011, p. 24.[28]

Imperial extraction was state led but illegitimate, insofar as it was made possible by force alone. This makes it an obvious contender to be the first global episode of illicit financial flows (IFFs). The looming end of empire in the twentieth century saw the beginning of what might reasonably be characterised as the second imperial age of IFFs. This took a more familiar form to the current period, motivated by the removal of wealth and income streams from the jurisdictions where they arose.[29]

'Financial flows that are illicit in origin, transfer or use, that reflect an exchange of value and that cross country borders ... A flow of value is considered illicit if it is illicitly generated (e.g. originates from criminal activities or tax evasion), illicitly transferred (e.g. violating currency controls) or illicitly used (e.g. for financing terrorism).'[30] What Ogle terms 'funk money' can be argued to meet this definition both because the ownership of the underlying assets and income streams, stemming from imperial extraction, is illegitimate; and because their transfer to the emerging financial secrecy jurisdictions was illicit, being designed to circumvent tax responsibilities that would have arisen upon their repatriation to the metropolis (although without losing the protection of empire, when they stay within the remaining dependent territories).

This last point, coupled with Katharina Pistor's findings on the importance and convenience of familiar rules for the regulation of capital,[31] and the attraction of common law for international commerce,[32] may explain why the dependent territories of the largest empire, the British, became so important subsequently. The economic governance of the British Empire contributed in important ways to the conditions in which the dependent territories were able to expand their role in this way.

At the same time, it seems unlikely that this development could have been sustained, and be so widespread, without support of the metropolis. Archival research has shown how the debate played out within the British government and financial institutions in the 1950s and 1960s, with concerns over the potential threat to UK tax revenues eventually giving way to more positive views of the opportunity for the dependent territories to become self-sustaining as financial centres, and to support the maintenance of the City of London as a leading international centre.[33]

In addition to the City of London, the UK's network of financial centres is made up of the Crown Dependencies (Jersey, Guernsey, and the Isle of Man) and the Overseas Territories (of which the most relevant here are Bermuda, British Virgin Islands, Cayman Islands, Gibraltar, and Turks & Caicos). The claim that the UK network today is the biggest single actor globally is motivated by three different analyses.

The first is the Financial Secrecy Index (FSI), the longest-standing ranking of financial secrecy jurisdictions published by the Tax Justice Network since 2009. The FSI was established to provide an independent measure, based on objectively verifiable criteria, in response to the reliance of international institutions such as the OECD and IMF on 'tax haven' lists which had no such criteria. Such lists consistently identified smaller and politically weaker jurisdictions, while ignoring larger financial centres including major economies[34] – just as the EU 'blacklist' does today.[35]

The FSI combines two components: a secrecy score for each jurisdiction based on twenty indicators (themselves based on more than one hundred components); and a global scale weight that reflects each jurisdiction's share of the global total of financial services exports. In this way, the index avoids targeting highly secretive but entirely marginal players, that pose little risk to others, and instead puts the spotlight on jurisdictions whose lack of transparency represents a major threat – because they provide both the secrecy necessary for illicit financial flows, and the scale of activity to facilitate substantial volumes.

The FSI's sister ranking is the Corporate Tax Haven Index (CTHI), which focuses more specifically on the provision of conditions that incentivise and facilitate the profit shifting of multinational companies.[36] Published since 2019, the CTHI takes a parallel approach to the FSI in combining a 'haven score' based on twenty indicators of the legal and policy conditions, with a scale weight that reflects the importance of each jurisdiction in multinationals' global activity.

Each index can be used to generate measures of the total global risk posed. That allows identification of the proportion of the global risk associated with individual jurisdictions, in order to support a comparative analysis of the relative importance of each.

The third approach to measuring the importance of the UK's network is to draw on the estimates of the State of Tax Justice 2020 report.[37] This new annual report provides consistent country-level estimates, with near-global coverage, of the revenue losses suffered each year to corporate tax abuse and to offshore tax evasion by individuals. At the same time, the analysis generates estimates of the responsibility of each country for the harm done to others by the facilitation of corporate and individual tax abuse. Again, the relative importance of each jurisdiction can be derived from this analysis, in this case by taking the estimated losses imposed on others as a share of the global total.

Table 14.1 summarises this range of measures of importance – in terms of risks posed and revenues losses caused – for the UK and selected dependent territories, and for the UK network as a whole. On each of the measures, the UK network – if taken as a single actor – is responsible for far greater global damage than any other. In terms of financial secrecy risks and revenues lost to individual offshore tax evasion, the United States is identified consistently as the next greatest threat. In terms of corporate risks – both tax abuse risks and revenue losses – the Netherlands is the next greatest threat.

As a single actor, the UK network would stand at the top of the Financial Secrecy Index, at the top of the Corporate Tax Haven Index, and is responsible for substantially almost half of the global revenue losses associated with offshore tax abuse, and more than a quarter of those associated with corporate tax abuse.

These losses of revenue are inflicted upon most countries in the world. The largest losses in absolute terms fall on the largest economies, by and large. But the losses fall most intensely, as a share of current tax revenues, on countries with lower per capita incomes – including most former colonies except those in the UK network of dependent territories. In this way, the UK network plays a central role in delivering the stark inequality that characterises the global distribution of taxing rights, which denies the ability to raise revenues through direct taxation to those states whose people would most benefit.

Table 14.1 The UK spider's web is the dominant 'tax haven' actor.

	Financial Secrecy Index 2020	State of Tax Justice 2020: Revenue losses, offshore abuse	Corporate Tax Haven Index 2019	State of Tax Justice 2020: Revenue losses, corporate abuse
	%	%	%	%
UK	1.57	15.74	2.81	5.58
Jersey	1.37	1.88	4.05	1.82
Guernsey	1.66		2.34	
Isle of Man	0.76	0.18	2.11	1.49
Bermuda	0.85	1.63	6.98	4.44
British Virgin Islands	1.82	3.22	7.29	4.25
Cayman Islands	4.63	26.04	6.67	9.32
Other Overseas Territories	2.02	0.05	2.35	1.58
UK network	14.68	48.75	34.60	28.48
Next biggest actor	4.37	12.92	6.29	10.86
	USA	USA	Netherlands	Netherlands

Source: Tax Justice Network.

The revenue losses are in turn associated with an erosion of governance, of state effectiveness and legitimacy – of statehood. While less immediately visible than foregone public funds, this damage inflicts a further cost, creating or exacerbating inequality in the global distribution of the *right to statehood*.

Dependent territories and post-imperial extraction: Hunter and hunted?

Under the Mughal Empire there were two main forms of revenue: 'Crown lands (*khāliṣa*) [which] deposited their taxes directly into the royal treasury [while the] rest of the state's lands provided the basis for a complex system of "place-holdings" (*jāgīr*), according to which the state bestowed a share in its tax revenues and powers on individual "place holders" (*jāgīrdār*) in exchange for their services.'[38] Four types of such place-holding were granted: one to high-ranking officials of the empire, in lieu of salary; one to those of particular military or civil rank in exchange for specific duties;

one to individuals deemed worthy, such as scholars or holy men; and one to local chieftains, of which only the latter was non-transferable but passed directly to the heir.

The jāgīrs were typically assigned for three-year periods, with the apparent benefit of preventing a powerbase being established. With the most important holders often having lands scattered across the empire, local officials and authority figures would assist in raising the revenue, in the role of *zamindars* (literally, landowner or landholder, *zamin* meaning 'land' in the original Persian):

> As long as the imperial center remained powerful, this system worked fairly well. Even at its height, however, the Mughal state permitted some large zamīndārs ... to possess the same tax- free jāgīrs for life ... and to pass them on to their children. These hereditary jāgīrs quickly grew in size and allowed their possessors to construct exactly the sort of localized power networks that the system had been designed to prevent.[39]

With the growth of international economic opportunities and the weakening of the Mughal empire by the early eighteenth century, it became increasingly common for zamindars to resist the centre, retaining greater revenues for themselves and even entering directly into trading relationships with European charter companies:

> The Bihari zamīndārs admitted their subordination to the Mughals when dealing directly with the imperial authority, but within the borders of their fiefdoms they thought and behaved like any independent sovereign. European companies such as the East India Company (EIC) thus found ample opportunities for inserting themselves into this process of 'regional centralization' pioneered by the zamīndārs and other Mughal rank holders. When the EIC moved into Bengal in the 1760s, for example, it appeared to be acting no differently from other zamīndārs: like other zamīndārs, it diverted trade and tax revenues to fund its private armies and pursued political aggrandizement while remaining formally subordinate to the Mughal throne.[40]

The 'Permanent Settlement of Bengal' began the wider formalisation of a zamindari system under the British, as they permanently displaced the Mughal Empire. The zamindars were again empowered economically and socially, but also – again – instrumentalised by the imperial power.[41]

A parallel with the UK's dependent territories can be considered. On the one hand, they have obtained the right to participate, with little objection from the former imperial powers, in the diluting of taxing rights from most of the world. On the other hand, the territories themselves are able to operate only at the continuing sufferance of those powers, and find themselves firmly trapped in a 'finance curse' from which exit – even if politically possible – would be highly costly.

Two instances of conflict are perhaps useful to consider. The major, coordinated pushback of the early 2000s, when the dependent territories organised against the OECD's 'harmful tax practices' effort to demand a level playing field versus OECD members; and the current efforts to resist the UK's encouragement to end anonymous company ownership.

The harmful tax practices effort generated perhaps the most famous and contested of the many 'tax haven' lists. It was ultimately defeated through the United States reversing its support, in response to a combination of mobilisation from right-wing organisations that praised tax havenry, and the (relatively left-wing) Congressional Black Caucus (CBC) which had come to see the OECD effort as fundamentally unfair, and likely to see rich countries do grave damage to poorer ones through unjustified financial sanctions. Some of the same people from the CBC effort were key players in the subsequent Obama administration's Foreign Account Tax Compliance Act, which played a key part in breaking the resistance of banking secrecy jurisdictions including many small havens but also the long-time leader, Switzerland.[42]

This analysis leads US tax law professor Stephen Dean to the conclusion that tax policy is better made by more diverse groups:

> Tax law tends not to be the most diverse of fields, and international tax often seems even less so. All the more remarkable then that two high-profile Black policymakers played marquee roles in FATCA's creation. On the one hand, that story appears to be a rather conventional one of greater diversity changing minds by sharing information. The OECD's 2000 list – referred to universally, if not officially, as a blacklist – had at least one striking omission. To some, the United States itself deserved to be included. But looking back on the OECD effort, it is hard to dispute that Switzerland, a member of the OECD, should have been included. In 2001 one could still debate whether Switzerland belonged on the list, but more glaring than that exclusion was the inclusion of another state. Absurdly, Liberia, wracked by years of civil war, earned a spot ... But treating diversity as a built-in focus group is a mistake. To suggest that Obama, Rangel, or Christensen needed to be Black in order to both support FATCA and oppose the OECD would be disingenuous. Men can, and do, oppose tampon taxes despite their gender. Does being a woman make it easier to see the unfairness in tampon taxes, or does being Black make the injustice of threatening Liberia with economic sanctions for crimes committed by whiter, wealthier states seem more obvious? Undoubtedly.[43]

A more recent piece of the story has been the reaction from some of the Overseas Territories to the UK's ongoing attempts to have them commit to public registers of the beneficial owners of companies (which the Crown Dependencies have already signed up to, following UK and EU adoption). As Cayman Compass reported:

The decision by the U.K. parliament to threaten an order in council to force the overseas territories to make their beneficial ownership registries public has caused consternation in Bermuda, the BVI and other territories. Bermuda's premier and finance minister David Burt called the vote 'a significant backwards step in the relations between the United Kingdom and the Overseas Territories' and 'a return to base colonialism' that has no place in 2018.[44]

The UK's dependent territories have power to negotiate and to find their own economic path; but they are also heavily conditioned by the path upon which the British Empire set them, and the continuing power of the UK over them. In that sense, as well as the 'farming' of taxing rights from others, the UK network exhibit parallels with the zamindars.

Where formal empire denied self-determination and statehood through outright domination, the current phase of imperial extraction undermines the right to statehood of former colonies and others in a less direct way. Where formal empire gathered the spoils directly and to its wealthy elite and its multinational companies, the current phase supports continued exploitation by ensuring that direct taxation of those groups operating around the world is only of limited efficacy; and sustains a continued flow of capital to the centre.

But recognising that the power behind this situation does not lie uniquely, or even primarily, with the dependent territories is important to seeing possible futures. A return to blacklisting on the basis of political power like the OECD lists of old is untenable – and the current makeup of the EU's list of non-cooperative jurisdictions is strikingly non-white, even as it excludes the US and any consideration of the bloc's own member states.[45]

If the UK recognises its responsibility for the dependent secrecy jurisdictions sufficiently to demand greater transparency from them, it should also recognise its much deeper responsibility for the development path that they are on – and for offering wholehearted support for a 'Plan B'. If the financial implications of supporting a new economic route for the islands' populations are significant, perhaps the UK can consider it as some combination of reparations for the costs of empire; of the compounded savings from all the financial support not provided since the 1960s; and for the aggregate benefits to the City of London, and unevenly to the rest of the UK, from the enormous flows of capital to the centre that the UK's network has delivered.

Reparations for the damage of formal empire are likely to be beyond the UK's economic capacity, even before the commitment to a deeply costly form of separation from the European Union. But the UK could do much to ameliorate the continuing costs of its choices in the period since the end of formal empire. That could include steps today to end the continuing damage that the UK network does to the taxing rights and statehood of so many countries, coupled with substantial support to the dependent territories to establish viable alternative economic and political strategies. The economic governance of the British Empire underpins these ongoing harms. The UK could leverage some of the disproportionate wealth that forms part of its own post-colonial legacies in order to draw a line under these harms and to partially offset them.

Notes

1 Both threads are explored, for example, by W. Rodney, *How Europe Underdeveloped Africa* (London: Verso, 2018; originally published 1972).
2 M. Hampton and J. Christensen, 'Offshore pariahs? Small island economies, tax havens, and the re-configuration of global finance', *World Development* 30 (2002), 1657–73; R. Palan, 'Tax havens and the commercialization of state sovereignty', *International Organization* 56 (2002), 151–76.
3 N. Shaxson, *Treasure Islands: Tax Havens and the Men Who Stole the World* (London: Bodley Head, 2011).
4 Original analysis in J. Christensen and N. Shaxson, *The Finance Curse: How Oversized Financial Centres Attack Democracy and Corrupt Economies* (Chesham, UK: Tax Justice Network, 2014), available at https://www.taxjustice.net/cms/upload/pdf/Finance_Curse_Final.pdf (last accessed 28 March 2022), and J. Christensen, N. Shaxson, and D. Wigan, 'The finance curse: Britain and the world economy', *British Journal of Politics and International Relations* 18.1 (2016), 255–69, doi: 10.1177/1369148115612793. See also G. Epstein and J. Montecino, *Overcharged: The High Cost of High Finance* (Washington, DC: Roosevelt Institute, 2016), available at http://rooseveltinstitute.org/overcharged-high-cost-high-finance/ (last accessed 28 March 2022); A. Baker, G., Epstein, and J. Montecino, *The UK's Finance Curse? Costs and Processes* (Sheffield: Sheffield Political Economy Research Institute, 2018), available at http://speri.dept.shef.ac.uk/wp-content/uploads/2019/01/SPERI-The-UKs-Finance-Curse-Costs-and-Processes.pdf (last accessed 28 March 2022); N Shaxson, *The Finance Curse: How Global Finance Is Making Us All Poorer* (London: Penguin, 2018).
5 Tax Justice Network, Global Alliance for Tax Justice, and Public Services International, *The State of Tax Justice 2020: Tax Justice in the Time of COVID-19* (London: Tax Justice Network, 2020).
6 A. Cobham and P. Janský, *Estimating Illicit Financial Flows: A Critical Guide to the Data, Methodologies and Findings* (Oxford: Oxford University Press, 2019).
7 A. Cobham,' Taxation policy and development', *Oxford Council on Good Governance: Economy Analysis, No. 2* (2005), available at http://www.taxjustice.net/cms/upload/pdf/OCGG_-_Alex_Cobham_-_Taxation_Policy_and_Development.pdf (last accessed 28 March 2022).

8 D. Brautigam, O. Fjeldstad and M. Moore, *Taxation and State Building in Developing Countries* (Cambridge: Cambridge University Press, 2008); R. Broms, 'Taxation and government quality: The size, the shape, or just Europe 300 years ago?', *Quality of Government Institute (University of Gothenburg) Working Paper* 16 (2011).
9 M. Ross, 'Does taxation lead to representation?', *British Journal of Political Science* 34 (2004), 229–49; J. Mahon, 'Liberal states and fiscal contracts: Aspects of the political economy of public finance', Paper presented at the annual meeting of the American Political Science Association (2005); W. Prichard, P. Salardi, and P. Segal, 'Taxation, non-tax revenue and democracy: New evidence using new cross-country data', *World Development* 109 (2018), 295–312.
10 M. Zockun, H. Zylberstajn, S. Silber, J. Rizzieri, A. Portela, E. Pellin, E. and L. Afonso, 'Simplificando O Brasil: Propostas de reforma na relação econômica do governo com o setor privado', *FIPE Texto Para Discussão* 03 (Brasilia: Fundação Instituto De Pesquisas Econômicas, 2007); CDES, 'Inequity indicators of the national tax system', *Observation Report* 2 (Brasilia: Economic and Social Development Council of Brazil, 2011).
11 B. Torgler, 'Tax morale and compliance review of evidence and case studies for Europe', *World Bank Policy Research Working Paper* 5922 (2011).
12 M. Jursa (ed.), *Aspects of the Economic History of Babylonia in the First Millennium BC: Economic Geography, Economic Mentalities, Agriculture, the Use of Money and the Problem of Economic Growth* (Münster: Ugarit Verlag, 2010).
13 E. Kiser and D. Kane, 'The perils of privatization: How the characteristics of principals affected tax farming in the Roman Republic and Empire', *Social Science History* 31.2 (2007), 191–212.
14 K. Fleet, 'Tax-farming in the early Ottoman state', *Medieval History Journal* 6.2 (2003), 249–58.
15 D. Naoroji, *Poverty and Un-British Rule in India* (London: Swann Sonnenschein, 1901). An important exception is U. Patnaik, 'Revisiting the "drain", or transfer from India to Britain in the context of global diffusion of capitalism', in S. Chakrabarti and U. Patnaik (eds), *Agrarian and Other Histories: Essays for Binay Bhushan Chaudhuri* (New Delhi: Tulika, 2019), pp. 277–318.
16 US Treasury, *Colonial Systems of the World: The Colonies, Protectorates, Dependencies, and Spheres of Influence of All Nations Exercising Authority Outside Their Immediate Territory; Showing Form of Government, Area, Population, Revenue, Etc* (Washington, DC: US Government Printing Office, 1899).
17 G. Metcalfe, 'After Maclean: Some aspects of British Gold Coast policy in the midnineteenth century', *Transactions of the Gold Coast & Togoland Historical Society* 1.5 (1955), 178–92.
18 As quoted by G. Serra, '"Hail the census night": Trust and political imagination in the 1960 population census of Ghana', *Comparative Studies in Society and History* 60.3 (2018), 659–87, p. 668.

19 As quoted in D. Akin, *Colonialism, Maasina Rule, and the Origins of Malaitan Kastom* (Honolulu: University of Hawai'i Press, 2013), p. 44.
20 Patnaik, 'Revisiting the "drain"'.
21 W. Treacher, *British Borneo: Sketches of Brunai, Sarawak, Labuan and North Borneo* (London: Lang, 1891/2020, reprinted).
22 This discussion follows closely that in A. Cobham, *The Uncounted* (Cambridge: Polity, 2019).
23 J. Williamson, 'What Washington means by policy reform', in J. Williamson (ed.), *Latin American Adjustment: How Much Has Happened?* (Washington, DC: Institute for International Economics, 1990), available at https://piie.com/commentary/speeches-papers/what-washington-means-policy-reform (last accessed 28 March 2022).
24 Williamson, 'What Washington means by policy reform'.
25 C. Adam and D. Bevan, 'Fiscal policy design in low-income countries', and C. Heady, 'Taxation policy in low-income countries', both in T. Addison and A. Roe (eds), *Fiscal Policy for Development* (Basingstoke: Palgrave Macmillan/UNU-WIDER, 2004).
26 A. Cobham, 'The tax consensus has failed!', *Oxford Council on Good Governance Economy Section Recommendation* 8 (2007), available at http://taxjustice.net/cms/upload/pdf/Cobham_Tax_Consensus_Failed_08.pdf (last accessed 28 Marach 2022).
27 V. Ogle, '"Funk money": The end of empires, the expansion of tax havens, and decolonization as an economic and financial event', *Past & Present* 249.1 (advance copy, 2020), pp. 6–7.
28 Shaxson, *Treasure Islands*, p. 24.
29 As detailed in Ogle, '"Funk money"'.
30 UNODC & UNCTAD, *Conceptual Framework for the Statistical Measurement of Illicit Financial Flows* (Vienna: United Nations Office on Drugs and Crime, 2020), p. 12.
31 K. Pistor, *The Code of Capital: How the Law Creates Wealth and Inequality* (Princeton, NJ: Princeton University Press, 2019); D. Berkowitz, J.-F. Richard, and K. Pistor, 'Economic development, legality, and the transplant effect', *European Economic Review* 47.1 (2003), 165–95; S. Fennell, 'Vorlesung international law and the economy in a postcolonial world: Colonialism, institutions and development' [online video, 14 November 2017], available at https://timms.uni-tuebingen.de:443/tp/UT_20171114_001_intlaw_0001 (last accessed 28 March 2022).
32 P. Rubin, 'Why is the common law efficient?', *Journal of Legal Studies* 6.1 (1977), 51–63.
33 Shaxson, *Treasure Islands*.
34 A. Cobham, P. Janský, and M. Meinzer, 'The Financial Secrecy Index: Shedding new light on the geography of secrecy', *Economic Geography* 91 (2015), 281–303.
35 W. Lips and A. Cobham, 'Paradise lost: Who will feature on the common EU blacklist of non-cooperative tax jurisdictions?', Open Data for Tax Justice, 2017,

available at http://datafortaxjustice.net/paradiselost/ (last accessed 28 March 2022).

36 L. Ates, A. Cobham, M. Harari, P. Janský, M. Meinzer, L. Millán, and M. Palanský, 'The Corporate Tax Haven Index: A new geography of profit shifting', in B. Unger, L. Rossel, and J. Ferwerda (eds), *Combating Fiscal Fraud and Empowering Regulators: Bringing Tax Money Back into the COFFERS* (Oxford: Oxford University Press, 2021).

37 Tax Justice Network, Global Alliance for Tax Justice, and Public Services International, *The State of Tax Justice 2020*.

38 M. K. Jha, 'South Asia, 1400–1800: The Mughal Empire and the Turco-Persianate imperial tradition in the Indian subcontinent', in J. Fairey and B. Farrell (eds), *Empire in Asia: A New Global History,* vol. I: *From Chinggisid to Qing* (London: Bloomsbury, 2018), pp. 141–70, p. 145.

39 Jha, 'South Asia, 1400–1800', p. 146.

40 *Ibid.*, pp. 149–50.

41 *Ibid.*; R. Ray, 'The Bengal Zamindars: Local magnates and the state before the permanent settlement', *Indian Economic Social History Review* 12.3 (1975), 263–92, doi: 10.1177%2F001946467501200303.

42 S. Dean, 'FATCA, the U.S. Congressional Black Caucus, and the OECD blacklist', *TaxNotes Special Report* 2 July2020, available at https://www.taxnotes.com/special-reports/competition-and-state-aid/fatca-us-congressional-black-caucus-and-oecd-blacklist/2020/07/02/2cns4 (last accessed 28 March 2022).

43 Dean, 'FATCA, the U.S. Congressional Black Caucus, and the OECD blacklist'.

44 M. Klein, 'Overseas territories accuse Britain of "modern colonialism"', *Cayman Compass*, 2 May 2018, available at https://www.caymancompass.com/2018/05/02/overseas-territories-accuse-britain-of-modern-colonialism/ (last accessed 28 March 2022).

45 On this, and broader questions of structural racism in international tax policy-making, see S. Dean and A. Waris, 'Ten truths about tax havens: Inclusion and the "Liberia" problem', *Emory Law Journal* 70.7 (2021).

15

The Crown Agents and the CDC Group: Imperial extraction and development's 'private sector turn'

Paul Robert Gilbert

Introduction: Taxation and development 'after' colonialism

The UK's Department for International Development (DFID) has focused significant attention on the relationship between taxation and development, particularly between 2012 and 2020, when DFID was absorbed into the Foreign, Commonwealth & Development Office. DFID's taxation and development policies have focused in recent years on providing technical support for 'capacity building' initiatives in the national revenue collection authorities of the Global South, and on the tax policies of DFID-backed development finance institutions.[1] This focus on institutional capacity building is a significant departure from mid-twentieth-century development economists' and tax advisers' Keynesian emphasis on taxation as an instrument to support development (via employment and redistribution), following a turn towards 'market-led' (rather than redistributive) development policy paradigms during the 1980s–1990s.[2] DFID's approach to tax reform and development does not merely reflect normative policy prescriptions. Calls for ensuring improved development 'outcomes' through DFID's work in the Global South are frequently coupled to concerns about 'value for money' for an imagined British taxpayer. In a 2015 inquiry into the finances of the DFID-backed Private Infrastructure Development Group (PIDG), for instance, parliamentarians were as concerned with PIDG's wasteful expenditure of 'taxpayer money' as with the need to 'support countries to build their tax base to support their own development', something which PIDG seemed to be partly undermining by investing via low-tax jurisdictions.[3]

This dominant framing presents taxation and development initiatives as a matter of one nation-state, responsible to its taxpayers, making resources available for the benefit of another distinct nation-state. In seeking to ensure aid money is 'delivering value for money for the taxpayer',[4] exclusionary racialised imaginings of the British welfare state as accountable only to *deserving* citizens are activated.[5] At the same time, the focus on a transfer of fiscal resources between nation-states elides the degree to which British public finances, the perceived 'lack' of fiscal capacity in former colonies, and the patterns of inequality which aid money purports to address cannot be understood outside a history of colonial expansion and extraction. Here the UK is not merely spending 'hard-earned taxpayers' money'[6] to strengthen revenue collection capacity in the South. Rather, it is repurposing quasi-governmental organisations which evolved as organs of colonial administration, at times complicit in the undermining of colonies' tax bases and welfare regimes for the benefit of Britain's nascent welfare state in the post-war period, and continuing to provide opportunities for aid money to recirculate among elites in the Global North.

In this chapter, I examine two UK-based development bodies, the Crown Agents and the CDC Group, drawing on work in economic history, as well as contemporary efforts to hold these bodies to account by scholars and civil society organisations. I focus on moments of controversy surrounding these organisations' impacts on public finances, both those of the UK and of former colonies. The aim is not merely to emphasise seamless continuity with colonial practices, as a counterpoint to the tendency to introduce a rupture between colonial administration and development practice. Instead, it is to highlight how 'colonial constraints and imperial dispositions have tenacious presence in less obvious ways', such that contemporary inequalities are not merely 'mimetic versions of imperial incarnations', but oblique reworkings of durable imperial formations.[7] After probing the Crown Agents and CDC Group in turn, the chapter concludes by revisiting recent work on the emergence of a 'retro-liberal' aid regime that privileges aid disbursements to for-profit private contractors, and an emphasis on supporting donor country exports through aid spending, and situates this regime within a longer history of colonial finance.

This retro-liberal regime displaces earlier development policy emphases on addressing state fragility while 'making markets work for the poor', as well as neoliberal approaches which sought to 'roll back the state' and dispense with redistributive taxation in the 1980s–1990s.[8] Under the retro-liberal regime, the state exists to sponsor and facilitate the private sector – yet is increasingly entangled with private, for-profit agencies through a range of state–capital hybrids that may benefit donor states in the Global North and development professionals more than they do 'beneficiaries' in the Global South. I would argue that the retro-liberal regime is also a 're-colonial' one, which sees aid flowing through UK-based intermediaries that are once again presented as bearers of the expertise that can address development challenges while demonstrating 'value for money' for the UK taxpayer.[9] Situating these seemingly recent turns in terms of the colonial entailments of development bodies like the Crown Agents and CDC Group draws attention to the persistence of imperial inequalities that are too often overlooked in attempts to hold present-day development agencies to account.

The Crown Agents: Colonial currency and modern contracting

The Crown Agents have suffered a curious neglect at the hands of economic historians, despite the instrumental role they played in the management of colonial currency reserves and public procurement – and by extension, in the shaping of forms of imperial revenue extraction which had significant (if divergent) consequences for public finances in the UK and their colonies. Perhaps more surprising is the lack of attention given to the durability and plasticity of the Crown Agents by scholars of development. After becoming embroiled in a series of financial scandals in the 1970s, the Crown Agents re-emerged as a celebrated development contractor. In 2020, they were shortlisted by British Expertise,[10] a trade body supporting UK businesses to receive aid-funded contracts, for the 'Best Non-Physical Development Project' for their work on the 'Provision of Value for Money Assessment Services to the Ministry of Finance, Ghana'.

The Agents have played a particularly significant role in aid procurement for the Japanese government, and, in the words of the former director general of the UK's Department for International Development (DFID), their 'consultancy services have been particularly important in helping to reform and strengthen countries' revenue services and debt monitoring and management, particularly in Africa'.[11] As of 1 October 2020, the Crown Agents are participants in sixty-two active DFID-funded projects, and received £83.8 million of DFID's procurement spending in 2019/20. In the remainder of this section, I briefly sketch the history of the Crown Agents since their formalisation in 1833. The focus is on two aspects of their operations through which the Agents formed a bridge between imperial forms of extraction, and differential impacts on the public finances of the imperial core and (former) colonies: first, their management of colonial currencies between the 1920s and 1940s; and second, their contemporary success in the aid contractor assemblage[12] for which previous iterations of the Crown Agents themselves laid the foundations.

Currency management and monetary colonialism

Crown Agents were first appointed as administrators of parliamentary grants in North America in the mid-eighteenth century. As an agency under the Treasury, the Crown Agents were appointed by Parliament in 1833 to hold the monopoly rights on procurement for the colonies, providing everything from railways to postage stamps from a select list of approved British firms. Formalised as the Crown Agents for the Colonies in 1863, with responsibility for them transferred from the Treasury to the Colonial Office, they were also granted exclusive intermediary rights between colonies and their investment brokers in the City of London. They came to act as both 'bankers and national debt commissioners'[13] for the colonies, earning a commission on both procurement contracts (1%), loan repayments (0.5%), and interest payments (0.25%).[14] In the 1900s, debates frequently arose in Parliament about the extent to which the Crown Agents' preferred list of suppliers undermined principles of 'free trade', and concerns were also raised regarding the excessive burden on the colonies' public finances as a result of the Agents' monopoly purchase rights – not to mention the lack of contracts available to colonial firms.[15]

Much is often made in Anglocentric scholarship of the high regard in which Crown Agents were held by government ministries, the expertise they were understood to have regarding colonial finances, and their concern for colonial welfare.[16] Nonetheless, economic historians such as Krozewski[17] and Sunderland[18] have drawn attention to the role that the Agents' management of colonial currency reserves played in maintaining advantageous public finances for the UK, while restricting development opportunities and increasing tax burdens in the colonies. The implementation of currency boards in British colonies enforced full backing (sometimes 110% backing) of circulating currency with sterling reserves, to be held and invested in London by the Crown Agents. The result of 'unrequited exports' of primary goods from the colonies to the UK and the US, large currency reserves were built up under the Agents' management between 1939 and 1958, compounded by 'austere policies' in exporting territories,[19] that were no doubt experienced along racialised lines, given the far lower tax burden placed on white European settlers in many of Britain's colonies. To keep down the costs of nationalisation, and the development of a nascent welfare state in post-war Britain, a solution needed to be found that could maintain cheap money policies, prevent inflation, maintain full employment, and deal with the dollar shortages making imports expensive: 'Colonial balances, therefore, had to be kept out of circulation, whether by physical import controls, taxation, or both.'[20]

The Treasury and the Bank of England began to enforce a policy whereby colonial funds were held in cash or invested in government securities, to provide public finances and prevent the export of sterling reserves (or their reinvestments in the colonies from which they were accumulated).[21] This policy resulted in the rate of interest earned on sterling investments being *lower* than the interest owed on loans taken out from City banks, and colonies began to air their grievances. Sunderland dismisses as 'untrue' the charges that these reserves were used to fund the 'establishment of the welfare state, and capital flows to countries in the independent sterling area, such as Australia, India and South Africa',[22] and yet capital flows from the City to Rhodesia and South Africa during the 1940s–1950s far outstripped their contributions to sterling reserves (and hence investment in British government finances), while the reverse was true for India and the colonies.[23] In certain ways analogous to the 'drain'[24] of resources that had operated through Home Charges imposed on India,[25] 'the sterling reserves of the colonies and India were effectively financing British investment into South Africa and Rhodesia. The implicit benefit of the sterling area – the holding of sterling in exchange for capital from Britain – was not realised in the colonies'.[26] In Malaya too, sterling balances (accrued from favourable rubber trade with the US) were transferred to London during the post-war period to pay corporate taxes and dividends (or simply be placed in reserve). In addition, British negotiators leveraged racial schisms in newly independent countries to convince elites to continue pegging their currency to the pound, and to avoid using sterling assets 'too quickly' to fund its independent development.[27]

Revisiting Krozewski and Sunderland in light of new archival evidence, Narsey reveals the lengths to which the Treasury and Bank of England went to overrule the Crown Agents when they wished to manage reserves for colonies' benefit. Narsey[28] also details the efforts to which the Treasury went to *deliberately* mislead the colonies regarding policies designed to extract monetary rent from imperial possessions, and bolster the public finances of post-war Britain – all while keeping taxes high, curtailing investment opportunities, and restricting colonies' ability to afford dollar denominated imports. While restrictions were made on how much of their reserves could be invested in anything other than UK government securities, colonies were also expected to meet development finance needs 'from their own funds', having recourse to investment from the CDC (see below) only as a 'supplement'.[29] And, the management of colonial reserves by the Agents under Treasury instructions laid foundations for monetary colonialism that continued even after independence. Upon Ghana's independence, figures on the quantity of their reserves were not available to the finance minister, and, on travelling to London, Nkrumah found reserves both diminished due to unsound investment, and tied up in long-term UK government securities with maturation dates well into the 1970s.[30]

Scandal and return to procurement

The end of the Crown Agents' monopoly in colonial procurement, as well as the desire of newly independent states to find other intermediaries through which to invest their reserves, forced the Agents to reinvent themselves. They continued to do business with independent governments, their municipalities and parastatals, and came under the responsibility of the Minister for Overseas Development in 1964, finding business within the emergent aid regime. But the loss of their 'captive market'[31] in the colonies led to declining reserves and put the Agents on a path towards reckless financial experimentation. Claude Hayes, who took over as senior Crown Agent in 1968, seemed to preside over questionable and at times potentially illegal investments on the Agents' own account – in some instances using the funds still invested with them by sixty-seven former colonies. Hood describes the Agents' schemes, revealed by a series of parliamentary inquiries (1972, 1977) and a tribunal (1981), as including 'back-to-back loans with insurance companies to circumvent legislation, tax-avoidance deals of labyrinthine complexity, exchange control avoidance, and "window-dressing" of balance sheets and accounts'.[32] The Agents managed to concentrate their investments in some of the most disastrous firms and property schemes around, implicating themselves in the fringe banking crises of the 1970s, and making losses near to £250 million that were effectively written off by the government.

The Agents' near collapse and subsequent bailout[33] set them on a path to becoming established as a statutory corporation in 1979, where they would no longer have a monopoly on business in the former colonies but *would* still procure for recipient governments all capital and imports financed by Britain's tied aid programme,[34] which was formally dissolved in 1997. Also in 1997, the Crown Agents metamorphosised once again, into a limited company wholly owned by a foundation funded by a £5.5 million government loan. They would now provide consultancy services in development, reinvesting their surplus in their own capacity or other development initiatives.

The curious organisational form taken by the Crown Agents over time is often invoked as one of the main reasons for their failures in the 1960s and 1970s. As Moore and Newbigging put it, those 'ultimately responsible for the activities of the Crown Agents do not appear to have consciously asked themselves what was the purpose of the organisation after the dissolution of the Empire. This failure allowed the Crown Agents to adapt as they saw fit without effective scrutiny from outside'.[35] The Agents and their employees had long viewed themselves as a 'private mercantile firm doing work for the Government but outside the Government'.[36] This curious feature of the Agents – lacking a constitution, not quite civil servants but subject to influence by the Treasury, sometimes merchants and brokers, acting 'for' the colonies but devising their own preferred list of contractors – laid the foundation for a form of public–private governance or 'development by contract'[37] that is increasingly of concern to scholars of international development.

As the UK intensifies its embrace of government by contract domestically, its international development spending has followed suit. While numerous parliamentary inquiries have raised concerns about the 'value for money' offered by for-profit development contractors (see below), vast sums continue to be spent. In 2019, £1.25 billion of DFID's funds were spent on private sector contractors, and at times this spending is heavily concentrated on a handful of firms: the 'Big Four' professional services firms alone were awarded £517 million worth of contracts by DFID between 2015 and 2018. As such, a percentage of funds disbursed through DFID (or as of 2020, the Foreign, Commonwealth & Development Office), as part of Britain's Official Development Assistance (ODA) or aid commitments, frequently circulate back into the UK.

Writing of the beltway consultants and contractors who have been increasingly able to capture USAID development spending, Susan Roberts[38] nods towards Cain and Hopkins'[39] argument about the service sector and rising incomes in southeast England during the late nineteenth century. 'Just as the southeast of England's prosperity grew up with finance capital based in the City of London, but with tentacles all over the globe, I venture that the greater Washington, D.C., area's recent extraordinary accumulation has grown up with the rise of contractor capital.'[40] Regardless of the Crown Agents' 'reputation for impartiality, and probity',[41] and the celebration of their extensive advisory work on taxation and revenue reform notwithstanding,[42] there has been no clear 'rupture' with the imperial past when it comes to their operations. While no longer having a monopoly on colonial procurement, nor an informal monopoly over procurement arising from 'tied aid', their promotion of the global tax reform agenda reproduces the very form of development by contract for which (an earlier version of) the Crown Agents provide the archetype – and such contracts include advisory services as well as the direct administration of customs and revenue services in the Global South.[43] And, while no longer explicitly repurposing colonial currency reserves to bolster the UK's public finances, the Agents continue to benefit from a retro-liberal aid regime[44] which is concerned as much with development assistance as it is with promoting the 'export' of British consultancy and fostering their ability to win 'aid-funded business'[45] – from the UK, as well as from other donors.

In the next section, I examine the fortunes of another state–capital hybrid founded to administer development in the British colonies, the CDC Group, which has likewise come back from the brink of failure to play a central role in the current retro-liberal aid regime. Where the Crown Agents played a key role in diverting potential fiscal resources from the colonies to bolster

Britain's efforts to found a post-war welfare state, the CDC Group today benefits from (and indeed contributes to) a global tax architecture that deprives states in the Global South of tax revenue and perpetuates the myth that incentives are required to attract investment to 'unstable' and 'capital-starved' developing states.

The CDC Group: Private equity, international development, and tax avoidance

The CDC Group has a shallower history than the Crown Agents, being founded in 1948 as the Colonial Development Corporation, renamed the Commonwealth Development Corporation in 1963, and permitted to invest beyond the Commonwealth in 1969. It has also been subject to far greater levels of public scrutiny than the Crown Agents, both within and beyond Parliament, as journalists and campaigners raise concerns about CDC's use of 'tax havens', high executive pay, and lack of demonstrable development impact. The CDC's use of a private equity funding model has intensified the criticism is has received, compounding private equity's place as the face of unacceptable capitalism in the UK,[46] and appearing particularly at odds with any kind of development mandate.[47] In the remainder of this section, I briefly review the CDC's history and evolving funding model, before examining the recurrent criticisms about tax practices levelled at the CDC by both parliamentarians and civil society organisations. I situate these concerns in terms of current evidence that capital flows in 'the wrong direction', from the Global South to the Global North, as well as debates about attempts donors like the UK are making to redefine aid and ODA to *further* amplify the private capital mobilised by CDC Group.

Colonial to Commonwealth to 'catalysing' development

One of DFID's former directors general has suggested that the rationale for the CDC under the 1945 Labour government was found in 'a gap between what the public sector should do and what the private sector was prepared to do'.[48] Yet the hasty establishment of the Colonial Development Corporation in 1948 had more to do with a desire to cultivate food and material supply chains that did not have to be paid for with dollars – and which created sterling reserves that could be managed in the interest of the UK's public finances (see above). As such, 'the criteria for establishing colonial enterprise were neither of corporate profitability nor of colonial social welfare but of vaguely defined propensities for dollar saving according to British national terms of account'.[49] If assessed purely in terms of its schematic success, Hyam and Louis observe 'that the CDC survived in any form is perhaps surprising, granted its poor track record and huge losses. At least thirty out of thirty-five CDC schemes for producing food were failures'.[50]

By 1955, however, CDC was breaking even, and by the 1970s was generating surpluses thanks to returns over and above the rate at which funds were advanced by DFID's predecessor, the Overseas Development Ministry. Borrowing limits were increased through the 1980s, and CDC's mandate was confirmed in 1993 as investing in 'viable projects which cannot attract sufficient private funds'.[51] Under the 1997 New Labour government, the CDC became CDC Group PLC, wholly owned by government, with existing government loan advances converted into equity, and funds being managed by two companies (Actis and Aureos) spun out of CDC staff. Between 1995 and 2016, CDC was 'self-financing', and from 2004 until 2012 managed entirely on a 'fund of funds' private equity model through Actis and Aureos. After 2012, new investment models (including direct equity and debt) were introduced, following a series of unfavourable audits and reviews.

In 2008, the National Audit Office (NAO)[52] raised concerns about CDC sitting on £1.4 billion in cash, held in the UK Debt Management Office – exceeding its total overseas investments – and a failure to bring about any putative 'pipeline' of investments towards which those funds might be allocated. Following the NAO review, the Public Accounts Committee[53] not only raised questions about how such high cash balances might better be allocated to development and poverty reduction in the Global South, but also noted that 'remuneration agreements led to extraordinary levels of pay in a small publicly-owned organisation charged with fighting poverty, with the Chief Executive receiving £970,000 in 2007'.[54] A lack of information on how CDC contributed to development and poverty reduction was also noted in the National Audit Office review, and despite a number of changes introduced since 2012, the Independent Commission on Aid Impact awarded, in 2019,[55] an 'amber-red' score for aid effectiveness, due in part to a lack of targets for development impact and a continued preference for commercial returns over 'higher risk' projects with potential development impact.

One of the principal ways in which CDC has responded to concerns about a lack of demonstrable impact was to design a 'Development Grid' in 2013, which scores investments according to job creation potential as well as the 'difficulty' of investing in a given country. The Development Grid[56] was central to the 2015 Business Case which encouraged further investment in 'harder geographies' as well as laying the groundwork for the CDC's spending funding cap to be raised from the 1999 level of £1.5 billion to £6 billion, and £12 billion with parliamentary approval.[57]

The Grid, however, only provides an *ex ante* approximation of development impact (limited to job creation without attention to exploitation), and measures of 'hard geographies' derive from the World Bank's controversial Doing Business Indicators which were discontinued in September 2021. Bizarrely (see below), CDC and other Development Finance Institutions often justify the use of offshore jurisdictions or 'tax havens' precisely because they provide easier operating environments, even as they tie markers of putative 'development success' to investing in territories marked by supposed measures of 'difficulty'. It is the summary measures of 'difficult geographies' that provide CDC with its rationale (even as it seeks to bypass this difficulty), to the extent that it purports to support development by 'crowding in' *additional* private finance where projects would not be feasible or investors would not be willing without CDC participation – yet such additionality can almost never be confidently measured.[58]

An emphasis on leveraging or catalysing private investment through development finance institutions like CDC is central to the contemporary retro-liberal aid regime according to which the public sector should never 'crowd out' private finance, and to the promotion of 'blended' finance as a means to meet the Sustainable Development Goals.[59] OECD donors are in fact pushing for new measures of aid which take into account publicly mobilised private financing – and allow donor countries to count as aid 'the support they provide to their own profit-making private sector'.[60] Development ministers and DFID civil servants have even hinted at the possibility of,[61] or endorsed,[62] inclusion of profits from CDC's investments in official aid measurements. This is particularly notable given that the majority of development finance institutions' investments are in fact in Global North-domiciled companies.[63] The retro-liberal aid regime thus repurposes earlier instruments of monetary colonialism (such as the CDC, which was mobilised to bolster sterling during the early years of the welfare state) in order to promote a form of 'development' investment that defies evaluation and frequently transfers funds to firms in the North while inflating measures of 'aid'. Perhaps far more concerning, however, is the extent to which institutions like the CDC utilise offshore jurisdictions or 'tax havens' to structure their investments.

'Tax havens' and taxpayer subjectivities in international development

Notwithstanding persistent shortcomings in CDC's capacity to demonstrate development 'impact' or 'additionality', they have typically used as measures either job creation figures (total jobs associated with an investment, or *ex ante* via the Development Grid), or taxes paid by businesses they have invested in. Giving evidence to the International Development Committee, the CDC Group justified this measure on the basis that the 'private sector provides the taxes for governments to invest in public services, health and education',[64] giving as an example their investment via Actis in Accra Mall which generated US$4.3 million worth of sales tax in 2009. And yet, as critics have observed, the Accra Mall was granted a five-year tax holiday and Actis, 'through its knowledge of foreign investments in Ghana', applied for rebates worth at least $3 million.[65] As numerous civil society observers have noted, the use of tax paid as an indicator of development contribution, without reporting on tax paid by companies in which development finance institutions like CDCs invest, is troubling.[66] Perhaps more concerting is the widespread use of offshore jurisdictions or 'tax havens' by CDC and other development finance institutions.

As Cobham and colleagues argue,[67] the language of 'tax havens' and even 'offshore' financial centres can be misleading. To speak of 'tax havens' and 'offshore' centres draws disproportionate attention to micro-states and island nations, and away from the relationships between legal jurisdictions which allow for reductions in tax paid on business activities or private wealth to be minimised, in the absence of clear legal guidelines for the conduct of multinational economic activity. Secrecy jurisdictions, by contrast, can be understood as administrative units that create regulation known to be of use to those outside of their jurisdiction and create secrecy to prevent those using these regulations from being identified. If all of the UK Crown Dependencies and overseas territories are included within the United Kingdom as one country, then the UK would top the Tax Justice Network's (2018 and 2019) Financial Secrecy Index.

A report prepared for a coalition of European non-governmental organisations noted that, in 2009, 48% of CDC's funds were in secrecy jurisdictions, as measured by the Financial Secrecy Index, excluding the UK.[68] Using IMF data on tax havens from 2007, the International Development Committee notes that 80% of CDC's funds (by number, not value) were invested through tax havens in 2010. Nonetheless, CDC claimed that investing their funds offshore was the 'most efficient way of pooling capital for investment' and insisted they only move funds through the OECD 'white list'.[69] At the end of 2013, 118 out of 157 fund investments made by the CDC went through jurisdictions in the top twenty of the Financial Secrecy Index, and between 2000 and 2013 these funds received $3.8 billion, including $553 million in 2013 alone,[70] and CDC's direct portfolio investments also made use of secrecy jurisdictions.[71] Numerous commentators have highlighted that the OECD Global Forum on Transparency and Exchange of Information for Tax Purposes – according to which the 'white list' on which the CDC relies is determined – conducts peer review that is not fit for purpose, focusing mainly on banking secrecy rather than tax minimisation and excluding Global South countries from policy design while admitting 'tax havens' to the negotiating table.[72]

CDC's policy on taxation claims that they use intermediate jurisdictions to 'meet its development priority of mobilising capital into African and South Asian businesses and to protect UK taxpayers' money', and that such jurisdictions will only be used to 'provide a stable financial, legal and regulatory environment' in order to 'mobilise commercial investors' – never to avoid tax or transparency.[73] While CDC does report taxes paid by companies in its portfolio, this is only a measure of taxes paid *per country*, without reference to the ratio of tax paid to economic activity or size of investment.[74] Given that there are recorded cases of significant tax minimisation strategies being deployed by firms in which CDC has majority stakes (such as Mineral Deposits in Senegal, which paid £20,000 tax in 2008 and appeared to avoid £6 million worth of charges via Mauritius), questions must be asked about why 'intermediaries' should be used to 'mobilise commercial investors' or provide legal 'stability'. As Murphy notes, the 'risk of [an] underlying investment is not altered by the legal form given to the [offshore] transaction that records its existence'.[75]

Some development scholars have pushed back on concerns about the use of offshore or secrecy jurisdictions by development finance institutions like CDC, based on the fact that double taxation agreements would allow, for example, CDC funds to avoid paying capital gains tax on the sale of equity whether funds operate out of London or an intermediary.[76] Double taxation treaties frequently put Global South jurisdictions on the back foot, by putatively avoiding taxation both at source *and* at destination for repatriated funds, but disadvantaging source countries.[77] The OECD-model double taxation treaty rules 'preclude source countries from taxing the business profits of non-resident enterprises made outside their permanent establishments within their jurisdictions'.[78] That is, a source country can exercise taxation rights on permanent establishments, but not establishments maintained by non-resident enterprises for storage, display, or purchasing goods. Source countries are further forbidden from taxing royalties and limited from taxing dividends.

In theory, double taxation agreements are justified by the assumption that capital flows from the North to the South, and that investment needs to be encouraged by tax treaties favourable to foreign investors.[79] Yet, as work by Léonce Ndikumana and colleagues[80] shows, 'capital is flowing in the wrong direction' for much of Africa.[81] Through trade mis-invoicing, transfer pricing, and repatriating profits via offshore intermediaries, capital flight *out* of Africa far outstrips official aid, and *increases* with rises in foreign direct investment: as such, the capital flight cannot be accounted for in terms of 'difficult geographies' deterring investment or encouraging fund managers to readjust their portfolios. The CDC Group, and development finance institutions like it, justify their (largely undemonstrable) development impact in terms of taxes paid, while participating in arrangements that whether by intention or not, enable tax minimisation and may well contribute to well-documented capital flight from Africa and elsewhere. They play a central part in the elaboration of the retro-liberal aid regime that sees not only the promotion of 'expertise exports' via Northern-domiciled consultants who acquire aid-funded business contracts (see above) but attempts to redefine Official Development Assistance[82] to include leveraged investment and flows of public money to private firms, including those from the Global North. As noted in the CDC's official policy on the use of taxation and tax havens,[83] the interests of the *UK taxpayer* are increasingly used to justify these reformulations of imperial extraction.

Conclusion: Retro-liberal or re-colonial aid regimes?

The interests of the British taxpayer have long been invoked to justify and evaluate both the Crown Agents and the CDC Group. Kresner[84] observes that the Crown Agents were highly regarded in the early twentieth century, since they were 'self-supporting, costing the British taxpayer nothing while appearing to serve his imperial interests admirably'. In response to questions following a public lecture he had given in his capacity as Deputy Chairman of the Colonial Development Corporation, H. Nutcombe Hume likewise defended the Corporation's decisions not to invest in railways in Tanganyika with reference to the taxpayer: 'I think that unless a railway holds out the prospect of becoming self-supporting, it would not perhaps be right to use the British taxpayer's money for its construction.'[85] That the CDC was established in such haste (leading to many failed agricultural schemes), and the Crown Agents directed to manage colonial reserves in order to bolster British public finances *against* the interests of colonial subjects, is not of course acknowledged in either case.

In this chapter, I have revisited the contemporary role of the Crown Agents and CDC Group in light of their imperial past. While no longer actively complicit in undermining pre- and post-independence colonies' public finances for the benefit of Britain's nascent welfare state (in the case of Crown Agents), nor investing in 'development' initiatives in order to salve Britain's public finances via providing raw materials within the sterling area (in the case of CDC Group), both organisations continue to act within a development finance assemblage that sees significant funds being diverted from the Global South to private funds or contractors in the North. But this is not merely a matter of failing to work hard enough to achieve 'value for money' for the British taxpayer, as parliamentary watchdogs and proponents of 'One World Conservativism' have argued.[86] Instead, it speaks to the solidification of a 'retro-liberal'[87] aid regime that privileges aid disbursements to for-profit private contractors, and emphasises supporting donor country consultancy 'exports'. The study and practice of international development is, as Olivia Rutazibwa reminds us, 'constitutively defined by colonial amnesia',[88] and there is now little space in consultancy circles for recalling the Keynesian models of taxation-for-development that dominated international tax advice in the mid-twentieth century.[89] Yet the degree to which Keynesian models of national economy and taxation were indelibly shaped by, and yet hostile to, anti-imperial economic thought[90] are erased in 'necro-Keynesian'[91] attempts to resuscitate mid-century models of the welfare state. As we have seen above, such models have only been cultivated in tandem with fiscal colonialism.

As much as the colonial durabilities manifested in the Crown Agents and CDC Group partake in a 'retro-liberal' aid regime, they also bespeak a 're-colonial' aid regime. There are continuities with British imperial practice, but also continuities with the fiscal colonialism enacted by New York's City Bank in its acquisition of contracts to collect, secure, and profit from collection of Haitian and Dominican revenue and receipts in the 1920s.[92] Elsewhere, there are parallels with today's durable remnants of the French Empire in west and central Africa, where austerity is forced upon 'independent' francophone nations by virtue of being subordinated to policy concerns of the French treasury, and thus unable to pursue employment and productive investment.[93] The amnesias besetting international development stand in the way of accounts that foreground the colonial durabilities which are so deeply embedded within aid flows, government by contract, and even 'value for money' models of accountability that structure the retro-liberal aid regimes. There can be no repurposing of development towards an anti-colonial fight for global justice and reparation without, at the very least, displacing the amnesiac models of fiscal nation-states that underpin contemporary policy regarding taxation and development finance.

Notes

1 International Development Committee, *Tax in Developing Countries: Increasing Resources for Development* (Westminster: House of Commons, 2012).
2 Roel Dom and Mark Miller, *Reforming Tax Systems in the Developing World: What Can We Learn from the Past?* (London: Overseas Development Institute, 2018).

3 Public Accounts Committee. *Oversight of the Private Infrastructure Development Group. HC 675* (Westminster: House of Commons, 2015).
4 'Spending UK aid to tackle poverty', *DFID*, last modified 9 June 2020, available at https://dfidnews.blog.gov.uk/2020/06/09/spending-uk-aid-to-tackle-poverty/ (last accessed 28 March 2022); also 'TaxPayers' Alliance report on future of foreign aid spending', *DFID*, last modified 18 March 2019, available at https://dfidnews.blog.gov.uk/2019/03/18/taxpayers-alliance-report-on-future-of-foreign-aid-spending/ (last accessed 28 March 2022).
5 Joanne Sharp, Patricia Campbell, and Emma Laurie, 'The violence of aid? Giving, power and active subjects in One World Conservativism', *Third World Quarterly* 31.7(2020), 1125–43.
6 Andrew Mitchell, 'One World Conservativism', *CapX*, last altered 13 June 2019, available at https://capx.co/one-world-conservatism/ (last accessed 28 March 2022).
7 Laura Stoler, *Duress: Imperial Durabilities in Our Times* (Durham, NC: Duke University Press, 2016), pp. 4–5.
8 Emma Mawdsley, Warwick Murray, John Overton, Regina Scheyvens, and Glenn Banks, 'Exporting stimulus and 'shared prosperity': Reinventing aid for a retroliberal era', *Development Policy Review* 36.S1 (2017), O25–O43.
9 Patricia Noxolo, 'Decolonial theory in a time of the re-colonisation of UK research', *Transactions of the Institute of British Geographers* 42.3 (2017), 342–44.
10 British Expertise emerged from the British Overseas Engineering Services Bureau, which was initially established in 1965 with government support, to assist British engineers in carrying out feasibility studies for developing countries seeking World Bank or similar funding.
11 Barrie Ireton, *Britain's International Development Policies: A History of DFID and Overseas Aid* (Basingstoke: Palgrave Macmillan, 2013), p. 176.
12 Susan Roberts, 'Development capital: USAID and the rise of development contractors', *Annals of the American Association of Geographers* 104.5 (2016), 1030–51.
13 Richard Kresner, 'Builders of empire: The role of the Crown Agents in imperial development, 1880–1914', *Journal of Imperial and Commonwealth History* 5.3 (2008), 314.
14 Kresner claims there is 'no evidence to suggest that any Crown Agent personally benefited from such gains', though Nyeck notes that the 'difference between market price and the Agency's price helped pay Crown Agents' salaries and provided them with good retirement plans'. Further archival work is required to settle this question of pecuniary benefit from the Agents' operations. See Kresner, 'Builders of empire', p. 325; Sybille Ngo Nyeck, 'The implicit dimensions of public procurement contracts: African history and debates', in S. Nyeck (ed.), *Public Procurement Reform and Governance in Africa* (Basingstoke: Palgrave Macmillan, 2016), p. 40.
15 The degree to which these concerns related exclusively to settler colonial-run firms is not always made clear in the academic literature or the sources from which they draw.

16 Kresner, 'Builders of empire', p. 324; David Sunderland, *Managing British Colonial and Post-Colonial Development: The Crown Agents, 1914–74* (Woodbridge: Boydell Press, 2007), p. 79.
17 Gerold Krozewski, *Money and the End of Empire: British International Economic Policy & the Colonies, 1947–58* (London: Palgrave Macmillan, 2001).
18 Sunderland, *Crown Agents*.
19 Krozewski, *Money and the End of Empire*, p. 33.
20 *Ibid.*, pp. 72–3.
21 In 1935, 5% of colonial funds managed by the Crown Agents were invested in local or municipal stock (in 1958 the figure was 3.3%); on average, just over half in total was invested in government securities, and 41% was invested colonial and dominion securities. Holdings in UK government securities rose from 11% of funds in 1935 to 74% 1962. See Sunderland, *Crown Agents*, p. 72.
22 Sunderland, *Crown Agents*, p. 88.
23 Krozewski, *Money and the End of Empire*, p. 48.
24 Utsa Patnaik, 'Revisiting the "drain", or transfers from India to Britain in the context of global diffusion of capitalism', in Shubhra Chakrabarti and Utsa Patnaik (eds), *Agrarian and Other Histories: Essays for Binay Bhushan Chaudhuri* (Delhi: Tulika, 2017), pp. 277–317.
25 By requiring that foreign purchasers of Indian goods used Bills of Exchange denominated in rupees, which were exclusively available for purchase with gold or sterling in London, the British prevented foreign exchange flowing back to Indian producers and exporters. Instead, Indian producers were paid out of the portion (approximately one third) of tax revenue that was transferred to London as 'Home Charges'. Thus, Indian producers were paid out of their own taxes, while British trade deficits were subsidised by Indian producers in the form of sterling or gold deposited in London by foreign purchasers of Indian goods. As such, the 'large capital exports from Britain from the 1870s onwards, which built US roads, railways and factories, depended crucially on Britain's ability to siphon off India's forex [foreign exchange] earnings'. See Patnaik, 'Revisiting the "drain"', p. 302.
26 Wardan Narsey, *British Imperialism and the Making of Colonial Currency Systems* (Basingstoke: Palgrave Macmillan, 2016), p. 193.
27 Maureen Sioh, 'Pricing race, circulating anxieties, and the fate of Malaya's currency reserves at independence', *Cultural Critique* 65 (2007), 115–39.
28 Narsey, *British Imperialism*, p. 190.
29 Krozewski, *Money and the End of Empire*, p. 70.
30 Matteo Landricina, *Nkrumah and the West: 'The Ghana experiment' in the British, American and German Archives* (Hamburg: Lit Verlag, 2020), p. 18.
31 Ireton, *Britain's International Development Policies*, p. 169.
32 Christopher Hood, 'The Crown Agents affair', *Public Administration* (1978), 297.
33 The terms involved making a 'recoverable grant' of £85 million in 1975, followed by £90 million in 1978, but the 'liability of the unincorporated Crown

Agents to replay the £175m of recoverable grants paid to them by government ceased the day before incorporation'. See Ireton, *Britain's International Development Policies*, p. 173.
34 *Ibid.*, p. 173.
35 Christopher Moore and Eric Newbigging, 'Environmental change and public enterprise: The dilemma of the Crown Agents', *Journal of General Management* 8.2 (1982), 80.
36 Vincent Ponko, 'History and the methodology of public administration: The case of the Crown Agents for the Colonies', *Public Administration Review* 27.1 (1967), 44.
37 Nyeck, 'The implicit dimensions', p. 44.
38 Roberts, 'Development capital'.
39 Peter Cain and Anthony Hopkins, *British Imperialism: 1688–2000* (London: Routledge, 2001).
40 Roberts, 'Development capital', p. 17.
41 Ireton, *Britain's International Development Policies*, p. 174.
42 Odd-Helge Fjedlstad, 'Tax and development: Donor support to strengthen tax systems in developing countries', *Public Administration and Development* 34.3 (2014), 182–93; Graham Harrison, 'Clean-ups, conditionality and adjustment: Why institutions matter in Mozambique', *Review of African Political Economy* 26.81 (1999), 323–33.
43 Beatrice Hibou, *Privatising the State* (London: Hurst & Co, 2009), p. 4.
44 Mawdsley *et al.*, 'Exporting stimulus'.
45 The Department for International Trade contains a team dedicated to helping UK firms 'win aid-funded business', and organisations like British Expertise run seminars to assist firms in 'tapping' this 'market'.
46 Christian de Cock and Daniel Nyberg, 'The possibility of critique under financialized capitalism: The case of private equity in the United Kingdom', *Organization* 23.4 (2014), 465–84.
47 Private equity involves the use of funds (usually provided by pension funds and other vehicles) and debt to leverage a controlling interest in companies, restructure them, and resell at a later date in return for capital gains, pre-sale dividends, and fund management fees. Criticisms are levelled at private equity firms, due in part to the decline in working conditions that often characterises 'restructuring', and the reduction in corporation tax from the use of debt in initial buyouts (in some cases, this debt is repaid to 'offshore' jurisdictions, further reducing tax liabilities and increasing profits for private equity investors, or even transferred to the purchased company).
48 Ireton, *Britain's International Development Policies*, p. 159.
49 Mike Cowen, 'Early years of the Colonial Development Corporation: British state enterprise overseas during late colonialism', *African Affairs* 83.330 (1984), 64.
50 Ronald Hyam and William Roger Louis, *The Conservative Government and the End of Empire 1957–64* (London: The Stationery Office, 2000), p. xi.
51 Ireton, *Britain's International Development Policies*, p. 164.

52 National Audit Office, *Investing for Development: The Department of International Development's Oversight of CDC Group plc.*, HC 2008–09 18 (Westminster: House of Commons, 2008).
53 Public Accounts Committee, *Investing for Development: The Department for International Development's oversight of CDC Group plc.*, HC 2008–09 94 (Westminster: House of Commons, 2009).
54 Accenture were commissioned by DFID to review pay at CDC in 2011, and found that it was, across the board, higher than median pay in comparator institutions – with CEO pay 123% above median sector pay, and Managing Director pay 137% higher. Investment Manager/Executive pay was 53–54% above the media. The National Audit Office noted in 2016 that average pay had reduced from £123,000 to £90,000 after DFID severed the peg to commercial pay.
55 Independent Commission for Aid Impact, *CDC's Investments in Low-Income and Fragile States* (London: ICAI, 2019). See also National Audit Office, *Department for International Development: investing through CDC (HC 2016–17 784)* (Westminster: House of Commons, 2016).
56 Curiously, the Grid is also now central to CDC's 2017 remuneration strategy, which ties performance/variable pay to a measure of Development Potential (meeting the target score on the grid of 2.4%), as well as Development Outcome, which is measured by the purely financial metric of a return on portfolio in excess of 3.5%.
57 Following a £753 million increase in funding in 2015.
58 International Development Committee, *The Future of CDC*, HC 2010–11 607-I (Westminster: House of Commons, 2011).
59 Emma Mawdsley, '"From billions to trillions": Financing the SDGs in a world "beyond aid"', *Dialogues in Human Geography* 8.2 (2018), 191–195.
60 Neissan Besharati, 'New development finance measure should be TOSSD out the window!' *South African institute of International Affairs, Policy Insights* 45 (2017), 4.
61 Sophie Edwards, 'DFID promises "no accounting tricks" to count CDC profits as aid', *Devex*, 30 November 2018, available at https://www.devex.com/news/dfid-promises-no-accounting-tricks-to-count-cdc-profits-as-aid-93917 (last accessed 28 March 2022).
62 Henry Mance, 'UK seeks reforms on overseas aid spending', *Financial Times*, 9 October 2018.
63 Maria Jose Romero, *A Private Affair: Shining a Light on The Shadowy Institutions Giving Public Support to Private Companies and Taking Over the Development Agenda* (Brussels: Eurodad, 2014).
64 International Development Committee, *Future of CDC*, Ev 60.
65 Alexander Eduful, 'Reconsidering the entrepreneurial city in an African context: Accra's shopping malls' development and the new private sector actors in a neoliberal Ghana', *Geoforum* 106 (2019), 271.
66 Sara Jespersen and Mark Curtis, 'Development Finance Institutions & responsible corporate tax behaviour: Where we are and the road ahead', Joint Agency

Briefing Paper prepared by Latindadd, Eurodad, CounterBalance, Diakonia, Bretton Woods Project, Kepa, Action Aid, TJN-Africa, Christian Aid, & Oxfam (Oxford: Oxfam: 2016), pp. 8–9.
67 Alex Cobham, Petr Jansky, and Markus Meinzer, 'The financial secrecy index: Shedding new light on the geography of secrecy', *Economic Geography* 91.3 (2015), 281–303.
68 Richard Murphy, *Investments for Development: Derailed to Tax Havens*. Report prepared for IBIS, NCA, CRBM, Eurodad, Forum Syd and the Tax Justice Network (Copenhagen: IBIS, 2010), p. 6.
69 International Development Committee, *Future of CDC*, Ev. 88.
70 Mathieu Vervynckt, *Going Offshore: How Development Finance Institutions Support Companies Using the World's Most Secretive Financial Centres* (Brussels: Eurodad, 2014).
71 Jespersen and Curtis, 'Development finance institutions', p. 12.
72 Vervynckt, *Going Offshore*, pp. 8, 17; Jespersen and Curtis, 'Development finance institutions', p. 14.
73 CDC, *Policy on the Payment of Taxes and the Use of Offshore Financial Centres* (London: CDC, 2018).
74 See https://www.cdcgroup.com/en/our-impact/key-data-2/ (last accessed 31 March 2022).
75 Murphy, *Investments for Development*, p. 10.
76 Paddy Carter, *Why Do Development Finance Institutions Use Offshore Financial Centres?* (London: Overseas Development Institute, 2017).
77 Vervynckt, *Going Offshore*, p. 11.
78 Oladiwura Eyitayo-Oyesode, 'Source-based taxing rights from the OECD to the UN model conventions: Unavailing efforts and an argument for reform', *Law and Development Review* 13.1 (2020), 207.
79 Jalia Kangave, '"Taxing" TWAIL: A preliminary inquiry into TWAIL's application to the taxation of foreign direct investment', *International Community Law Review* 10 (2008), 389–400.
80 Léonce Ndikumana and Mare Sarr, 'Capital flight, foreign direct investment and natural resources in Africa', *Resources Policy* 63 (2019), 101427.
81 Léonce Ndikumana, 'Causes and effects of capital flight from Africa: Lessons from case studies', *Africa Development Review* 28.1 (2016), 2.
82 Or Total Official Support for Sustainable Development (TOSSD), as a proposed alternative is known.
83 CDC, *Policy on the Payment of Taxes*.
84 Kresner, 'Builders of empire', p. 316.
85 H. Nutcombe Hume, 'The work of the Colonial Development Corporation", *Journal of the Royal Society of Arts* 104.4984 (1956), 779.
86 Mitchell, 'One World Conservatism'; Sharp, Campbell and Laurie, 'The violence of aid?'.
87 Mawdsley *et al.*, 'Exporting stimulus'.
88 Olivia Rutazibwa, 'On babies and bathwater: Decolonizing International Development Studies', in Sara De Jong, Rosalba Icaza, and Olivia Rutazibwa

(eds), *Decolonization and Feminisms in Global Teaching and Learning* (London: Routledge, 2018), p. 165.
89 Dom and Miller, *Reforming Tax Systems*.
90 Eleanor Newbigin, 'Accounting for the nation, marginalizing the Empire: Taxable capacity and colonial rule in the early twentieth century', *History of Political Economy* 52.3 (2020), 469; Manu Goswami, 'Crisis economics: Keynes and the end of empire', *Constellations* 35.1 (2018), 26.
91 Max Haiven, 'Undead ideologies: Necro-neoliberalism, necro-Keynesianism and the radical imagination', *The Media Co-op*, 27 June 2011, available at https://www.mediacoop.ca/blog/max-haiven/7610 (last accessed 28 March 2022).
92 Peter James Hudson, *Bankers and Empire: How Wall Street colonized the Caribbean* (Chicago, IL: University of Chicago Press, 2017), p. 89.
93 Fanny Pigeaud and Ndongo Samba Sylla, *Africa's Last Colonial Currency* (London: Pluto Press, 2021), p. 116.

Afterword: Imperialism and global inequalities

Heloise Weber

The essays in this volume offer important, critical, and original knowledge that centres imperialism and its legacies for understanding both international and global inequalities. In particular, they demonstrate connections between the institution of 'private property' and 'taxation and redistribution' in the context of colonialism and its implications and legacies, identifying these 'as integral to the configuration of structures of contemporary inequality'.[1] An important analytical thrust developed throughout the volume is that the processes through which (economic) wealth, privilege, and status of former imperial states were realised is a central explanatory factor of contemporary inequalities. The general approach is critical historical, rendering enduring legacies of imperialism for contemporary relations of inequality.

The contributors eschew the traps laid by methodological nationalist frames of analysis in favour of a critical historical global analytic in order to explicate that 'global inequality has global, that is colonial, conditions for its emergence'.[2] A key point is that 'the wealth of the nation-states of the Global North and their capacity to provide welfare, together with the poverty of the nation-states of the Global South, are connected through the histories of colonialism'.[3] Therefore, a key theme disclosed through the diverse and important case examples is 'the link between colonial extraction on the one hand and state and public expenditure in the domestic national interest on the other'.[4]

Taken as a whole, this volume is at the frontier of critical debates on imperialism, taxation, and inequalities. As Bhambra notes in her discussion of imperialism and welfare, 'the historical provenance of the material resources available to be redistributed was broader than the nation; it was imperial. ... the end of empire did not bring about an end to the legacies of its social structure, including their modes of legitimation'.[5] The institutions of imperialism – epistemic (justifications of 'progress' and 'improvement') and concrete (such as the construction of 'legal' systems for taxation, ordering social hierarchies, including for the purposes of tax collection) – shaped and constricted the ways in which anti-colonial struggles could pursue projects of 'just settlements' in the context of decolonisation. The conditions of the possibility of establishing more than a modicum of welfare for citizens of the formerly colonised states were not only structurally constricted by the colonial division of labour, but actively undermined. For example, the Haitian revolution instituted the first constitution dedicated to the welfare of the most vulnerable, excluded, and dispossessed,[6] even as Haitians faced the wrath of colonial violence which included the demand that they pay for their rightful freedom.[7] One of the consequences of this has been the Haitian state constantly having to manage spiralling debt and interest payments, especially as conditions attached to loans demand further privileges for the commercial private sector without the necessary requirements for progressive taxation that could be directed towards welfare.

While not exactly the same, Jamaica's experience is similar. At independence in 1962, Jamaica's economy was in deficit (trade deficit), and between 1962 and 1971 this trade deficit increased from £15 million to £85.6 million.[8] Jamaica was colonised by Spain and England. As with Haiti, colonialism in Jamaica transformed social and political relations through the establishment of plantations as well as enslaved and indentured labour. Extraction (bauxite and alumina) was also key among the sources of foreign income ('foreign multinationals owned upwards of 80% of known bauxite reserves in Jamaica').[9] In 1975, prime minister Michael Manley 'remarked that 53% of the land in Jamaica was in the hands of one thousand people'.[10] He attempted to reorient Jamaican development, prioritising social welfare 'within a new social structure',[11] and part of this strategy included nationalising key sectors of the economy (including Barclays Bank). His political project was aggressively undermined, especially by the World Bank and the International Monetary Fund.[12]

Thus, while anti-colonial struggles resulting in the wave of decolonisation in the post-1945 context *did* significantly shift international power relations, their intersection with Cold War politics stymied efforts to successfully consolidate a solidarist internationalism through the project of Third Worldism.[13] That the Bandung Declaration and the struggles for the New International Economic Order (NIEO) were undermined by the United States and the core capitalist bloc is also clear.[14] What is crucial, though, and this is a key theme of this volume, is how imperial rule was organised through a racially grounded project of colonial capitalism with enduring legacies.[15]

Unequally connected histories were analytically disarticulated by the international development framework of the post-1945 context. Instead, a hierarchy between states was justified by reference to formal categories taken as comparative markers of progress (such as through a comparison of GDP). The comparative framing of states as discrete units in time and space serves both as an analytic that simply stands in as an explanation of different stages (premised on this comparative logic) and as an ideological framework through which to reproduce the colonial logics of development in terms of 'catch up'.[16] Accepting 'objects of development' (states as 'units of development') as given[17] thus not only disregards imperialism in the constitution of global inequalities but also analytically conceals unequal relations of development (nationally and globally). Of course, dependency theorists, and I would explicitly include Samir Amin[18] and Walter Rodney,[19] drew our attention to the implications of the colonial division of labour, and the international inequality it helped to sustain. As Frantz Fanon put it pointedly:

> Europe is literally the creation of the Third World. The wealth which smothers her is that wealth which was stolen from the under-developed peoples. ... So when we hear the head of a European state declare with his hand on his heart that he must come to the help of the poor underdeveloped peoples, we do not tremble with gratitude. Quite the contrary; we say to ourselves: It's a just reparation which will be paid to us.[20]

The meticulous national accounting systems instituted as part of the logic of colonial rule, however, already disarticulated how exploitation and expropriation – following Fanon, wealth *stolen* from the colonies – were consolidated under the frame of international development. In our contemporary context, when concerns of progress are associated with the state unit taken as 'the object of development', the historically instituted structures of inequality serve to further entrench relations of injustices and inequalities. This is compounded in a global context where sectors associated with public goods and services are increasingly commodified. Today, the Sustainable Development Goals (SDGs) agenda explicitly comprises a commercial approach to development deeply aligned with an agenda to shore up the World Trade Organization.[21]

This takes me back to the issue of *global* inequalities. While not commensurate with colonial violence, including genocide, there was poverty and destitution in Europe alongside immense wealth and privilege.[22] The subjection of the impoverished to 'free labour',[23] with the promises of freedom associated with colonial capitalism, was part of the myth of the 'liberal reward of labour'.[24] Of course, many were subsequently beneficiaries of welfare enabled through imperialism. Inequalities and impoverishment in the Global North[25] exist alongside relations of wealth, impoverishment, and authoritarian rule in the Global South. How then, today, do we engage in repair towards a just reparation?[26] Before I briefly draw out key themes of each chapter, I recall Fanon's critical insights and his call for an alternative to colonial capitalism, cautioning against pursuing development centred on accumulation: 'what matters is to stop talking about output, and intensification, and the rhythm of work'.[27] And he continued: 'Humanity is waiting for something other from us than such an imitation, which would be almost an obscene caricature.'[28] Sixty years on, this statement holds true with added urgency.

Rendering how imperial violence was organised, David Brown's compelling analysis demonstrates how wealth of the elite of the United Kingdom was consolidated through colonisation of Ireland. His provides a detailed analysis of colonial rule, including the institution of the Quit Rent for the Crown in England. At the same time, he shows how 'Oliver Cromwell's brutal Irish campaign, 1649–50, paid for by English taxpayers for the benefit of private investors, laid a foundation for England's early modern empire',[29] including enabling the financing of the trade in enslaved persons. The analysis complicates approaches that account for inequality and injustices in terms of a North–South dynamics. Madeline Woker examines the how French colonialism justified the extraction of resources and finances to fund its concrete instruments of rule, including military expenditure. This raises, though, the question of what exactly it means to attest a 'low cost empire' in 1900? Who benefited from French colonialism? Did the resort to discourses of cost–benefit analysis serve as a distraction or a complement to the justification of colonialism in terms of the 'civilising mission' and the agitations in France following the French Revolution? Woker brings out the distinctively different justifications of rule and taxation in France and in the colonies. In the case of the former, they were increasingly tethered to questions of justice and progress, while for the latter they rested on 'dual mandate' tropes and on the intent 'to force colonial subjects into wage labour'.

This is also a point elaborated by Samuel Sanchez who shows how French colonial rule in Madagascar was organised through extractivism based on forced labour and taxation of local communities. Yet, as he shows, they were up against challenges as the French 'failed to develop an ethic of reciprocity'[30] that would have corresponded with a normative ordering principle of Malagasy peoples. At the same time, the concessionary companies benefited enormously from the extraction of 'gold, rubber, hides, and raffia'[31] while, as he notes, 'the state gained no benefits from this extraction'.[32] Sanchez concludes with an important statement about the contemporary policy of 'very low taxation of corporation and extractive industries', which ties in with critical analysis of the enduring legacies of colonial structures of rule. Emma Park provides an incisive explication of how the Imperial British East Africa Company (IBEA) reorganised social and political relations not only – though primarily – through the extraction of land, labour, and taxation in order to serve the objectives of the imperial mission even as it was justified in terms of the dual mandate. Park demonstrates how, and with what implications, the IBEA 'was also the bearer of sovereign authority'.[33] Importantly, the colonial administrator Lugard was also a former company employee. Here, again, we see the overlapping of private interests with the making of public government, a point that resonates with the final chapter of the volume by Paul Gilbert. But Park's argument also bears out the problematic assumption of associating political relations only with centralised authority rather than a multitude of 'local sovereigns' relating through reciprocity and tribute. The IBEA strategically focused on transforming a shift from 'work to labour' where value was to be mediated via money.

The subsequent regime of direct taxation persisted after the demise of the IBEA and was used to shore up the interests of the white settlers. This is a theme that resonates in most contexts of colonialism. Laura Channing offers an insightful account of taxation and expenditure in relation to inequalities in Sierra Leone. Again, this is an interesting and detailed account of the social transformations engendered through the rule of empire, and the role of taxation as both a means of covering the costs of modernisation (roads, sanitation etc.) but also as a means of extraction, especially payment to colonial administrators. The revenue collected in hut tax is telling – just over £60,000 in 1924 – and a potent reminder about how important this was as a strategy in colonial rule more broadly. Channing offers a detailed account of expenditure, including contestation by different communities for 'development'-related goals rather than the 'export potential of certain areas'.[34]

Julia McClure provides important insights on the unequal and unjust taxation system of the Spanish Crown and how it helped structure inequalities. She demonstrates how private wealth and power were amassed through the constitution of sovereign rule, through taxation of the peasantry including through competitive taxation regimes (tax farming contracts). She also shows the corresponding emergence of redistribution through the poor laws. A similar logic occurs in colonial Latin America, with the difference there being the expropriation of indigenous lands and labour, and genocide. Racialised rule was directly reflected in the laws of segregation in Latin America. Again, this is a policy that has been shared in other contexts, including the British in India. Andrew Mackillop offers an insightful account of the interplay between 'empire' and the British Union by focusing on the case of Scotland and, in particular, the policy of 'improvement'. His reconstruction shows how the latter was funded through 'social philanthropy by those associated with' colonialism and its violence.[35] How they used this as means to consolidate their status and power at 'home' explicates the link between the imperial state and (global) inequalities, evidenced by rising destitution and 'four famines between 1695 and 1699'.[36] At the same time, anxieties about racial 'corruption' were central at home given migration to India (via the East India Company). Mackillop also draws connections between Orcadian communities and the Hudson's Bay Company. His chapter leaves us with the question of what sustained the assumption that 'empire ought to have generated positive commercial and human connection'?

Camille Sallé provides a detailed account of the use of forced indigenous labour which was taxed in the context of mining extraction in the Andes. She shows how claims to, and justification of, a modicum of health and welfare services ultimately rested on status and hierarchy, reflecting again racial inequalities. Maarten Manse offers a similar analysis, noting how 'ninety per cent of export taxes in the Dutch East Indies ... was levied from agricultural production by indigenous people', much of which was derived from coerced labour.[37] A question this line of inquiry raises is whether these inequalities were a deviation from what he refers to as 'ethical colonialism', or an expression of it? Gurminder K. Bhambra makes a compelling case about the limits of methodological nationalism as an analytic to understand development. As she notes, 'the British state was an imperial state with a national project at its heart,' while the 'national project comes into being through "relations of redistribution", or welfare'; 'the imperial state was constituted, in part, through "relations of extraction"'.[38] The latter played a key, if not significant, part in the possibility of providing welfare as a public entitlement. Yet, the implications of justifying the latter in exclusionary terms (focused predominantly on white working-class labour) denies the broader context through which such entitlements were established through imperialism. She offers an excellent, empirically substantiated, critical intervention into prominent perspectives and debates on distributive justice conceived in terms of entitlements of bounded communities. These debates work from abstract and problematic understanding of the history of colonialism and associated extraction which have enabled the establishment of entitlements such as welfare and the welfare state (noting the differentials in inequality in the UK). As she shows, the racialised rule of the British in India served to deny those subjected to abject poverty even a modicum of protection similar to the Poor Laws in England and Wales.[39] Debates on distributive justice would benefit from engagement with Bhambra's and similar arguments.

Alexia Yates gives an account of how justice claims against French imperialism instead translated into a 'debt relationship' that only further constricted the enslaved Haitians' struggles for freedom while further privileging unjust claims of planters and slaveholders. What transpired was not restorative justice to enslaved Haitians but rather a form of extraction that only served to uphold and reward the cruelty of the planters and slavers. Lyla Latif combines detailing methods of rule to extract labour and tax from (colonial) Kenya with insights on how 'the tax system of colonised territories was designed to support colonial capitalism'.[40] In particular, she demonstrates how the colonial logic of taxation was disconnected from expenditure on public welfare (in Kenya), and how such a logic continued in the post-colonial contexts, not least because of structural power exerted by the OECD. The colonial legacies of post-colonial Kenya thus compromised what was promised to its people, African socialism. Gregory Rawlings offers an insightful and detailed reconstruction of the impacts and implications of different taxation regimes in the Pacific under exclusive British imperial rule in the Solomon Islands, on the one hand, and joint British and French administration in what was to become Vanuatu (then the New Hebrides), on the other. He also provides timely reminders of the significance of resistance by local communities to imperial taxation regimes and to the often brutal measures through which the latter were enforced. The discussion of resistance to taxation by leaders on the island of Malaita (Solomon Islands) and the retaliation by the colonisers is a chilling reminder of the violence of colonialism, particularly in the face of sustained resistance. Rawlings's analysis is scoped to give a broader account of colonialism and extraction (the institution of plantations, for example), demonstrating the social and political backdrop to taxation as enforced extraction and exploitation.

Alex Cobham focuses on a key political dynamic linked to taxation, namely political representation and accountability. He draws on examples of colonially imposed taxes, including in Ghana, India, and the Solomon Islands. These include poll taxes on every person (including children), often tied to strategies aimed at extraction of labour and expropriation of land (for plantations). He also demonstrates how tax havens inhibit development and the potential for redistribution and welfare provisions. Paul Gilbert develops critical insights on the link between colonial financial strategies and the Colonial Development Corporation (renamed the Commonwealth Development Corporation [CDC]). He demonstrates how colonial logics of taxation and extraction (privileging private interests closely aligned with public rule) are reflected in contemporary UK 'development policy'. The CDC Group 'today benefits from (and indeed contributes to) a global tax architecture that deprives states of the Global South of tax revenue and perpetuates the myth that incentives are required to attract investment to "unstable" and "capital starved" developing states. Instead, they are beneficiaries of private sector-oriented development with the consequence of capital flowing "from the Global South to the Global North"'.[41]

As Gilbert shows, the CDC even justifies the use of 'offshore "tax havens" to structure their investments'.[42] And thus, we come full circle to the logics of imperialism, exploitation, and taxation as the means of supporting not only, but primarily, private commercial interests overlapping with public political interests of the colonial state(s).

Imperialism and global inequalities

This collection of essays does more than disclose the connections between imperialism, taxation, and injustices. Together, they also reveal the entanglements between colonial capitalism and institutions ostensibly for the public interest; whether the imperial state, settler-colonial states, or (we could add to this) post-colonial states committed to reproducing colonial logics in the service of dynastic and private interests. Consequently, a question that arises is how to conceptualise well-being without taxation tethered to institutions of colonial capitalism: thinking instead in terms of the commons, and thinking about the commons as not mediated through structures and relations of dispossession.[43]

Notes

1 Bhambra and McClure, this volume, p. 1.
2 *Ibid.*, p. 2.
3 *Ibid.*, p. 5.
4 *Ibid.*, p. 6.
5 Bhambra, this volume, pp. 211–12.
6 See Siba N. Grovogui, 'To the orphaned, dispossessed, and illegitimate children: Human rights beyond republican and liberal traditions', *Indiana Journal of Global and Legal Studies* 18.1(2011), 41–63.
7 Robbie Shilliam, 'What the Haitian Revolution might tell us about development, security and the politics of race', *Comparative Studies in Society and History* 50.3(2008), 778–808.
8 Caroline Thomas, *In Search of Security: The Third World in International Relations* (Boulder, CO: Lynne Rienner, 1987), p. 148.
9 Thomas, *In Search of Security*, p. 150.
10 *Ibid.*, p. 156.
11 *Ibid.*, p. 174.
12 *Ibid.*
13 For example, see Vijay Prashad, *The Poorer Nations: A Possible History of the Global South* (London: Verso, 2012).
14 See Caroline Thomas, *New States, Sovereignty and Intervention* (Aldershot: Gower, 1985), especially pp. 122–55; Quynh N. Pham and Robbie Shilliam

(eds), *Meanings of Bandung: Postcolonial Orders and Decolonial Visions* (London: Rowman & Littlefield, 2016).
15 On this, see Onur Ulas Incem *Colonialism, Capitalism and the Dilemmas of Liberalism* (Oxford: Oxford University Press, 2018).
16 See Heloise Weber, 'A political analysis of the formal comparative method: Historicizing the globalization and development debate', *Globalizations* 4.4 (2007), 559–72.
17 Timothy Mitchell, *Rule of Experts: Egypt, Techno-Politics, Modernity* (Berkeley: University of California Press, 2002). See especially pp. 209–43.
18 Samir Amin, 'Underdevelopment and dependence in Black Africa: Historical origin', *Journal of Peace Research* 9.2 (1972), 105–20.
19 Walter Rodney, *How Europe Underdeveloped Africa* (Nairobi, Kenya: East African Educational Publishers, 1995 [1972]).
20 Frantz Fanon, *The Wretched of the Earth* (London: Penguin, 1990 [1961]), p. 81.
21 See for example Heloise Weber, 'Politics of "leaving no one behind": Contesting the 2030 Sustainable Development Goals', *Globalizations* 14.3 (2017), 399–414; Heloise Weber and Martin Weber, 'When means of implementation meet ecological modernization theory: A critical frame for thinking about the Sustainable Development Goals initiative', *World Development* 136 (2020). doi: 10.1016/j.worlddev.2020.105129.
22 Silvia Federici, *Caliban and the Witch* (New York: Autonomedia, 2004); William P. Quigley, 'Five hundred years of English poor laws, 1349–1834: Regulating the working and nonworking poor', *Akron Law Review* 30.1 (1996), 73–128.
23 Karl Polanyi, *The Great Transformation: The Political Economic Origins of Our Time* (Boston, MA: Beacon Press, 1957 [1944]). See especially pp. 77–85.
24 Robbie Shilliam, 'The past and the present of abolition: Reassessing Adam Smith's "liberal reward of labour"', *Review of International Political Economy* 28.3 (2021), 690–711.
25 Indicatively, see R. Margaret Somers and Fred Block. 'From poverty to perversity: Ideas, markets, and institutions over 200 years of welfare debate', *American Sociological Review* 70.2 (2005), 260–87; Vera Weghmann, 'The making and breaking of solidarity between unwaged and waged workers in the UK', *Globalizations* 16.4 (2019), 441–56; Philip Alston, 'Statement on visit to the United Kingdom, by United Nations Special Rapporteur on extreme poverty and human rights', 16 November 2018, available at https://www.ohchr.org/sites/default/files/Documents/Issues/Poverty/EOM_GB_16Nov2018.pdf (last accessed 28 Marach 2022).
26 For an excellent orientation in this direction, see Robbie Shilliam, *Decolonizing Politics: An Introduction* (Cambridge: Polity, 2021).
27 Fanon, *Wretched of the Earth*, p. 253.
28 *Ibid.*, p. 255.
29 Brown, this volume, p. 23.
30 Sanchez, this volume, p. 58.
31 *Ibid.*, p. 67.

32 *Ibid.*, p. 74.
33 Park, this volume, p. 80.
34 Channing, this volume, p. 113.
35 Mackillop, this volume, p. 159.
36 *Ibid.*, p. 160.
37 Manse, this volume, p. 178.
38 Bhambra, this volume, pp. 198–99.
39 Of course, the Poor Laws were highly problematic and not always even aligning with the requirements to live in dignity.
40 Latif, this volume, p. 140.
41 Gilbert, this volume, p. 305.
42 *Ibid.*, p. 307.
43 See for example Robert Nichols, *Theft is Property! Dispossession and Critical Theory* (Durham, NC: Duke University Press, 2020). See also his response to a forum of this book. 'Histories and afterlives of dispossession: Symposium on Robert Nichols' *Theft is Property!*: *Dispossession and Critical Theory*, Durham: Duke University Press, 2020', *Political Theory* (2021), 1–25; Angela Y. Davis, Gina Dent, Erica R. Meiners, and Beth E. Richie, *Abolition. Feminism. Now* (Chicago, IL: Haymarket Books, 2022); Shilliam, *Decolonizing Politics*.

Index

Africa 4, 25–30, 37–40, 44–8, 57, 66, 79, 83, 84, 90, 91, 98–101, 105, 107, 109, 110, 208, 211, 240, 242, 243, 246, 248, 252, 253, 287, 300, 309, 310, 311
   Algeria 37, 38, 45, 47, 49, 51, 53, 54
   Congo xvi, 46, 50
   Ghana 210, 283, 300, 302, 308
   Kenya xv, xvii, 13, 98, 116, 248–58, 324
   Madagascar xvi, 11, 42, 46, 49, 57–78, 321
   Nigeria 210, 211
   Rhodesia 303
   Sierra Leone xvi, 11, 13, 98–118, 322
   South Africa 208, 302, 303
   Zanzibar 79
African socialism 246, 248–53, 324
Asia 38, 157, 160, 163, 164, 165, 167, 170, 171, 287
   Southeast Asia 37, 38, 39
autonomy 10, 11, 37, 38, 45–9, 52, 53, 67, 73, 122, 125, 126, 130, 182, 246, 249

British East Africa Company xvi, 11, 79–97, 321
British East Indies Company (also written as East India Company) 80, 82, 163–71, 178, 201, 204, 279, 283, 284, 285, 291, 292, 323

British Empire 7, 9, 10, 12, 13, 19, 91, 101, 157–71, 198, 207, 208, 241–54, 259, 260, 283, 284, 287, 288, 293, 294
British North Borneo Company 284

Caribbean xv, 4, 19, 20, 29, 30, 37, 46, 49, 168, 201, 287
   British Virgin Islands 280, 288, 290
citizen xvi–xviii, 1, 5–7, 37, 38, 39, 44, 71, 76, 93, 100, 141, 186, 199, 202, 208, 211, 220, 221, 224, 228, 247, 248, 250–4, 263, 265, 269, 279, 282, 285, 298, 299, 319
civilisation xvi, 10, 47, 54, 79, 84, 87, 90, 91, 100, 139, 161, 229, 238
colonial capitalism 240, 242, 252, 253, 319–21, 324, 325
Company of Royal Adventurers 27, 28, 29, 30
corvée labour 69, 181, 182, 183
Council of Trade 21, 22
Cromwell, Oliver 22–7
Crown Colony 99–105, 107, 109
Crown Dependencies 288, 292, 308

debt xv, 13, 44, 48, 60, 75, 85, 86, 91, 202, 205, 207, 209, 210, 211, 219–22, 223, 225, 228, 229, 231, 233, 234, 241, 300, 301, 306, 307, 314, 319, 323

decolonisation xvii, 5, 7, 12, 13, 157, 219, 243, 261, 270–4, 319
democracy xiv, xvi, xvii, 11, 39
  fiscal democracy xvi, xvii
Dutch East India Company 80, 178
Dutch Empire 177–93
Dutch West India Company 25, 30

fiscal governance 2, 242
France 6, 11, 13, 37–56, 57–74, 199, 219–34, 262–5, 268, 270, 273, 274, 276, 321
French Empire xvi, 7, 37–49, 57–74, 219–34

Germany 62, 65, 66, 93, 262
gift 31, 86, 95, 209
Great Britain 61, 65, 74, 158, 198–212, 242, 247, 276, 280–95, 299–312
  England 6, 19–32, 160, 162, 164, 165, 198, 202, 206, 301, 302, 304, 319, 321, 323
  Ireland 11, 19–32, 159, 160, 163, 164, 166, 170, 198–200, 205, 206, 212, 321
  Scotland 12, 19, 23, 157–71, 198, 204, 322
  Wales 19, 165, 206, 323

Haiti 6, 13, 219–34, 311, 319, 323
Holland *see* Netherlands
Hudson's Bay Company 160, 164, 323

India 166, 169, 200, 202, 204–11, 284, 302, 313, 322–4
Indochina xvi, 44–8, 66, 68
Indonesia 12, 177–93
inequality xvii, 1–13, 49, 55, 99, 121, 129, 134, 157, 158, 162, 166, 177, 178, 181, 182, 185, 189, 190, 192, 193, 241, 243, 250, 254, 282, 291
International Labour Organization 102

joint stock companies 20, 80
justice 123–8, 131–3, 138, 141, 146, 150, 151, 153, 191, 200, 212, 230, 311, 321
  distributive justice 125, 131, 146, 199, 203, 241, 323
  tax justice xvii, xviii, 42, 48, 151, 290, 308

League of Nations 102
legislative council 246
local native councils 242, 246

Majimboism 242
Malaya 210
mercantilism 50, 57
Merina Kingdom 53, 58, 74
  see also Madagascar
modernising 48, 158, 177, 190
monopoly 21, 26, 30, 44, 63, 73, 80, 164, 179, 182, 189, 228, 247, 284, 301–5
mortgage 21, 23, 27, 30

Netherlands 25, 123, 126, 179, 180, 289, 290
North America 161, 288, 300
  California xvi
  United States 98

Pakistan 210, 211
peasant 69, 70, 72, 101, 122, 129, 136, 179, 181–8, 200, 221
poor 1, 69, 122, 125, 130, 133, 138, 139, 144, 145, 160, 161, 162, 166, 169, 194, 184, 187, 203, 205, 206, 220, 300
Portugal 231
Portuguese Empire 57
poverty 117, 126, 130, 131, 133, 160, 162, 163, 166, 167, 168, 170, 205, 226
protectionism 44, 50, 53, 61

Royal Africa Company 29, 31

slavery (including other forced / coerced labour) 19, 26, 28, 32, 42, 58, 62, 76, 99, 102, 128, 143, 167, 183, 221, 222, 225
Solomon Islands xvi, 260–7, 270, 271, 274, 283, 324
sovereignty xvii, 11, 12, 38, 40, 47, 79, 81–91, 101, 121–6, 131, 138, 160, 219, 223, 226, 229, 231, 279, 291
  corporate sovereignty 79
  sovereign seizures 47, 87, 90, 91
Spain 19, 25, 27, 121–34, 224, 231, 282, 318
Spanish Empire 7, 20, 30, 121–34, 138–53

taxes 42, 47, 48, 49, 57, 62, 63, 68, 69, 70, 71, 72, 73, 79, 80, 83, 87, 88, 89, 91, 99, 101, 111, 143
  auto-taxation 103, 122, 123
  capita tax (also known as head tax) xvii, 28, 69, 71, 122, 129, 182, 183, 190
  colonial tax 7, 38, 41, 46, 48, 49, 69, 99, 105, 111, 140, 177, 179, 182, 184, 191, 192, 240–8, 254, 300
  customs tax 27, 30, 33, 42, 45, 102, 181, 59, 60, 61, 83, 285
  direct tax 91, 104, 106, 122, 184, 185, 283, 294
  double tax agreements 245, 249, 310
  head tax 122, 129, 189
  hearth tax 28
  holpatan tax 133
  hut tax xvi, 102–5, 242, 243, 245
  income tax 12, 41, 44, 53, 98, 122, 181, 184, 186, 191, 199–207, 187, 243, 249, 259, 260, 270–2, 283
  indirect taxation 104, 105, 106, 250, 283, 284

land tax 44, 46, 53, 182, 185, 221, 242
  labour tax
  see also tribute labour 102, 103
  medio peso 139, 140, 143, 144, 147, 150, 152
  metropolitan tax 39, 41, 42, 49, 58, 178
  'native tax' 102, 103, 260
  opium tax 202
  poll tax xvi, 242, 243, 267, 271, 283, 324
  protectorate tax 113
  regressive taxation 102, 130
  sales tax (including alcabala and sisa) 139, 151, 308
  salt tax 203
  taifa tax 228
  tax avoidance 69, 303, 305
  tax exemption 44, 62, 64, 73, 121, 122, 123, 124, 202, 207, 309
  tax farming 26, 27, 28, 29, 30, 31, 284, 294
  tax havens 284, 288, 289, 291, 297, 298, 308, 309, 310, 311
  tax revolt 47
  tomín de hospital 132, 133, 142, 151
tribute 73, 128, 177, 200
  tribute labour 69, 102
  encomienda 128, 129
  repartimiento 129, 141, 146, 148

welfare 3, 8, 37, 41, 70, 71, 126, 127, 131–59, 177, 182, 185, 186, 187, 199, 203, 204, 207, 209, 220, 241, 252, 300
  charity 9, 10, 132, 139–46, 151, 153, 166–9, 204
  hospitals 9, 71, 131, 132, 138–53
  poor relief 109, 124, 126, 127, 138, 142, 166, 167, 168
  public good 7, 9, 127, 128
  public services 58, 107
  public utility 89

welfare (*cont.*)
  public works 9, 102, 107, 109, 110, 111, 182
  redistributive expenditure 106
  social goods 101
  social welfare 241, 244, 251, 306
  spiritual welfare 139

welfare Acts 210
welfare institutions 157
welfare philanthropy 165, 170
welfare state 8, 131, 199, 208, 209, 210, 211, 240, 243, 244, 249, 250, 254, 302, 306

EU authorised representative for GPSR:
Easy Access System Europe, Mustamäe tee 50,
10621 Tallinn, Estonia
gpsr.requests@easproject.com

www.ingramcontent.com/pod-product-compliance
Lightning Source LLC
Chambersburg PA
CBHW051557230426
43668CB00013B/1883